Longitudinal Data Analysis

If you can look into the seeds of time,
And say which grain will grow and which will not,
Speak then to me,

SHAKESPEARE, *Macbeth*, 1, iii, 58–60

Longitudinal Data Analysis

Designs, Models and Methods

Catrien C. J. H. Bijleveld & Leo J. Th. van der Kamp
with Ab Mooijaart, Willem A. van der Kloot,
Rien van der Leeden, Eeke van der Burg

SAGE Publications
London • Thousand Oaks • New Delhi

First published 1998

 SAGE Publications Ltd.
6 Bonhill Street
London EC2A 4PU

SAGE Publications Inc.
2455 Teller Road
Thousand Oaks, California 91320

SAGE Publications India Pvt. Ltd.
32 M-Block Market
Greater Kailash - I
New Delhi 110 048

British Library Cataloguing in Publication data

A catalogue record for this book is available from the British Library

ISBN 0 7619 5537 2
ISBN 0 7619 5538 0 (pbk)

Library of Congress catalogue record available

Printed in Great Britain by The Cromwell Press Ltd, Trowbridge, Wiltshire

Contents

List of Figures

List of Tables

Preface

Why this book came about   This book is the end result of a postgraduate course on longitudinal data analysis that all authors taught at Leiden University in September 1992. We felt that most books on longitudinal data analysis were too 'mono-method', in the sense that they dealt either with log-linear methods only, or with analysis of variance techniques only, etc. Presenting a broad variety of longitudinal methods would offer also a variety of approaches to the analysis of change. At the same time, presenting these seemingly different models in one book makes it possible to expand on the conceptual similarities between the various models.

What this book is about   Longitudinal research has many faces. The common trait is that the entity under investigation or unit of study is observed or measured at more than one point in time, possibly repeatedly, and that it develops over time. Of necessity, measurement or observation is part of longitudinal research, as well as the utilization of experimental, quasi-experimental, or non-experimental designs to collect the data. As soon as the data have been collected, the tools of data analysis are used to bring not only order but also insight into the phenomena studied. Ideally, measurement, design and analysis are well-integrated. Many modern textbooks on research methodology testify to the close link between the three.

In this book not much attention is given to measurement as such. To wit, in longitudinal research the concerns with measurement and the quality of data collection procedures where the measurement instruments are concerned are grosso modo similar to those in non-longitudinal research. Repeated observation, however, brings in the phenomenon called serial dependence, which has been called a disease that infects our data collected over time.

Chapter 1 presents a classification of designs for longitudinal studies. Collecting data in a certain design leads to an arrangement of observations in a data matrix. The latter data matrix is a design-specific exemplar of the basic data relation matrix. How the longitudinal design and corresponding data matrix link with the method of analysis is treated in Chapter 1. Validity threats are discussed in the context of (quasi-experimental) longitudinal designs, as well as other methodological concerns particular to or of particular relevance to longitudinal research. We focus on those issues in the framework of the three modes along which data are gathered in longitudinal studies: the person mode, variable mode and occasion or time mode. The last mode is of particular relevance: with this third temporal axis along which data are collected, the data matrix becomes a data box, which complicates standard statistical analysis. Indeed, this book is centred on the fact that the data constitute a data box, as well as on the fact that one of the axes of this box (the temporal axis) is a particular type of axis, along which time evolves and temporal dependence occurs. This book is intended to conceptualize, formalize and illustrate a number of relatively widely used exploratory and statistical techniques, that can accommodate in various ways both the temporal properties of the data as well as the three dimensions of the data box.

Chapter 2 is a self-contained thorough introduction and overview of explorative analysis of (categorical) longitudinal data. The reason for the length of this contribution (the longest chapter in this volume) is that the techniques are relatively unfamiliar to researchers in the social and behavioural sciences. Recently, the debate in statistical hypothesis testing has been revived, and as a result of this debate so-called practical significance is stressed – sometimes as a replacement, sometimes as a useful addition to statistical significance. Typically, Chapter 2 does not pretend to formulate statements in terms of statistical significance. It aims at description and exploration, and in doing so, at obtaining insight into the field of study and practically significant results.

Analysis of variance is the classical approach to analysing data obtained through experimental designs. Although it can be debated whether time may be conceived of as an experimental factor, analysis of variance has been extended to include longitudinal designs as well.

Analysis of variance of longitudinal data or repeated measures has been around for half a century. Chapter 3 gives an overview of (generalized) analysis of variance for longitudinal data.

Undoubtedly prominent in multivariate statistical analysis is the advent of structural equation modelling. The main techniques, discussed in Chapter 4, aim at confirmation, viz. statistical hypothesis testing. Most underlying models are developed for continuous data for which assumptions have to be made if statistical testing is the purpose. As structural equation modelling amounts to the testing of particular path models, by envisaging temporal dependence as simply one type of path, models for temporal dependence can be formulated and tested with these techniques. Recent developments, such as growth curve analysis through structural equation modelling, receive attention as well.

Multilevel analysis is a relatively new offspring of the multivariate analysis branch. The term as such refers to the way the data are structured, or, more precisely, hierarchically structured. As time is a structuring variable, the extension of multilevel analysis to longitudinal data is straightforward. The essentials of multilevel analysis are outlined in Chapter 5, together with the extension to longitudinal data. Attention is also given to recent developments.

Chapter 6 deals with categorical longitudinal data, highlighting log-linear analysis and Markov modelling. That is, statistical modelling is aimed at, and hypothesis testing is performed as a form of confirmation. In log-linear analysis various models for the association between temporal versions of variables may be tested. In Markov modelling, dynamic models for the transitions from one category to another can be tested. Either model can be used to test hypotheses about change, although the model specification is not identical.

Finally, Chapter 7 ties the chapters devoted to techniques together in terms of model specification as well as characteristics such as the presence of latent variables, assumptions on the distributions of the variables, and the like. It also presents rough guidelines for the choice of analysis technique given a research question and given a dataset.

Although chapters have been written by different authors, we have attempted to make the formats of the respective chapters as similar as possible. Whenever appropriate, each chapter starts out with an introduction to the cross-sectional application of the technique, and moves on to its longitudinal extension. All techniques are illustrated through empirical examples. All chapters devote a special section to the problem of missing data, which is generally more serious in longitudinal than in cross-sectional research. Most chapters end with a discussion, as well as with a short enumeration of the relevant literature. Unless too much out of line with standard notation for a specific model, notation is also uniform, and nomenclature for parameter matrices inasfar as possible is uniform as well.

Dependence among chapters   Chapter 1 is a general chapter. In Chapter 3 manifest variables only are used, while in Chapter 4 latent variables also are included in the models. Chapter 5 may, in principle, be subdivided into a manifest variable part and a manifest-plus-latent variable part. Because of the characterization of its first part it is connected to Chapter 3; because of the characterization of its second part it is connected to Chapter 4. Chapter 2 and Chapter 6 both tackle categorical longitudinal data. Their distinctive feature is the type of analysis: exploration versus confirmation in a statistical analysis. This all gives the reader a choice between various trajectories through the book. One can follow the explorative trajectory, or the categorical variable trajectory, the growth curve trajectory, or the latent variable trajectory.

Moving through the book will be facilitated by a working knowledge of statistics, including regression, as well as elementary multivariate analysis and matrix algebra.

Acknowledgements   Our thanks go to Ali van Teijlingen and Job van der Raad for secretarial support. Wim den Brinker assisted us greatly with his keen insight and expertise in data analysis. Many colleagues kindly lent the use of their data to us; they are referred to at the appropriate places in the text. We thank an anonymous reviewer for his comments which we feel considerably improved various versions of this text. Floor Luykx and Femke Heide diligently checked our manuscript. Frits Bijleveld was responsible for the synchronization and technical editing of the various chapters. We are endebted to him for his expertise, support and patience. Any remaining errors are solely ours.

Leiden   Leo J. Th. van der Kamp
                                                     Catrien C. J. H. Bijleveld

Chapter 1

Methodological issues in longitudinal research

Leo J. Th. van der Kamp
Catrien C. J. H. Bijleveld

1.1   Introduction

Longitudinal data can be defined as data resulting from the observation of subjects (human beings, animals, organizations, societies, countries) on a number of variables (employment status, depression, attachment, arithmetic skills) over time. This definition implies the notion of repeated measures, i.e. the observations are collected on a certain number of occasions. In fact, we speak of longitudinal data whenever we have observed more than once. Or: whenever the number of observation points or measurement occasions (T) is more than one, we have longitudinal data. The number of subjects may vary from one to many, and the number of variables may also vary from one to many. Thus, replication over time distinguishes longitudinal research from cross-sectional research: in cross-sectional research $T = 1$, in longitudinal research $T > 1$.

Collecting longitudinal data is more costly than collecting cross-sectional data. The increased cost is caused not only by the fact that we measure a sample of N subjects at least twice and that we thus have to collect $2N$ measurements or more, but mainly by the fact that we have to *follow* the subjects over time: we have to track subjects who move house, who move to another municipality. We have to ensure cooperation at all subsequent measurement occasions of those who participated at the first measurement occasions, as we cannot replace subjects who refuse or are lost by others who did not participate at the previous measurement occasions. Obviously this is much more time-consuming and thus much more costly than the collection of T samples of N subjects at any one time point, or even the collection of T samples of N subjects at T time points.

Apart from the actual research costs themselves, the organizational costs of longitudinal research are tremendous: not only do we have to ensure that the same subjects can be measured repeatedly over the course of often many years, we also run great risks if the research team cannot be preserved over the duration of the study.

A relevant question therefore seems to be: why at all would one want to conduct a longitudinal study, if the costs and organizational difficulties are that inhibitive? There are two major rationales for wanting to conduct a longitudinal study.

The first and most compelling rationale is that when *change* itself is the object of study, the only way to investigate change is by collecting repeated measurements. For instance, we might want to investigate through what mechanisms young children become attached to their mothers, or we might want to assess the various stages in maths skill acquisition. The only way to investigate such processes is by adopting a longitudinal approach. We simply cannot see the evolvement of development if we do not observe repeatedly. This is one instance in which longitudinal research is warranted.

Secondly, change itself, or the temporal ordering of events, is often the closest we get to causality. Scientists have always been interested in causality, in uncovering the mechanisms that cause the world and its subjects to behave as they do. When conducting cross-sectional research, we can at most assess the correlation between variables and thus ascertain whether variables co-vary. It is hard to assess any temporal ordering in such cases. For instance, we might discover that girl delinquents have very low esteem, but we cannot – on the basis of the cross-sectional data – assess whether the low self-esteem precedes delinquency (and thus whether low self-esteem in girls leads to delinquency) or whether delinquency precedes low self-esteem (and thus whether delinquency leads to low self-esteem in girls). However, if we had conducted a longitudinal study, we could for instance find that girls who have very low self-esteem at ages 10 to 12, have higher chances to become delinquent later on in life. In this manner, longitudinal research gives a much better insight than cross-sectional research into the causal relations between variables.

In general, the costs of longitudinal designs pay off in terms of the appropriateness with which certain research questions can be addressed.

Broadly speaking, there are three possible aims in a longitudinal investigation. First, we may want to *describe* subjects' intraindividual and interindividual changes over time; in doing so, we may want to describe both the magnitude of certain changes as well as the pattern of changes. Secondly, we may want to *explain* these changes in terms of certain other characteristics. These characteristics can be stable (for instance, randomly assigned interventions in experiments or non-randomly assigned characteristics such as gender and religious affiliation) or unstable (for instance, time-varying characteristics such as medication or mood). Ultimately, we might want to *forecast* subjects' scores on the variables of interest.

Our research questions may be purely explorative, or we might be interested to test certain hypotheses regarding the relations between the variables. In all instances, we are interested in change as a function of time. The time axis may be in time units such as days, seconds or years, or in age-periods, or in stages such as intake, the onset of therapy and the end of therapy.

In longitudinal research, it is generally assumed that the measurement occasions are equally spaced, or equidistant. Many techniques work from this constraint. Equidistance is indeed very often the case in practice, as subjects are generally observed or interviewed with a certain regularity. But, as may be apparent from the example above, it may not be feasible to require equal intervals between the successive measurement occasions, and intervals may even vary over subjects. If we investigate subjects' psychological well-being at intake, during onset and towards the end of therapy, the two intervals are generally not the same and are bound to vary over individual patients as well.

Even when a longitudinal study has been conducted successfully, and data have thus been gathered repeatedly for a number of subjects on a number of variables of interest, the researcher may still face complications. The remaining ones are methodological and are caused by the fact that through repeated measurement of the same variables, the assumption of independence of the measurements – which is one of the standard assumptions in statistics – is not met. In fact, the measurements on the successive occasions are *serially dependent*: the observations at time point $t + 1$ can be predicted to a certain extent from the observations at time point t. Such serial dependence invalidates many test statistics. More on serial dependency will be given below (Section 1.5).

In addition, when data are gathered repeatedly, the data constitute a data *box*: subjects (a first axis) are observed on variables (the second axis) over successive time points or occasions (the third axis). This complicates matters further, as most statistical techniques have been designed to analyse a data *matrix*. For instance, when subjects have been measured on a number of variables for one measurement occasion, the ensuing data matrix can be analysed by cross-sectional techniques. When variables have been measured on a number of time points for one subject, we also have a data matrix; this data matrix can be analysed by so-called time series techniques. As soon as a third axis appears, that is, when measurements take place over subjects as well as over variables as well as over occasions, special provisions have to be made for analysis to be possible.

This chapter gives a general conceptual framework for longitudinal data analysis. This framework is part of Cattell's Basic Data Relation Matrix, BDRM for short, a data box of which the axes or facets are defined by subjects, variables, and time points or occasions. We present a number of designs for longitudinal studies and discuss matters regarding age, cohort and period as possible explanations for temporal effects. Generalizability and validity issues particular to longitudinal research are discussed, after which a number of remaining methodological issues are treated, such as missing data.

We will cite relevant references throughout the text. At the end of the chapter, we give a number of further references, both for general introductory textbooks as well as for literature on more advanced subjects.

Before continuing, we must remark that this chapter (as well as this book) is limited to techniques that investigate change in discrete time. The main reason for this limitation is that most longitudinal data in behavioural and social research (on which this book particularly focuses) are collected in discrete time. Another reason for not analysing in continuous time is that continuous time analysis techniques are much more complicated than their discrete time counterparts. Thirdly, many discrete time approximations of continuous processes are in practice quite adequate for capturing the essentials of the process under investigation, as long as the spacing and span of the time points is appropriate given the object of study. Also, in some instances changes do not occur gradually and continuously but suddenly or in distinct stages, so that in those instances non-continuous data would be adequate for describing the transitions. More on continuous time techniques can be found in Bergstrom (1984), Dembo & Zeitouni (1986) and Singer (1993), amongst many others.

1.2   The data box

Longitudinal data can be conceptualized in the framework of a data box, the axes of which are defined by persons (N), variables (M), and occasions (T) (see Figure 1.1). Given the three dimensions or axes, each measurement constitutes a cell or datum of the three-dimensional data box, denoted as Y_{ijt} $(i = 1, 2, \ldots, N; j = 1, 2, \ldots, M; t = 1, 2, \ldots, T)$. Cattell (1946) was the first to present a taxonomy employing the categories persons $\times$ variables $\times$ occasions to form his so-called covariation chart. This covariation chart served as a framework for defining the six primary factor analytic techniques which are proposed for the analysis of six correlational or relational matrices obtained by selecting particular slices of the three-dimensional data box of Figure 1.1.

The six correlational or relational matrices and techniques obtainable from the three facets persons, variables and occasions are shown in Figure 1.2. Each matrix corresponds with a layer, or rather a slice, of the data box. Thus if we take the matrix of persons $\times$ variables (Figure 1.2a), we have T such matrices in the data box. Each of these T matrices can be analysed by for instance factor analysis or principal components analysis. The latter methods exemplify the R-technique. Similarly, each of the matrices (a) to (f) in Figure 1.2 can be identified in the three-dimensional data box: the R-technique and corresponding Q-technique, the P-technique and corresponding O-technique, and, lastly, the S-technique and corresponding T-technique.

Figure 1.1: *Basic Data Relation Matrix (BDRM) or Data Box Proposed by Cattell (1946, 1952, 1988)*

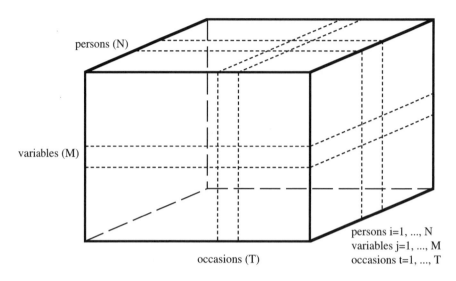

In Figure 1.2, the so-called R-technique analyses the covariation between variables computed over persons given one occasion of measurement. This is the classical cross-sectional data matrix. The Q-technique tackles the covariation between persons computed over variables given one occasion. Although less obviously applicable, this design is sometimes used when the number of variables exceeds the number of subjects: by transposing the data matrix, the data can be analysed by standard cross-sectional techniques once more. Both the R-technique and the Q-technique are less relevant in a longitudinal context.

The P-technique analyses the covariation between variables over occasions for one person: this slice of the data matrix can be analysed through multivariate so-called time series techniques (see Section 1.4). Both the O-technique and S-technique have less direct ties with common (longitudinal) analysis methods. The T-technique analyses subjects over time points for one variable, and is therefore again more relevant in a longitudinal context.

This book focuses on extensions to the R-, P-, and T-technique, in the sense that we will discuss techniques in which measurements have been obtained for several individuals (mostly many), generally for more

Figure 1.2: *Six Correlational or Relational Matrices and Techniques Obtainable from the Three Facets Persons, Variables and Occasions (After Cattell, 1988)*

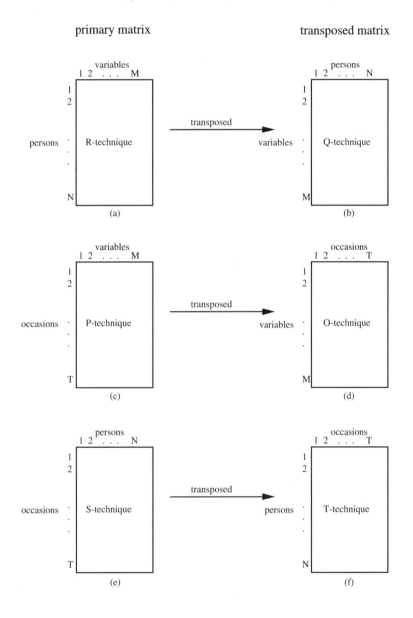

than one variable, over more than one (and generally more than two) time points (although the number of time points may vary substantially). Thus we have sometimes univariate, but mostly multivariate, multiwave data collected for a sample of subjects. We will give limited attention to single-subject studies, or case studies, where $N = 1$ and a non-extended slice such as depicted for the P-technique is analysed. Researchers in the field of developmental psychology, who are particularly interested in inter- and intraindividual change, have given much attention to the P-technique (see e.g. Nesselroade & Ford, 1985; Nesselroade & Featherman, 1991, for recent reviews).

The full data box as given by Cattell (1966, 1988) can have more facets or dimensions (maximally ten), but for our purposes a three-dimensional representation with dimensions persons, variables and occasions suffices. These three dimensions are also called *modes of classification*. The person mode may also be called subjects, individuals, units of observation, measurement units, and the like. And terms like points of time, times of measurement, measurement times, time-points or waves are used interchangeably with the term occasion. The term wave, for instance, is used often in the context of analysis of variance and in structural equation modelling, as in the terminology: 'two-wave two-variable' models (2W2V models) and 'multi-wave multi-variable' models. However, instead of actual points in time, the waves may also be less temporally defined stages such as stages in a therapeutic process. Also, concepts reflecting temporal distance such as 'father' and 'son' may be used in lieu of time points.

Quasi-experimental designs can also be embedded in the BDRM formulation. The total group of persons is then simply divided into an experimental and a control group, and the separate measurement occasions are subsumed within the two larger classes of occasions 'before treatment' and 'after treatment'. This applies as well to the so-called 'regression-discontinuity design' (see for instance Plewis, 1985).

More methodological points on the BDRM framework can be found in the literature already mentioned, as well as in Baltes, Reese, & Nesselroade (1977), Nesselroade & Baltes (1979), Nesselroade & Ford (1985, 1987), Nesselroade & Jones (1991), Nesselroade & Von Eye (1985), Rudinger (1979), and Rudinger & Wood (1990).

1.3   The three modes of the data box: selection effects

The BDRM or data box presented in the previous section is defined in terms of the three modes persons, variables and occasions. Longitudinal observations or measurements stem always, in one way or another, from this $(N \times M \times T)$ hypothetical universe. That is, a specific set of longitudinal observations or measurements is a multimodal selection from the $(N \times M \times T)$ universe. Selection of persons, variables, or occasions produce what is called selection effects (see e.g. Nesselroade, 1991; Nesselroade & Jones, 1991). As such, unimodal as well multimodal selection more often than not threatens the generalizability of research findings. Let us therefore consider the effect that selection may have in each of the modes of the data box separately. In doing so, we will focus on those selection effects and those threats to generalizability that are particular to the longitudinal nature of our designs, or are aggravated by the longitudinal aspects.

Person mode   In designing and conducting empirical studies, the selection of persons or subjects is often given considerable attention. What the investigator aims at is to generalize findings obtained from a sample of subjects to a population of interest. Usually, this is not an unspecified population of subjects but a well-defined one. What the researcher then wants is a purposive or a well-defined representative sample for this specific population. Not only have sampling theory and procedures been elaborated for the inference of sampling results to the population at large, but also for more specified generalization towards a population of interest. The latter type of generalization has been studied in the context of survey research (see e.g. Kish, 1987; Rossi, Wright, & Anderson, 1983; Skinner, Holt, & Smith, 1989), and many sampling designs have been proposed to minimize unwanted sampling effects. So far, longitudinal studies do not differ greatly from their cross-sectional counterparts.

However, the concept of random sampling for obtaining a sample that is representative for the population, may not always be applicable in longitudinal research. The problem lies – not surprisingly – in the longitudinal nature of the investigation. Suppose that we draw at the starting point of a certain study, at t_1, a random sample that is representative for some specified population. Suppose furthermore that we are able to follow up on all subjects at the subsequent time point t_2, so that we observe at t_2 100% of the respondents we had observed at t_1: none of the subjects has died or emigrated etc. This is apparently an ideal situation. However, while we were conducting our observations, the population changed: some members of the population died, others emigrated, again others immigrated into the population, etc. Thus, the sample is not representative for the population anymore, because the population has changed in the meantime.

Working with such *panels* (a panel is generally defined – somewhat interchangeably with the term sample – as a group of subjects that is measured repeatedly), it is hard to solve for this. If we attempt to circumvent the problem by drawing a random sample from the population at each time point, we are faced with a difficulty of a different nature: the samples at the various occasions contain different individuals so that it has become impossible to assess intraindividual change. This situation is sometimes dealt with by studying a panel of varying composition: one part of the panel is a 'true' panel in the sense that it contains a sample of subjects who are measured repeatedly, and a second part of the panel is a random sample at each time point (this design is often called a revolving panel design, see Section 1.4). Working in this way, it is possible to assess intraindividual change for the permanent subjects in the sample as well as total or aggregate change for the part of the sample that is representative at each occasion. Firebaugh (1997) gives a number of illustrative examples of the analysis of change for such panels of varying composition.

While the population from which the sample has been drawn may change during the course of the study, it is all too well known that the sample itself may also change. In fact, from a great many examples of longitudinal research, drop-out rates of 40 to 60% have been shown to be not uncommon. What is more, it seems that for a number of years, subjects' refusals to cooperate have become more numerous, perhaps indicative of an increasingly assertive attitude in the general population. While drop-out (or non-response) already constitutes a problem in short-term cross-sectional research, in longitudinal research the repeated nature of observations, and the time-span over which studies stretch, aggravate the situation. The longer the time-span of the study, the higher drop-out generally is. In addition, the repetitive nature of the longitudinal study actually induces drop-out in the sense that when people are asked after their private thoughts, opinions and attitude, they may be willing to disclose them once or twice, but they are less willing to do so as the questions are repeated more often. Drop-out is progressive and accumulative. Subjects lost once, generally cannot and do not re-enter the sample. In this context drop-out is often referred to as *attrition*.

If drop-out were a random phenomenon, all this need not be of great concern. It could then be dealt with simply by starting with a large enough sample: one would only have to ensure that sufficient numbers of subjects were left towards the end of the observation period for statistical testing or for some required level of statistical power. The problem in longitudinal research, however, just as in cross-sectional research, is that drop-out or attrition is not random: those who drop-out, who disappear, who refuse to cooperate, who die or fall ill, usually deviate in a *systematic* manner on a number of relevant characteristics that usually bear relevance to the topic under investigation. For instance, in a study on delinquency by Farrington, Gallagher, Morley, Stledger, & West (1990) it was shown how elusive and uncooperative subjects were in general more mobile, more often offenders, more often living alone, had more frequent problems with their children, had been involved more often in fights, etc. All this means that, even if we start out with a random sample at t_1, the sample will generally not be random anymore after drop-out has occurred. In other words: drop-out affects the generalizability of the results from the sample to the population. In longitudinal research, it is therefore of the utmost importance to attempt to retain as many subjects of the original sample as possible. And, even though high drop-out rates are not at all uncommon, low drop-out is by no means impossible. Nice examples can be found in several studies (stretching as long as 20 years and over) where very high retention rates could be achieved, through diligent and hard work, and inventive tracking. If drop-out does occur, its effects can be mitigated somewhat by the fact that we have information on the missing subjects from the waves during which they were present: we will thus be able to ascertain (and we should indeed do so) whether they deviated systematically on one or more variables of interest. See also Murphy (1990). More will be said on missing values in longitudinal research in Section 1.6.3.

The most important thing to remember in the area of drop-out is that prevention is better than cure. Important suggestions for preventing drop-out are to collect as much information as possible at the first measurement occasion on the network of the subjects, such as relatives' addresses, general practitioner, etc., to keep in touch with respondents through yearly birthday cards (on which one can simultaneously ask to pass on any change of address), payment of interviewers not per interview but per hour, doing everything to ensure the cooperation of the subjects, such as ensuring a pleasant atmosphere, ensuring that the interviewers are similar to the interviewed in terms of age, dress, and social class, stressing the importance of the subject's cooperation, etc. See also Farrington et al. (1990).

After elaborating on the need for complete representative samples, we need to mention as well that it is also possible that an investigator in a longitudinal study deliberately refrains from drawing a random sample from a population. A motivation to draw a biased sample is, for instance, to warrant the presence of a phenomenon in which the researcher is interested. Evidently, findings from such a study jeopardize external validity or generalizability. Still, researchers in developmental and other fields of psychology sometimes usesingle-subject designs for collecting data, because the nature of the problem under study requires it. For instance a researcher on learning might be interested in how the individual's behaviour can be modified during a learning task consisting of numerous responses. In that case the focus is primarily on the behaviour of the individual, and only in the second place may the researcher be interested in possible similarities in task performance under equal circumstances in other subjects. Such single-subject studies are also germane to research in client-centred psychotherapy. To discuss generalizability of single-subject data in the context of the person mode is something of an anomaly, however, as many such single-subject studies are not intended to generalize over persons. At the most, they are conducted to generalize over the occasion mode (see below) and sometimes they serve solely for falsifying existing or generating new hypotheses about the behaviour under study. The carefulness with which the issue of generalization over the person mode is generally approached in single-subject research is in stark contrast with the parallel situation in cross-sectional research where generalization over the occasion mode is often assumed implicitly. There, it is more often than not unquestioned and unchallenged that cross-sectional findings are valid for future circumstances as well.

If more subjects or clients are involved in such an $N = 1$ study, we have replicated single-subject designs, and the group and single-subject designs can be combined into multivariate, replicated, single-subject, repeated measures designs (see e.g. Nesselroade & Jones, 1991). Clearly, we then have person mode selection, variable mode selection, as well as time mode selection or occasion mode selection.

Variable mode   How does an investigator know if he or she has made the correct choice of which manifest variables to include in a given study? Do the manifest variables represent a domain of variables, and if so, how adequately? Or, alternatively stated, are the manifest variables appropriate indicators of the domain of interest? Here, domain validity is the issue, that is, the selection problem of the variable mode in combination with the question how the selected manifest variables represent the domain of variables. Variable selection has, in general, not as explicitly and as intensively been studied as person selection from a statistical point of view, that is, in terms of distribution theory. Nevertheless some work has been done in the area of variable selection, and these studies can be classified into two categories of research on the effects of variable selection. The first one encompasses studies of selection effects in terms of effects on statistical distributional properties (e.g. means, variances, covariances, correlations), and the second category includes research on generalizability. In the latter case the generalizability question in a broad as well as in a narrow sense is posed. Broadly speaking, generalizability refers to the extent to which the relationships observed among manifest variables (i.e. operationalized constructs) can be generalized to theoretical constructs other than those specified in the original research hypothesis. This is what Cook & Campbell (1979), among others, call external validity. In a narrow sense generalizability refers to the accuracy that obtains using a person's observed score as his or her universe score (see e.g. Cronbach, Gleser, Nanda, & Rajaratnam, 1972).

    In classical test theory, selection effects are studied in the context of reliability estimation and prediction, and are known as the effect of restriction of range. So far, we have considered only univariate selection on manifest variables. Obviously there are also situations in which multivariate selection of manifest variables takes place. In the context of test theory, multivariate restriction of range has rarely been studied (see, however, e.g. De Gruijter & Van der Kamp, 1984), nor has it been studied in the context of statistical theory at large. A first systematic approach of such selection biases was formulated by Berk (1983). So far, this work on selection effects or selection bias has not yet filtered into empirical behavioural and social research.

In addition to selection on the manifest variables, one can also think of selection of latent variables or constructs. If we take anxiety as a latent variable or construct, this construct can be operationalized as a score on an anxiety scale or as a physiological measure (e.g., GSR). And more than one kind of manifest variable might be used as operationalization of the same construct. Thus, with respect to the selection mode a hierarchy of selection decisions can be distinguished ranging from selection on the construct level to selection on the level of indicators (Nesselroade & Ford, 1987). Whatever the level at which the selection decisions are taken, they all influence generalizability of findings, in other words, they may impair external validity.

The distinction between the first and the second category of studies on selection effects with respect to the variable mode is not clear-cut if we take the second category as a broad one, i.e. by interpreting it as external validity. A narrower treatment of generalizability would be in terms of Cronbach's generalizability theory. The basic idea is that a measurement taken on a person records a sample of behaviour: a score on a variable is only one of many scores that might serve the same purpose. The usefulness of this score largely depends on the extent to which it enables an investigator to generalize from the observations at hand to a universe of generalization, that is, to similar behaviour in some wider set of situations. Generalizability theory recognizes that behavioural measurements may contain many sources of variance: among others, sources due to selection in the variable mode as well as in the time mode. Other modes may also give rise to variation, such as situations or experimental units. Experimental conditions may be a source of variance. Using an analysis of variance framework and postulating the existence of a universe of similar conditions allows an investigator to estimate relevant sources of variance. In other words, this framework enables us to assess the generalizability of the measurements.

However, the concept of a universe of generalization has been criticized already more than a quarter of a century ago by, among others, Loevinger (1965). The crux of the critique is that the concept of universe of generalization is not comparable to that of a population of subjects: whereas sampling subjects from a population makes sense, drawing a random sample from a universe of admissible variables does not make sense. Subjects in a population are interchangeable and independent, variables in a universe are not. One might define strata in the universe of variables and confine random sampling to separate strata, but this hardly solves the problem. Indeed, this postulate of a universe of measurement conditions (or universe of generalization) constitutes the Achilles' heel of generalizability theory. To date, rebuttals of these criticisms still remain forthcoming. The work on generalizability, however, has influenced the manner in which evaluations and social programmes are designed. Here also the basic framework is that of sampling. Sampling is now to be described in terms of units, treatments, observations and settings. In generalizability theory, sampling is intended with inference from the sample back to the original domain or another domain. In planning a study, the investigator has to define, i.e. to mark off, a domain of studies, all of which address the same or similar questions. The samples, of course, differ in the units and in the other conditions of observation or measurement. Specifying the treatment domain, the admissible procedures and observation conditions for data gathering on a certain variable (or on more than one of them), and the population intended marks off the relevant domain of an evaluation study. This basic orientation is implicit in the general framework of Cattell's (1966, 1988) BDRM or data box. These considerations on generalizability apply equally for longitudinal as well as cross-sectional research.

Apart from these theoretical and philosophical considerations, researchers in longitudinal studies may also be confronted with more pragmatic aspects of generalizability. The foremost of these is the effect of instrumentation on generalizability of the observed scores on the manifest variables to a behavioural domain, or a domain of hypothetical constructs. Let us give an example. Suppose that we have observed rebelliousness in a sample of youngsters. The youngsters are followed in a longitudinal study for 35 years. The first measurements took place in the 'roaring sixties'. Suppose for the sake of argument that after 35 years all sample subjects have children who are in their teens, and that we are interested to see whether the children of the parents who were rebellious are also rebellious. We are then faced with the fact that, at the start of the study rebelliousness was operationalized in a manner that reflected what was understood by rebelliousness in those days, 35 years ago. Now, we would have to use fairly different variables to measure what we now understand rebelliousness to be. In fact, to take the matter beyond the level of operationalization, one may even question whether the construct itself has the same meaning after 35 years? Therefore, not only the variables themselves, but also the manner in which the variables are indicators of the constructs we are investigating may change. Similar examples can be given for constructs such as 'social intelligence' or 'socio-economic status'.

Thus, even if a selection of manifest variables or a selection of latent constructs has been made that represents the universe of behaviour we would like to generalize to, this selection may well become wholly inadequate during the course of the longitudinal study. There are no easy solutions for this problem. If one retains the original operationalizations of the constructs, one can compare subjects over time points, but the interpretation of the more recent observations may be less meaningful. If one replaces the original variables by updated operationalizations, problems with the interpretation of the phenomena under investigation are solved, but – strictly speaking – one cannot compare subjects over time points any more.

Occasion mode   Longitudinal research and the measurement of change are defined across occasions or times of measurement. According to our definition, there are at least two occasions of measurement and the information gathered forms the basis on which statements on change and stability are made. In longitudinal studies the temporal units, whether in terms of duration (i.e. the length of the observational period from beginning to end) or of intervals constitute a crucial mode. One can think of this mode as being discrete (or continuous, but we limit ourselves to the discrete case), and two-occasion and multi-occasion inferences can be contrasted. However, the occasion mode causes temporal selection effects.

A first question that needs to be addressed in this respect is: what is the optimal number of occasions for a change study, optimal in the sense that stable longitudinal effects can be estimated. Thus, the question is essentially the same as the questions posed when discussing generalizability issues in the person mode and in the variable mode, except that generalizability now refers to the 'population' of time points. Thus, when discussing generalizability in the occasion mode, we essentially refer to the question whether, with the (number of) time points we use in our design, we can make valid and accurate predictions for the future. Answering the optimality problem with respect to the number of occasions without a further specification in terms of research question, design and data analysis is not possible. Even if a longitudinal study has been specified in more detail, it remains to be seen whether a satisfactory and generally acceptable answer can be given to the question how many occasions should be chosen. Essentially, the reason for this is that the occasion mode is not comparable with either the variable mode or the person mode. The researcher can, of course, define a universe of occasions and consider designs with a number of times of measurement. But can this investigator simply generalize from the sample to the universe of admissible observations? If one accepts the tenet that behaviour changes (systematically) over time, no matter how behaviour and time are related to each other, then the sampling orientation of the occasion mode must be considered critically and carefully.

Cronbach's generalizability theory has been around for more than a quarter of a century. In the meantime, much attention has been paid to a wide variety of designs that include various conditions or facets. To date, occasions or times of measurement have received only scant attention in this context. The reason for this is that generalizability analysis might well be inappropriate if behaviour cannot be assumed to be in 'a steady state', that is, not changing systematically over time, and not even so within a short time period (Shavelson, Webb, & Rowley, 1989, p. 926). As a measurement approach, generalizability theory (not unlike classical test theory) assumes that behaviour remains constant over observations. *"The best way to meet the steady state assumption is to restrict the time interval so that the observations of individuals' behaviour represent the same phenomenon"* (Shavelson et al., 1989, p. 926). Clearly, the ultimate restriction of the time interval is taking one time unit. Then, however, a longitudinal study is no longer involved.

Temporal generalizability poses a serious and in principle unsolvable problem. To illustrate the matter, we cite Nesselroade: *"Seeking lawful relationships that generalize over time, is something of a dilemma. One cannot sample the future in some representative way, and if one defines the population of interest so that its elements are all ac-*

cessible to sampling at a given time, that population is in some senses obsolete with the next tick of the clock" (Nesselroade, 1988, p. 22).

In a sense, all this constitutes a paradox. On the one hand, general-izability over the occasion mode (which can only amount to forecasting the future) is impossible, as we cannot sample the future. On the other hand, a first and foremost reason for conducting longitudinal studies is to be able to assess temporal changes, and for obtaining forecasts or projections for the variables of interest. The idea is that by investigating phenomena longitudinally, or dynamically, one may uncover the causal or generating mechanisms that produce the observed scores. If one knows the mechanisms, or has approximated them, one can, through extrapolation, or other assumptions about the relation between the time axis and the scores on the variables, obtain estimates of future scores.

Parallel to the situation in cross-sectional research, where the re-searcher has to decide how many subjects have to be observed to be able to estimate with a certain precision the level of some variable in the population, so the researcher in a longitudinal study has to decide how many occasions have to be used in order to be able to assess change validly and to forecast future levels of the variable(s) with a certain pre-cision. In practice, this question may translate in very different ways. For instance, in studies on the psychological adaptation processes of patients after presymptomatic DNA testing for Huntington's disease, it has been shown that observation periods of up to three years at least are necessary for assessing the psychological balance that patients have to reach to come to terms with their status (Tibben, Timman, Bannink, & Duivenvoorde, 1997). In time series analysis, a generally used rule of thumb is that the number of time points must be more than approxim-ately 50 for obtaining sufficient stability of the parameter estimates. It is not surprising that the use of time series studies in behavioural science has for this reason sometimes been regarded as impracticable.

Thus, generalizability over the occasion mode is an important issue. And in spite of the many criticisms that can be envisaged regarding the fundamental impossibility of generalizing towards something one has not sampled, and in spite of the pitfalls and uncertainty regarding the optimal or even minimum number of time points, it cannot be denied that longitudinal studies offer more opportunity for discovering tem-poral effects or temporal regularities than cross-sectional studies do. In fact, many so-called time series studies (in which the slice referred to as the P-technique is analysed, see Figure 1.2) have been designed to generalize over the occasion mode. Most of these models analyse one subject with respect to one variable, some analyse one subject with respect to several variables; in all instances, the main issue is to predict or forecast the future levels of the variables. Examples are the Dow Jones index, grain prices, the size of the prison population, etc.

The generalizability issues of the occasion mode and person mode embody important paradigmatic differences between classes of techniques. Most cross-sectional studies investigate a sample of subjects at one occasion, and attempt to generalize to a universe or population of subjects. Most time series studies investigate one subject over several occasions, and attempt to generalize to a universe of occasions. In order to be able to make these predictions, it is important that the dynamics of the process under investigation are captured. To capture this process, often a fairly complex representation with many parameters is needed. In that sense, time series models, or models that attempt to make accurate predictions of the future, are generally not even required to be parsimonious. More on this subject will be said in Section 2.4.1.

Surveying the three modes discussed above, one cannot conclude but by recommending that in a longitudinal study the researcher should specify the modes or dimensions of the hypothetical databox as explicitly as possible. This allows for a fair anticipation of possible selection effects in longitudinal research.

1.4 Designs for longitudinal studies

Longitudinal studies may vary in sample size, number of variables and number of occasions. The choice of particular samples and occasions and their combination, define what is called the longitudinal design. Broadly speaking, five main types of longitudinal designs can be distinguished:

1. simultaneous cross-sectional studies

2. trend studies

3. time series studies

4. intervention studies

5. panel studies

(see e.g. Keeves, 1997; Kessler & Greenberg, 1981; Menard, 1991). Before discussing these designs, we first outline three basic explanations for observed change. The reason to do so is that these explanations provide a means by which to evaluate the usefulness of the respective designs for answering substantive questions about change.

In a hypothetical example, suppose that we want to know how religious sentiments change over the course of the life cycle. We might postulate that, as people grow older, they become more religious. To answer our question, we take one sample of individuals, that harbours three subsamples: in one subsample all subjects are 20 years of age, in the second subsample all are 40 years of age, and in the third subsample all are 60 years of age. We measure religiousness for each age group.

Suppose that we find that the young are least religious, those in middle age are more religious, and the old are most religious. Are we right in concluding that people become more religious as they grow older? We are not, as this assertion (that religiousness is a function of age) is but one explanation for the observed effects. This explanation is called the *age effect*. A rivalling explanation is that the different levels of religiousness are simply linked to the age groups themselves: those born 20 years ago (the youngest cohort) are less religious, those born 40 years ago are more religious, and those born 60 years ago are most religious. In this manner, religiousness is formulated as a *cohort effect*: subjects' religiousness is determined by their time of birth. In that case, if we would measure religiousness again after 20 years, we would find that all three age groups are still at the same level of religiousness. Thus, there are two equally likely explanations for the results. We have no way of deciding which of the two is more likely.

To circumvent this problem, we redesign our experiment. We start out with one sample of individuals, and we assess their religiousness at 20 years of age, we measure again after 20 years, and assess their religiousness, and we repeat this after another 20 years. Suppose that again we find that when subjects are 20 years of age, they are least religious, and that as they grow older, they become more religious. Can we now confidently conclude that the observed increase in religiousness is an age effect? No, we cannot, and now there is an other rivalling explanation: it may be that the increased religiousness from the first measurement point to the second to the third is caused by an overall increased religiousness in the population over the course of the study. Then, the increased religiousness is a *period effect*.

This problem is commonly referred to as the age-period-cohort problem. Many textbooks on longitudinal data analysis discuss it (for instance the volume edited by Mason & Fienberg, 1985). The problem is caused by the fact that age, period and cohort effects – though conceptually different – are linearly dependent, in formula:

$$\text{Cohort} + \text{Age} = \text{Period}.$$

In our first hypothetical example, period was kept constant: we observed three samples of individuals at one time point. Thus any effects found can not be period effects, but they can be explained as either an age or as a cohort effect. In our second hypothetical example, cohort was kept constant: we observed one cohort of individuals, but now any effects we found could be explained as either age or period effects.

A practical way to deal with this problem is by imposing certain assumptions. For instance, in the first hypothetical example, we can assume that there are no cohort effects, after which we can decide that an age effect is present. And in the second example, we can decide that there is an age effect once we have made the assumption that there are no period effects. Of course we have no way of testing these assumptions, so the solution is essentially trivial.

We now move to the five designs enumerated above. The first of these is the *simultaneous cross-sectional design*. It is schematically represented in Table 1.1. In this design there are G groups of subjects (G different age groups) sampled by each cross-sectional study at the same occasion. Each age sample is observed with respect to M observed variables (e.g. the same predictor and criterion variables). The longitudinal dimension in this design is incorporated in the distinction of the different age groups. (This is in fact the same design we used in our first example on religiousness above.) This design has been employed in educational research for, e.g., the assessment of educational progress in mathematics achievement. We illustrated above how any changes between the various age groups can not only be explained as an age effect, but as a cohort effect as well. A related problem is that we can never assess intra-individual change with such a simultaneous cross-sectional design: the age groups are formed by different individuals. Some examples of analyses of simultaneous cross-sectional designs are given in Chapter 6, where analyses will be illustrated of the relation between father's socio-economic status (S_1 in the schematic representation) and son's socio-economic status (S_2 in the schematic representation – there are two groups in these examples in Chapter 6). Advantages of this design are efficiency: a longitudinal study is approximated, but measurements need to be made at one time point only. More on simultaneous cross-sectional studies can be found in for instance Keeves (1997) and Rudinger & Wood (1990).

Table 1.1: *Schematic Representation of the Simultaneous Cross-Sectional Design (After Keeves, 1997)*

Age group	Sample	Occasion	Observed variables
A_1	S_1	t_1	$X_1, X_2, X_3, \ldots, X_M$
A_2	S_2	t_1	$X_1, X_2, X_3, \ldots, X_M$
.	.	.	.
.	.	.	.
.	.	.	.
A_G	S_G	t_1	$X_1, X_2, X_3, \ldots, X_M$

The second design is a *trend study*. In *trend studies*, two or more related cross-sectional studies are performed with identical or comparable age groups at a number of occasions (T). Trend studies are schematically represented in Table 1.2. At each new occasion or time of measurement new, comparable (i.e. of the same age group in educational research) samples are drawn, while the same variables are observed over time. Such trend studies are conducted, for instance, in response to the perpetual and perennial problem posed by educational policy makers: 'Is the nation's educational level (for instance language skills in primary school) deteriorating?'. To answer this question, we could administer a language test to a sample of primary school children in the highest grade. If we repeat this every year, we will have a yearly assessment of language skills. If the scores decrease for several consecutive years, we have an indication that the nation's educational level is decreasing. Another substantive question for which the trend study design is appropriate is 'Is the level of petty crime rising among urban youth?'. To answer

Table 1.2: *Schematic Representation of a Trend Study*

Age group	Sample	Occasion	Observed variables
A_1	S_1	t_1	$X_1, X_2, X_3, \ldots, X_M$
A_1	S_2	t_2	$X_1, X_2, X_3, \ldots, X_M$
.	.	.	.
.	.	.	.
.	.	.	.
A_1	S_T	t_T	$X_1, X_2, X_3, \ldots, X_M$

this question, we can draw a random sample of urban youth every year, and ask them by some kind of self-report questionnaire the number of petty crimes they committed during the past year. Conducting our study this way, we are able to assess the trend in petty crime among urban youth. Again, as in the simultaneous cross-sectional design, we are unable to investigate intra-individual differences, as different samples are investigated at the various measurement occasions. Any changes can be identified at the aggregate level only.

Our second hypothetical example on religious affiliation represented a *time series design*. The design for time series studies is shown in Table 1.3. In a time series study, the same subjects (of the same sample)

Table 1.3: *Schematic Representation of a Time Series Study*

Age group	Sample	Occasion	Observed variables
A_1	S_1	t_1	$X_1, X_2, X_3, \ldots, X_M$
A_2	S_1	t_2	$X_1, X_2, X_3, \ldots, X_M$
.	.	.	.
.	.	.	.
.	.	.	.
A_T	S_1	t_T	$X_1, X_2, X_3, \ldots, X_M$

are followed at successive points in time. Thus, with this design it is possible to investigate intra-individual change. Table 1.3 gives a very general framework for time series studies, and for the sake of comparison with the data matrices in Table 1.1 and 1.2, here also age groups and samples are distinguished. A time series study, however, may also involve one subject followed over successive points in time and measured on only one variable (for instance blood pressure). Evidently, more subjects and more groups of subjects, and more variables can be involved in time series studies. Comparing the schematic representation of this design with the representations in Table 1.1 and Table 1.2, the advantages of this type of design over the simultaneous cross-sectional design and the trend design are once more illustrated. Since repeated observations are made of the same subjects, intra-individual changes as well as inter-individual differences can be studied. And if more age groups are included in the study, differences between groups in the intra-individual sequences of development will become clear.

The time series design is often encountered under the generic term *panel study*; in practice, the term time series study is used for designs with many occasions, and the term panel design for designs in which the number of waves is limited, in behavioural practice somewhere in the vicinity of 3 to 5 waves. The term 'panel' itself, as stated above, is often used for a group of subjects that is as a whole retained in a study and measured repeatedly. More on this design can be found in Finkel (1995) and Keeves (1997).

Thus, the time series or panel design is very suitable for investigating matters of intra-individual as well as inter-individual change. If it is used as a *prospective design*, that is, if the researchers actually start their measurements at t_1, and follow their sample up to t_T, it has many advantages over its main alternative, the simultaneous cross-sectional design. These advantages are primarily in the area of internal validity. This matter needs further consideration here.

In a prospective design one starts out with a sample of subjects. The subjects are measured repeatedly on a number of variables relevant to the phenomenon of interest. For instance, we are interested in the relation between personality characteristics, life events and disease. One of our research questions is: what is the relation between personality profile, life events and disease? To answer this question, we assess a number of personality traits at the start of the research, and follow the subjects through the course of their lives, registering life events and registering when subjects fall ill. In this manner we are able to give fairly conclusive answers to the research questions.

Prospective studies have unmistakable methodological strengths, but they are expensive and time-consuming, and thus costly and risky. Especially when the phenomenon of interest has low frequency of occurrence, one has to start out with huge samples in order to obtain sufficient numbers of subjects who can be investigated on the phenomenon of interest. Thus, prospective studies are practicable only for the investigation of phenomena that occur relatively often. An additional disadvantage is that the time-lag with which results become available is often quite long, and in many instances too long for practical purposes.

In many instances researchers have therefore attempted to conduct panel studies with all the methodological advantages of a prospective design, but without the accompanying cost, organizational complications and long waiting time. One option for circumventing the disadvantages related to repeated tracking, is to conduct the so-called 'instant' version of the panel study, which is the *retrospective design.* In a retrospective design, one starts at t_T, and, as it were, conducts the study looking backwards. One thus starts at the last measurement occasion in the design and asks after events retrospectively. In our example on personality, life events and disease, we could draw a sample of subjects, of whom some have a certain disease C, and some do not. We can not anymore measure the subjects' personality traits at t_1 as we would have done in a prospective study, so we measure the relevant personality traits at t_T. Furthermore we ask the subjects to indicate what major life events happened to them and when these took place in the course of their lives.

This looks like an elegant solution to a nasty problem. There are a few associated complications, however. Firstly, the sample one investigates in a retrospective study is non-random. This is so because attrition has taken place in the sense that if one would have started with a certain sample at t_1, part of the sample would have moved house, died, refused, etc. It appears as if there is no such loss to follow-up as sampling takes place at t_T, but units of measurement are excluded from the data collection (such as subjects who died during the period under consideration), so that the data do suffer from sampling bias.

Secondly, to answer our research question, we have to correlate the scores on the variable indicating presence of disease C to the personality variables and variables indicating the life events. Suppose that a positive association between, say, personality type A and disease C is found, we conclude that people with personality type A are more likely to develop disease C. Is this conclusion justified? The answer is no. To start with, as we are observing correlations, cause and effect can not be inferred. Statistically speaking, it is just as likely that personality type A causes disease C, as that disease C causes personality type A. We are unable to decide (as we could have done in a prospective study) that the personality structure was already there when disease C developed, or whether both developed simultaneously, or even whether the observed pattern of personality traits emerged after onset of the disorder. In other words: it has become much harder to distinguish whether personality structure is cause, correlate, or effect of the disorder.

Apart from these complications, long-term retrospective data also tend to be more unreliable than prospective data. This is so because respondent's (lack of, or biased) recall may influence the quality of the data (in our hypothetical example the occurrence and timing of life events). Five reasons are generally identified for this: memory loss, retrieval problems, telescoping, false positives or negatives, and the so-called 'modification to fit a coherent scheme'.

To start with the first two, many subjects simply forget the occurrence of events, feelings, considerations. And even when events have not been wholly forgotten, subjects may have trouble recalling them. Therefore, in retrospective studies, it is often advised to use so-called 'aided recall', by which is meant that subjects are presented with a checklist of possible events.

However, even if all relevant events have been correctly remembered, if asked *when* certain events happened, respondents tend to report those events as having taken place more recently than they actually did. This tendency of bias in reporting towards the more recent past is known as *telescoping*. The inverse also occurs, in which (some) subjects place events further away in the past than they actually happened. This results in false positives (or negatives): events are reported as having occurred within (or outside of) the period under investigation when they actually occurred in another period. An additional validity problem is that subjects can easily accommodate questions they feel uncomfortable with as: 'did not occur', or 'do not remember'.

Lastly, subjects tend to interpret and re-interpret events, opinions and feelings so that they fit in with subjects' current perception of their lives and their past lives, and constitute a sequence of events that bears some logic. This tendency is called the 'modification to fit a coherent scheme'.

In general, it applies that the longer the recall period is, the more unreliable retrospective data tend to become. Retrospective designs are particularly unsuitable for assessing past attitudes, opinions, behaviour with an evaluative connotation, abilities, as well as the measurement of gradual changes (see Janson, 1990). Retrospective data are also known to be sensitive to social desirability. On the other hand, the more factual the questions that need to be asked, the more suitable a retrospective study is. And for investigating phenomena that occur with low incidence (such as for instance studies into health, demographic and other correlates of infant cot death – which has very low incidence), retrospective studies are often the only practicable way to proceed. These and other issues regarding retrospective data are outlined in more detail by for instance Janson (1990). See also Farrington et al. (1990) and Menard (1991).

Before moving on to the next design, we remark on a special kind of time series or panel design, the so-called *revolving panel design*. In a revolving panel design, at each occasion a (fixed) part of the sample is replaced or so to say 'refreshed' by new subjects. This has the advantage that subjects will less easily develop 'survey boredom', that there will be fewer testing and learning effects, and that there will be less panel mortality. Certain types of bias can be traced when using this design. When the entire sample is replaced or sampled anew at every time point, we are left with the type of design that is used in opinion polls, family budget surveys and the like.

The fourth design is the *intervention study*. A schematic representation for *intervention studies* is presented in Table 1.4. Here again the representation is more elaborate than strictly necessary, but again this is for comparison's sake. The intervention or treatment affects only the subjects in the experimental group(s), but pre-intervention and post-intervention data are collected over successive time-points for the subjects of all groups. The most simple intervention study would be the well-known pretest-posttest control group design, in which one experimental and one control group are involved, and where the effects of an

Table 1.4: *Schematic Representation of Intervention Studies*

Age	Experimental Treatment	Control group No treatment	Sample	Occasion	Observed variables
A_1	E_1	C_1	S_1	t_1	$X_1, X_2, X_3, \ldots, X_M$
A_2	E_1	C_1	S_1	t_2	$X_1, X_2, X_3, \ldots, X_M$
.	.	.	.	.	.
.	.	.	.	.	.
.	.	.	.	.	.
A_T	E_1	C_1	S_1	t_T	$X_1, X_2, X_3, \ldots, X_M$

intervention or treatment are studied by analysing pretest and posttest scores of the subjects in both groups. If the experimental and control groups are not comparable, for instance because they have not been formed through random assignment of subjects, the design is called a non-equivalent control group design, which is a popular design in quasi-experimentation (see Cook & Campbell, 1979). Another design that is popular for intervention studies is the so-called *regression-discontinuity design* (see for instance Cook & Campbell (1979)). The design for an intervention study resembles that of the panel design. The only difference is that two types of subjects are investigated: subjects who receive a certain treatment, and subjects who do not receive the treatment.

The last design we discuss is the *longitudinal panel study*. The longitudinal panel study, also often referred to as a multiple cohort design, a cohort study, or – confusingly – a panel study, investigates multiple cohorts at multiple occasions. Because of the fact that the design is in fact an agglomeration of the simultaneous cross-sectional design and the time series design, period, age and cohort effects may be easier to identify. Both the trend study design, the time series design and the simultaneous cross-sectional design can be retrieved from this design.

In the design underlying panel studies, the same sample of subjects is observed at each time of measurement. A longitudinal panel design in addition includes multiple cohorts. If the number of times of measurement and of cohorts is sufficient, virtually any type of longitudinal data analysis is possible. Table 1.5 gives a schematic representation of a longitudinal panel study.

Table 1.5: *Schematic Representation of a Longitudinal Panel Study*

		Period					
		1936	1956	1966	1976	1986	1996
		1946	1966	1976	1986	1996	2006
Cohort		1956	1976	1986	1996	2006	2016
		1966	1986	1996	2006	2016	2026
		1976	1996	2006	2016	2026	2036
Age			20	30	40	50	60

In Table 1.5 the columns constitute trend studies: for instance in the first column we see that 20-year olds are investigated in 1956 (they were born in 1936), a new sample of 20-year olds is investigated in 1966 (born in 1946), etc.

The rows constitute time series studies: for instance in the last row a sample of subjects all born in 1976 is investigated in 1996 (when they are 20 years old), in 2006 (when they are 30 years old), in 2016... etc.

The anti-diagonals constitute simultaneous cross-sectional studies: for instance the anti-diagonal contains a study in which 20-year olds (born in 1976) are investigated in 1996, 30-year olds (born in 1966) are investigated in 1996, 40-year olds... etc.

1.5 Validity issues in longitudinal research

The tenability and generalizability of empirical research in general and of longitudinal research in particular are influenced by four classes of threats that deal with the following questions:

1. statistical conclusion validity This is defined as the extent to which the design of the study is sufficiently sensitive or powerful to detect outcome effects. It addresses the question whether the relationship(s) observed in the sample are due to chance.

2. internal validity – the extent to which the detected outcome effects are due to the operationalized causes rather than to other rivalling causes. This is often rephrased as: are there no alternative explanations for the detected effects?

3. external validity – the extent to which the detected outcome effects can be generalized to theoretical constructs, subjects, occasions and situations other than those specified in the original study. In most instances, this type of validity is used to refer to the question whether the effects that were found in the sample can be assumed to exist in the population as well.

4. construct validity – the extent to which the theoretical constructs in a study have been successfully operationalized. In other words: does the measurement on a certain variable represent the phenomenon it is supposed to represent?

These and similar definitions of research validities can be found in textbooks. Elaborations have been proposed; a succinct overview is given by Cook & Shadish (1994).

Each of these four types of research validity may be under threat. This is not only so in longitudinal research, but as well in cross-sectional research. Cook & Campbell (1979), Cook, Campbell, & Peracchio (1990), Judd & Kenny (1981) and Pedhazur & Pedhazur Schmelkin (1991) are among the most important authors to consult on these matters. They also discuss relationships and priorities among validities (for recent discussions, see Cook & Shadish, 1994). In the following we will elaborate on threats to the first three types of validity as far as they are particular to or particularly important for longitudinal research. The fourth type of validity, construct validity, is of a qualitatively different nature, and as such will be discussed below in Section 1.6.1. For a general exposition of threats to validity the reader is referred to, among others, Cook & Campbell (1979) and Messick (1989). Statistical conclusion validity and construct validity in the context of longitudinal research is discussed by e.g. Bergman & Magnusson (1990) and Rudinger & Wood (1990).

The validity issues that will be raised in this section have to do with longitudinal designs in general. Particular longitudinal designs have their own, particular threats of validity. Some examples will be mentioned in passing. For more specific validity issues with respect to measurement instruments, other data collection methods, aggregation of data, and the like, and for other aspects of data quality in longitudinal research the interested reader is referred to for instance Bergman & Magnusson (1990), and Magnusson & Bergman (1990).

1.5.1 Statistical conclusion validity

The most important threat to statistical conclusion validity that is due to the longitudinal nature of the data is serial dependence. When the measurements on the successive occasions are *serially dependent*, the observations at time point $t + 1$ can be predicted (to a certain extent) by the observations at time point t. Such serial dependence invalidates many commonly used test statistics.

Suppose that we have collected T measurements for N subjects. However, as the measurements at time point t can be partly accounted for by the past measurements at time points $t - 1, t - 2, \ldots$, we cannot extract as much information from the T dependent measurements as we could extract from the same number of independent measurements. Thus, the number of degrees of freedom in the dependent case is actually lower. In practice this means that test statistics will be judged significant too easily. In addition to the inflated degrees of freedom, the serial correlation will also mask part of the within variation in the data, which causes additional inflation of the statistics.

Serially correlated errors may also lead to least squares estimators that have increased variance. However, if one were to try to assess the precision of the estimates, that same precision would then be judged as smaller than it would be in the non-serially dependent case. The serially correlated errors thus give way to a misleading picture where the variances of the estimators are inflated, but appear in fact to be much better than they really are. In general, serial correlation may affect the bias, efficiency and consistency of estimators. See Brillinger (1981), for references on various studies into the behaviour of standard techniques when the assumptions are not met. Thus, most standard (statistical) techniques cannot be used for repeated measures, and specially designed techniques have to be used if we want to attain statistical conclusion validity. This book will discuss a number of such techniques.

1.5.2 Internal validity

Internal validity is concerned with the plausibility of the observed relationship among presumed antecedent and consequent variables. This plausibility question can be rephrased as: are there no alternative explanations for the observed association between variables? Apart from the threats to internal validity that are also present in cross-sectional studies, longitudinal studies face additional threats to internal validity as the time-axis itself may act as a confounder. This can be envisaged as follows. Suppose that two variables X and Y, measured for N subjects at 3 time points, have at each time point a correlation of almost zero. However, at each new time point, the scores on X and Y increase. Analysis of the data over time points then produces a positive correlation between X and Y (see Figure 1.3).

Figure 1.3: *Positive Correlation Computed over Time Points*

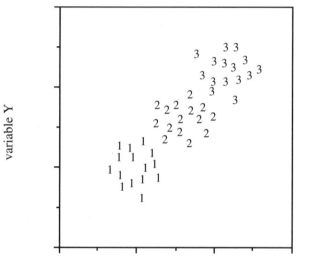

variable X

Technically speaking, such a correlation is spurious. If we were to compute the correlation per time point it would be zero: the correlation between X and Y vanishes if we control for the third variable 'time'. Other time-induced relationships can be imagined, such as the one presented in Figure 1.4, where the scores at each time point have a positive correlation, but analysis over time points results in a negative correlation.

Such situations occur frequently in longitudinal research, and researchers should always heed their conclusions, and not feel safe to present their findings until after close scrutiny of potential alternative

Figure 1.4: *Negative Correlation Computed over Time Points*

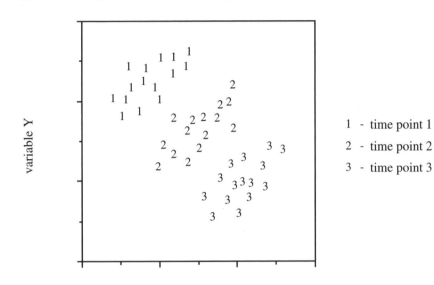

variable X

explanations for the effects. A classic example stems from a study on the relation between lung volume and smoking among secondary school pupils, where researchers came up with the surprising result that smoking increased lung volume. Upon closer inspection, it was found that the two variables were confounded through age. Pupils in the lower grades smoked less on average, and also had smaller lung volume; pupils in the higher grades tended to smoke more often, and had bigger lung volume. When corrected for age, the relation between lung volume and smoking indeed became negative, as expected.

We briefly discuss the threats to internal validity that are most pertinent to longitudinal studies.

(a) *History.* History is directly connected with time-of-measurement effects: typical events may modify the observations or measurements of a group of subjects. Examples are external events, coming from the outside world. For instance, if one investigates subjects' fear of flying in a training programme, designated to reduce subjects' fears, and a plane from the national airline crashes somewhere in the world, this is bound to interfere with subjects' fear levels. In that case, the effects of the training programme, and the effects of the publicity on the airline crash have become undistinguishable. The change in fear of flying cannot be attributed solely to the training programme anymore, as there is an alternative explanation (the airline crash).

(b) *Maturation*. Irrespective of possible historical events taking place, subjects may show differential maturational change in the course of the longitudinal study. Thus, one may investigate the effect of certain maths training courses on students' maths proficiency. However, the students also mature cognitively in an autonomous manner during the course of the study. Thus, any changes in maths skills cannot be attributed exclusively to the training courses anymore. There is an alternative explanation (maturation) and thus internal validity is threatened.

(c) *Testing*. Testing reflects the effects of the measurement process itself, as it may lead to practice because of repetitive testing. For instance, repeated language proficiency tests may increase students' skills in filling out those tests. For the same reason outlined above, there are several explanations for any found effects.

(d) *Instrumentation*. Statistically speaking, instrumentation amounts to the fact that differences in the measurement procedures may covary with the times of measurement. In Section 1.3, some of the possible threats to validity due to instrumentation were already mentioned in passing.

(e) *Statistical regression towards the mean* is the phenomenon that variables containing errors of measurement tend to regress toward their mean from one occasion of measurement to the next. In experimental situations, observed changes may thus be due to regression towards the (group) mean, or may also be attributed to the interventions.

(f) *Mortality* or sample attrition, was discussed previously in Section 1.3 in the context of generalizability, that is, in terms of the fact that non-random drop-out of subjects may cause the sample to become unrepresentative of the population. Moreover, differential drop-out may also threaten internal validity. This is so because any changes in the levels of the variables of interest may also be caused by the changed composition of the sample. Mortality or sample attrition can be a serious problem because of the cumulative effect of attrition over time leading to incomplete data. Mortality generally worsens with longer periods of observation. A similar validity issue arises in studies in which revolving panels are used, or repeated samples. Firebaugh (1997) discusses ways to separate effects due to sample turnover from effects due to intraindividual change.

(g) *Compounds* or combinations of these threats of internal validity.

More threats to internal validity have been listed in the context of, e.g., intervention studies and developmental research (Cook & Campbell, 1979; Judd & Kenny, 1981; Nesselroade & Labouvie, 1985).

Two solutions are available to counteract most of these threats. The first of these is also used extensively in the context of cross-sectional research. It amounts to employing a control group. When the control group is chosen in such a way that it differs from the experimental group only with regard to the intervention, then any differences between the two can be ascribed to the intervention only. Any or all the above mentioned threats to validity may well be present, but because they are present in the experimental group as well as in the control group, differences between the groups are unaffected by them. Another solution sometimes put forward is to use a time-series design. Measuring with greater frequency makes it possible to detect the presence of a number of these threats (particularly maturation and testing), so that conclusions can be adapted accordingly.

A threat to internal validity particular to longitudinal studies of longer duration, which is somewhat out of line with the previous threats is the *effect of publication* of the results for the separate waves. For instance, publication of the preliminary results (say, mid-term, or after a number of waves) of research on maths proficiency in secondary schools, may influence mathematics teachers' teaching behaviour. This may affect maths results of school children, and thus invalidate findings.

1.5.3 External validity

External validity defines the limits of valid generalizations from the findings of a given longitudinal study over experimental units, settings, measurement variables, and occasions or times of measurement. Generalization over experimental units refers to the extent to which the findings from a longitudinal study on one sample of a population permit inference to other populations. In this respect longitudinal studies do not differ from cross-sectional studies. If intervention studies are intended as longitudinal research, also generalization over treatments is as well a form of external validity. In Section 1.3, in connection with the three modes of observation, the most pertinent problems of external validity in the context of longitudinal research were already discussed.

1.5.4   Reliability and other aspects of construct validity

Different types of longitudinal data can be gathered depending upon the data collection methods (e.g. psychological test data, data arising from questionnaires, observations, interviews and the like). Construct validity is an important property of such measurements, cross-sectional as well as longitudinal. Construct validity is generally considered as reflecting various psychometric aspects. The first of these is *reliability*. Reliability can be described as the extent to which the measures on some variable represent the phenomenon of interest accurately. Reliability is a necessary (but not a sufficient) condition for construct validity.

The definition of reliability of longitudinal data depends upon the test score model chosen. If the classical test score model is chosen, reliability is defined as the ratio of true scores and observed scores. One procedure then to estimate this reliability coefficient is to calculate the correlation coefficient of scores between repeated measurements, i.e. the test-retest reliability or stability coefficient. The latter coefficient indicates how stable the obtained test scores are over time. But if the researcher is interested in change measures, defined for example as the difference between posttest and pretest scores, does it make sense to estimate a stability coefficient or must one rely on the reliability of the difference scores? In the latter case, however, the well-known problem arises of the lack of reliability of difference scores and of change scores in general (see any elementary textbook, such as Traub, 1994). These problems will not be pursued here; we return to this subject in Section 1.6.1. See also Willett (1988), and Bergman & Magnusson (1990).

Construct validity may also be under threat due to the repeated nature of the data. Generally speaking, data are said to be valid when they reflect those aspects of individual characteristics or behaviour that they are purported to reflect and not something else. Construct validity refers to the measurement procedure as a whole given its momentary character, and cannot be assessed once and for all. Several types of construct validity are distinguished: *criterion-related validity, content validity* and *construct validity in a narrow sense*. Each of these validities gives rise to its own problems if considered in a longitudinal situation. If criterion-related validity is the issue, validity is established by the use of external criteria. For instance, do scores on a certain surgery examination predict operating skills? External criteria, however, may also change and be unstable. Content validity refers to the issue whether for instance certain tests intended to measure a personality trait capture the entire breadth of the spectrum of aspects that are important for describing that trait. If we take intelligence as an example, we see that ideas of what constitutes intelligence have also evolved over the years and that the number of elements that are purported to constitute intelligence have increased considerably. Similar difficulties arise in a longitudinal context with content validity in the narrow sense (for instance we have a test that is supposed to measure the hypothetical construct social intelligence). Again, the conceptualization of the construct itself may be under the influence of time, and thus changing. To make matters worse, suppose that a researcher is interested in cognitive development – how is the concept of cognition defined, as a stable or as a changing concept? These and related issues are elaborated in, e.g., Bergman & Magnusson (1990), Rutter & Pickles (1990), and Magnusson, Bergman, Rudinger, & Törestad (1991).

1.6 Other methodological concerns in longitudinal research

In addition to the general problems attached to cross-sectional research, longitudinal research has critical issues and problems of its own arising from the nature of longitudinal data per se. In the following a number of important issues will be briefly reviewed.

1.6.1 Conditional or unconditional analysis

There has been quite a bit of controversy over the issue of unconditional versus conditional analysis of repeated measures. Briefly, the issue can be sketched as follows (see also Bock, 1975). Suppose that we have measured subjects' score on some variable, say we have measured body weight, at two occasions, t_1 and t_2. The subjects are men and women enrolled in a weight loss programme, and we are interested to investigate whether men and women differ with respect to their weight loss from t_1 to t_2.

Two options are available for analysis. First, we can simply compute the differences between the two measurements ($\text{WEIGHT}_2 - \text{WEIGHT}_1$), and assess whether men's and women's weight loss differs. This is called an *unconditional* analysis. Secondly, we can tackle the research question by adopting a covariance approach for comparing men's and women's weight loss. We regress weight at time 2 on weight at time 1, in formula: $\text{WEIGHT}_{i2} = a + b\text{WEIGHT}_{i1} + e_i$. If the slopes for the regression lines of weight at time 2 on weight at time 1 are the same for men and women, it is possible to compare the intercepts of the two groups. This is called a *conditional* analysis: the value of WEIGHT_2 is regarded as conditional on WEIGHT_1. Both models would appear to answer the question about change in the same way. However, in many practical instances, this turns out to be not the case.

This can be understood if we realize that the two methods address different inferential problems. In the unconditional method, one simply assesses whether the average weight loss in the two populations is the same. In the conditional method, one addresses the question: is the expected weight loss the same in the two groups, given equal weight at time 1? Phrased differently, with the conditional method one thus assesses whether a man and a woman with equal weight have the same expected weight loss. It is obvious that this can not be the case in general: if a man and a woman have the same weight, either the man is relatively underweight and is thus expected to lose less weight, or the woman is relatively overweight and is thus expected to lose more weight. This seemingly paradoxical situation is commonly known as Lord's paradox. The paradox is due to the covariate initial weight.

The paradox is not surprising as the two models answer essentially different questions. Where the unconditional model addresses the issue of change per se, the conditional model evaluates the score on time point 2 conditional on the score on time point 1. Statistically speaking, a different criterion is optimized, so that the two methods may turn up with different answers to what are different questions. For more information, see Bock (1975). This implies that the researcher will have to make a choice for either of the two models.

Difference scores (the variables analysed in unconditional models) have a number of limitations. Firstly, they can be used only for variables that have been measured at least at interval level. Thus, if we have categorical variables (ordinal or nominal), we cannot use difference scores. Secondly, difference scores can only be used in a straightforward manner if the variances of the variables at the time points are the same. Since, in longitudinal research, the levels of the scores on the variables generally increase with time, also the variances increase. This makes it harder to express the differences between the scores on t_2 and t_1. To deal with this, the variables may be standardized, but this induces the complication that interpretation in terms of the raw scores is not possible anymore, and only relative individual change can be assessed. Thirdly, in the social and behavioural sciences, many variables are measured with error. And as the scores on the respective time points do not represent the 'true' scores, also the difference scores do not represent the true difference. In fact, it can be shown that the reliability of difference scores is in practice generally worse than that of either of the two measurements from which that difference score was formed. This issue of unreliability of difference scores has received quite a bit of attention. A number of authors have recently argued that for certain purposes difference scores are quite acceptable. Recommended reading in this area is Rogosa, Brandt, & Zimowski (1982) as well as Rogosa (1995). While difference scores constitute a pragmatic solution for flattening the data box when there are two time points, this advantage soon disappears when more measurement occasions are present. In general, with T time points, $T - 1$ variables with difference scores can be constructed, and dealing with $T - 1$ such scores is less straightforward again.

Another issue related to the question of whether to use conditional or unconditional models, is the fact that in many instances the score on an initial measurement such as a pretest is correlated with the subsequent change. A classic example is regression towards the mean: those with high scores on the pretest tend to have lowered scores on the posttest, and those with low scores on the pretest tend to have higher scores on the posttest. When regression towards the mean occurs, change is negatively correlated with initial score. The reverse also occurs: for instance animals with high birth weight tend to grow faster than animals with lower birth weight. Whenever such relations are present in the data, difference scores are clearly inadequate as they do not take into account initial score at all. In such cases, conditional models are warranted.

In general, models with latent variables are considered to offer adequate solutions for dealing with measurement error. As such, they offer a solution for the reliability problems associated with differences scores. In addition, they provide a natural framework for modelling causal concepts. In a regression model in which the score on a posttest is predicted from the score at the pretest, the idea that causes (pretest) occur before effects (posttest) is incorporated, as well as the idea that later occurrences can be predicted from previous occurrences. As such, conditional models bear close links to the so-called causal models, or structural equation models. In addition, as will be shown below, also categorical variables can be analysed in conditional models. Rogosa (1995) provides an eminently readable overview on these issues. Further references are Plewis (1985) and Bock (1975).

This book focuses on conditional models, although a number of examples of unconditional models will be given in Chapter 3.

1.6.2   Aggregation

Aggregation of data amounts to collecting data and amalgamating them, either across subjects, across situations or interventions, across subvariables, or across time. If behaviour is situation-specific, then data aggregated across situations cannot be used for the analysis of cross-situational variation in individual behaviour. Aggregation across subvariables (e.g. subscales or items of a questionnaire) also has its limitations. For instance, it is common practice to aggregate across subgroups of items of the Beck Depression Inventory (BDI), which gives overall depression scores. Factor analyses of items of the BDI have led time and again to three underlying factors of the BDI. Can we conclude from this that aggregation over items for the BDI is justified?

In general, aggregation of data has consequences for the psychometric properties of the data, that is: for reliability, internal consistency, homogeneity and validity. The reliability of the BDI as a whole, for example, is higher than the reliability of its three factorially homogeneous subscales. Also the reliability of ratings aggregated across raters are generally higher than the individual rater reliabilities. However, this result does not imply that aggregated ratings (or for that matter, aggregated scores in general) are more valid. It is well-known that reliability is a necessary condition for validity, but it is not a sufficient one.

Aggregation over groups has consequences for the statistical properties of parameter estimates. For instance, the estimate of the effect of teacher instruction on language proficiency is suboptimal if we do not take into account the fact that students are grouped in classes, and that this grouping itself has an effect on students' scores on the language test in the sense that students in one class are generally more alike than students in different classes. Chapter 5 discusses multilevel models that have features to deal with the so-called aggregation bias due to such groupings.

More problematic issues arise if aggregation of data across time is considered. Some of the problems can easily be surmised if we consider, e.g., physiological (re)activity in terms of adrenaline excretion, aggressiveness and motor restlessness of schoolchildren in a longitudinal study. For example, if the physiological measures are collected weekly, but the other measures daily, how does the researcher treat these data? In very general terms this question may be phrased as how does the researcher treat data that are collected over different occasions? The time-disaggregated treatment and analysis of such data is the central question in the chapters to follow.

1.6.3   Missing data

Many are the sources of incomplete data in social science research. In behavioural research in general, missing data occur because of the fact that individuals either refuse to participate or are not willing to answer certain questions for one reason or another. In the cross-sectional research situation, the first source generates what is called drop-out or non-response; this was dealt with in a previous subsection. The second type generates what is generally referred to as missing values.

In the longitudinal case we can use a further classification relevant for the longitudinal focus, along the level at which missing data occur. In doing so, we distinguish between missing subjects, missing occasions and missing values.

We may have subjects who refuse to cooperate at all. Just as in the cross-sectional case, these subjects constitute the non-response. Such a non-responder may be called a *missing subject*. A missing subject is thus a subject who refused to cooperate, could not participate, could not be traced, in other words: who did not partake in the longitudinal study at any measurement point. Such missing subjects affect the representativeness of the sample and thus affect generalizability. Missing subjects evidently also affect sample size, but this can be accommodated by starting out with a larger sample, so that one ends up eventually with a large enough one. Missing subjects constitute as much of a problem in longitudinal research as they do in cross-sectional research. Most problematic is the situation where we have no background information on the missing subjects, in which case we have no way of assessing in what respect and to what extent non-responders differ from responders.

Missing occasions arise when a subject participates in the study during a number of occasions, but not all. At some occasions measurements are available for the subject, at some all measurements are missing. This situation typically arises when subjects drop out. For instance, subjects are present during the initial waves of the study, but do not reply anymore from a certain wave onwards, either because they have moved house or have died or for any other reason. Also, some subjects may enter the study after the study has started, that is, after a number of waves. In such cases we have longitudinal data for a group of subjects, but the series collected are of unequal length. Of course it is also possible that subjects are absent from one or more waves, but reenter the sample after a while. Then, we have number of series with gaps, or interrupted series. If subjects drop out after a number of occasions, the consequences are not as serious as they are in the case in which subjects do not participate at all. When subjects drop out during the course of the study, we have important information on them: not only as regards background characteristics, but also with respect to the variables of interest. Thus, we are able to compare subjects who remain in the sample with those who drop out.

A last category is the *missing value* problem. This may arise when subjects are available at a certain wave, but do not fill in all the questions at their answering sheet: measurements are thus available on some, but not on all variables. This situation is often more problematic in the longitudinal case than in the cross-sectional case. Many longitudinal analysis techniques need complete series of data. For such techniques, (any) missing data at a certain occasion cause not only that occasion for that subject to be useless, but also the entire series for that subject. Formulated differently, where in the cross-sectional case missing data for a subject cause the measurements for that subject to be unusable, in the longitudinal case missing data for a subject on one occasion may cause the measurements for that subject on all occasions to be unusable.

The differential occurrence of missing values (that is, as entirely missing occasions or as missing values within an occasion), has different implications for the way they can be dealt with. Longitudinal analysis techniques discussed differ in the extent to which they are sensitive to the various types of missing data: some can handle series of unequal length and others can not, again others can easily deal with missing values, while others need complete data etc.

In addition, the manner in which missing data can be dealt with is also largely determined by the mechanism through which missing data are generated. Little & Rubin (1987, 1989) distinguish three such mechanisms. Data are said to be *missing completely at random* (MCAR) when the probability that a measurement is missing does not depend on its own (unknown) score or on the score on any of the other variables. (In practice, this situation is often – confusingly – referred to as missing at random.) Data are said to be *missing at random* (MAR) when the probability that a measurement is missing may depend on the value of any of the manifest variables, but is unrelated to the scores on any of the latent variables. For instance, the probability of a missing measurement may be related to the values on for instance an IQ test, but is unrelated to the true scores or the latent ability. Whenever the probability of a measurement being missing is related to not only values of the manifest variables, but to those of the unobserved variables as well, the data are *non-ignorable missing*. This is the most serious, and unfortunately also the most frequently occurring type of missing data. It is also the type of missing for which the least degree of amendment can be made.

When data can be assumed to be missing completely at random, a pragmatic approach is to just run computations with the nonmissing part of the data (obtained either through listwise or pairwise deletion) and generalize the results to the population from which the sample was drawn. However, this is a very strong assumption, which is hardly ever met. In most cases data are not missing completely at random, and not even missing at random. Usually, those who drop out during the course of the study deviate from those who remain throughout the study, either on background variables, or on one or more of the variables that are of specific interest in the study. Drop-outs are generally: more criminal, more depressed, less adaptable, etc. Thus, simply leaving out these subjects altogether may seriously invalidate the findings.

If data can not be assumed to be missing completely at random, weighting procedures and imputation methods can be used. Weighting methods are often used for handling unit nonresponse, for instance when entire units such as questionnaires, are missing. The imputation-based procedures estimate the missing data on the basis of the nonmissing part and insert these estimations to create a complete data set which can subsequently be analysed by standard statistical methods. The problem of missing data and its remedies have been treated only briefly and generally here. More can be found in Little & Rubin (1987), Rovine & Delaney (1990), Rovine (1994), and Little & Schenker (1995). Although many procedures are around for handling missing data, it should be kept in mind that *"the most important step in dealing with missing data is to try to eliminate it as much as possible during the data collection stage"* (Little & Schenker, 1995, p. 69).

1.7   Further reading

An introduction to longitudinal research is given by Menard (1991). The volume edited by Nesselroade & Baltes (1979) will probably in due time turn out to be a classic on longitudinal research in the study of behaviour and development. Methodological issues in aging research are considered in a volume edited by Schaie, Campbell, Meredith, & Rawlings (1988), data quality in longitudinal research is treated in a volume edited by Magnusson & Bergman (1990), while problems of stability and change are the main topic of the contributions collected by Magnusson et al. (1991). Informative reviews have been published by Kowalski & Guire (1974), Schaie & Hertzog (1982), Cook & Ware (1983), Schaie & Hertzog (1985), Von Eye (1985), Keeves (1997), and Willett (1988). Henning & Rudinger (1985) edited a volume on the analysis of qualitative data in developmental psychology, Visser (1985) wrote a monograph on the analysis of quantitative longitudinal data, Von Eye (1990) edited two volumes of statistical methods in longitudinal research, and a companion volume containing applied computational statistics is written by Rovine & Von Eye (1991). Von Eye &

Clogg (1994) collected contributions to the application of latent variable analysis for developmental research. The measurement of change is
a topic by itself, that can be subsumed under longitudinal data analysis.
The most recent volumes in this field are the ones edited by Collins &
Horn (1991), with problems relevant for psychological research, Dale &
Davies (1994), who focus on the analysis of social and political change,
and Gottman (1995) with applications particularly relevant for developmental psychology. In addition to the publications which emphasize
applications in the social and behavioural sciences, an important statistical handbook in which causal inference, structural equation modelling,
multilevel modelling, latent class models, panel analysis for metric as
well as qualitative variables and event history analysis are treated, is the
book edited by Arminger, Clogg, & Sobel (1995). A monograph on
panel analysis with emphasis on structural modelling is Finkel (1995).
Hand & Crowder (1996) present a number of methods of longitudinal data analysis, among which are (multivariate) analysis of variance
for repeated measures, regression methods, random effects models and
structural equation models as well as models based on non-normal error
distributions.

Chapter 2

Analysis of longitudinal categorical data using optimal scaling techniques

Catrien C. J. H. Bijleveld
Eeke van der Burg

2.1 Introduction

In many areas of behavioural research, researchers investigate the relations between variables of which some have been measured at noninterval measurement level. For instance, psychologists may be interested in the relation between type of activity and urge to smoke, or therapists may be interested in the relation between employment status, marital status and depression. In these examples, 'type of activity', 'employment status' and 'marital status' are categorical measurement level variables: the measurement scale of these variables consists of a set of categories.

Such categorical measurement level variables may also occur when longitudinal studies are conducted: researchers may be interested in the relation between the type of activity subjects are engaged in during a number of time points and their urge to smoke, or medical psychologists may be interested in the psychological adaptation processes of the chronically ill in relation to their type of diagnosis, medication, and the like.

When faced with categorical longitudinal data, there are basically two options for analysis. One is the class of log-linear and Markov models for categorical data that will be presented in Chapter 6. The second is the class of multivariate techniques that use optimal scaling, and that can handle variables of mixed measurement level. These are the subject of the present chapter.

Optimal scaling techniques can handle categorical variables. Many of these techniques can handle in fact any mixture of nominal, ordinal or numerical (interval level) categorical variables. Categorical variables partition the subjects into different categories, like 'marital status' (married, divorced, single, widowed) or 'employment status' (permanent job, temporary job, volunteer work, unemployed). The term categorical thus refers to variables with a limited number of categories. This means that ordinal variables as well as numerical (interval level) variables with a limited number of categories are also called categorical. In the literature such variables are often referred to as 'ordered categorical' and 'interval categorical', or 'discrete interval', respectively. See Agresti (1990).

Generally speaking, optimal scaling techniques assign numerical or scale values to the categories of variables, optimizing a particular criterion. This scaling process is called quantification or optimal scaling. After the variables have been quantified they can be treated as if they were continuous variables. This approach is different from the approach adopted in log-linear models, in which variables are analysed as they are, in a special set-up that accounts for their character.

Many multivariate analysis techniques based on optimal scaling are described by Gifi (1990). These techniques, also called nonlinear multivariate analysis techniques (here nonlinear refers to the optimal scaling), are discussed in this chapter. They can be used when the analysis objective is not so much confirmatory data analysis or statistical model testing, but rather data exploration and summarization. The techniques give ample opportunity for exploration and interpretation of the structure in the data, without providing information on the statistical properties of the solution, however. As such, they are typically suited for preliminary investigations and the analysis of survey data.

All optimal scaling techniques discussed in this chapter use an Alternating Least Squares (ALS) algorithm to arrive at a solution. ALS algorithms generally consist of two alternating steps. In both steps, solutions are found that minimize a loss function. Alternating the two steps, the algorithm converges to one solution for the parameters of the (linear) analysis model as well as for the new values for the categories of the categorical variables.

In the field of longitudinal analysis, to date these optimal scaling techniques have not been applied widely. As we will show below, they can be applied fruitfully and with versatility in many areas of longitudinal data analysis. There are several reasons for this. Firstly, optimal scaling techniques do not make distributional assumptions. As such, they are untroubled by problems that may arise from phenomena common to repeated measurement such as serial correlation. Because of this, these techniques can be used for longitudinal data without the need to consider the impact of the time dependence on the distribution of variables or on the properties of the tests. Secondly, optimal scaling techniques have, because of their algorithms, efficient options to deal with missing values. Drop-out or attrition, often a complication in longitudinal research, is thus not augmented by any missing values, and analyses can be performed on as many observations as are available. Thirdly, those optimal scaling techniques that analyse two or more sets of variables, can be used to perform monotone or categorical versions of time series regression. In ordinary time series regression the (criterion) variables are regressed on the time axis, or some function thereof. When we use optimal scaling techniques to perform time series regression, it is possible to include categorical variables in our set of criterion variables. In addition, we can treat the variable representing the time axis itself as a categorical variable, which makes it possible not only to regress the variables of interest on a variety of possible shapes of growth curves that may be of interest to the researcher, but also to explore the data in order to find the best fitting or optimal growth curve. Particularly this property will be used extensively in the following sections.

In addition to a number of essentially cross-sectional applications of optimal scaling techniques in the analysis of categorical longitudinal data, optimal scaling extensions have been proposed to time series models as well. We will focus on an optimal scaling extension to state space or linear dynamic systems analysis, in which a solution is obtained for one subject, with parameter estimates and quantifications for the categories of the categorical variables. Stability is attained by requiring fairly long series (long at least for the behavioural sciences). Such linear dynamic systems with optimal scaling are extended to the case where not one, but several subjects have been measured. We will introduce them in Section 2.5.2 below.

We will start by introducing a number of nonlinear multivariate techniques that use optimal scaling in the next section, Section 2.2. Nonlinear multivariate techniques based on optimal scaling can be used for the analysis of long as well as short series of categorical data obtained for several subjects. Repeated measures can be accommodated in a variety of ways, and intraindividual changes and interindividual differences explored. Several possibilities exist for doing so; we will present a number in Section 2.3. A number of multivariate dynamic models are introduced in Section 2.4. Optimal scaling extensions of these models are discussed in Section 2.5. In all these sections, the techniques are illustrated with empirical examples; the explanation and interpretation rely mostly on graphical representations. Formulas have been kept down to a minimum, and are given merely for completeness. The chapter ends with a section on the treatment of missing data, a discussion and suggestions for further reading.

We need to stress that the introduction to optimal scaling techniques given here is limited. For more detailed information on optimal scaling techniques we refer to De Leeuw (1983, 1989), Gifi (1990), Van de Geer (1993), Greenacre (1984, 1993), Nishisato (1994) and Van der Heijden (1987).

2.1.1 Assumptions

The optimal scaling techniques discussed in this chapter do not rely on distributional assumptions. This is an advantage in the sense that findings do not depend on the (often untestable) validity of such assumptions. On the other hand, no statistical tests are provided, particularly no statistical test is provided for the goodness of fit of the model. This may be a disadvantage. If a researcher wants to test the stability of a solution, permutational methods such as bootstrapping or jackknifing have to used. We return to this subject in the discussion (Section 2.7).

2.2 Multivariate analysis using optimal scaling

In this section several techniques will be introduced that are part of the so-called Gifi-system of multivariate analysis (Gifi, 1990). The Gifi-system is a class of analysis techniques that use optimal scaling for quantifying the categories of various types of categorical variables. Three types will be distinguished: nominal, ordinal and numerical variables.

For nominal variables (for instance, religious denomination) the values of the categories reflect a partitioning, or similarities and differences, between the categories; any transformation (or quantification) should preserve this structure. Ordinal variables are measurements of which the categories reflect both a partitioning and a rank order. The rating scale is a typical example of an ordinal variable. When rescaling an ordinal variable, the partitioning and rank order must be preserved. This means that monotone transformations are allowed. The third type of categorical variable is numerical or interval level. As we are dealing with categorical variables, also interval variables are generally measured in a restricted number of categories; an example is a variable 'number of offences committed during the past month', with categories 0, 1, 2, 3, etc. An interval variable may also be a continuous variable, with its values grouped into a small number of categories, for instance length in centimetres, with categories '<150', '150–159', '160–169', '170–179', '180–189' and '>189'. For numerical variables, only linear transformations are permitted, as in ordinary multivariate analysis techniques. See also Agresti (1990), Gifi (1990). Using the techniques of the Gifi-system, mixtures of nominal, ordinal and numerical variables can be analysed simultaneously (compare Young, 1981).

Two classes of techniques can be distinguished within the Gifi-system. The first class of techniques analyses the relations between the variables not differentiated into sets, or all belonging to one set. The second type analyses the relations between the variables, where these are distinguished into two or more sets. Examples of one-set techniques are (multiple) correspondence analysis and nonlinear principal component analysis. A more-sets technique is nonlinear generalized canonical (correlation) analysis.

We will first discuss multiple correspondence analysis. Next we discuss nonlinear principal components analysis. Even though the latter technique is not used in any of the longitudinal examples in the second part of this chapter, we believe that a number of important principles are best introduced through it. Also, it would be hard to move in one step to the last technique we shall introduce: nonlinear generalized canonical analysis.

We need to stress that the computer programs that perform these techniques all produce a wealth of output and material through which the solutions can be interpreted. It would be impossible to discuss all that material in detail here, and for more in-depth discussions of both the models, techniques and output we will each time refer the reader to the appropriate references.

2.2.1 Multiple Correspondence Analysis

Suppose that, in a survey on socio-economic status, we have interviewed a number of subjects with respect to their living conditions. We have asked them whether they are married, cohabiting, divorced or single, we have asked them whether they are employed or not, we have asked them after their profession, what type of pets they own, whether they are engaged in any sports, what type of music they prefer, and so on. All these variables are indicators of our concept 'living conditions'. We know that a number of these variables are interrelated. We presume, for instance, that people who are married will more often have a dog, and that people who are married will more often like classical music. We want to differentiate our subjects with respect to their living conditions. However, as the variables are nominal (that is, the respective categories cannot be assumed ordered), to investigate the manner in which these aspects covary and people can be differentiated on the basis of certain combinations of categories that are typical for them, we would have to cross-tabulate the variables. If we are investigating M variables, we are then faced with the task to inspect $M(M-1)/2$ cross-tabulations of bivariate relations. Obviously, the larger the number of variables, the more cumbersome this procedure is. In addition, as we are interested in data reduction, we do not want to end up with the intricacies of many bivariate relations. Rather, we would like to summarize the most pertinent multivariate relations in the data. We are thus striving for a solution that enables us to investigate the multivariate relations between all categorical variables simultaneously. One technique to find such a solution is multiple correspondence analysis.

Multiple correspondence analysis, introduced as early as 1941 under a different name by Guttman, is an analysis technique for nominal data (Benzécri, 1973). In multiple correspondence analysis, the categories of nominal variables are quantified, that is, scale values are assigned to the categories of the variables (the *category quantifications*). This is done in such a way that the correlation or similarity between all quantified variables is maximal. If for instance a large number of subjects have similar scoring patterns on two variables, the category quantifications of these two variables will be chosen similarly, maximizing the correspondence between the two variables.

The starting-point in multiple correspondence analysis is always the nominal treatment of the variables. A nominal variable is completely characterized by its so called *indicator matrix*. The indicator matrix contains dummy variables that show to which categories a subject belongs (1) and to which categories he or she does not belong (0) (see Figure 2.1). Suppose that we have measured N subjects on M categorical variables. The indicator matrix of variable j with k_j categories is denoted by $\mathbf{I}_j(N \times k_j)$. (In the Gifi-system $\mathbf{I}_j$ is generally referred to as $\mathbf{G}_j$.) The quantifications of the categories (denoted in the example in the figure for the first variable by q_a, q_b and q_c) are stacked in $\mathbf{b}_j(k_j \times 1)$. Then the expression $\mathbf{I}_j\mathbf{b}_j(N \times 1)$ gives the transformed or quantified variable (Figure 2.1). Note that the matrix product $\mathbf{I}_j\mathbf{b}_j$ contains the k_j respective quantifications and that their values are identical to those in $\mathbf{b}_j$.

The maximization of correspondence is approached by searching for the similarity between all the variables, or, as in principal components analysis, by searching for the direction that explains most variance. For this, multiple correspondence analysis uses a vector $\mathbf{z}$ $(N \times 1)$ of so-called *object scores* (comparable to factor scores in principal components analysis). Multiple correspondence analysis then aims at maximizing the similarity or *homogeneity* between the quantified variables, that is, at maximizing the average squared correlation between the object scores and the optimally scaled variables. Maximum similarity or maximum homogeneity is attained when *all* the quantified variables are – simultaneously – as similar as possible (Gifi, 1990). Maximization of similarity amounts to minimization of differences. Therefore, when the

Figure 2.1: *Nominal $N \times 3$ Data Matrix, Corresponding Indicator Matrices, and Quantifications of the First Variable*

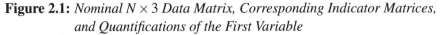

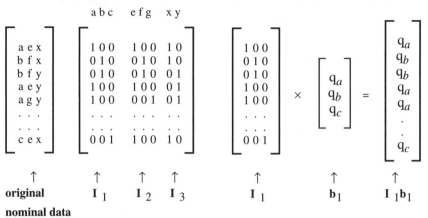

difference between object scores $\mathbf{z}$ and rescaled variables $\mathbf{I}_j\mathbf{b}_j$ is minimal for all j (with $j = 1, \ldots, M$), the homogeneity is maximized. This amounts to minimizing the following loss function:

$$\sigma(\mathbf{z}, \mathbf{b}_1, \ldots, \mathbf{b}_M) = \sum_{j=1}^{M} \mathrm{SSQ}\left(\mathbf{z} - \mathbf{I}_j\mathbf{b}_j\right), \tag{2.1}$$

where $\mathrm{SSQ}(\mathbf{v})$ stands for the sum of squares of the elements of vector $\mathbf{v}$[1]. As Equation (2.1) can be – trivially – solved by setting both $\mathbf{z}$ and $\mathbf{b}_j$ equal to zero, a normalization restriction is needed to avoid such a degenerate solution. One possible restriction is to normalize $\mathbf{z}$ to $\mathbf{z}'\mathbf{z} = N$. In addition, it is generally requested that the object scores be in deviation from the mean, or $\mathbf{z}'\mathbf{u} = 0$, with $\mathbf{u}$ an N-dimensional vector of ones.

Solving expression (2.1) under the conditions $\mathbf{z}'\mathbf{u} = 0$ and $\mathbf{z}'\mathbf{z} = N$ gives a one-dimensional solution: each subject receives one object score, and each category one quantification. As in principal components analysis, it is possible to find higher-dimensional solutions as well. For each subject, we then find not one object score, but several or p

---

[1] As we will always use a data vector $\mathbf{v}$ in deviation from the column mean, this definition of $\mathrm{SSQ}(.)$ corresponds with the usual sum of squares notation. Below, we use the SSQ-notation for matrices (in deviation from column means) as well, where $\mathrm{SSQ}(\mathbf{V})$ stands for the sum of squares of all elements of $\mathbf{V}$, or trace $(\mathbf{V}'\mathbf{V})$.

object scores. Formulated differently: for each subject we then find a point in p-dimensional space. Similarly, for each category, we do not find one quantification, but p *quantifications*, or: one quantification in p-dimensional space. Such p-dimensional category quantifications are labelled *multiple nominal*.

In order to achieve such a p-dimensional solution, we extend the N-dimensional vector $\mathbf{z}$ to an $(N \times p)$ matrix $\mathbf{Z}$, and we combine the p category quantifications for each category of each variable in $M(k_j \times p)$-dimensional matrices $\mathbf{B}_j$. If we define $\mathbf{0}$ as a p-dimensional vector of zeroes, maximum homogeneity for a p-dimensional solution is obtained by minimizing:

$$\sigma(\mathbf{Z}, \mathbf{B}_1, \ldots, \mathbf{B}_M) = \sum_{j=1}^{M} \text{SSQ}(\mathbf{Z} - \mathbf{I}_j \mathbf{B}_j) \qquad (2.2)$$

under the conditions $\mathbf{Z}'\mathbf{u} = \mathbf{0}$ and $\mathbf{Z}'\mathbf{Z} = N\mathbf{I}$.

As we want the respective dimensions to be independent, we restrict $\mathbf{Z}$ to $\mathbf{Z}'\mathbf{Z} = N\mathbf{I}$. Similar to the one-dimensional case, also here we restrict the object scores to be centred on zero: $\mathbf{Z}'\mathbf{u} = \mathbf{0}$.

An important property of multiple correspondence analysis is that solutions of varying dimensionality are *nested*. That is, if we were to compare the results of, e.g., a two-dimensional and three-dimensional solution, the first two dimensions would be identical (same quantifications, same object scores). Nestedness implies that the p dimensions of a p-dimensional analysis are thus identical to the first p dimensions of a $p+1, p+2, \ldots$-dimensional analysis.

Expression (2.2) in combination with the restrictions gives the formal definition of multiple correspondence analysis or *homogeneity analysis* (Gifi, 1990; Greenacre, 1984; Nishisato, 1980; Tenenhaus & Young, 1985; Van de Geer, 1993). In case of only two variables, multiple correspondence analysis is commonly referred to as correspondence analysis. However, correspondence analysis is usually introduced using a cross-tabulation, and not via maximization of the homogeneity, so that those who are familiar with correspondence analysis may not see its correspondence with Equation (2.2) immediately. We refer to the literature for more information (Benzécri, 1973; Gifi, 1990; Van de Geer, 1993; Van der Heijden, 1987). The computer program for multiple correspondence analysis we will use below is HOMALS (short for HOMogeneity analysis through Alternating Least Squares; Van de Geer, 1985,

1993). HOMALS is available in the SPSS procedure CATEGORIES (SPSS, 1990). Many more programs perform multiple correspondence analysis, for instance the SAS procedure CORRESP (Kuhfeld & Young, 1988).

A first measure for interpreting solutions is the badness-of-fit or *loss*, the minimum value of $SSQ(\mathbf{Z}, \mathbf{B}_1, \ldots, \mathbf{B}_M)$, as defined in Equation (2.2). The badness-of-fit is inversely related to the goodness-of-fit, which is defined as the number of dimensions minus the loss.

Another way to define the goodness-of-fit is in terms of the so-called *eigenvalues*. Each dimension of the solution has an eigenvalue. The eigenvalue of a dimension corresponds to the mean variance of all the quantified variables accounted for by that dimension, in short as an indication of explained variance. The eigenvalues in multiple correspondence analysis are thus comparable to the eigenvalues in principal components analysis, although it should be kept in mind that the eigenvalues in multiple correspondence analysis reflect the explained variance of the quantified variables, not that of the original variables. Eigenvalues are useful for assessing the importance of the respective dimensions. The eigenvalues are always ordered according to their magnitude: the first dimension has the highest eigenvalue, then the second dimension, and so on. One possibility for choosing the dimensionality of a solution, is thus to apply an elbow-type of criterion or the graphical scree test (see Stevens, 1992, Chapter 11.4).

Apart from assessing the importance of the respective dimensions, we can also assess the importance of the respective variables using the so-called *discrimination measures*. These are best understood as follows: if subjects can be distinguished well on the basis of a variable, then that variable discriminates well between subjects. The variable then has a high discrimination measure. Discrimination measures are a function of the category quantifications: the further apart the category quantifications of a variable are, the wider the spread of subjects along the categories of this variable, and the larger the discrimination measure. The maximum is 1, the minimum is 0. As each category receives a separate quantification for each dimension, discrimination measures are thus also computed per variable per dimension. Discrimination measures correspond to the explained variance of the quantified variables. For details, see Gifi (1990) or Van de Geer (1993). Discrimination measures are useful for assessing the contribution of the respective variables to the respective dimensions of the solution.

Eigenvalues and discrimination measures are thus both indicators of goodness-of-fit. They are linked, as the eigenvalue of a dimension is computed as the average of the discrimination measures of all variables for that dimension. The sum of the p-eigenvalues equals the goodness-of-fit of the total solution.

Each subject is assigned a point in p-dimensional space. The object scores can be represented in an orthonormalized system. They then form a swarm of points with unit variance for each dimension. As stated above, the categories of variables on which subjects score simultaneously, receive similar quantifications. Conversely, because the quantifications are chosen in this manner, the object scores of subjects whose answering patterns are close will bear resemblance, and subjects who have different answering patterns will have different object scores. This correspondence between category quantifications and object scores can be formalized as follows. The quantification of a category is equal to the centroid of the object scores of all subjects who have scored that category. Conversely, the object score of a subject is equal to a multiple of the average category quantification of all categories that belong to this subject.

Thus, category quantifications and object scores are intrinsically linked. Both are part of the same solution, and should therefore be interpreted in relation with one another. Subjects can be characterized by the categories that have been placed in their vicinity. Subjects close to each other share this characterization and may thus be identified as belonging to the same subgroup of subjects. Subjects far from each other have dissimilar patterns and belong to different subgroups. Categories in the periphery of the solution characterize homogeneous subgroups of subjects. Categories in the centre of the solution are shared by many subjects, and can generally not be used to characterize distinct subgroups.

Example of multiple correspondence analysis   We analyse an artificial small example data set to illustrate the performance and interpretation of multiple correspondence analysis. The data set is composed of the scores of 20 subjects on 7 variables. The data, variables and categories are given in Table 2.1 below. The first column of the data table shows the subject number. The subsequent columns correspond to the follow-ing variables: educational level, gender, marital status, age, drinking habits, health and number of children. The labels used for the varia-bles are: EDUCATION, GENDER, MARITAL, AGE, DRINK, HEALTH, CHILDREN.

Table 2.1: *Artificial Data: Subject Number, Raw Data, Variables and Categories*

1	3 1 1 1 3 1 2	EDUCATION	
2	2 2 1 4 2 1 1	1 = primary school	
3	4 1 2 3 2 2 3	2 = secondary school	
4	2 1 3 3 3 2 3	3 = vocational training	DRINK
5	4 2 2 3 3 2 4	4 = university	1 = not at all
6	2 2 3 3 2 1 2		2 = once a week
7	3 2 3 3 3 1 3	GENDER	3 = more than once
8	4 1 1 2 2 1 1	1 = male	a week
9	3 2 2 3 3 2 4	2 = female	4 = every day
10	2 2 2 3 1 2 3		
11	3 1 1 2 3 1 1	MARITAL	HEALTH
12	2 2 2 1 3 1 1	1 = single	1 = good
13	4 1 2 2 3 2 3	2 = married/cohabiting	2 = reasonable
14	2 1 3 2 3 2 3	3 = divorced/widowed	3 = not so good
15	4 2 2 4 2 2 4		
16	2 2 3 3 2 1 1	AGE	CHILDREN
17	3 2 3 4 3 1 3	1 = 18–25 years	1 = none
18	4 1 3 2 2 1 2	2 = 26–35 years	2 = 1 child
19	3 1 2 3 3 2 3	3 = 36–45 years	3 = 2 children
20	3 2 1 3 1 2 4	4 = > 45 years	4 = >2 children

We ran HOMALS in two dimensions for this data set. The discrim-ination measures of the quantified variables on the two dimensions are given in Table 2.2. From these discrimination measures, we can con-clude that the variables HEALTH and CHILDREN are the most import-ant variables on the first dimension, with a second place for MARITAL and AGE. The second dimension is constituted mainly by GENDER

Table 2.2: *Artificial Data:* HOMALS *Eigenvalues and Discrimination Measures*

	Dimension	
Variable	1	2
EDUCATION	0.031	0.206
GENDER	0.087	0.749
MARITAL	0.455	0.052
AGE	0.411	0.516
DRINK	0.299	0.164
HEALTH	0.757	0.096
CHILDREN	0.866	0.323
Eigenvalues	0.415	0.301

and AGE, with a second place reserved for CHILDREN. The variables EDUCATION and DRINK play a much smaller role. Apparently, HOMALS has not been able to fit the categories of these variables as well as the categories of the other variables. The eigenvalues reported in Table 2.2 are slightly on the low side, implying that the variables do not discriminate very well. To assess whether we have achieved an acceptable solution, we therefore interpret the solution. A graphical representation of the discrimination measures to aid this interpretation is given in Figure 2.2. The discrimination measures, represented as points, have been connected with the origin, so that every variable is represented as a vector. As the discrimination measures correspond to the explained variances of the optimally scaled variables they are all positive.

The graphical representation illustrates at a glance what we inferred from the table. The vectors of drinking habits and educational level are the shortest: the technique has not been able to fit these variables satisfactorily in the solution. The vector of marital status is quite short as well. It points in the same direction as the vector of health. Apparently, these two variables relate to the other variables in a similar manner, although the relation is less strong for marital status than it is for health. The vector of the number of children is quite long, it loads strongest

Figure 2.2: *Artificial Data: HOMALS Discrimination Measures*

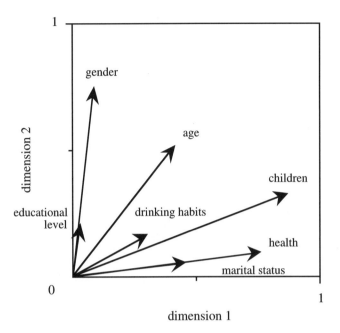

on the first dimension although there is some relation with the second dimension as well. The vector of age loads in a similarly moderate fashion on both dimensions. Apparently, the number of children bears some relation to subjects' reported health status and, to a lesser extent, to marital status and age. The most important variables for the second dimension are gender, age and the number of children. For our group of subjects, age, gender and the number of children are related.

The discrimination measures correspond to the explained variances of the optimally scaled variables. They tell us only that variables relate, but not how they relate, so that we have to inspect the positioning of the categories of the variables to uncover which categories of variables occur together. We refer to Table 2.3 which gives the variable labels, category number, frequencies of occurrence, category labels and category quantifications for this solution.

From Table 2.3 we can underline a number of our provisional conclusions. We see how indeed the categories of CHILDREN are well spread out over the first dimension. Over the second dimension, this

Table 2.3: *Artificial Data: Variables, Categories, Frequencies and* HOMALS *Category Quantifications*

Variable	Category Number	Category Frequency	Label	Category quantifications 1-dim.	2-dim.
EDUCATION	1	0	primary school	0.00	0.00
	2	7	secondary school	−0.24	−0.43
	3	7	vocational training	0.15	−0.14
	4	6	university	0.10	0.67
GENDER	1	9	male	−0.33	0.96
	2	11	female	0.27	−0.78
MARITAL	1	5	single	−0.77	−0.39
	2	8	married/cohabiting	0.80	0.15
	3	7	divorced/widowed	−0.37	0.11
AGE	1	2	18–25 years	−1.00	−0.47
	2	5	26–35 years	−0.72	1.13
	3	10	36–45 years	0.60	−0.16
	4	3	> 45 years	−0.13	−1.04
DRINK	1	2	not at all	1.34	−0.96
	2	7	once a week or less	−0.56	−0.22
	3	11	several times a week	0.11	0.32
	4	0	every day	0.00	0.00
HEALTH	1	10	good	−0.87	−0.31
	2	10	reasonable	0.87	0.31
	3	0	not so well	0.00	0.00
CHILDREN	1	5	none	−1.05	−0.56
	2	3	1 child	−1.16	0.15
	3	8	2 children	0.47	0.62
	4	4	> 2 children	1.23	−0.65

spread is less. The categories of HEALTH have a little less spread. (Note how the category quantifications of the two categories with equal frequencies are exactly equal in absolute value: this is because of the constraint that the average object score of all subjects must be zero or $\mathbf{Z'u} = \mathbf{0}$; as the third category was not scored by any subject it has received a quantification equal to zero.) The spread of the categories of GENDER on the second dimension is sizeable, as expected. At first glance, the spread of the categories of AGE is larger; however, upon closer inspection it can be seen that the two categories with large absolute quantifications have not been scored much (5 resp. 3 subjects) so that the total spread is not that high. For interpretation, it is again easier to revert to a graphical representation of these category quantifications. This is given in Figure 2.3.

From Figure 2.3 we can infer the following. Young subjects (18–25 years) are situated in the lower left part of the solution. These younger subjects are generally single, have no children, report their health as being good, drink once a week and have finished secondary school (both the number of children and their educational level is not surprising given their age). Moving counter clockwise, we find that quite close by are situated the oldest subjects (over 45 years of age) and the average object score of the female subjects. Moving on, we find subjects who have more than two children and who report drinking nothing at all. Moving in the same direction, we find subjects in the age range 36–45 who have had vocational training (although this category is less peripheral, and not too much meaning should be attached to it). Married and cohabiting subjects report reasonable health, and drinking several times a week. They are situated quite close to the uppermost region, which is occupied predominantly by male university graduates who are 26–35 years old and have 2 children. In the left part of the solution we find subjects with one child, who are generally divorced or widowed.

A tentative overall description of our results would be that in the sample young male university graduates typically have 2 children. The youngest subjects have fewer children and feel quite healthy, drink once a week and are of lower educational level. Those with more than 2 children are generally somewhat older and tend not to drink at all. Married subjects drink several times a week and are less healthy. Subjects with one child are generally somewhat younger, are either single or divorced

Figure 2.3: *Artificial Data:* HOMALS *Category Quantifications*

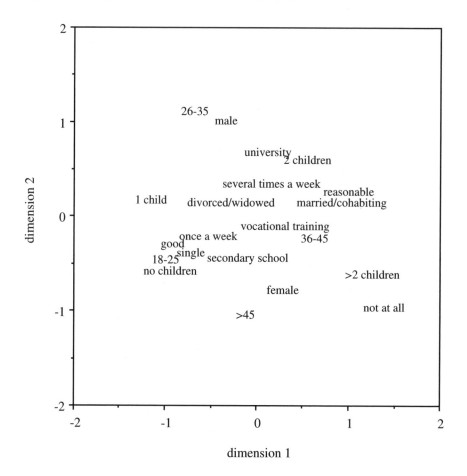

or widowed, drink once or several times a week and are reportedly in good health.

Figure 2.4 gives the positioning of the subjects in this solution. This figure may be viewed as superimposed upon the previous figure with category quantifications. We can distinguish four peripheral clusters of subjects in the solution. The bottom-left cluster (subjects 2, 16, 2 and 6 - whether 17 belongs to it is a matter of contention) consists of generally young, single, healthy subjects with no children. Some subjects in this cluster may be over 45 years of age (by referring back to the original data we can see that this is subject 2). Moving counter

Figure 2.4: *Artificial Data:* HOMALS *Object Scores*

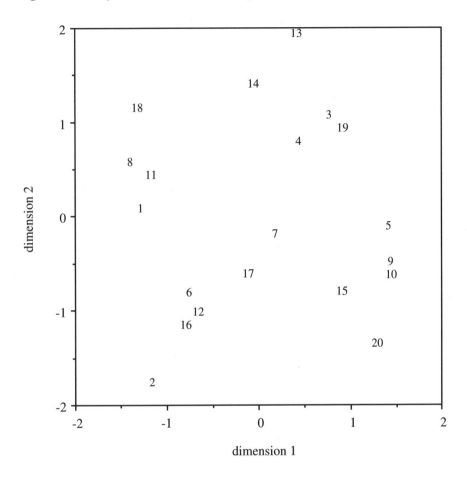

clockwise we encounter the second cluster composed of subjects 15, 20, 10, 9 and 5. Subjects in this cluster are generally female, drink not at all, most have more than two children and a number are over 45. The third cluster is formed by subjects 4, 3, 19, 13 and 14. These subjects are generally male, university educated, have 2 children, report feeling reasonably healthy and drink several times a week. They are either in the age range 36–45 or in the age range 26–35, as the quantification of this category is shared with the last cluster of subjects. This last cluster is composed of subjects 18, 8, 11 and 1. These subjects are generally younger (either 18–25 or 26–35) have one child or no children, are either divorced/widowed or single. They are generally male. Subject 7 has been quite centrally placed, meaning that the combination of categories scored by this subject is not in line with any of the other characterizations of subjects in the clusters. Subject 17 is also hard to place, although this subject belongs to the lower left cluster if any.

For a more in-depth discussion of the HOMALS program, its algorithm and output, we refer to Gifi (1990), Greenacre (1993), and Van de Geer (1993).

2.2.2   Nonlinear Principal Component Analysis

Suppose again that, in a survey on socio-economic status, we have interviewed a number of subjects with respect to their living conditions. We have asked them whether they are married, cohabiting, divorced or single, we have asked them whether they are employed or not, we have asked them their profession, what type of pets they own, whether they are engaged in any sports, what type of music they prefer, and so on. However, this time we have included a number of additional questions related to our subjects' financial situation: for instance, we have asked them after their monthly income, we have asked the number of bedrooms in their house, and we have asked them the price of the car they drive. Again, all these variables are indicators of our concept 'living conditions'. Again we know that a number of the variables are interrelated, for instance we still believe that people who are married often have a dog, and we also believe that people who are employed will often have a high income, and the like. We again want to differentiate our subjects with respect to their living conditions. However, this time not all variables are of nominal measurement level. The categories of the variables pertaining to the subjects' financial situation can be assumed ordered, that is, they can be assumed to have been measured at at least ordinal level. Therefore, we have now at our disposal a set of categorical variables of mixed measurement level: some are nominal, some are ordinal and some are numerical.

As also this time we would like to summarize the most pertinent multivariate relations in the data, investigating the multivariate relations between all variables simultaneously, we are thus looking for a technique like multiple correspondence analysis. However, this time we would like the technique to take into account the fact that the categories of a number of variables are ordered and/or at interval level.

A technique for analysing such data is nonlinear principal components analysis. Nonlinear principal components analysis has been implemented as an extension of ordinary principal components analysis, with optimal scaling of categorical variables (Gifi 1990, Chapter 4; Young, Takane, & De Leeuw 1978). Principal components analysis is discussed in many textbooks on multivariate analysis (e.g. Tatsuoka, 1988, Chapter 6). The optimal scaling extension to principal components analysis implies that options are available for transforming any nominal, ordinal or numerical variables. After defining the restrictions of the measurement level that give a class of permitted transformations for each variable, the technique chooses those permitted transformations that minimize the loss (Young, 1981).

Nonlinear principal components analysis can thus be viewed as a generalization of ordinary principal components analysis, with nonlinear and linear transformations of the variables. Conversely, it can also be considered as multiple correspondence analysis with restrictions on the transformations. This is best envisaged as follows. In multiple correspondence analysis, p-dimensional category quantifications are found such that the homogeneity between the variables is maximized. Every subject receives a p-dimensional object score. Category quantifications and object scores are chosen such that a loss criterion is minimized. In doing so, the p-dimensional category quantifications of a variable can in principle be found anywhere in the space of object scores. We can now introduce measurement restrictions on the variables by restricting the category quantifications. Suppose for instance that a categorical variable has been measured at ordinal level. We can then restrict the category quantifications to be ordered along a line. This type of measurement restriction is labelled *single ordinal* in Gifi (1990). For numerical (interval) variables we can restrict the category quantifications to be not only ordered on a line, but to be ordered such that also the intervals between the successive categories are of the same length. This type of measurement restriction is labelled *numerical* in Gifi (1990), which is similar to the standardization restrictions in ordinary principal components analysis. In nonlinear principal components analysis, it is possible to restrict the quantifications of a nominal variable as well to be in one-dimensional space. In that case, the quantifications are restricted to be on a line, with the ordering free. This type of measurement restriction is labelled *single nominal* in Gifi (1990). In all these latter cases, the quantifications have been reduced from a p-dimensional quantification to a one-dimensional quantification.

Nonlinear principal components analysis has been implemented in a program called PRINCALS (short for PRINCipal components analysis through Alternating Least Squares; Gifi (1990)). PRINCALS is available in the SPSS procedure CATEGORIES (SPSS, 1990). A similar program is available in SAS under the name PRINQUAL (Kuhfeld & Young, 1988). In the following, we will centre our introduction on the PRINCALS program.

Similarly to multiple correspondence analysis, nonlinear principal components analysis aims at maximizing the similarity between the quantified variables. Again, maximum similarity is attained when *all* the quantified variables are – simultaneously – as similar as possible, or when all the quantified variables are as similar as possible to the object scores $\mathbf{Z}$. This amounts to minimizing the same loss function as in multiple correspondence analysis, only the conditions are different. Defining $\mathbf{c}_j$ as a numerical, nominal or ordinal quantification, the loss function is:

$$\sigma(\mathbf{Z}, \mathbf{B}_1, \ldots, \mathbf{B}_M) = \sum_{j=1}^{M} \text{SSQ}\left(\mathbf{Z} - \mathbf{I}_j \mathbf{B}_j\right) \qquad (2.3)$$

under the conditions $\mathbf{Z}'\mathbf{Z} = N\mathbf{I}$, $\mathbf{Z}'\mathbf{u} = \mathbf{0}$ and $\mathbf{B}_j = \mathbf{c}_j \mathbf{a}'_j$ for variables treated as single.

The $\mathbf{B}_j$ are again $(k_j \times p)$, and the quantified variables can again be written as $\mathbf{I}_j \mathbf{B}_j$ $(N \times p)$, with $\mathbf{I}_j$ the indicator matrix well-known from multiple correspondence analysis. The object scores are gathered in $\mathbf{Z}$ $(N \times p)$. The single measurement restrictions are implemented in nonlinear principal components analysis by requiring that $\mathbf{B}_j$ be a rank-one matrix, or equivalently, that $\mathbf{B}_j$ can be represented as the product of two vectors: $\mathbf{c}_j \mathbf{a}'_j$. This restriction is also called a rank-restriction. The scores of the vector $\mathbf{c}_j$ $(k_j \times 1)$ are referred to as the *single category quantifications*. If there are no additional restrictions on the $\mathbf{c}_j$ these scores refer to a single nominal variable; if monotone restrictions are applied, it refers to an ordinal variable; if a linear restriction is used, the $\mathbf{c}_j$ refer to a numerical variable. The scores in the vector $\mathbf{a}_j$ $(p \times 1)$, which are the correlations between $\mathbf{I}_j\mathbf{c}_j$ (the transformed variable) and the object scores $\mathbf{Z}$, are named the *component loadings*. The unrestricted quantifications $\mathbf{B}_j$ are referred to as *multiple category coordinates*; the restricted $\mathbf{B}_j$ $(=\mathbf{c}_j\mathbf{a}'_j)$ are referred to as the *single category coordinates*. The transformed variables $\mathbf{I}_j\mathbf{c}_j$ are unit-normalized, which was not the case in multiple correspondence analysis.

Note that, if all variables are treated as multiple nominal, the restrictions of Equation (2.3) reduce to the restrictions of Equation (2.2). The latter equation with restrictions was the mathematical formulation for multiple correspondence analysis. This shows why one model can be seen as a special case of the other. If all variables in Equation (2.3) are numerical, (2.3) reduces to classical principal components analysis, in which case the columns of $\mathbf{Z}$ are the ordinary principal components.

The goodness-of-fit measures in nonlinear principal components analysis are similar to the goodness-of-fit measures in multiple correspondence analysis. In nonlinear principal components analysis, the average explained variance per dimension of the rescaled variables is reflected as an eigenvalue for each dimension. The eigenvalue is computed as the average of the squared correlations of the rescaled variables with the object scores. The eigenvalues have maximum 1 and minimum 0. The sum of the eigenvalues is again the total goodness-of-fit, which equals the number of dimensions minus the loss. The eigenvalues are always ordered according to their magnitude: the first dimension has the highest eigenvalue, then the second dimension, and so on. In choosing the dimensionality of a solution, an elbow-type of criterion is often used. As in multiple correspondence analysis, there is no objective criterion to decide whether a fit is high enough. Whether a solution is satisfactory or not is generally determined mainly by its interpretability.

Due to the rank restrictions on the quantifications of single variables, the solutions of nonlinear principal components analysis are not nested. Thus, the first p solutions of a p-dimensional analysis need not equal the first p solutions of a $p+1, p+2, \ldots$-dimensional analysis. In practice however, the first p solutions very often correspond to a large extent. If this congruence is important, one always has to check for it, by comparing the quantifications of the variables across solutions in different dimensions.

The contribution of the respective variables to the dimensions can be assessed using the *component loadings*, which were defined above as the correlations between the object scores and the rescaled variables. As component loadings are available for single variables only, for multiple variables we have to refer back to the p-dimensional category quantifications. The component loadings are points in the p-dimensional solution; by connecting these points to the origin, the component loadings can be viewed as vectors. The higher a component loading, the longer the corresponding vector will be. The length of the vector of a component loading thus reflects the importance of the rescaled variable in the solution.

As in multiple correspondence analysis, the object scores form an orthonormalized system. The categories of variables on which subjects score simultaneously receive similar quantifications, and the object scores of subjects who have similar answering patterns are close. As category quantifications and object scores are thus part of the same solution, they should therefore be interpreted in relation to one another. Subjects can be characterized by the categories that have been placed in their vicinity. Subjects close to each other share this characterization and may thus be identified as belonging to the same subgroup of subjects; subjects far from each other have dissimilar patterns and belong to different subgroups. Categories in the periphery of the solution characterize homogeneous subgroups of subjects. Categories in the centre of the solution are shared by many subjects, and generally can not be used to characterize distinct subgroups. The category quantifications in nonlinear principal components analysis can be much more restricted than the quantifications in multiple correspondence analysis. Both multiple correspondence analysis and nonlinear principal components analysis can be used for classification purposes.

Example of nonlinear principal components analysis   We analyse the same small example data set that was used in Section 2.2.1 above to illustrate the performance and interpretation of nonlinear principal components analysis. The data set, variables and categories were described in Table 2.1 above.

In multiple correspondence analysis all variables are always treated as multiple nominal variables (in fact, as we showed above, multiple correspondence analysis can be viewed as nonlinear principal components analysis with multiple nominal restrictions on all variables). As the categories of some variables in the example data set could be perceived

as intrinsically ordered, we will illustrate nonlinear principal components analysis by imposing ordinal restrictions on a number of these variables.

The variables and measurement levels we used for the PRINCALS
analysis are in Table 2.4.

Table 2.4: *Artificial Data: Variables and Measurement Levels used in*
           PRINCALS Analysis

Variable	Measurement level
EDUCATION	Ordinal
GENDER	Numerical
MARITAL	Multiple nominal
AGE	Ordinal
DRINK	Multiple nominal
HEALTH	Multiple nominal
CHILDREN	Multiple nominal

We thus restricted the variables educational level and age to have ordinal quantifications. In principle, for the categories of drinking habits,
and the number of children such an ordering may be envisaged as well.
However, for the choice of an ordinal (or numerical) restriction, it is important not whether such an ordering is inherently present in the categories, but whether the researcher presumes such an ordering to be present
in and relevant to the relations in the data. As an illustration imagine
a variable with ordered categories that relates in a nonlinear fashion to
another variable: ordinal restrictions on the categories of this variable
would obscure the nonlinear relationship. It may appear surprising that
we entered 'numerical' for the measurement level of GENDER; however, any variable with two categories *de facto* has numerical measurement level: two categories can always be ordered on a straight line. As
such, a variable with only two categories can be treated at any measurement level; this will lead to the same quantifications.

Again, we chose two dimensions for the solution. PRINCALS converged to a solution with eigenvalues for the first and second dimension
of 0.408 and 0.281 respectively. These eigenvalues are again on the low

side and slightly lower than the eigenvalues reported for the HOMALS
solution above but then a lower fit is expected as the PRINCALS solution is more constrained. However, we will again judge the usefulness
of the solution through its interpretability rather than from the fit values as such. We can get an indication of how much was lost by the
ordinal constraints by comparing the average object score of all subjects in each category of a single variable (the *multiple category coordinate*), with its constrained version (the *single category coordinate*).
(In the PRINCALS output the multiple category coordinates are called
category quantifications for multiple nominal variables.) This comparison is given in Figure 2.5(a) for the variable educational level and in
Figure 2.5(b) for the variable age. Figure 2.5(a) shows how for edu-

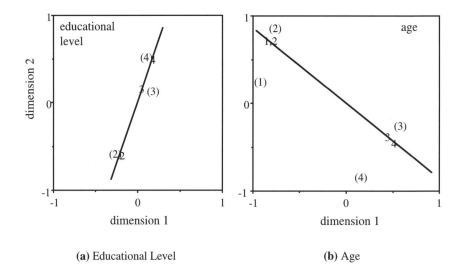

(a) Educational Level   (b) Age

Figure 2.5: *Artificial Data: PRINCALS Multiple and Single Category
Coordinates of Educational Level and Age*

cational level little is lost by constraining the variable to ordinal measurement level: the *multiple category coordinates* are very close to the
constrained *single category coordinates* on the line. For age this is not
so: some multiple category coordinates (category numbers 1 and 4) are
in fact quite far from the line. For category numbers 1 and 2 the ordering
would in fact become reversed if they were projected on the line. In such

cases, the technique projects them in the same spot (see Figure 2.5(b)). For single variables, identical category coordinates are often an indication that the ordering of the categories of the variables would not be preserved in the solution if left unconstrained.

Three variables thus had single restrictions (two with ordinal measurement level and one numerical), so that for these variables the component loadings can be given. However, for interpreting the solution the component loadings would have to be interpreted in conjunction with the category quantifications of the multiple nominal variables. In this situation, with multiple nominal as well as single variables, it is more efficient to immediately combine the interpretation of the categories of the multiple nominal variables (the *category quantifications*) with the constrained average category values of the single variables (the *single category coordinates*). If all variables are single, interpretation of component loadings is preferable, just as in ordinary principal components analysis. The category quantifications of the multiple nominal variables and the single category coordinates of the single variables are given in Figure 2.6. For each single variable the categories are connected. They lie on a line with the same direction as the component loadings (compare for instance Figure 2.5(a) or Figure 2.5(b)). A separate plot of component loadings is not shown for this example. Comparing this configuration of categories with the one produced for the HOMALS solution, we see that it has become somewhat more condensed. For the variable age, for which single ordinal restrictions apply, the categories '18–25' and '26–35' have been combined and been positioned close to the spot that '26–35' assumed in the HOMALS configuration; the categories '36–45' and '>45' have been moved to assume a fairly close position as well (compare Figure 2.5(b)). As expected (compare Figure 2.5(a)), little has changed in the positioning of the categories of educational level. For marital status, a (small) change has occurred in the positioning of the categories 'single' and 'divorced/widowed', which have moved to much closer spots. The interpretation is thus quite similar to the interpretation of the HOMALS configuration.

The object scores are graphically represented in Figure 2.7. The PRINCALS object scores are quite similar to the object scores in the HOMALS solution. The bottom-left cluster has changed a little, with subject 12 moving out towards the centre, and subjects 2, 16 and 6 moving closer. Moving counter clockwise, the cluster formed by sub-

Figure 2.6: *Artificial Data:* PRINCALS *Category Quantifications of Multiple Nominal Variables and Single Category Coordinates of Single Variables*

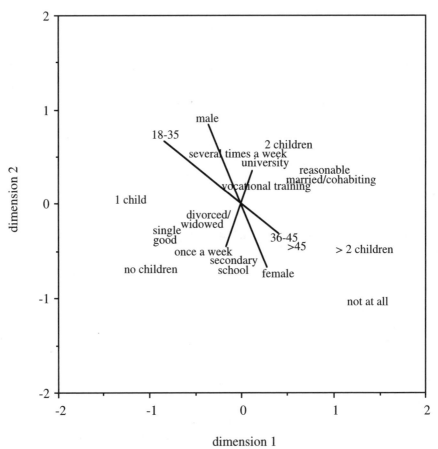

jects 15, 20, 10, 9 and 5 has become slightly more condensed on the first dimension. The cluster containing subjects 3, 4, 13, 14 and 19 has altered little. The last cluster formed by subjects 1, 8, 11 and 18 has also become more condensed. Subject 17 has now assumed a central position. The clusters of subjects have thus become more compact.

Thus, compared with the HOMALS solution, the configuration has changed but little. All in all, the interpretation derived from the positioning of subjects as well as from the category quantifications and

Figure 2.7: *Artificial Data:* PRINCALS *Object Scores*

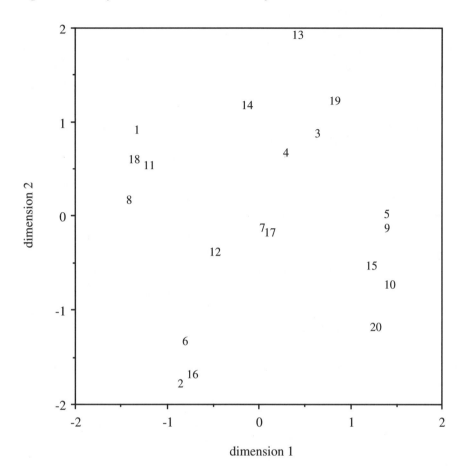

single category coordinates is quite similar to the interpretation of the
HOMALS solution. This is not remarkable, as restrictions on only two
variables were added and the restriction on one of these variables (educational level, see Figure 2.5(a)) constrained the solution very little.
Adding more constraints will probably induce more changes in the solution.

   For a more in-depth discussion of the PRINCALS program, its algorithm and output, we refer to Gifi (1990) and Van de Geer (1993).

2.2.3   Nonlinear Generalized Canonical Analysis

Suppose that, in our survey on socio-economic status, we have measured the same variables as introduced above for multiple correspondence and nonlinear principal components analysis. Again the variables are of mixed measurement level and serve as indicators of what we understand to be 'living conditions'. However, this time we have added another refinement to our understanding of the construct under investigation. We understand now that two distinct types of variables play a role in the living conditions of our subjects: on the one hand their financial situation (income and expenditures), and on the other hand their background characteristics (age, marital status, employment status and the like). We want to investigate to what extent these background characteristics are related to living conditions.

Thus, as in the examples above, we again want to differentiate our subjects with respect to their living conditions. However, this time we want to explicitly relate two distinct types of indicators. Thus, we are looking for a model that can investigate the relation between *sets* of variables of mixed measurement level. Nonlinear generalized canonical analysis (GCA) is such a technique. It is introduced by Van der Burg, De Leeuw, & Verdegaal (1988) and Gifi (1990, Chapter 5). Nonlinear GCA maximizes the correspondence between two or more sets of variables. Before the correlational structure between sets can be assessed, first an intermediary for sets has to be formulated. One way to go about this is by using weighted sums of the variables in the sets. For each set a weighted sum of variables serves as the representative of the set. The correspondence between the sets can be maximized by maximizing the correlations between the weighted sums, as in canonical correlation analysis or multiple regression analysis. Nonlinear GCA has been implemented in the computer program OVERALS, on which we will centre our discussion below. OVERALS is available in the SPSS procedure CATEGORIES (SPSS, 1990). A version of generalized canonical correlation analysis for two sets is available in the procedure TRANSREG in the SAS-package (Kuhfeld & Young, 1988).

Suppose that we have K sets of variables. The number of variables per set is denoted by M_k. The indicator matrix of variable jk is written as $\mathbf{I}_{jk}$ and the matrix of category quantifications as $\mathbf{B}_{jk}$ ($j = 1, \ldots, M_k; k = 1, \ldots, K$). The loss function to be minimized in nonlinear generalized canonical analysis can be formulated as:

$$\sigma(\mathbf{Z}, \mathbf{B}_{11}, \ldots, \mathbf{B}_{M_k K}) = \sum_{k=1}^{K} \text{SSQ}\left(\mathbf{Z} - \sum_{j=1}^{M_k} \mathbf{I}_{jk}\mathbf{B}_{jk}\right), \qquad (2.4)$$

subject to the conditions $\mathbf{Z}'\mathbf{Z} = N\mathbf{I}$, $\mathbf{Z}'\mathbf{u} = \mathbf{0}$, and $\mathbf{B}_{jk} = \mathbf{c}_{jk}\mathbf{a}'_{jk}$ for single variables.

In Equation (2.4), the vector $\mathbf{c}_{jk}$ contains the numerical, ordinal or nominal quantification and $\mathbf{a}_{jk}$ is the vector of weights, each time for the j-th variable in the k-th set. The badness-of-fit is defined as the loss as specified in Equation (2.4). This badness-of-fit or loss can be broken down by set and by dimension. Thus, for each set, and for each dimension, loss values can be specified. The eigenvalues of the respective dimensions are then defined as one minus the average loss (over the sets) for that dimension. The sum of the eigenvalues equals the goodness-of-fit, which can also be defined as the number of dimensions minus the loss averaged over sets over dimensions. Similarly to nonlinear principal components analysis, the eigenvalues reflect the explained variance of a dimension. Note that this explained variance now refers back to the weighted sums of variables, and not directly to the variables as in principal components analysis.

For single variables the vector $\mathbf{I}_{jk}\mathbf{c}_{jk}$ provides the transformed variable and the $\mathbf{c}_{jk}$ are called the *category quantifications*. The $\mathbf{a}_{jk}$-scores are the *weights* per dimension that sum the variables of one set into the weighted sum, also encountered in the literature under the name *canonical variate*. However, as in multiple regression, these weights depend for each variable not only on its own contribution, but also on the contributions of the other variables within the set, that is, they are susceptible to multicollinearity. It is thus hazardous to interpret the weights as such. To assess the importance of the respective variables in a set, the transformed variables $\mathbf{I}_{jk}\mathbf{c}_{jk}$ can be projected into the space of object scores. The coordinates of these projections are denoted by p-dimensional vectors $\mathbf{r}_{jk}$. The scores $\mathbf{r}_{jk}$ are the correlations between the transformed variables $\mathbf{I}_{jk}\mathbf{c}_{jk}$ and the object scores $\mathbf{Z}$; they are therefore equivalent to component loadings as defined for nonlinear principal components analysis. Thus, where in nonlinear principal components analysis the component loadings $\mathbf{r}_j$ were identical to the weights $\mathbf{a}_j$, in nonlinear GCA weights and component loadings are different entities. Given the fact that in nonlinear GCA the $\mathbf{a}_{jk}$ and $\mathbf{r}_{jk}$ are different, also the products $\mathbf{c}_{jk}\mathbf{a}'_{jk}$ (single category coordinates) and $\mathbf{c}_{jk}\mathbf{r}'_{jk}$ (projected centroids) are different. We will return to this subject below.

For variables considered as multiple nominal, the scores $\mathbf{B}_{jk}$ are the multiple quantifications of the categories. However, also for multiple nominal variables, interpretation of their relevance is less straightforward than in the one-set case. Analogously to the single variables situation, the p-dimensional quantifications of the categories of multiple nominal variables take into account the effect of the other variables within the set as well: the effect of multicollinearity is incorporated in the multiple category quantifications. Thus, whereas in multiple correspondence analysis the category centroids were identical to the category quantifications $\mathbf{B}_j$, in nonlinear GCA category centroids and category quantifications are different entities. To assess the importance of a multiple variable, it is advisable to inspect the category means or *category centroids* of the object scores instead.

This points to another important difference between one-set techniques such as multiple correspondence analysis and nonlinear principal components analysis on the one hand, and multi-set techniques such as nonlinear generalized canonical analysis on the other hand. This difference is determined by the different criteria through which the space of object scores is found. One-set techniques search for directions that explain maximum variance of the variables. Multi-set techniques search for directions to explain maximum variance of the sets, as represented by weighted sums of variables. This implies that in multi-set techniques the eigenvalues of the dimensions do not reflect the variance accounted for by the quantified variables, but the variance accounted for by the weighted sums $\sum_j \mathbf{I}_{jk} \mathbf{B}_{jk}$, the canonical variates. As such, the dimensions in a nonlinear GCA solution represent that which is most common between the sets – which need not be identical to what is most common between the variables. As a consequence it is theoretically possible to find a good congruence (high fit) between sets, but low explained variance of the variables.

The object scores again form an orthonormalized system. Category centroids, projected centroids, component loadings and object scores are thus part of the same solution and also the same space. Therefore they should be interpreted in relation to one another. Subjects can be characterized by the categories that have been placed in their vicinity.

Subjects close to each other share this characterization and may thus be identified as belonging to the same subgroup of subjects; subjects far from each other have dissimilar patterns and belong to different subgroups. Categories in the periphery of the solution characterize homogeneous subgroups of subjects. Categories in the centre of the solution are shared by many subjects, and generally can not be used to characterize distinct subgroups.

Whenever single quantifications are present, nonlinear generalized canonical analysis solutions are not nested, just like nonlinear principal components analysis.

Nonlinear generalized canonical analysis is related to several other techniques. If there are only two sets of variables and all variables are numerical, nonlinear GCA reduces to canonical correlation analysis (Hotelling, 1936; Tatsuoka, 1988, Chapter 7). In case of two sets of variables and mixed measurement level variables, nonlinear GCA is – but for superficial differences – identical to the model for nonlinear canonical correlation analysis introduced by Young, De Leeuw, & Takane (1976) and by Van der Burg & De Leeuw (1983). Given these relations with canonical correlation analysis, it is not surprising that nonlinear GCA bears the epithet 'canonical' in its name, and that the weighted sums are often referred to as canonical variates. If there is one variable per set, nonlinear GCA reduces to nonlinear principal components analysis. If there is one multiple nominal variable per set, nonlinear GCA reduces to multiple correspondence analysis. Note that, while nonlinear generalized canonical analysis was introduced as a k-sets technique, in the latter two formulations it corresponds to a one-set technique. Van der Burg et al. (1988) described a special version of nonlinear GCA in which all variables are multiple nominal, which they coined *homogeneity analysis with K-sets of variables* or *homogeneity analysis with additivity restrictions*. Carroll (1968) defined linear generalized canonical analysis or K-sets analysis; other possibilities for linear K-sets analysis were described by Kettenring (1971) and Van de Geer (1984), amongst others. These K-sets techniques differ in the maximizing criteria used.

For more details on nonlinear GCA see Van der Burg et al. (1988), Gifi (1990, Chapter 5) and Van der Burg, De Leeuw, & Dijksterhuis (1994).

Example of nonlinear generalized canonical analysis   We again analyse
the same small artificial data set that was used in Section 2.2.1 above
to illustrate the performance and interpretation of nonlinear generalized canonical analysis. The data set, variables and categories were
described in Table 2.1 above.

When variables can be considered as grouped into sets, nonlinear
generalized canonical analysis is an appropriate analysis technique. For
illustrative purposes, we thus grouped the variables in our example data
set in three sets: one for the demographic variables educational level,
age and gender, a second set for the 'family' variables marital status
and children, and a third set that contained the health related variables
drinking habits and health. We used the same measurement levels for
the variables that were used in the PRINCALS example above (Section 2.2.2). The sets, variables and corresponding measurement levels
we used for the OVERALS example are summarized in Table 2.5.

Table 2.5: *Artificial Data: Sets, Variables and Measurement Levels used in
OVERALS Analysis*

Set	Variable	Measurement level
Set 1	EDUCATION	Ordinal
	AGE	Ordinal
	GENDER	Numerical
Set 2	MARITAL	Multiple nominal
	CHILDREN	Multiple nominal
Set 3	HEALTH	Multiple nominal
	DRINK	Multiple nominal

Again, we chose two dimensions for the solution. OVERALS converged to a solution with eigenvalues for the first and second dimension
of 0.776 and 0.634 respectively. These are quite adequate eigenvalues. The eigenvalues are incomparable with the eigenvalues from the
HOMALS and PRINCALS analyses as the model is fundamentally different: we are not optimizing relations between variables, but between
sets of variables. A summary of the fit and loss values over sets and
dimensions is given in Table 2.6.

Table 2.6: *Artificial Data: Summary of* OVERALS *Solution: Loss per Set, Mean Loss, Fit and Eigenvalues*

		Loss per set	
			Dimensions
	Sum	1	2
SET 1	0.636	0.338	0.298
SET 2	0.472	0.201	0.271
SET 3	0.663	0.134	0.529
Mean	0.590	0.224	0.366
Fit	1.410		
Eigenvalue		0.776	0.634

Looking at the loss per dimension for each set, we can infer from Table 2.6 that the third set (drinking habits and health) has the lowest loss for the first dimension, and the highest loss for the second dimension. Apparently, this set is thus a quite important contributor to the first dimension. The second set plays a role in the first dimension as well as the second dimension. The first set fits about equally well in either dimension. The average loss over sets for the first dimension is 0.224, so that the eigenvalue for this dimension is $1 - 0.224 = 0.776$. The average loss over sets for the second dimension is 0.366, so that the eigenvalue for this dimension is $1 - 0.366 = 0.634$. Looking at the total loss for each set, we see how the second set has the smallest loss and thus the best overall fit.

We stated above that to interpret the OVERALS solution, one should, similarly to the interpretation of multiple regression results, not interpret the weights, but measures comparable to the correlations. In OVERALS terminology we should thus not interpret the weights but the component loadings. The component loadings for all variables with single restrictions (GENDER, EDUCATION, AGE and HEALTH – while

HEALTH has three categories, only two categories have entries, so that like GENDER it has actually numerical measurement level) are depicted in Figure 2.8. Figure 2.8 shows how HEALTH and AGE are important variables in the first dimension; GENDER and EDUCATION are important variables in the second dimension. If the component loadings are squared, only positive scores are obtained, comparable to the discrimination measures of multiple correspondence analysis.

Figure 2.8: *Artificial Data: OVERALS Component Loadings of Single Variables*

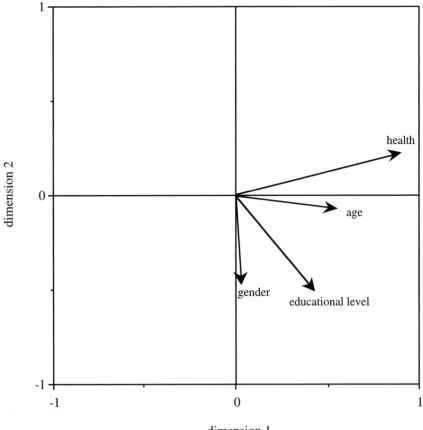

Like the weights, single category coordinates may suffer from the effect of multicollinearity. Thus, if one wants to interpret the average positioning of the categories of single variables in the solution, one should always inspect the *projected centroids*, as in the projected centroids the effect of multicollinearity has been corrected for. This can be verified by connecting the projected centroids of the various categories in single variables: the lines thus formed have the same direction as the component loadings of the variables.

A similar situation exists for multiple variables. As we said above, the category quantifications in OVERALS, because they are affected by multicollinearity, are not necessarily comparable to the centroids of the object scores of all subjects in a certain category. As such, to interpret the role of multiple variables in an OVERALS solution, one should always inspect the *category centroids*, from which the effect of multicollinearity has been removed.

To interpret the OVERALS results, we therefore give a graphical representation of the category centroids of the multiple variables and the projected centroids of the single variables in Figure 2.9. To mark them clearly, the projected centroids of the single variables have been connected with lines having the same directions as the component loadings. From Figure 2.9 we can infer the following. Starting in the bottom right of the configuration, we see that those with more than two children who are married or cohabiting, more often are females with a university education who drink once a week. Moving clockwise, we see that those with one child or no children, are often subjects in good health in the 18–25 or 26–35 age range. Single or divorced/widowed subjects are also often young with vocational training or secondary school. In the sample, male subjects often have 2 children, they drink either not at all or several times a week. Those who drink not at all more often tend to report feeling reasonably healthy. Note that Figure 2.9 resembles Figure 2.6. Although the loss function of generalized canonical analysis differs from the loss function of principal components analysis, and the two techniques answer different questions about the data, the results are still fairly similar. This is not always the case if the two techniques are applied on the same data.

As a last tool for interpretation, we give the object scores, labelled by subject number, in Figure 2.10. As mentioned already, object scores, category centroids and projected centroids belong to the same space (with the component loadings). Here the scales of the dimensions of the figures with object scores, category centroids and projected centroids

Figure 2.9: *Artificial Data: OVERALS Category Centroids and Connected Projected Centroids*

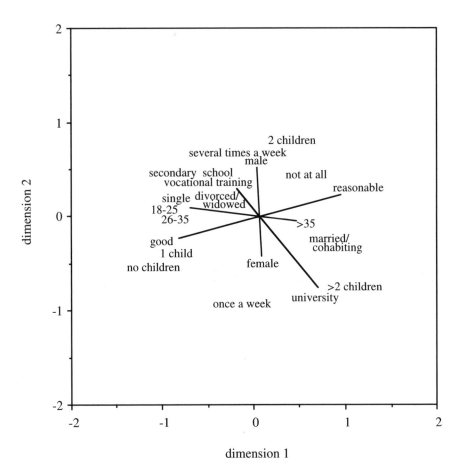

are the same, so that Figure 2.9 and Figure 2.10 can be viewed as super-imposed. Figure 2.10 shows how the subjects have been partitioned into two groups. A small cluster consisting of subjects 2, 6, 8, 12, 16 and 18 is positioned in the bottom left of the configuration. The category centroids and projected centroids show that this group can probably be characterized as healthy subjects with no children or one child. This group has been contrasted with the remainder of subjects who have been spread out like a fan over the bottom right-, upper right- and upper left-hand side of the figure. Those in the lower and middle right-hand side

Figure 2.10: *Artificial Data: OVERALS Object Scores*

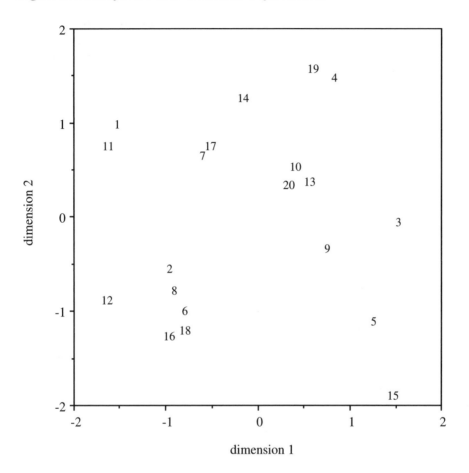

are generally older females, university educated and married with more than 2 children (subjects 15, 5, 9 and 3). Moving on counter clockwise, we encounter predominantly males who either abstain from alcohol or drink several times a week, report reasonable health and have 2 children (e.g. subjects 13, 4, 19 and 14). Ending in the upper left-hand side of the figure are younger single and divorced or widowed subjects with secondary school or vocational training (subjects 7, 17, 1 and 11).

The interpretation derived from the category centroids and projected centroids in combination with the object scores is different in a number of aspects compared with the interpretation derived from the HOMALS and PRINCALS solution (Sections 2.2.1 and 2.2.2) that used the same data set: particularly the role of educational level and marital status was altered. One should, however, always keep in mind that in an OVERALS analysis, one relates sets of variables, and the model fitted on the data is thus fundamentally different. Thus, different relations are modelled and different patterns of relationships may be stressed in the solution.

For an in-depth discussion of the OVERALS program, we refer to Van der Burg et al. (1988), Van der Burg et al. (1994), Gifi (1990) and Van de Geer (1993).

2.3   Longitudinal extensions to optimal scaling techniques

As discussed in Chapter 1, a major problem in longitudinal data analysis is that almost all existing data analysis techniques have been designed to analyse data matrices, and that in the longitudinal ($N > 1$) case, we have a data box. In this section we will discuss three strategies for analysing longitudinal categorical data using cross-sectional multivariate techniques. In all three strategies, the data box has to be flattened first.

In the first strategy, the data box is first as it were cut into slices, with one slice per time point (compare Figure 1.2(a)). Next, two options are available for amalgamating these slices into one matrix: vertical stacking and horizontal stacking. As we will show, the second option is in most cases unsuitable for the analysis of categorical data through optimal scaling techniques. We will therefore illustrate the application of only the first option using multiple correspondence analysis.

In the second strategy, time is introduced as a categorical variable into the model. We will illustrate this strategy through multi-set analysis, using the program for multi-set analysis OVERALS.

A third strategy comprises working with lagged variables: relating the variables for time t in one set with the same (or other) variables at time point $t - 1$ in another set (or working with higher-order lags), gives an indication of the dependence in time between variables. We will illustrate this strategy with a multi-set analysis as well.

For both the second and the third strategy the data box is first flattened through horizontal stacking.

2.3.1 Flattening the data box: time points adding subjects or time points adding variables

Suppose that we have measured in a sample of outpatients several scales that measure depression and general well-being, as well as demographic and other background variables, such as employment status, marital status, therapy and medication. Measurements have been obtained at a number of occasions, for instance at intake, at the start of therapy and at the end of therapy, so that $T = 3$. We want to investigate subjects' overall development over time, with respect to depression as well as with respect to the background characteristics. We do not want to do this univariately, but in a multivariate fashion. Thus, we are interested in summarizing the most pertinent relations between the variables. In addition we want to describe and interpret subjects' changes on these variables.

Formalizing the problem described above, we thus have a data box with N subjects, M variables and T time points. We denote the respective entries as Y_{ijt}, with i the index denoting the subject ($i = 1,\dots,N$), j the index denoting the variable ($j = 1,\dots,M$), and t denoting the occasion at which measurements took place ($t = 1,\dots,T$). For reasons described previously, we want to flatten the data box so that it becomes a data matrix.

Time points adding subjects The most popular choice for flattening the data box is by lateral slicing, and subsequent vertical stacking of the resulting data matrices. In that case, the data matrices for each time point, stacked vertically, form a super-matrix of observations (see Figure 2.11). The entries Y_{ijt} now become $Y_{i_t,j}$, with ($j = 1,\dots,M$) and i_t denoting subjects at the respective time points ($i = 1,\dots,N; t = 1,\dots,T$). The resulting super-matrix is often named the LONG matrix (Visser, 1985, p. 51), of order $(NT) \times M$. As the data box has been flattened into a data matrix, we can analyse the data using either ordinary cross-sectional techniques or cross-sectional techniques in a special design, or set-up, that takes account of the time dependence in the data matrix. Visser (1985, pp. 48–55) formalized the classes of techniques that will be presented here.

In flattening the data box, it is not important whether the matrices for each time point are stacked blockwise, or whether the time points for

Figure 2.11: *Slicing and Vertical Stacking of the Data Box*

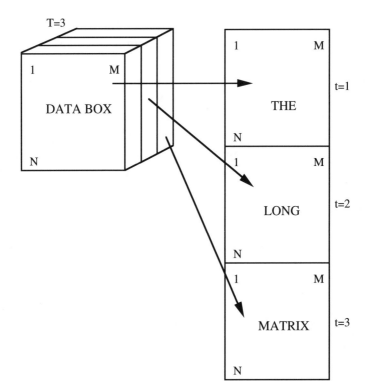

each subject are stacked blockwise, as long as one remembers where the subjects and time points can be found. For multivariate analysis to be feasible, NT has to be substantially larger than M, and in hardly any case will this be a problem. Instead of N subjects, the flattened data matrix has NT subjects, and submitting this super-matrix to any multivariate analysis technique, the time points at which the subjects were observed will thus be treated as independent replications, or equivalently, as new or added subjects. Note that when flattening the data box in this way, missing occasions do not constitute a problem: for each subject, all measurement occasions for which data are available can be entered, and those occasions for which no observations were collected are simply left out. This means that series of unequal length can be included, and even interrupted series may be entered. (This advantage applies as well to the other two strategies discussed in the remainder of this section.) In terms of notation this implies that T may differ for different subjects: $T_i \neq T$. In that case the dimensionality of the super matrix becomes $(\sum_{i=1}^{N} T_i) \times M$. However, in the following we will for ease of presentation often use the notation NT. Note that it is assumed, however, that the same variables have been measured at each time point.

Visser (1982, p. 65) recommends using this type of flattening when the serial correlation of the true scores is thought to be importantly higher than serial correlation of the error: for instance, in cases where the mean of variables is thought to vary considerably over time. In many instances, however, the first dimension of a principal component analysis-type of technique will then represent the changes over time, irrespective of the relations between the variables. This can be illustrated as follows. Suppose that two variables measured at a number of time points have at each time point a correlation of almost zero, but that for both variables, the values increase at each time point. Analysis of the vertically stacked super-matrix then produces a positive correlation between the variables (see also Figure 1.3 in Chapter 1).

Technically speaking, such a correlation is spurious: the correlation between the variables disappears if we control for the third variable 'time'. Other time-induced relationships may exist (see for instance the example in Figure 1.4 in Chapter 1), where the scores at each time point have a positive correlation, but analysis over time points results in a negative correlation.

Problems of this kind can be circumvented by applying the strategy put forward by Bentler (1973). Bentler proposes to first unit normalize the variables per time-point, laterally slicing the data box afterwards. The relations between the variables at the various time points then cannot be influenced anymore by changes in the mean over time points. This has the disadvantage that changes in the mean over time cannot be analysed anymore. Another solution, more relevant in our categorical context, would be to perform separate analyses per time point, and compare these respective solutions with the solution from analysis of the super-matrix.

Such time-induced relationships arise from the fact that by analysing the LONG matrix, one performs a single common analysis for all time points simultaneously, which produces one solution and thus one structure, which does not and can not reveal changes in structure. Analysing the laterally sliced vertically stacked data box in a longitudinal context, each subject is assigned a new object score for each new time point. As such, each subject appears T times in one single solution. While the solution is the same across time points, subjects may appear in a different position at each time point. Framed conceptually, analysing the LONG matrix, one thus models changing subjects in a stable world.

In the context of exploratory longitudinal multivariate analysis, this is an eminently useful concept. In a longitudinal data analysis situation, we are interested in intraindividual change as well as in interindividual differences in intraindividual change. As analysis of the LONG matrix produces coordinates for every subject for every time point, it is possible to visualize and interpret subjects' changes: looking at the coordinates we can see how subjects change over time. Because LONG analysis of T time points produces one solution, subjects' positions at the various time points can be compared and intraindividual differences investigated. In addition, it is possible to compare differences as well as similarities between the changes of (groups of) subjects.

Analysing the LONG matrix with multivariate techniques such as multiple correspondence analysis or nonlinear principal components analysis, we obtain a solution that can be interpreted using the category quantifications and component loadings. Given that the data matrix $\mathbf{Y}$ has entries $Y_{i_t,j}$, with j the index denoting the variables and i_t the index denoting subjects at the successive time points, the loss function for, for instance, nonlinear principal components analysis becomes (a similar formula can be written down easily for multiple correspondence analysis or nonlinear generalized canonical analysis):

$$\sigma(\mathbf{Z}, \mathbf{B}_1, \ldots, \mathbf{B}_M) = \sum_{j=1}^{M} \mathrm{SSQ}\left(\mathbf{Z} - \mathbf{I}_j \mathbf{B}_j\right), \qquad (2.5)$$

under the conditions $\mathbf{Z}'\mathbf{Z} = (\sum_{i=1}^{N} T_i)\mathbf{I}$, $\mathbf{Z}'\mathbf{u} = \mathbf{0}$ and $\mathbf{B}_j = \mathbf{c}_j \mathbf{a}'_j$ for variables treated as single,

with $\mathbf{c}_j$ a numerical, nominal or ordinal quantification, with the scores in the vector $\mathbf{a}_j$ the correlations between $\mathbf{I}_j \mathbf{c}_j$ (the transformed variable) and the object scores $\mathbf{Z}$, and with Z_{i_t} the elements of $\mathbf{Z}$. Note that, apart from the conditions, loss function (2.5) is identical to loss function (2.3). The object scores Z_{i_t} represent the subjects at the respective time points. For instance, Z_{1_1} is the position of subject 1 at time point 1, Z_{1_2} is the position of subject 1 at time point 2, etc. Subjects' changes can be made visible by connecting the object scores of subjects at the respective time points. If for instance, subject 16 travels from a spot at time point 1 close to the category quantification of severe depression, to a spot at time point 2 close to the category quantification of mild depression, we may conclude that subject 16 has become less depressed from time point 1 to time point 2.

However, to attempt to interpret a plot where the object scores at the time points have been connected for each individual subject, so that one has N individual trajectories, is generally not very elucidating. We recommend therefore to draw trajectories for subgroups of subjects, or to connect the average object score of all subjects at the time points (see the examples below).

Time points adding variables   A second, less commonly used method to flatten the data box is that of lateral slicing and horizontal stacking. Visser coins the resulting matrix the BROAD matrix (Visser, 1985, p. 54). An example for $T = 3$ is in Figure 2.12.

The data box entries Y_{ijt} become Y_{i,j_t}, with j_t now denoting the variables at the respective time points ($j = 1,\ldots,M; t = 1\ldots,T$) and i denoting the subjects ($i = 1,\ldots,N$). As can be seen from Figure 2.12, all subjects must have been measured at the same number of time points: $T_i = T$. Note, however, that strictly speaking it is not necessary that the same (number of) variables have been measured at all time points; in other words: $M_t \neq M$. The BROAD matrix is thus of order $N \times (\sum_{t=1}^{T} M_t)$. N has to be substantially larger than $\sum_{t=1}^{T} M_t$ for multivariate analysis to be feasible. One reason for the relative unpopularity of the use of the BROAD matrix is that in many cases this condition is not met. The technique will interpret the time points at which the subjects were observed as new or added variables, so that we usually end up with a relatively large number of variables with respect to the number of subjects. The problem becomes more serious the larger the number of time points is. A second complication particular to the analysis of categorical data in a BROAD matrix design emerges as a result of the optimal scaling of the categories of the variables. The analysis technique views every variable at each time point as a new, different variable. Thus, if we have for instance one depression scale measured at three time points, the technique will treat the variable at the three time points

Figure 2.12: *Slicing and Horizontal Stacking of the Data Box*

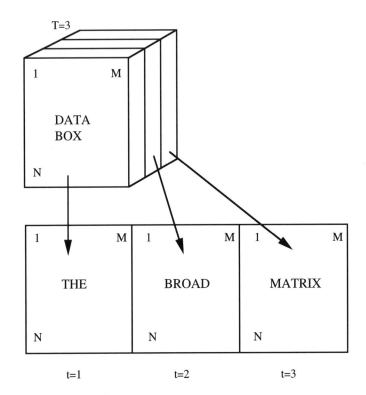

as three different variables. If the variable is categorical, the technique will quantify the three temporal versions of the same variable, such that the loss function is minimized. In doing so, quantifications are unconstrained across time points, so that there is no guarantee that the quantifications of the same variable at the various time points will be identical. And if the quantifications are indeed different, the rescaled variable is not comparable anymore across time points. This constitutes an additional practical limitation in using the BROAD matrix. Of course, given that the data box contains a sufficiently large number of subjects, we may analyse the BROAD matrix and check afterwards whether any categorical variables have been quantified in a comparatively similar way across time points. If the quantifications are identical or almost identical, interpretation can proceed; if the quantifications are different, there is no other option but to abandon further analysis through the BROAD matrix. Unfortunately no formal criterion is available to decide on sufficient similarity. For a further discussion of these points see Van Buuren (1990, 1997b).

Analysis of the BROAD matrix with multivariate techniques such as multiple correspondence analysis or nonlinear principal components analysis produces a solution in which the object scores represent the subjects at all time points. Given that the BROAD data matrix $\mathbf{Y}$ has entries Y_{i,j_t}, with j_t the index denoting the variables at the successive time points, and i the index denoting the subjects, the loss function for, for instance, nonlinear principal components analysis becomes: (again a similar formula can be written down easily for the case of multiple correspondence analysis or nonlinear generalized canonical analysis)

$$\sigma(\mathbf{Z}, \mathbf{B}_{1_1}, \ldots, \mathbf{B}_{M_T}) = \sum_{t=1}^{T} \sum_{j=1}^{M} \text{SSQ}\left(\mathbf{Z} - \mathbf{I}_{j_t} \mathbf{B}_{j_t}\right) \tag{2.6}$$

under the conditions $\mathbf{Z}'\mathbf{Z} = N\mathbf{I}$, $\mathbf{Z}'\mathbf{u} = \mathbf{0}$ and $\mathbf{B}_{j_t} = \mathbf{c}_{j_t}\mathbf{a}'_{j_t}$ for variables treated as single,

with $\mathbf{c}_{j_t}$ a numerical, nominal or ordinal quantification, the scores in the vector $\mathbf{a}_{j_t}$ the correlations between $\mathbf{I}_{j_t}\mathbf{c}_{j_t}$ (the transformed variable) and the object scores $\mathbf{Z}$, and with Z_i the elements of $\mathbf{Z}$. In Equation (2.6) the component loadings $\mathbf{a}_{j_t}$ are now the component loadings of the variables at the respective time points. The category quantifications $\mathbf{c}_{j_t}$ are the category quantifications of the variables at the respective time points. Note how the various quantifications of the respective temporal versions of the variables appear in Equation (2.6): every variable at every time point has its own indicator matrix, and its own vector of quantifications. Assuming that the category quantifications are stable over time, we can interpret changes in structure by comparing the component loadings of the variables at the successive time points. For instance, in the hypothetical depression example sketched above, analysis of the BROAD matrix might show that high scores on well-being at intake are related to low scores on depression, but that high scores on well-being at the end of therapy are related to employment and marital status. While interpretation of changes in structure is fairly straightforward, interpretation of subjects' changes is more cumbersome. One way to approach this is by comparing subjects' relative positioning at each time point towards the component loadings of the variables. For instance, if a subject's object score is located close to the arrow of depression at time point 1, and if the arrow of depression at time point 2 is further away from the object score of that same subject, we could infer that this subject has become less depressed from time point 1 to time point 2.

Multivariate analysis of the BROAD matrix is a particularly well-suited tool for investigating changes in structure over time. Analysing the BROAD matrix in a longitudinal context, one models stable subjects in a changing world: people stay put while the world evolves around them. As such, this type of analysis is also conceptually less attractive for studying (intra)individual change. Particularly in a behavioural or developmental context, where the focus is mostly on intra-individual change, the interpretation offered by this type of analysis is thus less attractive. Given its additional technical limitations for analysing categorical data through optimal scaling, we will therefore not illustrate analysis of the BROAD matrix with an example here.

Example of time points adding subjects: care-substitution for the elderly
The data set under consideration stems from a study on the effect of care-substitution for the elderly (Perenboom & Zaal, 1991) [2]. In the Netherlands, as in many Western countries, elderly people make up a growing proportion of the population. Elderly people need care, medical and otherwise, and in the Netherlands efforts are made to investigate means of containing the cost of such care. One strategy (or philosophy) in this field is that of care-substitution: such substituted care is not offered in standard form, but in bits that can be flexibly tailored to the specific needs of the elderly person. Where possible, care is shifted from intramural to extramural facilities, and from formal towards (volunteer) informal- and self-care. Supposedly, an added advantage of such care is that elderly people can remain living on their own for a longer time. Care-substitution is also hypothesized to be more cost-effective.

Care-substitution is not routinely provided in the Netherlands and elderly people generally receive care in one of three care packages:

- *sheltered accommodation*, where people live independently, but which is connected to a retirement home with nursing care (see

---

[2]The authors acknowledge permission by the TNO Institute for Prevention and Health to use material and data.

below), from which they can use facilities, such as the alarm system, meals, and some assistance in case of problems;

- *retirement home with nursing care*, where people live in rooms with shower facilities. Meals, entertainment assistance in household chores, plus, if necessary, some physical care is provided;

- *nursing home*, where not only elderly people live, but also many who are revalidating. People sleep in wards, they do not live independently at all, and are usually quite intensively cared for.

In 1987, a special home for the elderly in the Netherlands was started as an experiment, the so-called 'Care Home'. The Care Home was the first of its kind to offer integral facilities for substituted care. As substituted care is assumed to be cheaper, one of the aims of the quasi-experiment discussed here was to assess whether elderly people receiving the cheaper substituted care in the Care Home were not worse off than a comparable group of elderly in the same town, who still received the old three-tier, more expensive, custom-made care package.

Over a period of two-and-a-half years, 430 elderly people (150 in the Care Home who constituted the experimental group and 280 from regular care-institutions who constituted the control group) were interviewed at five time points, each approximately 6 months apart, except for the fourth and the last measurement which were one year apart. From the five measurements, a total of 1432 interviews had been obtained. Not only complete series were used, but shorter and interrupted series were included as well – from those subjects who had died, were ill at one or more measurements, or had otherwise disappeared from the sample. During the course of the study, a number of people newly moved into the Care Home, and interviews with them were included as well. Thus, the longitudinal study is conducted on a panel of varying composition.

We analyse the eight selected variables from the data set, that indicate physical and mental well-being, as well as need for care and care consumption. Loneliness and well-being had been measured at the first, third and fifth time point; the other variables had been measured at all five time points. Thus, not all variables had been measured at all measurement points. This is not a problem as the optimal scaling technique can deal with these missing values efficiently. The variables and their categories are listed in Table 2.7.

Table 2.7: *Care Substitution Data: Well-being and Care Variables*

Variable	Categories
HEALTH	Good to bad
PHYSICAL COMPLAINTS	None to 5 or more complaints
PSYCHOLOGICAL COMPLAINTS	None to 5 or more complaints
LONELINESS	Very lonely to not lonely
WELL-BEING	Low to high
MOBILITY PROBLEMS	Slight to serious
INFIRMITY	No infirmity to severe infirmity
MEDICAL CONSUMPTION	None to 3 or more

The measurements for the subjects were stacked vertically into a LONG matrix. Each time point for a subject is thus treated as a new subject, and subjects appear at the most five times in the solution. Using default measures for convergence, we ran HOMALS in two dimensions for the eight variables and 1432 data rows.

The algorithm converged to a solution with eigenvalues measures for the first and second dimension of 0.433 and 0.236 respectively [3]. For interpretation we use the plot of category quantifications (see Figure 2.13).

The solution has a straightforward interpretation. As subjects' object scores (that are not shown here) are located close to the categories that they scored, we find in the right hand side those subjects that fare well. These subjects have no or one physical complaint, no psychological complaints, they feel healthy, not lonely, and they score high on well-being; most subjects, however, do have some (minor) mobility problems. They also score low on medical consumption. Towards the centre bottom of the picture are located those subjects who feel relatively healthy, say they have no or few infirmity problems, and some mobility problems. Their medical consumption is somewhat higher, they have more physical and psychological complaints; their well-being is slightly lower. Towards the top left of the picture are situated those elderly who do not fare well at all: they report a high number of phys-

---

[3] Analyses per time point of the dataset had shown approximately the same structure, leading to the same interpretation (viz. Section 2.3.1).

Figure 2.13: *Care Substitution Data: Category Quantifications of the*
HOMALS Solution

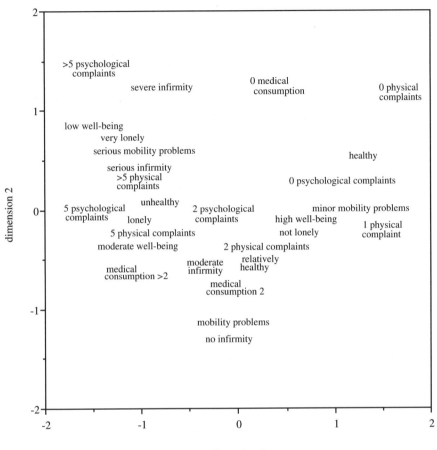

ical and psychological complaints, their sense of well-being is low, they
feel quite lonely, have serious mobility problems and feel unhealthy.
The very upper left of the picture is occupied by those subjects who
are worst off: subjects located here report more than five psychological
complaints and severe infirmity.

In order to investigate subjects' developments over the time points,
and in order to compare the elderly in the Care Home with the elderly
in the control group, we graphically represent subjects' average object

scores at the five time points, for the experimental and control subjects separately, as well as separately for the three care packages (sheltered accommodation, retirement home and nursing home). While the experimental subjects in the Care Home had not been housed in accommodation corresponding to any of the three standard indication types (they were all housed in the Care Home receiving flexibly tailored care), for reasons of comparability we classified each experimental subject into the category in which he or she would have been housed normally. The average object scores of the three indication types in the experimental and control group, for each of the respective time points are given in Figure 2.14; the (zig-zagging) arrows point from time point 1 to time point 5. For reasons of overview, separate figures are given for experimental and control groups. Both figures should be viewed as superimposed upon Figure 2.13.

For both figures it applies that the elderly in the sheltered accommodation indication types as well as the experimental group retirement home subjects appear in the lower right-hand side of the picture. Towards the left-hand side are located the control group retirement home subjects. Towards the upper left we find the two nursing home groups.

From Figure 2.14, we see that the experimental and control groups are located in more or less the same positions in the configuration. Thus, it appears as if the experimental subjects in the Care Home group did not fare worse than their counterparts in the traditional care system. One notable exception is the retirement home experimental group, which performs even better than the retirement home control group, in fact almost as well as the sheltered accommodation group. Apparently, these subjects are in much better shape than their counterparts in the traditional care facilities.

As remarked above, both those who feel very well in the sheltered accommodation as well as those being cared for as invalids in the nursing homes score low on medical consumption: this can be understood for subjects who report feeling quite well, but it is hard to imagine for people in nursing homes with lists of complaints. However, in the nursing homes, medical care is provided routinely with doctors visiting patients (in principle) every day, so that medical consumption is not registered separately.

Interpreting the changes of the respective indication categories for experimental as well as control group, a first striking observation is that

Figure 2.14: *Care Substitution Data: Average Object Scores of Indication Subgroups in Experimental and Control Group at the Measurement Occasions*

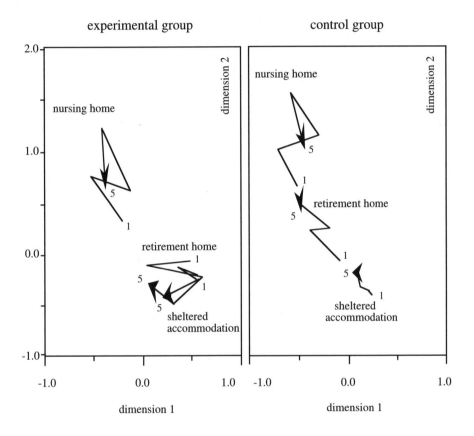

the development curves described by the groups are quite jagged. Apparently the groups do not develop smoothly over the years, but have ups and downs. Some of this whimsical behaviour might be due to the season, as time points 1 and 3 are situated mostly more to the right-hand side and 2, 4 and 5 more to the left-hand side (measurements 1 and 3 were conducted in spring, and measurements 2, 4 and 5 in autumn). A first explanation is thus that the effect has been caused by a seasonal variation, with subjects apparently feeling better in spring than in autumn. Overall, subjects develop from the right towards the left, moving upward more or less along the left part of the structure that emerged in the plot of category quantifications. The overall changes are marked by a decrease in health and well-being. As subjects move upwards in the left-hand side of the picture, they reach the categories of many complaints, loneliness, low well-being, mobility problems and severe infirmity. Changes are largest, and most dramatic, for the nursing home groups and the control group retirement home subjects.

2.3.2 Time as a categorical variable

Suppose, as usual, that we have a data set of N subjects measured on M variables over T time points: for instance depression, general well-being and background variables, such as age, marital status, employment status and the like, measured for N outpatients at three time points. We are again interested to investigate subjects' developments. However, this time we are particularly interested in summarizing subjects' psychological well-being at the respective time points to characterize the various phases in the therapeutic process. For instance, one of our research questions is: what are the differences between subjects when they enter therapy compared with when they are dismissed from therapy? As such, we not only want to summarize the sample's average psychological state at each time point, but we also want to actually discriminate the time points in terms of the psychological variables, in order to obtain a profile of each time point in terms of the variables of interest. As such we have two types of variables: the psychological variables, and the time points that we want to discriminate. Our research question can be answered by analysing the data set using multi-set or nonlinear generalized canonical analysis, with the data box flattened in a special way, using a categorical time variable constructed specifically for our purposes.

   To do so, again we start with a data box that is $N \times M \times T$. As above, we first stack the individual data matrices in a flattened super-matrix that is of size $(NT) \times M$. We now want to use two sets of variables, so we designate the psychological variables in the first set as Y, and the variables (actually the time variable) in the second set as X. Thus, we then have entries Y_{ijt} that become $Y_{i_t,j}$, with $(j = 1, \ldots, M)$ and i_t denoting the subjects at the respective time points $(i = 1, \ldots, N; t = 1, \ldots, T)$. This matrix constitutes the first set, the so-called variables-set. Next, a categorical time variable is constructed as an $(NT) \times 1$ vector, a supervector, that contains the time points that have been numbered in such a way that each t-th time point has a unique identification. If we name the categorical time variable X, the entries for X are $X_{i_t,j}$, with j denoting the variables (here $j = 1$) and i_t denoting the subjects at the respective time points ($i = 1, \ldots, N; t = 1, \ldots, T$). For the values of the categorical time variable, we can take for instance the number of the time point. Then:

$$X_{i_t,j} = t, \qquad \text{with } t = 1, \ldots, T.$$

The categorical time variable constitutes the second set, the so-called time-set. For a schematic representation see Figure 2.15.

Figure 2.15: *Categorical Time Variable Set-up*

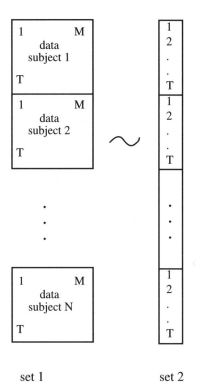

set 1   set 2

If we relate the variables in set 1 to the categorical time variable in set 2, as depicted in Figure 2.15, we in fact correlate the set of X-

variables to the time axis. If we do this with nonlinear generalized canonical analysis, treating the categorical time variable as a numerical
variable, we attain a type of time series regression. The difference with
ordinary time series regression is that we can rescale any nominal or
ordinal variables in the set of predictor variables.

However, further possibilities can be envisaged. It is not only possible to rescale categorical variables in the set of predictors, but it is also
possible to rescale the categorical time variable itself. For instance, we
can treat the time variable in the time-set as an ordinal variable. We can
then model monotone versions of time series regression: the technique
fits values for the categories of the time variable that are in ascending
(or descending) order. We can also treat the categorical time variable
as a (single) nominal variable. The category values of the time points
are then not restricted to be ordered, so that many more different developmental trajectories can be explored (for instance, developments with
ups and downs). This approach will be elaborated and illustrated in the
remainder of this section.

Using multi-set analysis for such a design, which has a variables-set
(with M_1 variables) and a time-set (in the general case with M_2 variables), the loss function based on Equation (2.4) (cf. Section 2.2.3)
becomes:

$$\sigma(\mathbf{Z}, \mathbf{B}_{11}, \ldots, \mathbf{B}_{M_2 2}) = \sum_{k=1}^{2} \text{SSQ} \left(\mathbf{Z} - \sum_{j=1}^{M_2} \mathbf{I}_{jk} \mathbf{B}_{jk} \right), \qquad (2.7)$$

subject to the conditions that $\mathbf{Z}'\mathbf{Z} = (\sum_{i=1}^{N} T_i)\mathbf{I}$, $\mathbf{Z}'\mathbf{u} = \mathbf{0}$ and
$\mathbf{B}_{jk} = \mathbf{c}_{jk}\mathbf{a}'_{jk}$ for single variables,

with $\mathbf{c}_{jk}$ a numerical, ordinal or nominal quantification, $\mathbf{a}_{jk}$ the weight,
each time for the j-th variable in the k-th set of variables, and with Z_{i_t}
the elements of $\mathbf{Z}$. Note that, apart from the conditions, loss function
(2.7) is identical to loss function (2.4).

Because multi-set analysis maximizes the correlation between the
object scores and the variables in the two sets, the relation between the
variables-set and the time-set is optimized. Consequently, the category
quantifications of the nominal time variable summarize the scores of
all subjects on the variables at each time point. The category quantifications of the single nominal time variable X thus give a profile of
subjects' average status in terms of the Y variables, at each time point.

Using this set-up, we can answer questions like: what distinguishes subjects who enter psychotherapy from subjects who complete psycho-therapy, in terms of a number of psychological and health indicators? Multi-set analysis of the data in this set-up is thus a suitable tool to char-acterize overall development on the variables over the course of time. An example of such an analysis is in Schoon (1992).

Variations on this theme are possible. The categorical time variable could be treated as multiple nominal, which gives a second, independ-ent, summary of the development over time. A similar result is obtained by adding a second categorical time variable to the time-set, labelled in a different fashion (otherwise the algorithm collapses). Both time var-iables can then be treated as single nominal, and higher dimensional canonical spaces can be analysed, opening up the possibility of invest-igating higher-dimensional development.

Another variation would be to incorporate several time variables in the time-set, of which the categories have been numbered such that they reflect various orthogonal developments. For instance, a time-set could be constructed that has three categorical time variables: the first one reflecting cross-sectional interindividual differences or intercepts, the second reflecting linear growth, and the third reflecting u-shaped or quadratic growth:

$$X_{i_t,1} = i \qquad\qquad \text{with } i = 1,\ldots,N, \qquad (2.8)$$

$$X_{i_t,2} = t \qquad\qquad \text{with } t = 1,\ldots,T, \qquad (2.9)$$

$$X_{i_t,3} = \left(t - \left(\frac{T+1}{2}\right)\right)^2 \qquad \text{with } t = 1,\ldots,T. \qquad (2.10)$$

Scaling the intercept categorical time variable $X_{i_t,1}$ as single (or mul-tiple) nominal, and scaling the linear and quadratic time variables $X_{i_t,2}$ respectively $X_{i_t,3}$ as ordinal (or even numerical), interindividual as well as intraindividual differences are captured. In this way, we approach hierarchical modelling or growth curve analysis. For instance, suppose that we find in our solution of the depression data described in the be-ginning of this section, that depression is related to the first and the second time variable, then we may infer that, firstly, subjects have in-terindividual differences in the level of depression throughout the study, and that, secondly, subjects exhibit linear development in terms of de-pression. Inspection of the category quantifications in combination with the component loadings is necessary to interpret the nature of the linear development in depressive symptoms.

This framework is very useful for investigating change. While in Equation (2.8) a number of fairly explicit explanations for the observed variation in the data are postulated (interindividual differences, linear and quadratic growth), it is possible to generalize the application of categorical time variables to an exploratory framework by using simply:

$$X_{i_t,1} = i \qquad \text{with } i = 1, \ldots, N, \qquad\qquad (2.11)$$

$$X_{i_t,2} = t \qquad \text{with } t = 1, \ldots, T, \qquad\qquad (2.12)$$

and requesting that not only $X_{i_t,1}$, but also $X_{i_t,2}$ be treated as a nominal variable. In that case, interindividual differences are reflected in the quantifications of $X_{i_t,1}$, intraindividual differences are reflected in the quantifications of $X_{i_t,2}$. As the categories of $X_{i_t,2}$ can be rescaled freely, any type of change over time can be uncovered: linear as well as monotone as well as curvilinear as well as step-wise etc. Note that it is not necessary that the Y variables have mixed measurement level. In fact, it can be envisaged that we have entirely numerical data, but that in order to explore growth optimal scaling methods are used simply for nonlinear modelling of development.

The analysis of time-dependent data using the categorical time variable set-up is different from the type of analysis described in Section 2.3.1, that analysed the LONG matrix as such. By adding one or more categorical time variables, and defining them as a separate set, we in effect give the technique the explicit assignment to discriminate the time points on the basis of the variables in the other set. We then perform a type of nonlinear discriminant analysis in which we attempt to discriminate between the time points. As such, analysis of longitudinal development using a categorical time variable set-up (generally) gives different results than one that analyses the time points – as it were – unconstrained. Introduction of the time variable generally increases the similarity between subjects within time points, decreasing the similarity between subjects between time points.

Other attractive properties can be added to an analysis that uses a categorical time variable set-up. It is for instance possible to add a number of discriminatory variables, that may be constituted of indicator variables such as group membership or gender. An example of such an analysis will be given below.

Example of time as a categorical variable: development of attachment in young children   The data used for this example stem from a study into the development of attachment in infants (Van den Boom, 1988) [4]. According to prevailing theoretical insights, infants can develop three types of attachment relationship to their mothers: secure attachment, resistant attachment and avoidant attachment. Infants who are securely attached use the mother as a secure base from which to explore, reduce their exploration and may be distressed in her absence, but greet her positively on her return, and soon return to exploring. This is the pattern shown by two-thirds of infants in normative samples. It has been associated with responsive care in the home during the first year. Infants whose attachment pattern is avoidant, explore with minimal reference to the mother, are minimally distressed by her departure, and seem to ignore or avoid her on return. In normative samples, this pattern characterizes one in five infants. Prior maternal home behaviour in this group has been described as intrusive and reflecting discomfort with physical contact. Theoretically, avoidant attachment in infancy is associated with later antisocial and aggressive behaviour, but the subject is controversial. The third major pattern is described as insecure resistant. It is marked by minimal exploration, reflecting inability to move away from the mother. These infants are highly distressed by separations and are difficult to settle on reunions. In normative samples, approximately one in seven babies show this pattern; it is considered to reflect a history of inconsistent maternal responsiveness, and subsequent social development vulnerable to social withdrawal. However, since this is also the least frequent pattern, it has been impossible to provide strong empirical tests of these propositions (for details and references see Van den Boom, 1988).

The design of this study had been as follows. Thirty mothers with their children had been observed for 40 minutes on two occasions in each month during the 6 months after birth. During these observations, a number of behavioural variables had been scored. Each time the mother or child exhibited a certain type of behaviour, this was scored, so that the measurements were actually frequencies of occurrence of types of behaviour in small (6 second) time intervals. The mother and child variables are in Table 2.8. After 12 months, it was assessed whether the

---

[4]The authors acknowledge permission by Dr van den Boom to use material and data.

Table 2.8: *Attachment Data: Mother and Child Behaviour Variables*

Child variables
POSITIVE SOCIABLE BEHAVIOUR
OBSERVING PERSONS AND OBJECTS
VOCALIZING
WHINING/CRYING
EXPLORATION
SUCKING

Mother variables
OBSERVING BABY
EFFECTIVE STIMULATION
VOCALIZING/OFFERING OBJECTS
PHYSICAL CONTACT
COMFORTING
UNINVOLVED
RESPONSIVENESS TO CRYING
RESPONSIVENESS TO POSITIVE BEHAVIOUR

child had developed a secure, resistant or avoidant attachment. Attachment type thus constituted the (non-time-varying) criterion variable.

It was assumed that mothers influenced children, and children influenced mothers. As a longitudinal design had been chosen, any time-dependence was of explicit interest. The research question was how attachment type related to mother and/or child (developments in) behaviour during the 6 months after birth.

To investigate the general development of mothers' and children's behaviour in relation to attachment, we chose the following analysis design. First, the data box was flattened into a LONG matrix. The mother and child variables were put in separate sets. The type of attachment constituted the third set. A fourth set contained a categorical time variable, constructed as described above, such that for each mother and child pair 6 time points were available. See Figure 2.16. Thus, in the flattened data box, each mother and child pair appears as 6 subjects (one new observation unit at each time point). One child had been admitted

Figure 2.16: *Attachment Data: Design of Categorical Time Variable OVERALS Analysis*

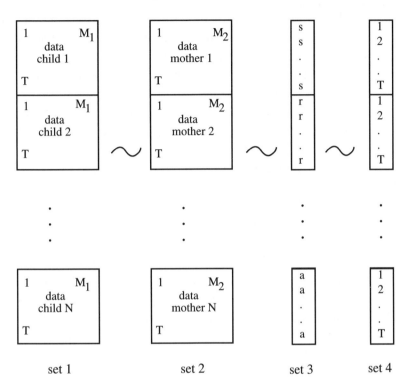

(a=avoidant attachment, r=resistant attachment, s=secure attachment)

to hospital in the last two months, which, with lots of crying, caused rather deviant scores, so for this mother and child pair we deleted the last 2 months from the data set.

All variables were treated ordinally (we had recoded the original frequencies of behaviour into 7 or 8 categories). Both the categorical time variable and the attachment variable were treated as multiple nominal, which gave the chance to model higher dimensional temporal developments. By choosing this set-up, OVERALS will try to maximize the relation between mother and child variables, the categories of the time axis, and the attachment variable. As attachment has only three categories, we perform a type of multiple group (longitudinal) discriminant analysis. This implies that attachment is predicted as well as possible on the basis of what is common in child behaviour, maternal behaviour and the development of these.

Default values were chosen for the convergence criterion (see Gifi, 1990). The algorithm converged to a solution with eigenvalues of the first and second dimension 0.630 and 0.560 respectively. Though not unsatisfactory, these eigenvalues are somewhat on the low side. This can be at least partly explained by the fact that attachment does not vary in time as the other variables do (attachment and the categorical time variable are in fact orthogonal), which suppresses the relation between sets. The component loadings are in Figure 2.17 (maternal behaviour variables have been typed in plain face, children's behaviour variables in italic face).

Interpretation of Figure 2.17 is as follows. In the centre top of the picture, crying has been placed close to comforting. This means that children who cry a lot, are usually comforted often (although the component loadings are not identical). Thus we can expect in the top of the plot, mother and child pairs in observation periods during which the baby cries a lot, and the mother does quite a bit of comforting; in the bottom of the plot we find mother and child pairs in observation periods during which the baby cries little, and the mother does little comforting. Starting from the centre top of the plot and turning clockwise, we find physical contact of the mother closest to responsiveness to crying. Next, we find children's positive behaviour, stimulation by the mother, and less strongly so, vocalizing by the baby and the mother's responsiveness to positive behaviour pointing in approximately the same direction. Vocalization by the child is thus apparently more related to the mother's stimulation than to her vocalizing, as we find the latter variable closer to exploration by the baby. Turning further, we find uninvolvement of the mother. Close by, watching of the mother by the baby can be found, and close to it, watching of the baby. Both watching variables and the sucking variable have low component loadings, implying that we should not attach too much importance to these variables.

To allow inspection of children's development, we have drawn in Figure 2.18 the average object scores of the mother child pairs for each attachment category in month 1 to 6. This figure should be viewed as superimposed upon Figure 2.17. Note, however, that the scaling of the two figures is different. The first thing that catches the eye is that the

Figure 2.17: *Attachment Data: Component Loadings of Quantified Mother and Child Variables*

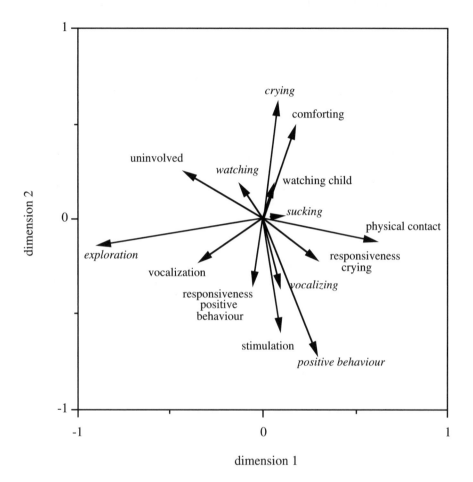

three attachment groups are markedly separated in the plot. The securely attached 'travel' through the bottom part of the plot, from month 1 to 6, and both the avoidantly and resistantly attached travel in the upper part. On average, children develop from right to left. The first dimension thus differentiates the time points. The second dimension discriminates the groups, although the separation is far from perfect. While the securely attached in the bottom of the plot have been separated quite distinctly from the two insecurely attached groups in the top of the plot, the technique has apparently not been able on the basis of the available behavioural information to discriminate between the resistantly and avoidantly attached. It might be that additional dimensions can achieve this discrimination, but we would pay the price of a considerable loss in overview, so that we will not attempt to do so here.

In this example, each dimension discriminates the subjects according to one separate criterion: discrimination in time is achieved in the first dimension, discrimination of the attachment types is achieved in the second dimension. Thus, attachment type and temporal development can be related to the behavioural variables in independent manners. It should be noted that this type of analysis does not always have this property: for instance it is distinctly possible that one dimension discriminates subjects on the basis of one criterion, and the second dimension discriminates on the basis of the first as well as other criteria (see for instance Timman & Bijleveld, 1996).

Figure 2.18 should be interpreted in connection with the component loadings of Figure 2.17. Combining the information from the two plots we can deduce that the avoidantly attached cry a lot in month 1, the mothers have lots of physical contact with the securely attached in month 1, and so on. We thus arrive at the following interpretation of the analysis results.

The mothers of those children who will eventually become securely attached, start out with lots of physical contact with their babies; they are very responsive to crying, especially in the second month. In the second and third month, these children show lots of positive behaviour, and, though less markedly so, start vocalizing, with their mother stimulating them. The mother's responsiveness to positive behaviour then increases towards the fifth month, as does her vocalizing and offering of objects. In the last month, the securely attached children start to explore to the full. Towards the end of the 6 months, mothers generally become less involved with their children. For the securely attached children, crying and comforting are at a more or less stable low level over the months.

Those children who do not develop a secure attachment pattern eventually, interact with their mothers along different lines. The resistantly as well as the avoidantly attached both start out with lots of crying. Mothers of resistantly attached children start out a little less involved than mothers of avoidantly attached children. In the second months, they swing to the right, with mothers probably trying to cope

Figure 2.18: *Attachment Data: Developments for Three Attachment Subgroups*

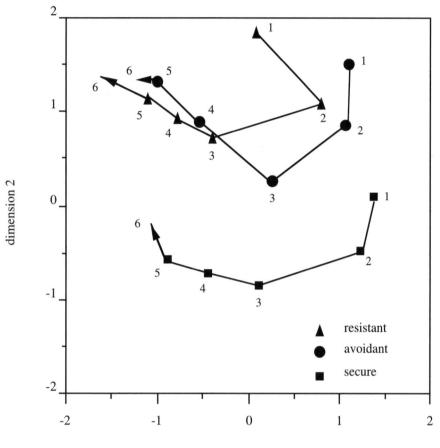

with her child's crying through lots of comforting and more physical contact. In the third month, however, physical contact decreases substantially, and mothers become less and less involved with their children towards the last months, with children becoming more explorative. The children who will become avoidantly attached do not make such a bad start as the resistantly attached, although also these children cry a lot in the first month. The mother has somewhat more physical contact than the mothers in the resistant group. In the third month, the mother and child move towards stimulation, positive behaviour, vocalizing, but this is counteracted by still relatively high levels of crying by the baby. In the fourth month, things take a turn for the worse, as mothers sweep to uninvolvement, a tendency which becomes stronger and stronger until the last month. From month 4 onwards, the avoidantly attached catch up with the resistantly attached, and exhibit very similar behaviour. Looking at differences between the avoidant and resistant group, it appears that the resistantly attached make an even more markedly bad start, and that their mothers are generally even less involved, and from an earlier stage onwards so, than the mothers in the avoidantly attached group.

Thus, it appears as if secure or insecure attachment can be predicted from as early on as the first month after birth: babies who become insecurely attached are characterized by lots of crying in the first months after birth. Somewhat contrary to expectation, the different types of attachment groups could not be distinguished on the basis of their developments on the mother and child behavioural variables during the first 6 months after birth. It should be noted that all babies develop in the direction of exploration, meaning that, irrespective of the eventual attachment type, explorative behaviour grows in time.

2.3.3   Modelling time with lagged variables

A third strategy to accommodate time dependence is to use so-called *lagged* variables. Suppose we have obtained daily recordings of the severity of a subject's headaches. Thus, we have one subject: $N = 1$. We name the headache variable Y, and the measurements at the respective days are indicated as Y_t, with $t = 1, \ldots, T$. Suppose furthermore that we are interested in the effect of alcohol consumption on headache complaints. We have therefore also registered the subject's daily alcohol intake, and we name the daily alcohol measurements X_t, with $t = 1, \ldots, T$. The measurements X_t and Y_t are stacked vertically in vectors, of size T, that thus contain X_1 to X_T and Y_1 to Y_T respectively. Our research hypothesis is 'liberal intake of alcohol on day t leads to headache on day $t + 1$'.

We can investigate this hypothesis by analysing so-called *lagged* versions of the variables. If the hypothesis were true, we would find a high positive correlation between the scores on the alcohol variable at days t and the scores on the headache variable on days $t + 1$. To investigate this hypothesis we alter the two variables, eliminating the last measurement of the alcohol variable and eliminating the first measurement of the headache variable. Next, we 'shift' the two vectors (that are now both $(T-1) \times 1$) so that they match once more. Now, correlating the shifted variables, we correlate X_{t-1} with Y_t. In the literature, the lagged version of the X-variable is often referred to as 'the lag(1) version of variable X' or 'the previous version of X'; the lagged version of Y is often referred to as 'the lag(0) version of Y' or 'the present version of Y'. An example of such a situation for six time points is presented in Figure 2.19.

Figure 2.19: *Relating Lag(1) Variable to Lag(0) Variable*

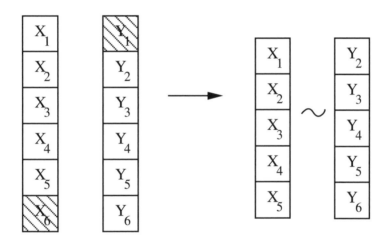

The most likely interpretation for a high correlation between the lag(1) version of X and the lag(0) version of Y is that X causes Y: that is, alcohol intake on day t causes headaches on day $t+1$. Theoretically, the high correlation could also mean that headaches at day $t+1$ cause alcohol intake on day t, but as causes are supposed to occur before or at the most simultaneously with effects, this alternative explanation need not be considered for practical purposes.

Other phenomena may be modelled using lagged variables. For instance, one might be interested to know to what extent certain physiological indicators depend on or can be predicted from their own past values. In that case, one would want to model the influence of a past version of a variable on its present version. Suppose for instance that such a variable is blood pressure, and that measurements have again been obtained at T time points, that have again been combined in a vector Y of size T. In order to assess to what extent blood pressure measurements can be predicted from their prior values, we would then have to duplicate the Y variable, eliminate from one version the first measurement (this is now the lag(0) version of the variable), and eliminate from the other version the last measurement (this is now the lag(1) version of the variable). Next, we shift them, so that they match again. The correlation between the lag(0) and the lag(1) version of the same variable gives an indication to what extent blood pressure depends on previous values, the squared correlation between the lag(1) and lag(0) versions of the variable equalling the percentage of the variance of blood pressure that can be predicted from its previous value. Relationships between lag(1) and lag(0) versions of the same variables model autoregressive or Markov-type dependencies (see Box & Jenkins, 1976 and see Section 2.4.1). An illustration of such a situation for six time points is in Figure 2.20.

Figure 2.20: *Relating Lag(1) Variable to its Lag(0) Version*

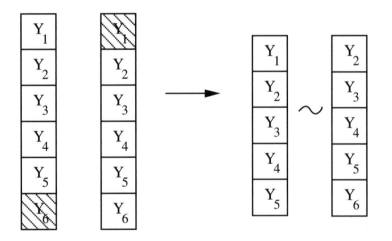

Other variations on this theme are possible. Higher-order lags may be specified, relating for instance lag(2) or lag(3) versions of variables to lag(0) versions of other variables, or of the same variables. One then approaches the ARMA-type models that were proposed by Box & Jen-

kins (1976). Conceptually most attractive are lagged versions of variables that can capture autoregressive phenomena, or cyclical occurrences
such as monthly cycles (28 days for instance in menstrual research) or
years. An example is a situation with daily measurements, where we
predict a set of lag(0) variables from their lag(1) versions, that thus captures the immediate past, as well as from their lag(7) versions, that thus
models the dependence on the measurements at the same day last week.
In that case, the lag(0) set would contain the measurements from $t = 7$
until $t = T$, the lag(1) set those from $t = 6$ to $t = T - 1$, and the lag(7)
set from $t = 1$ to $t = T - 7$. See Figure 2.21.

Figure 2.21: *Lag(7) and Lag(1) Versions of Variables Relating to Lag(0)*
Variables

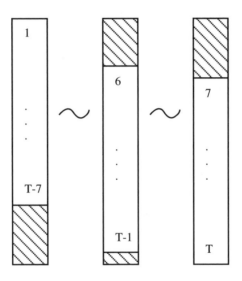

Lagged versions of variables can be used in any type of analysis.
In some analyses, the user need not do all the handiwork of constructing copies and lagged versions of variables, but can instead indicate the
order of the lag required for each variable, after which the analysis constructs the lagged versions. Such an analysis for categorical data can be
performed using the SERIALS program (Van Buuren, 1990).

It is possible to work with lagged versions of variables for $N > 1$
situations as well. In that case, one has to stack the shifted versions
of variables in a super-matrix (or LONG matrix). An example of such

a super-matrix with lag(0) and lag(1) versions of variables is given in
Figure 2.22. Next, it is possible to analyse the data in that matrix in the
manner described above in Sections 2.3.1 or 2.3.2, for instance through
multi-set analysis with the lag(0) versions of the variables in one set and
the lag(1) versions of the same variables (or lagged versions of other
explanatory variables) in the other set.

Figure 2.22: *Relating Lag(1) and Lag(0) Versions of Variables for N Subjects*

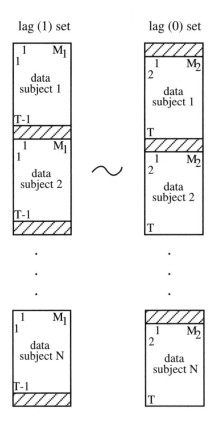

Working towards a more formal and more general notation, we have
thus observed N subjects on M_1 variables X and on M_2 variables Y,
in each case for T time points. We altered and shifted the X variables
such that the shifted X variables are the lag(m) version of the original X
variables and we altered and shifted the Y variables such that the shifted
Y variables are the lag(0) version of the original Y variables. We have

done this for each subject, and we have subsequently vertically stacked the data matrices for each subject. The entries in the data matrix X are then $X_{i_t,j}$, with ($j = 1, \ldots, M_1$) and i_t denoting the subjects at the respective time points ($i = 1, \ldots, N; t = 1, \ldots, T - m$). The entries in the data matrix Y are $Y_{i_t,j}$, with ($j = 1, \ldots, M_2$) and i_t denoting the subjects at the respective time points ($i = 1, \ldots, N; t = m + 1, \ldots, T$). For multi-set analysis of the X and Y set, Equation (2.4) for nonlinear multi-set analysis (cf. Section 2.2.3) becomes:

$$\sigma(\mathbf{Z}, \mathbf{B}_{11}, \ldots, \mathbf{B}_{M_2 2}) = \sum_{k=1}^{2} \text{SSQ}\left(\mathbf{Z} - \sum_{j=1}^{M_2} \mathbf{I}_{jk}\mathbf{B}_{jk}\right) \qquad (2.13)$$

subject to the conditions that $\mathbf{Z}'\mathbf{Z} = \left(\sum_{i=1}^{N}(T_i - m)\right)\mathbf{I}$, $\mathbf{Z}'\mathbf{u} = \mathbf{0}$ and $\mathbf{B}_{jk} = \mathbf{c}_{jk}\mathbf{a}'_{jk}$ for single variables,

with $\mathbf{c}_{jk}$ a numerical, ordinal or nominal quantification, with $\mathbf{a}_{jk}$ the weight, each time for the j-th variable in the k-th set of variables, and with Z_{i_t} the elements of $\mathbf{Z}$. Solutions should be interpreted just as solutions with ordinary variables, that is by using the component loadings or category quantifications. Normally, if two variables have similar (or opposite) component loadings, we say that these variables have a lot in common. In the case with lagged variables, if for instance the component loadings of a lag(0) and lag(1) variable are similar, one might conclude that the lag(1) variable has an impact on the lag(0) variable.

This type of analysis, though conceptually attractive, has a number of limitations. Firstly, one loses one time point for every lag: the higher the order of the lags the more time points have to be deleted at the end and the beginning of the lag(m) respectively lag(0) variables. Therefore, higher order lags can become unattractive or even impossible to model when there are few time points. A second technical limitation is that, in rescaling the lag(0) and lag(m) versions of categorical variables, there is no guarantee that the categories of these lag(0) and lag(m) versions will receive identical quantifications. (In the context of time series analysis, Van Buuren (1990) developed the so-called SERIALS program, that ensures that the quantifications of the various temporal versions of the same variable are identical; we will return to this topic below.) When no such guarantees can be given, the various lagged versions of the same variable may not be comparable. Again, the same rules apply as outlined in Section 2.3.1 regarding analysis of the BROAD matrix:if the quantifications are identical or virtually identical, analysis can proceed. If the quantifications are different, further analysis has to be abandoned. However, in practice, because the lag(0) and lag(1) versions of variables are usually fairly similar (especially for long series), widely different quantifications are unlikely. A number of authors (for instance Goldberger, 1971, and Rogosa, 1979) have warned that the analysis of cross-lagged correlations (for instance the correlation between the lag(0) version of one variable, and the lag(1) version of another variable) may be misleading. However, given sufficient replications over time, and with due caution in the drawing of conclusions, (cross-) lagged correlations may offer additional insights. The interpretation of analyses with lagged versions of variables is usually conceptually somewhat harder than the interpretation of ordinary types of analysis, however. Below, we will give an example of an analysis using lagged variables.

Example with lagged variables: the development of attachment in young children   The same data set that was used in Section 2.3.2 will be used here (Van den Boom, 1988). Mothers and children had been investigated at 6 time points. The frequencies of occurrence of 8 types of mother behaviour formed 8 variables in the mother set, the frequencies of occurrence of 6 types of child behaviour constituted 6 variables in the child set. For details and background on the data, see Section 2.3.2.

Having previously investigated the correlational structure in the data, we were now interested to obtain additional insights into the causal structure of the data. More particularly, we wanted to investigate what types of past behaviour precluded the various aspects of present behaviour. We thus wanted to investigate autoregressive (for instance of the effect of children's previous behaviour on children's present behaviour) as well as crossregressive dependencies (for instance of th effect of mother's previous behaviour on children's present behaviour).

In order to investigate the influence of prior mother behaviour on the present behaviour of their children and vice versa, and in order to investigate the dependence of present on past behaviour for mothers as well as children, we constructed data sets with lagged variables. In the first set, we stacked all mother measurements from time point 1 until time point 5, this is the so-called mother lag(1) set. In the second set we stacked all children measurements from time point 2 until time point 6, this is the so-called child lag(0) set. (If these latter two sets are analysed together, we model the influence of mother's behaviour in the previous month on children's behaviour in the present month.) Next, we constructed a third and a fourth set with lagged variables: in the third set, we stacked all child measurements from time point 1 until time point 5, the child lag(1) set; in the fourth set we stacked all mother measurements from time point 2 until time point 6, the mother lag(0) set. (If these two sets are analysed together, we model the influence of children's behaviour in the previous month on mother's behaviour in the present month.)

Instead of performing separate analyses of the influence of children upon mothers and vice versa, we analysed the four sets together in one analysis. This has the added advantage that a number of cross- and autoregressive influences are investigated simultaneously. For a schematic representation see Figure 2.23. The autoregressive structure of mother behaviour (past on present) is modelled by the combination of the mother lag(0) and mother lag(1) set (relation E in the figure). The autoregressive structure of children's behaviour is modelled by the combination of the child lag(0) and child lag(1) set (relation F in the figure). Cross-regressive influences are captured by relations A and B. Instantaneous relations between mothers and children are modelled by the combination of mother and child sets of same lag (relations C and D).

As we have more than one set of variables, we performed multi-set analysis, using the computer program OVERALS. All variables were treated as ordinal variables. Default measures were used for the convergence criterion.

The algorithm converged to a solution with eigenvalues for the first and second dimension of 0.801 and 0.730 respectively. The component loadings are graphically represented in Figure 2.24. (as in the example in Section 2.3.2, mother variables are typed plain face, child variables italic face). For reasons of overview, the component loadings are not connected to the origin, but the component loadings of lag(1) versions of variables are connected to the corresponding lag(0) versions, with the arrow pointing from past to present. To make the configuration more comparable to that of the former example, the first and second canonical axes have been switched.

The structure is slightly tilted counter clockwise with respect to that in Figure 2.17. The most striking feature of the picture is that, for al-

Figure 2.23: *Attachment Data: Lagged Analysis Design*

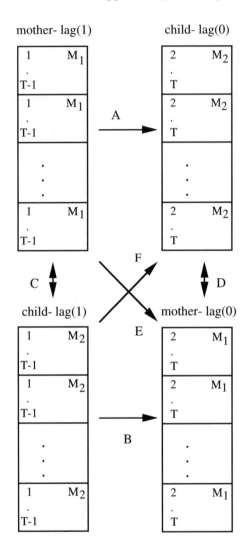

<u>relations modelled</u>

A. mother -> child   E. mother -> self
B. child -> mother   F. child -> self
C. & D. mother <-> child

most all variables, the lag(0) – or present – and lag(1) – or previous – versions are located very closely. This is most apparent in the periphery, for instance previous and present versions of exploration, vocalization by the mother, uninvolvement, watching by the mother as well as by the child, physical contact and vocalization by the child are situated very closely. This implies that many aspects of behaviour - mothers' as well as children's – are apparently strongly autoregressive. Thus, in preference over past or present behaviour of the other party in the mother–child pair, and in preference over past or present other behavioural aspects, the best predictor of present own behaviour generally is own past behaviour. One could translate this into saying that interindividual differences are larger than intraindividual differences, with mothers as well as children fluctuating at more or less individually determined levels of behavioural activity, which do not change dramatically in the course of the first 6 months after birth.

An exception to this pattern is the relation between past positive behaviour of the child and present effective stimulation by the mother (circled in the plot). These are located very close to one another, and closer to one another than to any other variable, indicating that positive behaviour of children in one month generally is followed by effective stimulation by the mother in the next month. Perhaps children's positive behaviour triggers the mother's stimulating behaviour; this result might be explained by supposing that mothers only start stimulating their children once the children give the signal that they are ready for it.

Another striking aspect of Figure 2.24 is how the lag(0) and lag(1) versions of both responsiveness variables differ quite a bit. Mothers' lag(0) responsiveness to positive behaviour is in fact closer to their children's lag(1) vocalizing and positive behaviour than it is to its own lag(1) version (which is the endpoint of a fairly short component loading and thus less important). This can be interpreted by saying that perhaps mothers can only become responsive to their children's positive behaviour once the children have expressed such behaviour. Secondly, as the mother's lag(0) responsiveness to positive behaviour is quite close to their children's vocalization, a child's vocalization apparently triggers the mother's responsiveness as well.

Another interesting feature of the plot is that the mother's lag(0) responsiveness to crying is inversely related to lag(0) crying (this can be seen if we draw the original vectors of the component loadings by

Figure 2.24: *Attachment Data: Component Loadings of Quantified Mother and Child Variables in Lagged Analysis*

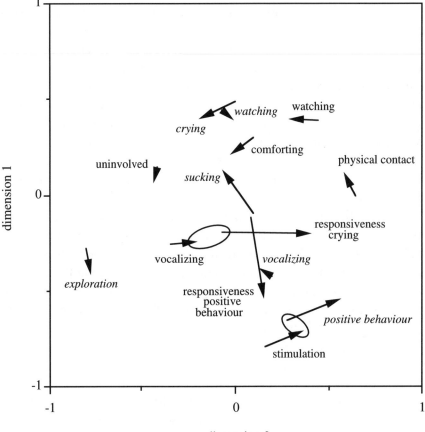

connecting lag(0) responsiveness to crying and lag(0) crying with the origin). The same applies to the lag(1) versions of these variables. This indicates that the more the child cries, the less responsive the mother is. The lag(1) version of responsiveness to crying is closest to the mother's vocalizing at lag(0). This can be translated by saying that higher levels of maternal responsiveness apparently preclude the mother's vocalization.

Tracking the three attachment groups' developments in the plot gave approximately the same results as in the previous analysis of these data. The resistantly and avoidantly attached travel in the upper part of the plot, characterized by a lot of crying. The securely attached travel in the bottom of the plot, starting out with a lot more responsiveness to crying, positive behaviour and stimulation.

The lagged analysis thus underlines the earlier results from the analysis that used a categorical time variable (presented in Section 2.3.2). It provided additional insights in terms of possibly causal relationships between the temporal versions of the behavioural variables.

2.4   Multivariate dynamic analysis

In this section, we introduce dynamic analysis techniques. By dynamic analysis techniques we mean techniques in which a particular model for the temporal dependence in the measurements is specified. Such techniques are intended for the analysis of data sets with a fairly large number of time points, although no explicit criteria exist for the number of time points required. The techniques introduced here have been designed to analyse single series only, that is, data obtained for a single subject, although some have been extended to the analysis of more than one subject.

We start with a class of dynamic models that are useful for understanding a number of important concepts in dynamic analysis.

2.4.1   AR(I)MA models

The basic model used in the last part of this chapter is the linear dynamic system or state space model. This model is closely related to the ARMA models (Box & Jenkins, 1976) referred to briefly in Section 2.3.3 above: in fact, Akaike (1976) showed how every ARMA model can be written as a linear dynamic system. A thorough discussion of ARMA models is beyond the scope of this chapter. Nevertheless, a number of central concepts that appear frequently in longitudinal and dynamic data analysis are best introduced through ARMA models, and are thus best discussed at least briefly. The term ARMA stands for autoregressive moving-average models: the models can be viewed as consisting of an autoregressive and a moving-average part. Sometimes the term ARIMA is also encountered, in which the 'I' stands for integrated, indicating the number of times the data were differenced: such differencing (replacing the Y_t by $Y_t^* = Y_t - Y_{t-1}$) is useful for smoothing erratic series; it is used often in econometric research but less frequently in behavioural science.

Suppose in a hypothetical example that we are measuring mood states, and that we have daily measurements for the mood of one subject undergoing light therapy for seasonal depression disorder. We believe that there is temporal dependence in the measurements in the sense that if a subject is cheery on a certain day, chances are high that the subject will also be cheery on the next day. If the subject is depressed, however, chances are high that the subject will be depressed as well the day afterwards. Thus mood at day(t) can be predicted to a certain extent from mood at the previous day. In other words: the development of the subject's mood states is autoregressive: it can be predicted from, or regressed on, a lagged version of itself. Note how we are dealing with data from a single subject only: $N = 1$. See the graphical representation in Figure 2.20, in which the variable measuring mood state at day t is indicated as Y_t.

Figure 2.25: *Autoregressive Model*

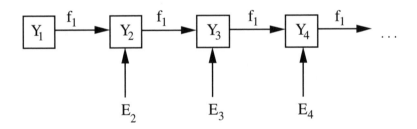

The model outlined in Figure 2.25 specifies the relations between the consecutive measurements: Y_t depends directly on Y_{t-1}, but only indirectly on Y_{t-2} (or on Y_{t-3}, or any measurements further back). The parameter f_1 is the regression coefficient for predicting Y_t from Y_{t-1}: $Y_t = f_1 Y_{t-1}$. Thus to predict Y_{t+1}, it is sufficient to know Y_t, as all information from the past relevant for the prediction of Y_{t+1} must be incorporated in the measurement Y_t. In other words: given Y_t, Y_{t+1} is independent of Y_{t-1}, Y_{t-2}, Y_{t-3}, etc. This property is an attractive conceptualization of a particular notion of 'memory' or survival: everything that is important for the future, must be retained at each consecutive time point, and anything that is lost, cannot be retrieved. Because the prediction of Y_{t+1} from Y_t is not perfect, a variable of residuals E_t is present in the model. (The variable at time point 1 has no such residual term, as it is not predicted from any previous measurement.) As the measurements depend only on the measurements one step backwards in time, this model is coined autoregressive: measurements at time point t can be predicted by regression on the measurements at $t - 1$. It is also popularly encountered under the names AR(1) model, or Markov chain or – series, where the (1) stands for the order of the process. Note how the model in Figure 2.25 is functionally equivalent to the model defined in Figure 2.20. Higher order autoregressive models can be envisaged by imagining how arrows point not only from Y_{t-1} to Y_t, but also from Y_{t-2} to Y_t, or also from Y_{t-3} from to Y_t, etc.

The general formula for the AR(p) model is:

$$Y_t = f_1 Y_{t-1} + f_2 Y_{t-2} + \cdots + f_p Y_{t-p} + E_t,$$

where f_k is the parameter for predicting Y_t from Y_{t-k}, and where p stands for the order of the process. For the special case where $p = 1$:

$$Y_t = f_1 Y_{t-1} + E_t,$$

which is the model of Figure 2.25.

In a moving average or MA model, the data are considered to arise from a weighted sum of random shocks $A_t, A_{t-1}, A_{t-2}, \ldots$. For instance, the values of shares on the stock exchange are steered by a number of unpredictable events, such as natural disasters, war, crop failure, summer temperatures and the like. In formula:

$$Y_t = \theta_0 A_t - \theta_1 A_{t-1} - \theta_2 A_{t-2} - \cdots - \theta_q A_{t-q},$$

where the $\theta_0, \theta_1, \theta_2, \ldots$ are the coefficients for the respective random shocks. Figure 2.26 gives a graphical representation of a MA(1) model.

Combining the MA and AR models, we arrive at the ARMA(p, q) model:

$$\begin{aligned} Y_t = & f_1 Y_{t-1} + f_2 Y_{t-2} + \cdots + f_p Y_{t-p} + \\ & \theta_0 A_t - \theta_1 A_{t-1} - \theta_2 A_{t-2} - \cdots - \theta_q A_{t-q} + E_t. \end{aligned}$$

Figure 2.26: *Moving Average Model*

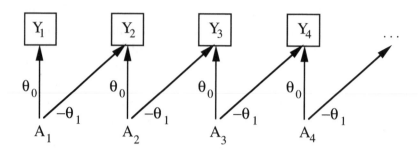

The parameters in autoregressive models can be estimated fairly straightforwardly (for instance by a multiple regression of the present on the p-lagged past), using least squares methods that are equivalent to maximum likelihood methods in case of normality. For estimating the parameters of the moving average part, fairly complicated iterative optimization methods are needed. As such, also the estimation of the parameters in AR(I)MA models is fairly complicated.

In time series analysis, the idea is that the time points at which observations have been collected constitute a representative sample of the domain over which generalizations have to be made. In this context, it is important to realize that time series analysis therefore generalizes over time points (and not over subjects). To obtain sufficient stability of the parameter estimates, the number of replications, and thus the length of the series, must be fairly large: 50 time points is generally regarded as the minimum.

A number of extensions of AR(I)MA models exist, the most notable being extensions to models for seasonal phenomena (SAR(I)MA models) and to multivariate models (VARMA) models (Box & Jenkins, 1976).

ARMA models are of major importance in time series analysis. They have found wide application in all branches of science in which the aim is forecasting, such as engineering, econometrics and the geophysical sciences. They have found but little application in behavioural data analysis, however, where the aim is not as much forecasting but rather interpretation. In addition, their applicability is limited because of the fact that the number of time points they require is quite large for behavioural research practice. Because they are essentially $N = 1$ techniques they are less fitting in the behavioural paradigm where the aim is to generalize over subjects rather than over time points. We will return to these points later. An enormous amount of literature is available on time series analysis; an important reference is of course Box & Jenkins (1976), and a very readable introduction is provided by Chatfield (1989).

While AR models contain useful formalizations (for instance 'memory') for phenomena we would be interested to investigate in behavioural research practice, the MA model remains somewhat elusive. Predicting the developments on theoretically important constructs from random influences has never been attractive to social and behavioural scientists. The main reason for this relative unattractiveness is that scientists from these disciplines are less interested in accurate forecasting than in explanation and interpretation. For this reason, the state space model or linear dynamic system, which combines autoregressive influences with extraneous steering mechanisms, has proven to be more appealing. We will discuss the linear dynamic system in the next section.

2.4.2 The linear dynamic system

Suppose that we have measured for one subject a set of physiological indicators such as blood pressure and heart rate at a number of time points, for instance at a number of 15 minute intervals. We are interested to find out whether and how these physiological indicators depend on situational variables such as mood and activity. Therefore, we have collected at the same time points measurements on several mood scales (that reflect important dimensions such as anger, arousal, and the like). We want to predict the physiological indicators from the scores on the mood scales. However, we cannot use standard methodology for this as the physiological indicators are dependent in time. If for instance the subject under observation has high blood pressure at a certain time point, it is quite likely that blood pressure will still be high at the next time point.

Switching to a more formal definition of our problem, suppose that, for one subject, we have measured at a number of time points T, a set of predictor variables X. We thus have observations X_{ijt}, with j denoting the input variables ($j = 1, \ldots, M_1$), i denoting the subjects ($i = 1$), and t denoting the time points ($t = 1, \ldots, T$). As $N = 1$, the observations can be stacked in a data matrix $\mathbf{X}$ of size $T \times M_1$. The second set of observations contains the Y_{ijt}, with j denoting the output variables ($j = 1, \ldots, M_2$), i the subjects ($i = 1$) and t the time points ($t = 1, \ldots, T$). As $N = 1$, again the observations can be stacked in a data matrix $\mathbf{Y}$ of size $T \times M_2$. Suppose further that the X are understood to influence the Y variables, and that the time dependence itself of the measurements is of interest. In technical terms: the X are the independent (or input) variables, exerting an influence on the dependent (or output) variables Y.

We now suppose that the impact of the input on the output is mediated by an unobserved factor, the so-called *latent state*, in the sense that the input variables influence the state, and the state in turn influences the output variables. At the same time, the state embodies the time-dependence in the measurements, transferring information from past time points to the future. There may be more than one latent state variable, or: the state may be more-dimensional (hence the term state space). In system analytic terms, the input variables X, output variables Y, the state variables that are called Z, and the relations between them, together constitute a *system*.

In the system as described above, the time dependence is modelled in such a way that the latent state at any time point t contains all information from the former time points that is relevant for the future. The latent state thus functions as the *memory* of the system. In the behavioural sciences, we want our models to be parsimonious. Therefore, just like in other techniques with latent variables, such as factor analysis, we want the dimensionality of the state, to which we refer as p, to be as low as possible. As such we want the dimensionality of the state to be lower than that of the input and/or the output. When the state has lower dimensionality than that of the input and output, the state serves as a *filter* between input and output. At the same time, the state serves as a filter between past and present: it filters the information from the past that is relevant for predicting the future. Thus, the state truly functions as the crux of the system.

This model is often encountered under the name of *state space model*. It is also referred to as linear dynamic system or longitudinal reduced rank regression model. The model can also be viewed as a chain of so-called MIMIC models, where the subsequent models are linked through the latent state (see also Chapter 4, Section 4.2.2 and Section 4.3.1). In the following we will preferably refer to this model as the linear dynamic system. A schematic representation of the model is given in Figure 2.27.

Figure 2.27: *Linear Dynamic System*

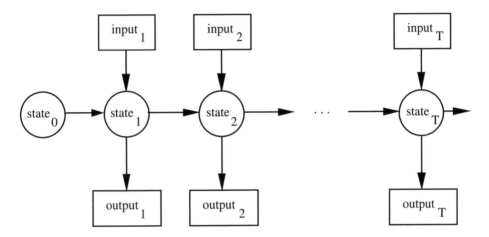

Thus, we have input variables, output variables, and latent state variables. The relations between input and latent state, latent state and output, and the relations between the subsequent latent states are specified by matrices of regression coefficients. For instance, the p latent state scores at any time point t depend on those of the former time point $t - 1$, weighted by a transition matrix $\mathbf{F}$, as:

$$\mathbf{z}_t = \mathbf{F}\mathbf{z}_{t-1} ,$$

with $\mathbf{z}_t$ and $\mathbf{z}_{t-1}$ the p-dimensional vectors of latent state scores at time points t and $t - 1$ respectively, and $\mathbf{F}$ a $p \times p$ matrix of regression coefficients. As, however, the latent state scores depend as well on a weighted contribution of the vector of input variables at time point t, $\mathbf{x}_t$, this means that the definition of $\mathbf{z}_t$ should be extended to the so-called *system equation*:

$$\mathbf{z}_t = \mathbf{F}\mathbf{z}_{t-1} + \mathbf{G}\mathbf{x}_t + \mathbf{d}_t \qquad \text{(system equation)}, \qquad (2.14)$$

with $\mathbf{x}_t$ the M_1-dimensional vector of input variables at time point t, $\mathbf{d}_t$ a p-dimensional vector of disturbances reflecting imperfect fit of the system equation at time point t, and $\mathbf{G}$ a $p \times M_1$ matrix of regression coefficients. Similarly, the output variables at any time point t are predicted from a weighted sum of the latent state scores at that time point, which is in formula written as in the so-called *measurement equation*:

$$\mathbf{y}_t = \mathbf{H}\mathbf{z}_t + \mathbf{e}_t \qquad \text{(measurement equation)}, \qquad (2.15)$$

with $\mathbf{y}_t$ the M_2-dimensional vector of output variables at time point t, $\mathbf{e}_t$ the M_2-dimensional vector of measurement errors reflecting imperfect fit of the measurement equation at time point t, and $\mathbf{H}$ an $M_2 \times p$ matrix of regression coefficients.

Equations (2.14) and (2.15) together describe the linear dynamic system. Note how the system needs a starting point at t_0: $\mathbf{z}_0$. Note that in the formulation above, the system is time-invariant: $\mathbf{F}_t = \mathbf{F}$, $\mathbf{G}_t = \mathbf{G}$, $\mathbf{H}_t = \mathbf{H}$. It is often assumed that the relations between the variables do not vary over time, even though the values of the latent state variable(s) may of course be time-varying. A representation of the linear dynamic system, including transition matrices and error terms is in Figure 2.28.

Figure 2.28: *Linear Dynamic System with Transition Matrices, Disturbances and Error Terms*

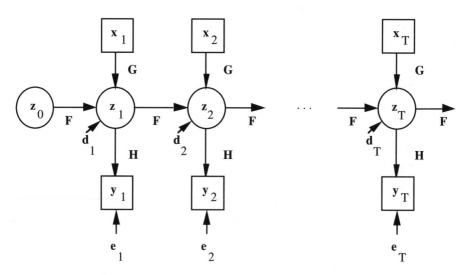

State space modelling was made famous by Rudolf Kalman (Kalman, 1960; Ho & Kalman, 1966). Given the parameter matrices **F**, **G** and **H** (reportedly named after Kalman's teacher F. G. H. Linear), and given information on the error in system and measurement equations and the initial state at time zero z_0, the Kalman filter is a least squares optimal procedure for estimating the latent state scores. The procedure is recursive: after estimates for z_t have been obtained, those for z_{t+1} are computed, next those for z_{t+2} and so on. The filter is very fast converging, elegant and efficient. Kalman filtering has been developed for the $N = 1$ case from the engineering framework of exact, if necessarily high dimensional, forecasting where information is available on the system under observation. In linear dynamic systems analysis, the dimensionality of the state space may be high and may in fact be a lot higher than that of the dimension of the input and output. This is necessary to be able to capture the dynamic mechanisms that generate the time-dependent process, especially cyclical processes. In many common applications of state space analysis, such as are to be found in engineering, econometrics or process control, the technique has been geared to find high dimensional exact solutions. This is so because the scientific paradigm in these branches of science is directed strongly towards accurate forecasting.

In behavioural research practice, we are faced with a different situation. In general, we have no information on the values of the transition parameters in **F**, **G**, and **H**, nor do we have information on the error terms or initial state. The so-called algebraic realization methods for estimating **F**, **G** and **H** that were developed in engineering and econometrics (Aoki, 1990; Hannan & Deistler, 1988), also arrive at high dimensional exact representations. Our aim, however, is data reduction and interpretation. Thus, we do not want to find an exhaustive, but a parsimonious model, and we are content with approximate, not necessarily exact, solutions. This means also that we want to find only a small, and actually very small, number of dimensions: for most real life applications 3 to 4 at the most. For these reasons, classical state space analysis as well as the newer realization methods are less widely applicable in a behavioural context, and the same extends, as noted above, to the closely related AR(I)MA models. It is therefore not surprising that the terminology 'state space modelling' for the type of models presented below has sometimes created unnecessary confusion and controversy, generated more by the differing paradigm and application of the models than by differences in model formulation.

In the following we will briefly outline the method presented by Bijleveld & De Leeuw (1991) for estimating the unknowns **F**, **G** and **H** as well as the latent state scores Z. The method attempts to find least squares optimal, low dimensional solutions. The latent state scores are found with a non-recursive least squares optimization procedure.

To describe the method, we first do a little rewriting. We can write the formulas for the linear dynamic system for all time points simultaneously if we use an auxiliary so-called shift matrix **S**, that serves to construct the latent state scores from time point $t = 0$ to $t = T - 1$ out of those from time point $t = 1$ to $t = T$. Figure 2.29 illustrates the structure of the shift matrix.

Figure 2.29: *Shift Matrix* **S**

$$
\begin{bmatrix} \mathbf{z}'_0 \\ \mathbf{z}'_1 \\ \mathbf{z}'_2 \\ \mathbf{z}'_3 \\ \cdot \\ \cdot \\ \cdot \\ \mathbf{z}'_{T-1} \end{bmatrix}
=
\underbrace{\begin{bmatrix} 0 & 0 & 0 & 0 & \ldots & 0 & 0 & 0 & 0 \\ 1 & 0 & 0 & 0 & \ldots & 0 & 0 & 0 & 0 \\ 0 & 1 & 0 & 0 & \ldots & 0 & 0 & 0 & 0 \\ 0 & 0 & 1 & 0 & \ldots & 0 & 0 & 0 & 0 \\ \cdot & \cdot & \cdot & \cdot & \ldots & \cdot & \cdot & \cdot & \cdot \\ \cdot & \cdot & \cdot & \cdot & \ldots & \cdot & \cdot & \cdot & \cdot \\ \cdot & \cdot & \cdot & \cdot & \ldots & \cdot & \cdot & \cdot & \cdot \\ 0 & 0 & 0 & 0 & \ldots & 0 & 0 & 1 & 0 \end{bmatrix}}_{\mathbf{S}}
\begin{bmatrix} \mathbf{z}'_1 \\ \mathbf{z}'_2 \\ \mathbf{z}'_3 \\ \mathbf{z}'_4 \\ \cdot \\ \cdot \\ \cdot \\ \mathbf{z}'_T \end{bmatrix}
$$

Note that the (hypothetical) state at time point 0, $\mathbf{z}_0$, is in this example constructed as a vector of zeroes. Other choices for $\mathbf{z}_0$ are possible, such as $\mathbf{z}_0 = \mathbf{z}_1$, or $\mathbf{z}_0 = \mathbf{z}_T$. It is also possible to estimate a best fitting $\mathbf{z}_0$ from the data. In the default case we will be dealing with here $\mathbf{z}_0 \equiv \mathbf{z}_1$. Thus, when **Z** is the $T \times p$ matrix of latent scores at all time points t (the right-hand matrix of Figure 2.29), **SZ** gives the matrix of latent state scores at time points 0 to $T - 1$. Using the shift matrix, the linear dynamic system can be written as:

$$\mathbf{Z} = \mathbf{SZF} + \mathbf{XG} + \mathbf{D} \qquad \text{(system equation)} \qquad (2.16)$$
$$\mathbf{Y} = \mathbf{ZH} + \mathbf{E} \qquad \text{(measurement equation)}, \qquad (2.17)$$

with $\mathbf{X}$ the $T \times M_1$ matrix containing the input variables from time point 1 to T, $\mathbf{Y}$ the $T \times M_2$ matrix containing the output variables from time point 1 to T, $\mathbf{D}$ the $T \times p$ matrix containing the disturbances in the system equation from time point 1 to T and $\mathbf{E}$ the $T \times M_2$ matrix containing the errors in the measurement equation from time point 1 to T.

It should be noted that model (2.16), (2.17) can be viewed as a combination of two models: (2.16) resembles a longitudinal regression model, (2.17) describes the factor analysis model. As such, the combined model encompasses a number of different models frequently used in social research. If for instance the state transition matrix $\mathbf{F} = 0$ (in which case there is no dependence of the former state on the present), we arrive at a reduced rank regression type of model. If $\mathbf{G} = 0$, there is no influence of the input on the developments in the system; the model then is reduced to a dynamic factor type of model.

Fitting the model (2.16), (2.17) to data using a least squares criterion we arrive at the minimization problem that was proposed by Bijleveld & De Leeuw (1991). The loss function is:

$$\sigma(\mathbf{Z},\mathbf{F},\mathbf{G},\mathbf{H}) = \mathrm{SSQ}\,(\mathbf{Z} - \mathbf{SZF} - \mathbf{XG}) + \mathrm{SSQ}\,(\mathbf{Y} - \mathbf{ZH})\ , \qquad (2.18)$$

under the conditions $\mathbf{Z}'\mathbf{Z} = T\mathbf{I}$ and $\mathbf{Z}'\mathbf{u} = \mathbf{0}$ [5].

The restriction $\mathbf{Z}'\mathbf{Z} = T\mathbf{I}$ is necessary to avoid trivial solutions. The minimization problem in (2.18) can not be solved analytically. Bijleveld & De Leeuw (1991) opted to minimize the loss function using Alternating Least Squares. Their choice was guided by the fact that the minimization problem can be divided into two parts: on the one hand solving for $\mathbf{Z}$, which is possible (by a pretty cumbersome majorization procedure with which we will not burden the reader) if $\mathbf{F}$, $\mathbf{G}$ and $\mathbf{H}$ are known, and on the other hand solving for $\mathbf{F}$, $\mathbf{G}$ and $\mathbf{H}$, which is possible analytically if $\mathbf{Z}$ is known. Thus, the minimization problem is divided into two subproblems, that are solved by an iterative least squares minimization procedure. Starting with an initial solution for $\mathbf{Z}$, one obtains a sequence of solutions in which the loss is each time decreased, and which always converges to one solution. The solution is a space for $\mathbf{Z}$,

---

[5] Bijleveld & De Leeuw (1991) propose to add a constant ω^2 to the part of the loss function that regards the system equation. This is necessary to eliminate the impact that scale differences may have on solutions. Not specifying ω, we effectively set $\omega = 1$, in which case the system and measurement part of the loss function are weighted equally. Unit-normalizing both input and output, the solution is then relatively unaffected by scale differences.

for which several bases can be chosen, which implies that some rotational freedom is left, just like in factor analysis. For details we refer to Bijleveld & De Leeuw (1991) and Bijleveld (1989).

2.5 Multivariate dynamic analysis of categorical data

Suppose, in the example described in the previous section, that we have collected at a number of time points not only physiological indicators – such as blood pressure and heart rate – and mood scales, but information on our subject's activities as well. Thus, we have also registered whether our subject is conducting a telephone conversation, engaged in sports, cooking, relaxing, etc. In that case, we are faced with an additional problem, as our variables are of mixed measurement level: at least one variable (type of activity) can not be considered to have been measured at interval level. We would thus need a technique that can handle categorical data.

A number of techniques appear in the statistical literature under the heading time series models for categorical data; we name a few: Harvey & Fernandes (1989), Ord, Fernandes, & Harvey (1993), Singh & Roberts (1990, 1992); Fahrmeir (1992) and Fahrmeir & Tutz (1996). Mostly these techniques amount to some kind of time series analysis for count data (also often confusingly referred to as qualitative data). Again, these techniques have found their application mostly in areas where the paradigm is oriented towards forecasting of single series, and the applicability of these models to a behavioural context is quite limited for reasons outlined above. A rudimentary approach to describing time series using mixture distributions was recently proposed for categorical variables by De Leeuw, Bijleveld, Van Montfort, & Bijleveld (1997).

In the following we will outline how optimal scaling extensions to the linear dynamic system that was described above can be used to accommodate categorical variables.

2.5.1 Optimal scaling extensions to linear dynamic analysis for N = 1

Bijleveld & De Leeuw (1991) chose the Alternating Least Squares algorithm described above for estimating the transition matrices and latent states in the linear dynamic system. Their choice was guided not only by the fact that the optimization problem could be divided into two steps, but mainly by the advantage that the optimal scaling algorithm could easily incorporate optimal scaling of any categorical variables. Extending the algorithm with a third substep, category quantifications can be computed along the lines of the optimal scaling procedures described in Gifi (1990). The minimization problem then becomes:

$$\text{minimize } \sigma\left(\mathbf{Z}, \mathbf{F}, \mathbf{G}, \mathbf{H}, \tilde{\mathbf{X}}, \tilde{\mathbf{Y}}\right) =$$
$$\text{SSQ}\left(\mathbf{Z} - \mathbf{SZF} - \tilde{\mathbf{X}}\mathbf{G}\right) + \text{SSQ}\left(\tilde{\mathbf{Y}} - \mathbf{ZH}\right),$$

under the conditions $\mathbf{Z}'\mathbf{Z} = T\mathbf{I}$ and $\mathbf{Z}'\mathbf{u} = \mathbf{0}$,

where $\tilde{\mathbf{X}}$ is the matrix containing the entries $\mathbf{I}_j^{X}\mathbf{B}_j^{X}$, with $\mathbf{I}_j^{X}$ the indicator matrix and $\mathbf{B}_j^{X}$ the matrix of category quantifications for the j-th variable of $\mathbf{X}$. $\tilde{\mathbf{Y}}$ is the matrix containing the entries $\mathbf{I}_j^{Y}\mathbf{B}_j^{Y}$, with $\mathbf{I}_j^{Y}$ the indicator matrix and $\mathbf{B}_j^{Y}$ the matrix of category quantifications for the j-th variable of $\mathbf{Y}$.

An additional advantage of the algorithm is that in a fourth substep, least squares optimal estimates of any missing values can be computed. The sequencing of the substeps can be varied, for instance it is possible to first let the algorithm converge to a solution, and then to quantify the categories of any categorical variables, and other variations are possible. The algorithm was implemented in a computer program named DYNAMALS[6]. As yet, only single nominal and ordinal transformations have been implemented. For details see Bijleveld & De Leeuw (1991).

DYNAMALS solutions should be interpreted in a fairly similar way to solutions from other exploratory analyses that use optimal scaling. DYNAMALS produces a normalized fit, that ranges between 0 and 1. Important instruments for interpretation are the latent state scores, which are comparable to object scores, except that the state space scores are of course ordered in time. In this context, a useful tool is therefore to plot the development of the state scores against time. When two or more dimensions have been modelled, one can also plot the development through the object space. As in OVERALS and comparable techniques, the weights (that is, for DYNAMALS, the values in the transition matrices $\mathbf{G}$ and $\mathbf{H}$) take into account the effect of the other variables as well. Solutions have some rotational freedom, for which DYNAMALS

---

[6]Various versions of DYNAMALS can be obtained for academic use from http://www.stat.ucla.edu/gifi/software/dynamals.

provides defaults upon request, see Bijleveld & De Leeuw (1991). If one wants to evaluate the impact of the respective variables, it is useful to interpret the matrix of correlations of the input and output variables with the dimensions of the latent state. The correlations of the rescaled variables with the latent state scores are thus useful for interpreting the dimensions of the latent state. When variables have been rescaled nominally or ordinally, just like in PRINCALS or OVERALS, the category quantifications have to be taken into account in the interpretation.

Another approach to assessing the impact of the input variables, which is in line with the longitudinal nature of the data, is to forecast future Y-values for various hypothetical values of the input. This is especially useful as the results of such forecasts need not be immediately obvious from the (essentially cross-sectional) correlations of the input variables with the latent state. For examples, see Olmstead (1996).

An additional tool for interpretation, particular to the dynamic nature of the model, is the state transition matrix $\mathbf{F}$. If $\mathbf{F}$ equals zero, the latent states do not depend on the past. As the largest singular value of $\mathbf{F}$, denoted by $|\mathbf{F}|$ and referred to as the *norm* of $\mathbf{F}$, increases, the time dependence becomes stronger and stronger. As long as $|\mathbf{F}| < 1$, we model what is in the literature referred to as a *stable* system: if left unperturbed by outward influences, the values of the latent state eventually converge to zero. If $|\mathbf{F}| > 1$, we model what is generally labelled an *unstable* system: if left unperturbed by outward influences, the values of the latent state would be ever increasing, a condition of explosiveness.

When $|\mathbf{F}| > 1$, the time series process that generates the values of the latent state is labelled non-stationary: the distribution of $\mathbf{z}_t$ is not the same for all t: for instance $E(\mathbf{z}_t) \neq E(\mathbf{z}_{t+k})$. In time series analysis, solutions where $|\mathbf{F}| > 1$ are considered problematic (comparable to a Heywood case in factor analysis) as stationarity is a necessary condition for identification in many types of time series analysis (see Box & Jenkins, 1976; Chatfield, 1989). For our type of exploratory least squares analysis technique, stationarity is not a necessary condition. In fact, in behavioural research we quite often expect to model processes in which subjects' starting values are essentially different from their end values. However, more research needs to be done to assess the seriousness of improper solutions, where $|\mathbf{F}| > 1$.

DYNAMALS has been designed for the analysis of datasets for one subject. When measurements are available for only one subject, and stability cannot be obtained from a large number of replications over subjects, stability has to be derived from a sufficient number of replications over time. In time series analysis such as ARMA-modelling (Box & Jenkins, 1976), an often used rule is that T be larger than 50. Aoki (1988) uses as a rule of thumb that the number of time points should be larger than 6 times the number of input and output variables. While no such explicit criteria have as yet been derived for DYNAMALS, solutions are known to become increasingly unstable for smaller numbers of time points. Given the fact that the algorithm has additional freedom from the quantification process, a reasonable rule of thumb would seem to be that T be larger than roughly 6 to 8 times the total number of variables – including the latent state variables to be on the safe side. This rule of thumb varies with the number of ordinal and particularly nominal variables. In general, when fewer restrictions are imposed on the category quantifications, more time points are needed to attain stability. As nominal variables are the least restricted, in principle more time points are needed to attain stability when the data consist of nominal variables than would be needed for ordinal or interval level variables. All in all, the minimum number of time points for which DYNAMALS is practicable would then be approximately 25. Although this is an uncommonly large number for social research situations with substantial replications over subjects, large numbers of time points are not uncommon in situations with one subject, or a limited number of subjects.

The choice of dimensionality of the state is generally guided by pragmatic rather than theoretical considerations. As interpretability decreases rapidly after two dimensions, it is uncommon that more than two dimensions be modelled for the latent state. However, because so much work has to be done in the latent state, a high number of dimensions may be needed to obtain a good fit, especially in situations where the fit is not enhanced by optimal scaling of any categorical variables. DYNAMALS solutions are not nested, although in a sequence of solutions of increasing dimensionality the solutions for the subsequent dimensions are often quite similar.

Similarly to the examples in Section 2.3.3, it is possible to model lags in DYNAMALS. We give an illustration below.

Example of linear dynamic systems analysis with optimal scaling for N = 1: blood pressure We analyse the relation between medication and blood pressure. The one subject in this example is a 57-year old, male Caucasian patient under medical treatment for hypertension. (The same data were analysed with a different DYNAMALS algorithm in Bij-leveld (1989).) For 113 days, this patient had recorded every morning his diastolic and systolic blood pressure. Added to this were two series of data. The first series, which we will call MEDICATION, registers changes in medication in the recording period. The patient started out on a daily dosage of 400 mg of metoprololtartrate. After 52 days, the patient switched to 240 mg per day of sotalolhydrochloride, to which a daily diureticum was added after 11 days. After another 16 days, the dosage of sotalolhydrochloride could be reduced to 160 mg per day. MEDICATION therefore has four categories.

As blood pressure can be influenced by work-related stress, we added a variable for investigating whether blood pressure might generally be lower in the weekends and higher during the working-week. This series, which we will call WEEKDAY, consists of the day of the week on which blood pressure was measured. MEDICATION and WEEKDAY were thus the input variables. The blood pressure measurements constituted the output variables.

We analysed these data using dynamic systems analysis with optimal scaling. As no *a priori* ordering of the categories is available for either of the two input variables, we treated them both as nominal variables. The diastolic and systolic blood pressure output variables were treated as numerical variables. We modelled one latent state variable, so that the dimensionality of the latent state is one. A number of missing blood pressure measurements had been interpolated previously. As MEDICATION does not take effect immediately, we imposed a lag of one day on the medication variable, thereby reducing the number of measurement points that could be used in the analysis to 112. A graphical representation of the resulting model is given in Figure 2.30.

The algorithm converged to a normalized fit of 0.883. The norm of **F** (**F** is in fact a scalar as the dimensionality of the state is one) was 0.787.

The correlations of input variables and blood pressure data with the one-dimensional state are shown in Table 2.9. From these, we can infer the following. Surprisingly, WEEKDAY correlates barely with the latent state. From the quantifications of the categories of WEEKDAY, it appears as if Monday and Friday are days with relatively lower blood

Figure 2.30: *Blood Pressure Data: Relation of* WEEKDAY *and Lag(1)*
Version of MEDICATION *with Diastolic and Systolic Blood*
Pressure

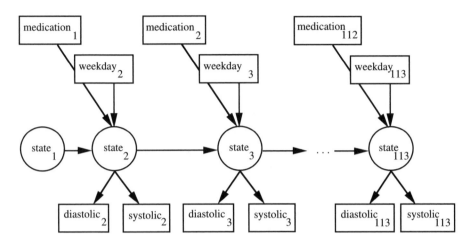

Table 2.9: *Blood Pressure Data: Correlations of Quantified Input Variables*
and Output Variables with the Latent State

MEDICATION	0.851
WEEKDAY	0.154
DIASTOLIC	0.924
SYSTOLIC	0.939

pressure, and as if blood pressure is increased on Tuesdays, Wednesdays, Thursdays and particularly Saturdays, which have on average the highest blood pressure. However, as the variable WEEKDAY has such a low correlation with the state, we cannot attach much importance to any patterns observed. Thus, it appears as if, within this one-dimensional solution, there is little to no effect of the working-week on the latent state values and subsequently blood pressure. MEDICATION, however, correlates quite strongly with the latent state. Because also the medication variable was treated as a nominal variable, the impact of the various medication categories has to be evaluated while taking into account the values of the quantifications. The category quantifications of the medication variable are presented in Table 2.10.

Table 2.10: *Blood Pressure Data: Category Quantifications of Medication*

Period	MEDICATION	Category quantifications
1	Metoprololtartrate 400 mg	1.13
2	Sotalolhydrochloride 240 mg	0.31
3	Sotalolhydrochloride 240 mg + Diureticum	−0.69
4	Sotalolhydrochloride 160 mg + Diureticum	−0.86

Given the fact that **F** equals 0.787, and that the values of the latent state are thus ever decreasing if unperturbed, and given the fact that the blood pressure values as well as MEDICATION are positively correlated with the latent state, categories of MEDICATION with a high quantification steer the latent state values upwards, away from its unperturbed autonomous trend of decrease. Categories with a low quantification lower the latent state values. Thus we may infer that – departing from the average value for the total number of 113 days – blood pressure is increased for the medication categories with high quantifications, and blood pressure is decreased for the categories with low quantifications. In the first period when metoprololtartrate was used, blood pressure was highest. The new sotalolhydrochloride medicine lowers blood pressure to slightly above average levels. Once the diureticum is added, blood pressure is lowered to almost its lowest levels ever. The lowered dosage of sotalolhydrochloride, from 240 to 160 mg a day gives an additional small improvement.

The conclusion that can be drawn from this analysis is thus that a dosage of 160 mg of sotalolhydrochloride, in combination with a daily diureticum, is the most beneficial medication for this subject. The largest decrease in blood pressure is gained by the addition of a diureticum to the daily medication. These conclusions are in accordance with clinical experience.

2.5.2 Optimal scaling extensions to linear dynamic analysis for N > 1

The DYNAMALS model can be extended to the analysis of $N > 1$ designs. The extension is fairly straightforward.

We have measured at T time points, for N subjects, M_1 input variables X, stacked in a data box $\mathbf{X}$ of size $N \times M_1 \times T$. The output variables, measured at the same time points, are named Y, and are stacked in a data box $\mathbf{Y}$ of size $N \times M_2 \times T$. If we formulate the linear dynamic system for these N subjects as in Equations (2.14) and (2.15), we arrive at:

$$\mathbf{z}_{i_t} = \mathbf{F}\mathbf{z}_{i_{t-1}} + \mathbf{G}\mathbf{x}_{i_t} + \mathbf{d}_{i_t} \, ,$$

with $\mathbf{z}_{i_t}$ and $\mathbf{z}_{i_{t-1}}$ the vectors containing the p latent state scores of subject i at time points t and $t-1$ respectively, $\mathbf{F}$ the $p \times p$ matrix of regression coefficients specifying the transition from the latent state scores from time point $t-1$ to time point t, $\mathbf{x}_{i_t}$ the M_1-dimensional vector of input variables of subject i at time point t, $\mathbf{G}$ a $p \times M_1$ matrix of regression coefficients, and $\mathbf{d}_{i_t}$ a p-dimensional vector of disturbances.

The output variables at any time point t are predicted from a weighted sum of the latent state scores at that time point, which is in formula written as:

$$\mathbf{y}_{i_t} = \mathbf{H}\mathbf{z}_{i_t} + \mathbf{e}_{i_t} \, ,$$

with $\mathbf{y}_{i_t}$ the M_2-dimensional vector of output variables of subject i at time point t, $\mathbf{H}$ an $M_2 \times p$ matrix of regression coefficients, and $\mathbf{e}_{i_t}$ an M_2-dimensional vector of measurements errors. The vectors with error terms are needed because we do not expect a perfect fit to real data. Again, the system needs hypothetical starting points at $t = 1$: $\mathbf{z}_{i_0}$.

Note that subjects share the same $\mathbf{F}$, $\mathbf{G}$ and $\mathbf{H}$, but that each subject has his or her own latent state scores.

To analyse the linear dynamic model for N subjects simultaneously, we flatten the data box by stacking the data matrices for the N subjects into an $NT \times M_1$ matrix $\mathbf{X}_{sup}$ and an $NT \times M_2$ matrix $\mathbf{Y}_{sup}$ in a similar way to the procedure outlined in Section 2.3.1:

$$
\mathbf{X}_{sup} =
\begin{bmatrix}
\mathbf{X}_1 \\
\mathbf{X}_2 \\
\mathbf{X}_3 \\
\mathbf{X}_4 \\
\cdot \\
\cdot \\
\cdot \\
\mathbf{X}_N
\end{bmatrix},
\qquad
\mathbf{Y}_{sup} =
\begin{bmatrix}
\mathbf{Y}_1 \\
\mathbf{Y}_2 \\
\mathbf{Y}_3 \\
\mathbf{Y}_4 \\
\cdot \\
\cdot \\
\cdot \\
\mathbf{Y}_N
\end{bmatrix}.
$$

The stacked super matrices are in fact LONG matrices, just like the LONG matrices discussed in Section 2.3. If we stack the latent state scores, similarly, into an $NT \times p$ matrix of latent state scores $\mathbf{Z}_{sup}$, we can then construct an $NT \times NT$ block diagonal super-shift matrix $\mathbf{S}_{sup}$ using for each of the N blocks the ordinary $T \times T$ shift matrix:

$$
\mathbf{S}_{sup} =
\begin{bmatrix}
\mathbf{S}_1 & & & & \\
& \mathbf{S}_2 & & \mathbf{0} & \\
& & \mathbf{S}_3 & & \\
& & & & \\
& \mathbf{0} & & \mathbf{S}_{N-1} & \\
& & & & \mathbf{S}_N
\end{bmatrix}
$$

and write the model ((2.16), (2.17)) as:

$$
\mathbf{Z}_{sup} = \mathbf{S}_{sup}\mathbf{Z}_{sup}\mathbf{F} + \mathbf{X}_{sup}\mathbf{G} + \mathbf{D}_{sup} \qquad \text{(system equation)}
$$
$$
\mathbf{Y}_{sup} = \mathbf{Z}_{sup}\mathbf{H} + \mathbf{E}_{sup} \qquad \text{(measurement equation)},
$$

with $\mathbf{D}_{sup}$ and $\mathbf{E}_{sup}$ two matrices of disturbances and error terms, respectively, of dimensionality $NT \times M_1$ and $NT \times M_2$ respectively.

Note that, as in Section 2.3, the series for the different subjects may be of unequal length. In that case the dimensionalities of the super matrices change somewhat: $NT \times M_1$ becomes $(\sum_{i=1}^{N} T_i) \times M_1$, and $NT \times M_2$ becomes $(\sum_{i=1}^{N} T_i) \times M_2$, with T_i the number of time points at which subject i has been measured.

Interpretation of solutions from $N > 1$ linear dynamic systems analysis is analogous to interpretation in the case where $N = 1$. The correlations serve for interpreting the dimensions of the latent state. The norm of $\mathbf{F}$ should preferably be lower than one in absolute value. The values of the latent state are useful for assessing intraindividual change, but can now also be used to assess interindividual differences. As in the examples given in Section 2.3.1 and Section 2.3.2, it is advisable to draw the latent state curves for subgroups of subjects.

Linear dynamic systems analysis for several subjects with optimal scaling has a number of advantages over time series modelling. The most prominent of these is the fact that categorical data can be analysed. A second type of advantage is in the area of stability. Where cross-sectional methods derive stability from a suitably large number of replications over subjects, and where time series models derive stability from a suitably large number of replications over time, the $N > 1$ method discussed here derives stability from time points as well as subjects. This is so because every subject adds T additional measurements to the data, or conversely: every time point adds N additional measurements to the data. Another way to phrase this is by saying that N and T boost each other in terms of stability. Contrary to the rivalling – essentially cross-sectional – methods like structural equation modelling that derive stability from sufficient (and for time series applications usually unrealistically large) numbers of replications over subjects, it is likely that under mild conditions the essentially three-way methods proposed here can derive sufficient stability of the estimates at lower N and/or T than conventional time series or cross-sectional two-way methods.

Example of linear dynamic systems analysis with optimal scaling for $N > 1$: concentration complaints and the menstrual cycle   We analyse an example from psychosomatic research. We have at our disposal daily measures of well-being and distress that had been gathered in 59 healthy women and men in a study on menstrual symptoms (Van den Boogaard & Bijleveld, 1988). The measures had been collected for 35 consecutive days; this time-span had been chosen to include at least one menstrual cycle for the female subjects. Men had been included in the sample to serve as control subjects. A self-administered questionnaire contained 53 items; it had been constructed from Moos's menstrual distress questionnaire (Moos, 1968) extended with 6 additional items reflecting positive moods that had emerged as relevant in a pilot study. Subjects had indicated every day on a rating scale ranging from 1 to 6 whether they had 'no complaints regarding this item' (1) to 'many complaints regarding this item' (6). A previous factor analysis on the flattened

$59 \times 53 \times 35$ data box had produced nine factors (Van den Boogaard & Bijleveld, 1988). In the example here, we will further analyse the relations between the variables that constituted three of these factors.

More particularly, we will investigate to what extent variables typically associated with pre-menstrual and menstrual distress such as water retention and abdominal pain influence concentration. For this purpose, we selected four variables reflecting symptoms of water retention and two variables reflecting symptoms of abdominal pain. These variables serve as input variables in our example. A variable reflecting concentration had been constructed by summing five indicator variables. This variable, labelled CONCENTRATION, serves as the output variable. The three-dimensional data for our example now have dimensionalities $59 \times 6 \times 35$ for the input variables, and $59 \times 1 \times 35$ for the output variable. See Table 2.11 for the variables.

Table 2.11: *Menstrual Distress Data: Concentration Complaints and Menstrual Distress Variables*

Input variables	Output variable
ABDOMINAL PAIN	CONCENTRATION
CRAMPS	
PAINFUL BREASTS	
SWELLING	
SKIN DISORDERS	
WEIGHT GAIN	

The research question we will analyse is to what extent the above mentioned factors typically associated with pre-menstrual and menstrual distress influence concentration. Female subjects could be divided into those using oral contraception (OC) and those using no oral contraception (NOC). The answers to all items had been poled such, that high scores are unfavourable, reflecting high levels of complaints. We modelled one dimension for the latent state. We treated the concentration variable as an ordinal variable. As we did not want to disallow possibly curvilinear or other nonmonotone relationships between the input variables and latent state, we treated all input variables as nominal.

The model converged to a solution with a standardized fit of 0.919. **F** was estimated at 0.91 (also in this example, **F** is a scalar), meaning that there is a strong influence of the previous state on the present state. For interpretation we use the correlations of the input variables and output variable with the latent state values, computed over subjects over time points. These are given in Table 2.12.

Table 2.12: *Menstrual Distress Data: Correlations of Quantified Input Variables and Concentration Variable with the Latent State*

Input variables		Output variable	
ABDOMINAL PAIN	0.29	CONCENTRATION	0.95
CRAMPS	0.00		
PAINFUL BREASTS	0.05		
SWELLING	−0.02		
SKIN DISORDERS	0.20		
WEIGHT GAIN	0.32		

From Table 2.12, it appears that the latent state variable – expectedly – very strongly resembles the output variable (the loading from the latent state to the output variable being 0.95). The correlations of the input variables with this latent state show that the latent variable is most strongly related to the input variables WEIGHT GAIN, ABDOMINAL PAIN, and SKIN DISORDERS. CRAMPS, PAINFUL BREASTS and SWELLING play a minor role.

The quantifications of the concentration variable were such that subjects with no concentration complaints had been contrasted with subjects with concentration complaints: the quantification of 'no concentration complaints' was negative, and the quantification of all other categories was positive – with the higher less frequently scored categories receiving quite high quantifications. We will not interpret the quantifications of the input variables with very low correlation with the latent state. The quantifications of WEIGHT GAIN were in ascending order; those of ABDOMINAL PAIN were, but for one disruption, also monotone. The categories of SKIN DISORDERS had been quantified in an ordinal fashion as well; the first five categories of this variable had received a negative quantification, and the last, sixth, category a positive quantification. This means that only very high scores on SKIN DISORDERS affected concentration complaints.

Thus, subjects in this sample tend to experience more concentration complaints with weight gain, abdominal pain, and with many skin disorders. Subjects without weight gain, without abdominal pain and with no or relatively few skin disorders tend to experience fewer concentration complaints. However, by far the strongest influence on concentration at a time point t, is concentration at the previous time point $t-1$ (the value of $\mathbf{F}$ being 0.91), as transferred by the chain of latent state values.

To facilitate interpretation and visual inspection, we have averaged the latent scores for each of the three groups in the study, i.e. men, women using oral contraception (OC) and women using no oral contraception. For the women, the latent scores have been synchronized such that for each female subject, the score at day 1 in the figure is the first day of her pre-menstrual phase. As the pre-menstrual phase had been defined as the week before the onset of menstruation, menstruation starts for all women at day 8. As women's cycles were of unequal length, the number of subjects decreases rapidly after day 28, so that we do not give the average latent scores after this day anymore, given that they are bound to become heavily influenced by attrition and therefore likely to be erratic. For men, scores were synchronized such that for all men, day 1 was the first Monday in the research period, this being the day that was most often shared by the men as the first day they participated in the research; the scores of the men extend up to day 35. A graphical representation of these averaged latent state scores is given in Figure 2.31.

Looking at the interindividual differences, that is, at the level of the curves in Figure 2.31, we see that women using oral contraception have on average the highest level; as the variables were all poled such that high values mean many complaints, this means that women using oral contraception generally report the highest level of complaints regarding concentration. Men assume an intermediate position. Women using no oral contraception report on average the lowest level of complaints. In a sense, this is surprising as one would expect women using no hormonal contraceptives and men to be on a somewhat equal footing, both being in a 'natural state'. However, as 'treatments' (contraception) were not

Figure 2.31: *Menstrual Distress Data: Synchronized Latent State Scores for Subgroups*

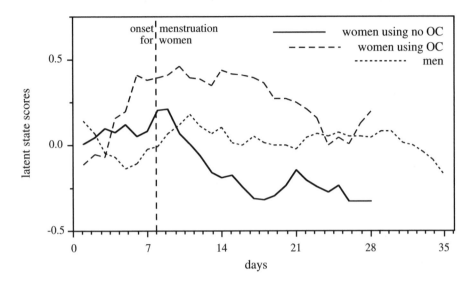

assigned randomly, it is quite likely that the groups that were formed by natural selection differ with regard to other relevant aspects (e.g. the women using oral contraception may more often have had a partner; the women not using oral contraception may have been younger). For privacy reasons, demographic information for investigating such presumptions had not been made available.

When we inspect the development of the average latent curves over time, we see that the women using no oral contraception start out at a relatively high group-specific level of complaints in the pre-menstrual phase. During day 1 and day 2 of the menstrual phase, concentration complaints are at their highest for this group. From day 3 onwards, complaints fall rapidly, remaining at a low level from day 14 onwards, i.e. after most women will have ended their menstrual period. We see a further lowering and subsequent increase and decrease between days 21 and 25, which might be related to mid-phase distress sometimes reported around the time of ovulation. However, given general levels of variability, it is hard to say whether this is a chance phenomenon or not.

For the women using oral contraception, we see a strong increase of concentration complaints, from low levels at day 1 to the highest group-specific levels from day 6 onwards, which is the day the women in the sample – who all used a combination-type of pill containing oestrogen and progesterone – finished their strip of pills. After two days, all women in this group started their menstrual period, this menstruation being an actual withdrawal bleeding. Concentration complaints climb a little more, and then level off in a stepwise fashion, rising again from day 26 onwards, perhaps moving in the same cyclical way towards the next pre-menstrual phase.

For the men, we see something of a swing during the first 7 days of reporting, from higher to lower levels and up again. After day 9, levels remain fairly constant, with some fluctuation. Even though the initial swing is not dramatic in the sense that it spans the range of values exhibited later on in the curve, it is remarkable. It is hard to say what may have caused it; one likely explanation for the initial decrease may be offered by the fact that, in menstrual research, subjects are well known to report generally higher levels of complaints during the beginning of the investigation period; as the men's average initial values are actually located at the beginning of the investigation period, this may thus emerge much more clearly for the men than for the women, the sequencing in whose series has become jumbled because of the synchronization to menstrual periods. For the men, the days were synchronous (day 1 being a Monday for all men, day 2 a Tuesday, etc.). No weekly cycles emerge from the figure, however.

While the developments of the women in the group using no oral contraception can thus be linked in an interpretable fashion to the menstrual cycle and pre-menstrual and menstrual periods therein, the fluctuations in the group of women using oral contraception relate in a different manner to the menstrual cycle. Levels are much higher in general. In fact, women using no oral contraception fluctuate at low levels, with a peak around the onset of menstruation. Women using oral contraception fluctuate at high levels, with a dip towards the end of the three weeks during which contraception is used. Men can be shown to be variable in their reported levels of concentration as well.

The analysis reported here emphasizes differences between subjects. This can be guessed from the figure where the average curves for the subjects are well-separated, and it can be seen from the low correlations between the input variables and the latent state in contrast to the value of the one element of the transition matrix $\mathbf{F}$, which equalled 0.91.

With such a high value for $\mathbf{F}$, the development of the latent state is very strongly autoregressive, and the latent state fluctuates at more or less individually particular levels, influenced only weakly by exogenous variables.

This means that the one-dimensional DYNAMALS solution emphasized interindividual differences (although temporal developments could very well be retrieved and interpreted in a meaningful manner). In general, when higher dimensional solutions are sought, $N > 1$-DYNAMALS tends to emphasize interindividual differences in the first dimension(s), and emphasizes intraindividual differences in the following dimensions.

A first explanation for this tendency lies in the fact that in many empirical situations interindividual level differences (or intercepts) are often larger than intraindividual changes. Secondly, given that in most practical situations the number of subjects is larger than the number of time points, algorithms can also generally gain more in terms of fit from emphasizing interindividual differences. In addition, in the dynamic systems models discussed here, the postulate of a latent state at time 0 ($\mathbf{z}_{i_0}$) facilitates or even induces this tendency: setting the estimate for the value of the initial state for each subject equal to that subject's average score on the criterion variable(s), and setting the estimate for $\mathbf{F}$ close to 1, the values of the latent state variable reflect the stable interindividual differences (intercepts). The impact of external time-varying influences such as measured by the input variables then does not emerge or is much less prominent. The tendency is even stronger when the data are optimally rescaled, as the technique then has more freedom to fit this type of autoregressive model. (In a previous analysis for this example that used no optimal scaling, we found substantially higher correlation coefficients for the relation between input variables and latent state.) Clearly, such autoregressive explanations may not be what one is looking for when one is attempting to assess the impact of external influences (as represented by the input variables) on the process at hand.

If that is the case, there are several possibilities for restricting the autoregressive emphasis. First, one may analyse a higher dimensional model, and look for temporal developments and the impact of external influences on these in the higher dimensions of the solution. However, such a model may be less attractive (for our example this would have meant fitting a two-dimensional latent state for a one-dimensional criterion variable). In case one wants to find a parsimonious (for instance one-dimensional) solution for the temporal developments, it is possible to remove the interindividual differences first. For that, one can define the observed output variables in deviation from the subject means, or:

$$Y_{ijt}^* = Y_{ijt} - \sum_{t=1}^{T_i} \frac{Y_{ijt}}{T_i}, \qquad (2.19)$$

effectively eliminating interindividual differences from the data set; of course, this is possible only – strictly speaking – when the output variables are at interval level. This procedure is analogous to the procedure often used in time series research, where in case of trend (that can be conceptualized as heterogeneity over time points), one first removes the trend, and next performs time series analysis on the de-trended data.

Summarizing, there are three solutions if one is searching particularly for (the impact of external influences on) intraindividual developments. One could start simply by not rescaling the variables. This is not a guaranteed solution, but generally reduces the autoregressive emphasis. This is less feasible when (a number of) variables are ordinal, and impossible when there are nominal variables. A second possibility is to remove the interindividual differences in the output variable beforehand; this is possible only when the output is at interval level. A third solution is to run the analysis in more dimensions; this may be the only solution when nominal variables are present.

2.5.3   Other multivariate dynamic analysis techniques for categorical data

Van Buuren (1990) developed the so-called SERIALS method that combines a state space or linear dynamic system-type of model with the Box–Tiao transform proposed by Box & Tiao (1977). The linear dynamic system was discussed above. The *Box–Tiao transform* is a method that extracts components from multiple time series, in such a way that these components are related as strongly as possible to lagged versions of themselves. Thus, the correlations between the lag(0) and lag(d) versions of a data set must be as high as possible. This implies that the technique seeks those components that can be constructed from the data that forecast themselves as well as possible. Because of the forecasting constraint, the extracted components are mostly pretty smooth, and the technique can thus also be viewed as a smoother of wild series. For details, see Box & Tiao (1977) and Van Buuren (1990).

Bijleveld, Bijleveld, & De Leeuw (1994) presented a version of DYNAMALS in which the constraint $\mathbf{d}_{i_t} \equiv 0$ is implemented. Their technique uses a different least squares algorithm and finds latent state scores that are non-orthogonal. Because of the constraint that $\mathbf{d}_{i_t} \equiv 0$, the latent state space series are usually also quite smooth.

2.6   Missing data

One of the advantages of the use of optimal scaling techniques for longitudinal data is that they can handle missing data relatively easily.

Missing values are easy to deal with in the techniques discussed above: when one uses HOMALS, PRINCALS or OVERALS, the techniques simply exclude any missing observations from the loss function. If one uses DYNAMALS, the techniques substitute missing values (one or a number of variables missing at a certain time point) by least squares optimal estimates.

However, the proportion of missing values should not become too high, because then these optimal scaling techniques may run into trouble as well. For instance, in HOMALS, the discrimination measures may become greater than one when there are many missing values. Unfortunately, no absolute guidelines on this proportion of missing values can be given. When the solution appears to be affected by the number of missing values, other options for dealing with missing data are available. For instance, if a variable is nominal, one may simply give any missing values a same (new) category value, and add this category to the variable. Instead of k categories, the variable then has $k + 1$ categories, with the $k + 1$-th category containing all missing values.

For ordinal variables in PRINCALS or OVERALS, one could run an analysis in two steps: in a first step, one runs the analysis without the missing values. Next one computes the average object score of all subjects who had a missing score on this variable, and compares it to the (for instance in case one uses OVERALS) projected centroids of the other categories. On the basis of this comparison, one assigns a new category to the missing values that fits in with the comparison of the average object score to the projected centroids. Next, one adjusts the values for the other categories, and reruns the analysis.

We give an example. Suppose that an ordinal variable has categories 1, 2, 3, 4, and 5. We run an analysis (for instance an OVERALS analysis), and treat the variable as single ordinal, disregarding the missings. Next, we inspect the projected centroids of the categories of the variable. Suppose that we find for the respective categories the centroids are as shown in Table 2.13 and suppose that the average object score of

Table 2.13: *Quantification of Missing Data*

Category number	Projected centroid
category 1	−1.31
category 2	−0.80
category 3	0.15
category 4	0.56
category 5	0.97

subjects with a missing value on this variable is 0.73. Then a best recategorization for the missing scores on this variable would be in between category 4 and 5. As this does not exist, we simply insert the missing value category in between, label it '5', and relabel the old '5' as '6', and rerun the analysis with the variable now having 6 instead of 5 categories. A similar procedure can be followed for numerical variables. Other options that are sometimes used to deal with missing data for ordinal or numerical variables are to assign all subjects with missing values an average category; however, this is generally suboptimal as subjects with missing values on a variable are usually deviant in some respect.

In case of *missing occasions* (all variables missing at a certain time point) DYNAMALS substitutes the missing values on all variables by least squares optimal estimates. When cross-sectional techniques are used such as HOMALS or OVERALS for longitudinal data entered into a LONG matrix format, only those records that are missing are left out of the data set. This is an advantage of our techniques as then we do not need to resort to listwise deletion to handle the problem of selection through attrition or drop out. As techniques such as MANOVA for repeated measures can use only complete series, subjects with incomplete (or interrupted) series are often disregarded. However, as is well-known, such subjects have differential characteristics from those who remain throughout the study, and often even characteristics that are of particular relevance to the topic of study. Excluding the dropouts may lead to different or even invalid conclusions (see also Section 1.6.3).

In both HOMALS and PRINCALS applications with the LONG matrix, all occasions at which at least one variable is non-missing can participate. In OVERALS or any other multi-set analysis, all occasions are retained for which, in each set, at least one variable is non-missing. When one uses cross-sectional techniques for data that have been cast into BROAD matrix format, missing occasions can be left in the data set. As the total number of variables is then MT, a missing occasion causes only part of the record to be missing. More particularly: it gives a gap of M missing values in a record with MT values.

If one uses lagged versions of variables, missing occasions create more complications. If for instance, in the case of a lag(0) and a lag(1) set, all measurements at time point t are missing, one cannot model the influence of the observations of time $t - 1$ on those of time point t, and one can also not model the influence of the observations of time point t on those of time point $t + 1$. Thus, when all measurements on one occasion are missing, two records have to be deleted from each set. See the example in Figure 2.32. When more complicated lags are modelled, an accordingly larger number of records has to be deleted in the same manner.

2.7 Discussion

In this chapter we introduced a number of exploratory techniques that use optimal scaling to quantify categorical data. The techniques can handle mixed-measurement level categorical data, that is, mixtures of nominal, ordinal and numerical variables. They do so by rescaling the values of the categorical variables in such a way that a loss function is minimized. The optimal scaling occurs in a substep of an iterative minimization procedure. After rescaling, the categorical variables are treated as continuous variables. Through this approach to the analysis of categorical data, optimal scaling techniques like PRINCALS, OVERALS and DYNAMALS are essentially linear techniques, that have been extended with a substep to transform any categorical data.

We discussed two approaches to the longitudinal analysis of categorical data using optimal scaling techniques. In the first, we adapt

Figure 2.32: *Deletion of Records in Lagged Analysis Because of Missing Occasion*

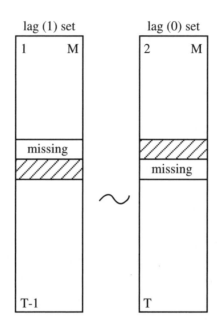

the data box in such a way that the data can be fed into the technique and analysed as if they are cross-sectional. Any categorical variables are transformed. When the technique produces a solution we return to the longitudinal properties of the data box, retrieving time points and subjects, and making visible any changes by drawing subjects' trajectories from one time point to the next. Even though this approach is not without methodological hazards – the most notable being the risk of relationships induced by heterogeneity over time points, it has proven to be flexible, easy to apply and conceptually attractive. The multi-set techniques can be adapted to investigate summary as well as group-specific changes in time. They can be used for rescaling noninterval level data, or they can be used to explore nonlinear growth for interval level data. They can incorporate specific additional research questions, such as questions into the discrimination between groups.

In the second approach, time series techniques for continuous data are extended with an optimal scaling substep. These techniques were designed originally for the analysis of single subject designs with long series. Extensions can be applied when there are replications over subjects. They are in a sense more appropriate for the analysis of longitudinal data than the techniques presented in the first approach, as they truly model (autoregressive) time-dependence. Our applications illustrated how the results from the two approaches may converge, with the first dimensions of the solution often tending to focus more on interindividual differences, and the higher dimensions highlighting intraindividual differences more. Such results may be conceptualized as a kind of growth curves, with intercepts and slopes emphasized in respective dimensions.

Compared with confirmatory techniques, the two approaches share the disadvantage that no stability information is provided. For those cases where we have sufficient replications over subjects, this can be overcome by jackknifing or bootstrapping. For the categorical $N = 1$ time series techniques in the second approach this is more difficult, as the observations are tied by the time axis, and in principle one thus cannot leave out or add observations at random, or permute the ordering of the measurements. Efron & Tibshirani (1993) describe permutational methods for longitudinal data that use so-called moving blocks. In this approach the stability of parameter estimates is investigated by re-positioning entire 'chunks' out of the time series, and investigating the influence this has on the parameters estimates. However, for behavioural data, the length of the time series is usually such that only chunks of small length can be moved about. This makes the method less practicable. A second possibility is to resample the residuals. However, Shao & Tu (1995) conclude that methods that resample the residuals are based on model assumptions, and that the results are sensitive to violations of these assumptions. In addition, many time series models for behavioural data are non-stationary by nature, as in behavioural applications we are usually investigating developmental processes in which there is growth of some kind (e.g. a decrease of anorectic symptoms under the influence of therapy, the formation of attachment). Any changes in the sequence of measurements give an unnatural and ill-fitting disruption of the flow of the series.

The time series techniques for categorical data still need to gain in applicability. Both DYNAMALS algorithms need to be improved and implemented in accessible software, although some advances have been made.

Other authors have proposed using the exploratory optimal scaling techniques in the context of longitudinal analysis. An example of an application of multiple correspondence analysis as a P-technique (see Chapter 1) is given by Van der Kloot (1981), who applied multiple correspondence analysis to the analysis of psychoneurotic symptoms of one psychiatric patient.

The work of Van der Heijden (1987) deserves mention as well, although it approaches the subject from a slightly different angle. Van der Heijden (1987) proposes to use correspondence analysis on various types of cross-tabulations derived from longitudinal data. In his work with De Leeuw (Van der Heijden & De Leeuw, 1985), correspondence analysis is used complementary to log-linear analysis. After removing various effects from the longitudinal data (such as the effect of the marginal distribution – see also Section 6.2), correspondence analysis is performed on the residuals, and any remaining relations in these interpreted.

All in all, the optimal scaling techniques presented here are essentially exploratory techniques useful for generating rather than testing hypotheses. They are relatively untroubled by technical problems due to dropout and attrition common in longitudinal research. They provide a flexible and conceptually attractive framework for investigating a variety of exploratory research questions of a longitudinal nature, incorporating categorical variables of mixed measurement level.

2.8   Further reading

More on optimal scaling and the application of optimal scaling techniques can be found in, amongst others, Gifi (1990), De Leeuw (1983, 1989), Van de Geer (1993), Greenacre (1984, 1993), Nishisato (1994).

Hands-on introductions to the various cross-sectional techniques are given in SPSS (1990).

Theory and applications of the longitudinal extensions to these techniques can be found in Van der Heijden (1987), Ouweneel & Bijleveld (1989), Van Buuren (1990, 1997b), Bijleveld & Monkkonen (1991), Bijleveld (1993), Timman & Bijleveld (1996), Olmstead (1996) and Bijleveld & Bijleveld (1997).

Chapter 3

Univariate and multivariate analysis of variance of longitudinal data

Willem A. van der Kloot

3.1   Introduction

In the first chapter it was shown that longitudinal data can be analysed by means of a multitude of different statistical and data-analytical methods. One family of such methods consists of univariate and multivariate analysis of variance (ANOVA and MANOVA for short) and of their extensions that are obtained by including covariates in the analysis. In this chapter, a variety of these methods will be described. It will be shown that the same set of data can be analysed in several ways and we will point out the differences and similarities between the alternative approaches.

As the (M)ANOVA family belongs to an even wider class of models, namely the general linear model, many relationships exist between the (M)ANOVA techniques of this chapter and the models and methods treated in the other chapters of this book. At the end of this chapter we will turn to some of these relationships. We will start, however, by giving a classification of the types of longitudinal data to be treated here.

3.1.1   Types of longitudinal designs

Longitudinal designs consist of *one or more groups* of 'objects' that are measured on *one or more variables* on *two or more waves*. In the simplest longitudinal design there is *one group* of N objects that are measured on *one variable* on *two waves*. The word 'objects' may refer to any kind of observation units: for example, persons, groups, animals, plants, or factory products. In the social and behavioural sciences such objects are usually persons, who traditionally are called 'subjects'. Therefore, from this point on we will use the term subjects, on the understanding that there are many examples of longitudinal data in which the role of the subject is taken by something other than a human individual. Subjects may belong to different groups, either because they are members of intact groups (such as the classes of a school), or because they belong to different categories of one or more block or background variables (such as sex, age, intelligence), or because they were randomly assigned to the levels of one or more experimental conditions or treatment factors. Such factors or variables constitute one or more *independent variables* that vary between the subjects.

   In the general longitudinal design, variation among the subjects, the so-called *between-subject* variation, is composed of two types of effects: the *between-groups* and the *within-groups* (or rather: the *subjects-within-groups*) variation. In addition to these two sources of variance, there is variation *within* each subject between his or her scores on the different waves. The term 'wave' refers to a particular occasion or particular 'point in time' at which the subjects are measured or observed. Different waves thus differ at least with regard to their location in time: each particular wave always comes before or after another wave. In addition to mere difference in time, waves may differ with regard to the (experimental) conditions under which the measurements were obtained. For instance, they may be classified into measurements taken before or after some sort of intervention that occurred between two successive occasions. From this point of view, the different waves thus constitute the levels of *one or more* independent variables that vary *within* the subjects.

   The measurements that are obtained on the different waves are called *repeated measures*. In fact, this term is used for three basic forms of design: (a) designs in which each unit is observed under several treatment *conditions*, (b) designs in which each unit is observed on two or more points in *time*, and (c) designs in which each unit or subject is measured on several *variables* or tests. The data obtained in this third form of design are often called *profile data* and their analysis is referred to as *profile analysis*.

In the less complex longitudinal designs, measurements are obtained on only one dependent variable, that is, the same variable on each wave. However, even though the data actually consist of measures on one and the same variable on all occasions (that is Variable Y at Time 1 through Time T), they can also be regarded *as if* they consist of measures on T separate variables (that is Variable Y_1 through Variable Y_T). This difference of interpretation marks a transition from univariate to multivariate analysis. In this chapter, both approaches will be treated in detail.

Examples of dependent variables are length, weight, performance score, attitude, reaction time, number of trials before reaching a correct answer, etc. Such dependent variables will be denoted by the symbol Y. The actual measurements can be written either as a column vector **y** with NT elements or as a matrix **Y** with NT cells. The choice between these notations depends on the particular type of analysis (univariate or multivariate) one has in mind. In the present chapter we will assume that all dependent variables are measured at the interval level. The longitudinal analysis of categorical (dependent) variables is treated in Chapters 2 and 6. In the context of the present chapter only independent variables can be categorical (i.e. ordinal or nominal).

Complex longitudinal designs Obviously, the simplest longitudinal design can be expanded, in three ways: by increasing (a) the number of waves, (b) the number of groups, and (c) the number of dependent variables measured on every occasion. In its most general form, a complex longitudinal design thus consists of G groups of $N_g(g = 1, \ldots, G)$ subjects each, which are measured on T occasions on M variables. As was mentioned before, the *occasions* may just be different points in time, or they may correspond to different levels of one or more within-subjects independent variables. The same holds for the *groups* of subjects in the design. These groups may consist of subjects randomly assigned to the conditions formed by the levels of one or more *between-subjects* variables. On the other hand, these groups may consist of intact groups such as the classes of a school, families in an apartment building, and so on. Or they may consist of members who belong to the same categories of one or more background variables, for instance, sex, socio-economic status, age, and intelligence[1].

The third way in which the simplest longitudinal design can be extended concerns the number of dependent *variables*. In that case we have a multivariate design with several dependent variables on which the subjects are repeatedly measured. Such a design is known as a *doubly multivariate* design. Obviously, the analysis of multi-variable designs is – at least computationally – more complicated. In a multi-wave/multi-variable design there is sometimes the option of treating the measures on the dependent variables as one set of TM variables. Usually, it makes more sense to treat the observations as separate sets of M variables obtained at T occasions.

In Section 3.2 we will describe the univariate and multivariate treatment of the one-group/one-variable/two-waves design. We will present several alternative analysis methods for this design and will show their relationships. Next, in Sections 3.3 and 3.4 respectively, we will consider the multiple-group/one-variable/two-waves and the one-group/one-variable/multiple-waves designs. Subsequently, we will extend this design to the multiple-group/one-variable/multiple-wave case (Section 3.5). This is followed by a discussion of the multi-variable extensions of these designs (Section 3.6). As we proceed from the less complex to the more complex designs, we will increasingly use MANOVA as the most appropriate analysis technique[2]. Finally, in Section 3.7, we will sketch some of the relationships between the various (M)ANOVA approaches and two other methods: *multilevel analysis* and *structural equation modelling*. We will start, however, by looking into the types and forms of hypotheses one generally wants to test in longitudinal studies.

3.1.2 Hypothesis testing

In the multiple-group/one-variable/multiple-wave design, we can distinguish between two general types of variation: the *between-subjects* and the *within-subjects* variation. The first source can be further sub-

---

[1] In the context of experimental design, such variables that can not be controlled by the experimenter are often called 'nuisance' variables. They can be used to form 'blocks' of subjects who are homogeneous with regard to their values on the particular non-experimental variable.

[2] For the computational work involved in the examples of this chapter we used the SPSS/PC 4.0 package of statistical computer programs.

divided into *between-groups* and *subjects-within-groups* components. These sources correspond to the between and within effects of a design in which the data consist of the mean scores of the subjects, averaged over the waves. The second source can be broken down in a *between-waves* effect, a *groups × waves interaction* and a *subjects-within-groups × waves interaction* (see Kirk, 1995; Maxwell & Delaney, 1990; Winer, Brown, & Michels, 1991).

In these designs, three types of hypotheses are usually of interest. Those hypotheses concern the between-groups differences, the between-waves differences and the groups × waves interactions. Univariate and multivariate analysis of variance techniques can now be used to obtain the sums of squares, degrees of freedom and mean squares that are necessary to test these effects.

Contrasts   In the multiple-group/one-variable/multiple-wave case, the sums of squares of each effect can be broken down into several sums of squares that belong to particular *contrasts* or hypotheses about (sub)sets of population means. Each contrast may be evaluated individually, to answer questions like 'Is the mean of Group *g* significantly different from the mean of Group *q*?', 'Is the mean of Wave 2 different from the mean of Wave 1?' and 'Is the difference between Waves 2 and 1 in Group 1 equal to that difference in Group 2?'. Contrasts, thus, are linear combinations of means (and therefore linear combinations of the data) that correspond to a particular hypothesis about a set of population means. Methods for answering such questions are called 'procedures for multiple comparisons' (see Hays, 1988; Kirk, 1995; Winer et al., 1991).

Tests of individual contrasts can be planned before the data are collected – one speaks of planned or *a priori* comparisons – or they are performed after univariate or multivariate analysis of variance has shown that a particular source of variation is significant. In the latter case we speak of *a posteriori* or *post hoc* comparisons. Planned and post hoc comparisons differ with regard to the critical values that are used for deciding whether a contrast is statistically significant or not.

Contrasts or comparisons can be independent of each other (*orthogonal*) or can be correlated. If the contrasts are orthogonal, the sums of squares of the individual contrasts add up to the sum of squares of the overall effect to which they belong (for instance, between-groups, between-waves or groups × waves). Given a design with G groups, there are $G - 1$ orthogonal contrasts into which the overall group effect can be decomposed. Similarly, in a design with T waves, there are $T - 1$ orthogonal contrasts by which the Wave-effect can be dissected.

Note that there exist an infinite number of different *sets of orthogonal contrasts* that can be used to decompose the overall effect. Each set decomposes the overall sums of squares in a different way, but in all cases the individual contrast sums of squares add up to the overall sum of squares. Therefore, if one is only interested in the overall effect, it is completely arbitrary which set of independent contrasts is chosen. If, on the other hand, one wants to test specific hypotheses about specific means, one should define contrasts that correspond to those hypotheses.

What a particular (set of) contrast(s) looks like, depends on the way in which the observations are represented, that is, as a *vector* or as a *matrix*. When the data are collected in one vector, the analysis obviously is univariate. When the data are collected in a matrix, the analysis can be either univariate or multivariate.

3.1.3   Differences among waves

When all data of a multiple-group/one-variable/multiple-wave design are collected in a vector $\mathbf{y}$ with $\sum_g N_g T$ elements, we can test the null hypothesis that the population means μ_1 and μ_2 of two waves are equal by defining a contrast vector $\mathbf{c}$ (also with $\sum_g N_g T$ elements) in which all observations belonging to Wave 1 are assigned the value -1 and all observations of Wave 2 are assigned the value $+1$ (observations in other waves are assigned 0). The null hypothesis $H_0 : \mu_1 - \mu_2 = 0$ is equivalent to $H_0 : \psi = 0$ where $\psi = (-1)\mu_1 + (1)\mu_2$ and ψ is estimated by $\hat{\psi} = \mathbf{c}'\mathbf{y}$. Note that the actual contrast values or coefficients are to a large extent arbitrary; the only requirement is that they add up to zero. Therefore it is allowed to choose coefficients that not only sum to zero but also have a sum of squares that equals one. Such coefficients are convenient because the sum of squares necessary for testing the null hypotheses then simply becomes

$$SS_\psi = \frac{\mathbf{y}'\mathbf{c}\mathbf{c}'\mathbf{y}}{\sum_g N_g}$$

If there are T waves, it is possible to test many contrasts between the waves. Altogether, $T - 1$ independent contrasts can be defined, whose coefficients can be collected in a $(\sum_g N_g T) \times (T-1)$ matrix $\mathbf{C}$. If we choose the coefficients of each contrast such that they are uncorrelated with the coefficients of the other contrasts and if we make sure that their sums of squares equal unity, we have a set of *orthonormal* contrast vectors that code the between-waves component of the within-subjects differences. For instance, with three waves, the first null hypothesis could be $H_0 : \mu_1 = \mu_2$ and the second one could be $H_0 : \frac{1}{2}(\mu_1 + \mu_2) = \mu_3$. In that case, the first contrast vector would consist of the coefficients $-0.707, 0.707$ and 0.000, and the second vector would contain the values $-0.408, -0.408$ and 0.816 for, respectively, the first, the second, and the third waves. Thus, to each hypothesis $\psi = 0$ corresponds a separate SS_ψ and a separate contrast vector $\mathbf{c}$.

Differences among groups   Identical procedures can be followed to test the null hypothesis that the population mean of Group 1 is the same as that of Group 2. To do so, we have to construct a contrast vector in which all observations in Group 1 are assigned, for example, the value $+0.707$ and all observations in Group 2 the value -0.0707. If there are G groups, it is possible to define $G-1$ independent contrasts for the groups, which can be added as extra columns to the matrix $\mathbf{C}$. The latter columns of $\mathbf{C}$ contain dummy-variables that code the between-group differences among the observations. The sums of squares necessary for testing the between-groups differences[3] then are

$$SS_\psi = \frac{\mathbf{y}'\mathbf{cc}'\mathbf{y}}{N_g \times T} \ .$$

If there are many groups, one can test several ψ-hypotheses each of which yields a separate SS_ψ-value which corresponds to the particular contrast vector $\mathbf{c}$.

Interactions between groups and waves   The matrix $\mathbf{C}$ can be further extended by adding $(T-1)(G-1)$ columns that correspond to the *group*

---

[3]The contrast coefficients for the between-groups effects presented here assume that the numbers of subjects in each group are equal. If the numbers of subjects in each group are different, the presented coefficients are no longer orthonormal and their respective sums of squares do not add up any more to the $SS_{\text{between groups}}$. Hays (1988) describes procedures for constructing orthonormal contrasts that are appropriate when the numbers of observations in different groups are not identical.

$\times$ *waves interaction.* These columns are obtained by multiplying each element of a particular between-groups contrast vector with the corresponding element of a given between-waves contrast vector. The sums of squares for testing the interaction effects then become

$$SS_\psi = \frac{\mathbf{y'cc'y}}{N_g}$$

where $\mathbf{c}$ is the corresponding contrast vector[4].

Example   We will demonstrate the above theory by means of an example consisting of the three-group/one-variable/three-wave design of Table 3.1 in which three groups of two subjects are measured on three occasions. Such a design can be labelled a *two-factor experiment with repeated measures on one factor*, a *Split Plot Factorial SPF 3.3 Design* (e.g. Kirk, 1995) or a *Two-factor Between-Within Design* (Keppel, 1982). For this design we can construct the eight contrast vectors that were introduced above (see Table 3.1). The first two vectors 'explain' the between-waves differences, the third and fourth vectors do so for the between-groups effect, and the last four vectors model the wave $\times$ group interaction. That this is true can be checked in Table 3.2, which contains the usual SPF-ANOVA results and the corresponding contrast sums of squares. The F-tests displayed in this table are valid only if the data meet certain assumptions, in particular the assumption of *sphericity*. These assumptions will be discussed later, after we have outlined the multivariate approach to these kinds of designs.

3.1.4   Multivariate approaches

In the matrix approach to the multiple-group/one-variable/multiple-waves case, the measurements of $\sum_g N_g$ subjects on T different waves are represented in the $\sum_g N_g \times T$ matrix $\mathbf{Y}$. The rows of this matrix correspond to different subjects in different groups, whereas the columns of $\mathbf{Y}$ correspond to the multiple measurements of each subject. Given this setup, one possibility is to perform separate univariate ANOVAs on each of the T variables. However, such an approach has three obvious disadvantages. Firstly, one would be performing T times as many

---

[4]The situation changes if the number of subjects in each group is different. See Note 3.

Table 3.1: *Example of Split Plot Design with Data Vector **y** and column **c**₁ through **c**₈ of the Matrix **C** of Contrast Vectors*

S^* G^* W^*	Y	c_1	c_2	c_3	c_4	$c_5 =$ $c_1 \cdot c_3$	$c_6 =$ $c_1 \cdot c_4$	$c_7 =$ $c_2 \cdot c_3$	$c_8 =$ $c_2 \cdot c_4$
1 1 1	1	−0.707	−0.408	0.707	0.408	−0.500	−0.289	−0.289	−0.167
1 1 2	3	0.707	−0.408	0.707	0.408	0.500	0.289	−0.289	−0.167
1 1 3	1	0.000	0.816	0.707	0.408	0.000	0.000	0.577	0.334
2 1 1	2	−0.707	−0.408	0.707	0.408	−0.500	−0.289	−0.289	−0.167
2 1 2	1	0.707	−0.408	0.707	0.408	0.500	0.289	−0.289	−0.167
2 1 3	4	0.000	0.816	0.707	0.408	0.000	0.000	0.577	0.334
3 2 1	2	−0.707	−0.408	−0.707	0.408	0.500	−0.289	0.289	−0.167
3 2 2	3	0.707	−0.408	−0.707	0.408	−0.500	0.289	0.289	−0.167
3 2 3	3	0.000	0.816	−0.707	0.408	0.000	0.000	−0.577	0.334
4 2 1	4	−0.707	−0.408	−0.707	0.408	0.500	−0.289	0.289	−0.167
4 2 2	4	0.707	−0.408	−0.707	0.408	−0.500	0.289	0.289	−0.167
4 2 3	2	0.000	0.816	−0.707	0.408	0.000	0.000	−0.577	0.334
5 3 1	1	−0.707	−0.408	0.000	−0.816	0.000	0.577	0.000	0.334
5 3 2	5	0.707	−0.408	0.000	−0.816	0.000	−0.577	0.000	0.344
5 3 3	3	0.000	0.816	0.000	−0.816	0.000	0.000	0.000	−0.667
6 3 1	1	−0.707	−0.408	0.000	−0.816	0.000	0.577	0.000	0.334
6 3 2	3	0.707	−0.408	0.000	−0.816	0.000	−0.577	0.000	0.344
6 3 3	5	0.000	0.816	0.000	−0.816	0.000	0.000	0.000	−0.667
Sum	48	0.000	0.000	0.000	0.000	0.000	0.000	0.000	0.000
SSQ	32.0	6.000	6.000	6.000	6.000	2.000	2.000	2.000	2.000
$c'y$		5.657	2.448	−4.248	−2.448	0.000	−2.885	1.731	−1.998
$y'cc'y$		32.000	6.000	18.000	6.000	0.000	8.323	2.996	3.990

* S=Subject; G=Group; W=Wave; '·'=elementwise product.

statistical test, which would inflate the usual level of significance to values larger than $\alpha = 0.05$. Secondly, since the different variables may be (and usually are) strongly correlated with each other, one would not know which of the ANOVA results give new and independent information about our hypotheses and which ANOVAs are redundant with one or more of the other analyses. Thirdly, performing T univariate tests with a more critical significance level (for instance, $\alpha = 0.05/T$) would reduce the *power* of our procedures. It is precisely these three problems that are avoided by either performing a univariate split-plot-factorial analysis (as above) or by using one of the multivariate approaches that are outlined below.

The usual approach in a multivariate analysis of several groups and several variables, is to simultaneously test the null hypothesis that the

Table 3.2: *Analysis of Variance of the Data of Table 3.1*

	Source	SS	df	MS	F	
1	Between subjects	5.333	$\sum_g N_g - 1 = 5$			
2	Groups	4.000	$G - 1 = 2$	2.000	[2/5]	4.500
3	Contrast 3	18.0/6 = 3.000	1	3.000	[3/5]	6.750
4	Contrast 4	6.0/6 = 1.000	1	1.000	[4/5]	2.250
5	Subjects-within-groups	1.333	$\sum_g(N_g - 1) = 3$	0.444		
6	Within subjects		$\sum_g N_g(T - 1) = 12$			
7	Waves	6.333	$T - 1 = 2$	3.167	[7/15]	3.000
8	Contrast 1	32.0/6 = 5.333	1	5.333	[8/15]	2.526
9	Contrast 2	6.0/6 = 1.000	1	1.000	[9/15]	0.474
10	Waves × Groups	7.665	$(G-1)(T-1) = 4$		[10/15]	0.908
11	Contrast 5	0.0/2 = 0.000	1	0.000	[11/15]	0.000
12	Contrast 6	8.323/2 = 4.162	1	4.162	[12/15]	1.971
13	Contrast 7	2.996/2 = 1.498	1	1.498	[13/15]	0.710
14	Contrast 8	3.990/2 = 1.995	1	1.995	[14/15]	0.945
15	Subjects-within-groups × Waves	12.667	$\sum_g(N_g-1)\times (T-1) = 6$	2.111		
16	Total	32.00	$(\sum_g N_g T) - 1 = 17$			

vector of means of each Group g comes from one and the same population as the vector of means of the other groups. For G groups this null hypothesis is

$$H_0 : \mu_{1X}, \mu_{1Y}, \ldots, \mu_{1Z} = \cdots = \mu_{gX}, \mu_{gY}, \ldots, \mu_{gZ}$$
$$= \cdots = \mu_{GX}, \mu_{GY}, \ldots, \mu_{GZ}$$

for the variables $\{X, Y, \ldots, Z\}$.

A second null hypothesis, which usually is of less interest, is, $H_0 :$ $\mu_X, \mu_Y, \ldots, \mu_Z = \{0, 0, \ldots, 0\}$. These two hypotheses concern what is called the group effect and the constant, respectively. Both hypotheses can be tested by a variety of statistics that are routinely printed by most computer programs for multivariate analysis of variance (MANOVA). Of these test statistics, Wilks's Λ is most widely recommended. Wilks's Λ has a corresponding F-value with degrees of freedom that are a function of G, T and N (see for instance Stevens, 1996).

If it is found that one or both of the null hypotheses should be rejected, then one usually tries to interpret the results by looking at the univariate ANOVAs of the separate variables. Although the level of significance is not inflated in this case (one uses the multivariate test of significance at a preset α for deciding whether there are any differences at all among the means), there is still the second problem of possibly redundant interpretations[5]. Moreover, this approach does not test differences between the T variables (that is, the waves) themselves, neither among their overall means, nor among their means in the separate groups. Below, we will outline a procedure that enables us to simultaneously test for group effects and differences among the waves.

3.1.5   Linear transformations of repeated measures

If the group effect H_0 is true, then it also holds that for all linear combinations of the variables the means in one particular Group g are equal to the corresponding means of all the other groups. Therefore, the H_0 for group effects can also be tested on a set of several 'new' variables which are independent linear combinations of the T original measurements (the columns of **Y**). Obviously, one can perform univariate ANOVAs on each of these linear combinations or one can submit the transformed variables to one overall MANOVA. In the case of two columns (e.g. waves) we can form two independent (or orthogonal) linear combinations **Yh**$_1$ and **Yh**$_2$. The actual coefficients of the linear combinations may be chosen *a priori* in such a way that they correspond to some hypotheses that are of interest. For instance, in the case of one variable measured on two waves it is reasonable to form the first linear combination by adding the two measurements of each subject, and the second combination by subtracting the first measurement from the second one. One possible analysis now consists of performing separate univariate ANOVAs on the independent transformations. In that case we have reduced the multivariate problem to several (here: two) independent univariate problems.

Now let us assume that there are T instead of two waves. Then we can construct T independent linear combinations of the data. The first one consists of the sum per subject of the T variables, the second to T-th combinations are functions of the differences among the T variables (see below). In doing so, we have decomposed the T-variable prob-

---

[5] A much better procedure for interpreting significant MANOVA results is discriminant analysis. Such an analysis looks for sets of uncorrelated linear combinations of the variables that are responsible for the differences between the groups (see for instance Stevens, 1996).

lem into two independent problems that can be solved by one univariate ANOVA of the sumscores and one multivariate MANOVA of the $T-1$ difference score variables. If these latter variables are independent, one can finally interpret the MANOVA solution by inspecting the univariate effects of each combination variable. This approach, one MANOVA on the sumscores and a MANOVA on $T-1$ transformed variables (instead of the T original variables), is known as *multivariate analysis of repeated measures* (see O'Brien & Kaiser, 1985).

3.1.6   Structured multivariate analysis of repeated measures

It should be noted that apart from the sumscores, there exists an infinite number of sets containing $T-1$ independent linear transformations. Therefore one should choose these transformations in such a way that they highlight the particular aspects of the data that one is interested in. For instance, with three wave data, one could choose transformation coefficients $\{-0.408, -0.408, 0.816\}$ in order to study differences between the third wave on the one hand and the first and second waves on the other hand. If the $T-1$ transformed variables are constructed in such a manner that they carry information that is of substantial interest, and if they are independent of each other (uncorrelated, orthogonal), it makes sense to just perform $T-1$ separate univariate ANOVAs instead of one overall MANOVA. Hand & Taylor (1987) call this the *structured multivariate approach*, in contrast to the *multiple univariate approach* (that consists of separate ANOVAs of each original variable) and a truly or *intrinsically multivariate analysis*, that is, MANOVA on the T original or the $T-1$ transformed variables.

In the structured multivariate approach, the particular combinations of the variables are either specified explicitly by the researcher or implicitly by a particular computer program. When there are many waves, there are many vectors $\mathbf{h}$ that can be constructed to test for effects of the between-subjects independent variables or *factors*. Altogether, T such independent vectors $\mathbf{h}$ can be constructed. They can be collected in a matrix $\mathbf{H}$ with T columns, of which the first column consists of elements which all have the same value.

With the exception of the first one, the linear transformations of the variables correspond to differences between the waves. Group differences on these transformed variables, therefore, demonstrate that a particular wave difference in Group g may not be equal to the corresponding difference in Group q. Differences between groups thus correspond to *interaction effects* between the within-subject factors Waves and the between-subjects factors Groups. The between-group differences (i.e. the wave $\times$ group interactions) can be studied in detail by constructing a matrix of contrast variables $\mathbf{C}$ with $\sum_g N_g$ rows and $G - 1$ columns. The columns of an $\mathbf{H}$-matrix may be chosen in an – in principle – infinite number of ways. The choices have consequences for the interpretation of the effects. Some computer programs (for example SPSS) use certain default contrasts on *transformation* vectors that are only printed if requested by the user. An example of $\mathbf{H}$ and $\mathbf{C}$ for the three-groups/one-variable/three-waves data of Table 3.1, written as a matrix $\mathbf{Y}$, is given in Table 3.3. The univariate and multivariate analyses of these data are presented in Table 3.4.

Table 3.3: *Example of Split Plot Design with Data Matrix $\mathbf{Y}$ and Matrices $\mathbf{H}$ and $\mathbf{C}$ of Contrast Vectors*

Subject	Group	y_1	y_2	y_3	h_1	h_2	h_3	c_1	c_2
1	1	1	3	1	0.577	−0.707	−0.408	0.707	0.408
2	1	2	1	4	0.577	0.707	−0.408	0.707	0.408
3	2	2	3	3	0.577	0.000	0.816	−0.707	0.408
4	2	4	4	2				−0.707	0.408
5	3	1	5	3				0.000	−0.816
6	3	1	3	5				0.000	−0.816

3.1.7 Trend analysis

If there are more than two waves, another kind of structured multivariate analysis consists of performing a *trend analysis* in order to investigate whether the population wave means are ordered as a linear, quadratic, cubic or higher order function of time. If there are three or more groups that differ in terms of a quantitative independent variable (for instance, stimulus intensity, drug dosage, exposure time) one can do similar trend analyses of the group effects. That is, one can study the form of the function that relates the population group means to the quantitative variable.

Table 3.4: *ANOVAs and MANOVA of the Transformed Data of Table 3.3*

	Source	SS	df	MS	F	
Transformed variable **Yh$_1$**:						
1	Total	5.333	$\sum_g N_g - 1 = 5$			
2	Groups	4.000	$G - 1 = 2$	2.000	[2/5]	4.500
3	Contrast **c**$_1$	6.0/2 = 3.000	1	3.000	[3/5]	6.750
4	Contrast **c**$_2$	2.0/2 = 1.000	1	1.000	[4/5]	2.250
5	Within groups (residual)	1.333	$\sum_g (N_g - 1) = 3$	0.444		
6	Constant	128.000	1			
Transformed variable **Yh$_2$**:						
7	Total	7.667	$\sum_g N_g - 1 = 5$			
8	Groups	4.167	$G - 1 = 2$	2.083	[7/11]	1.786
9	Contrast **c**$_1$	0.0/2 = 0.0	1	0.0	[8/11]	0.0
10	Contrast **c**$_2$	8.333/2 = 4.167	1	4.167	[9/11]	3.571
11	Within groups (residual)	3.500	$\sum_g (N_g - 1) = 3$	1.167		
12	Constant	5.333	1			
Transformed variable **Yh$_3$**:						
13	Total	12.667	$\sum_g N_g - 1 = 5$			
14	Groups	3.500	$G - 1 = 2$	2.000	[14/17]	1.750
15	Contrast **c**$_1$	3.000/2 = 1.500	1	1.500	[15/17]	0.491
16	Contrast **c**$_2$	4.000/2 = 2.000	1	2.000	[16/17]	0.655
17	Within groups (residual)	9.167	$\sum_g (N_g - 1) = 3$	3.056		
17	Constant	1.000	1			

MANOVA
Test involving 'Wave' Within-Subject Effect:
Group by Wave: Wilks' $\Lambda = 0.164$; $F = 1.466$; $df = 4,4$; $p = 0.360$
Wave: Wilks' $\Lambda = 0.181$; $F = 4.511$; $df = 2,2$; $p = 0.181$.

Both types of trend analysis are performed by constructing matrices of coefficients **H** and/or **C** that specify sets of *orthogonal polynomials* (see Hays, 1988, p. 944). If there are T waves, the maximum number of orthogonal polynomials is $T - 1$ plus a constant, which means that the highest degree of the polynomial function is also $T - 1$. For G groups there are $G - 1$ orthogonal polynomials plus a constant. The group $\times$ waves interaction can then be described in terms of $(G-1)(T-1)$ polynomials.

3.1.8 Relationships between univariate and structured multivariate analysis

At this stage it is important to point to the relationships between a univariate SPF ANOVA (as in Table 3.2) and the separate ANOVAs of the linear combinations **Yh** (as in Table 3.4). Each of the latter ANOVAs yields a set of sum of squares for which the following relations hold.

1. If $\mathbf{h}_1$ is the column of which all elements are equal, then the ANOVA of $\mathbf{Yh}_1$ yields an SS_{total}, an $SS_{\text{between groups}}$, and an $SS_{\text{within groups}}$ (or SS_{residual}) which are, respectively, identical to the $SS_{\text{between subjects}}$, the SS_{groups}, and the $SS_{\text{subjects within groups}}$ sums of squares of the SPF analysis. The ANOVA of $\mathbf{Yh}_1$ thus is identical to the between-subject part of the SPF ANOVA.

2. The transformed variables $\mathbf{Yh}_2$ through $\mathbf{Yh}_T$ are linear combinations of the waves that completely describe the between-waves, that is, the within-subjects differences. Therefore, the $SS_{\text{between groups}}$ terms of the separate ANOVAs of $\mathbf{Yh}_2$ through $\mathbf{Yh}_T$ add up to the $SS_{\text{groups} \times \text{waves}}$ interaction of the SPF analysis. Similarly, the $SS_{\text{within-groups}}$ of $\mathbf{Yh}_2$ through $\mathbf{Yh}_T$ add up to the $SS_{\text{subj.w.groups} \times \text{waves}}$ of SPF, and their terms for SS_{total} add up to the SPF $SS_{\text{within subjects}}$. Analogous relationships hold for the separate contrasts that describe the between-groups differences.

3. The SS_{waves} of the SPF analysis is equal to the sum of the SS_{constant} sums of squares of the $T - 1$ linear combinations $\mathbf{Yh}_2$ through $\mathbf{Yh}_T$, where

$$SS_{\text{constant } \mathbf{Yh}_t} = \frac{\sum_{i=1}^{N} (\mathbf{Yh}_t)_i^2}{N}$$

4. These relationships do not only hold for the sums of squares, but also apply to the corresponding degrees of freedom.

Even though the above relationships are always true *numerically* (they rest on a mathematical equivalence), it does not always make sense *statistically* to add the sums of squares of the separate analyses of $\mathbf{Yh}_2$ through $\mathbf{Yh}_T$ and perform one overall F-test using one composite error term as is done in an SPF-ANOVA of repeated measures (in some computer programs, such as SPSS MANOVA, these F-tests are referred to as *average tests of significance*). To do so would only be warranted if the following requirements are met: (a) the linear combinations $\mathbf{Yh}_2$ through $\mathbf{Yh}_T$ and their corresponding sums of squares should be statistically independent of each other, and (b) the (population) error variances of the $\mathbf{Yh}_2$ through $\mathbf{Yh}_T$ should be equal. If we take care that the **h**-coefficients are orthogonal (as in our examples so far), the first requirement is no longer a problem. What remains, however, is the second requirement, which in fact, is one of the basic assumptions of ANOVA of Split Plot and *Randomized Blocks Factorial* (RBF) designs. As we can see in Table 3.4, the residual sums of squares of $\mathbf{Yh}_2$ and $\mathbf{Yh}_3$ are far from equal (respectively 3.500 and 9.167). Therefore, it is not advisable to *pool* these sums of squares and compute one common error term for simultaneously testing the group effects on $\mathbf{Yh}_2$ and $\mathbf{Yh}_3$. In the following section we will turn to these assumptions, and we will describe some approaches that can be followed when the assumptions do not seem tenable.

3.1.9   Assumptions in univariate ANOVA of repeated measures

In the univariate ANOVA of the multiple-group/one-variable/multiple-waves design (see Section 3.1.3), the data are analysed as a *Split Plot Factorial* (SPF) design, which is usually conceived as a *mixed model* or *model III* design. In such an analysis, the subjects are regarded as a random factor and the waves and groups as fixed factors. In order that the statistical tests be valid, the data must satisfy a certain number of assumptions (see Stevens, 1996). First of all, the observations of the different subjects should be independent of each other. Secondly, in each group, the scores on the different waves or variables should come from a multivariate normal distribution. Thirdly, the variance–covariance (VCV) matrices of the measurements of each group should be equal to each other (this is the so-called *homogeneity assumption*). Finally, the within-group VCV-matrix should satisfy the so-called *circularity* or *sphericity assumptions*. These assumptions concern the particular *structure* of the respective VCV matrices; they will be discussed in more detail below.

In any practical application of SPF ANOVA one should check whether all assumptions are tenable. The best strategy to do so would be as follows (Stevens, 1996). First, one should ascertain the independence of the observations. Secondly, one should inspect the data for deviations from multivariate normality. If multivariate normality need not be rejected, one should test for homogeneity of the different VCV-matrices. If this assumption is not tenable, one should try and find a remedy for this situation (see the next paragraph). If, on the other hand, the homogeneity requirement is fulfilled, one is allowed to *aggregate* the separate VCV-matrices into one *pooled* VCV-matrix. Finally, this matrix should then be tested for sphericity.

The homogeneity assumption Lack of homogeneity of the within-group VCV-matrices may result in distortions of the actual significance level as compared with the nominal level α and may have consequences for the *power* of the statistical tests performed. There are various methods for testing the assumption of homogeneous within-groups VCV matrices[6]. One of those is a χ^2-statistic developed by Box (1950), which is described, for instance, in Morrison (1990), Stevens (1996), Timm (1975), or Winer et al. (1991). As the Box-procedure is very sensitive to deviations from multivariate normality of the measurements, Stevens (1996) recommends to first establish whether the variables within each group have multivariate normal distributions. If not, some variables could be transformed or discarded in order to secure multivariate normality. Only then should one use the Box test for assessing homogeneity.

If homogeneity of the VCVs does not hold, there is no simple solution. However, the following comments may be relevant.

1. The statistical test rejecting the hypothesis of equal VCVs may have been too sensitive (due to a large number of observations).

2. If the number of subjects in each group is approximately equal, unequal VCVs have only very small effects on the probability of making Type I errors but do somewhat decrease the power of the test procedure (Stevens, 1996). If the numbers of subjects in the different groups are markedly different (that is, $N_{largest}/N_{smallest} > 1.5$), then the (multivariate) significance tests will either be too

---

[6]Actually, it is not necessary that the within-group VCVs be homogeneous; it is sufficient that the products $\mathbf{H}'\Sigma_g\mathbf{H}$ are equal for all groups ($g = 1, \ldots, G$). A test for this condition developed by Box is given by Kirk (1981, p. 500)

liberal (largest VCV in smallest group) or too conservative (largest VCV in largest group) (Stevens, 1996).

3. One might look for a substantive interpretation of the unequal VCVs and act accordingly, for instance by transforming or eliminating certain variables or by discarding one of the experimental groups (i.e. the group responsible for a significant Box test).

Compound symmetry, circularity and sphericity   In order that the overall F-tests on the wave or within-subject effects be *unbiased*, it was originally assumed that the measurements of the different waves should meet the requirement of *compound symmetry* (Hays, 1988; Stevens, 1990, 1992; Winer et al., 1991). This requirement entails, first of all, that the variances on the diagonal of the (pooled) VCV-matrix should be equal, and secondly, that the covariances between any two waves should also be equal. Compound symmetry implies that the covariances of the waves can be explained completely by the between-subjects differences. That is, if the between-subjects differences are partialled out, the covariance between any two waves is zero, and the residual variances of the waves are all equal to the error variance. Lack of compound symmetry results in positive bias of the F-tests of within-subject effects, that is, the actual significance level is higher than the nominal level set at α.

An implication of compound symmetry is that the variance $\sigma^2_{(y_u - y_w)}$ of the differences between any two waves u and v is equal to a constant. That this is true can be seen from

$$\sigma^2_{(y_u - y_w)} = \sigma^2_{(y_u)} + \sigma^2_{(y_w)} - 2\sigma_{(y_u, y_w)} = \sigma^2_y + \sigma^2_y - 2\sigma^2_y \rho_{yy} = c, \quad (3.1)$$

where ρ_{yy} is the constant correlation between any two waves y_u and y_w. Any VCV matrix that satisfies the condition $\sigma^2_{(y_u - y_w)} = c$, is said to meet the so-called *circularity requirement* (see Winer et al., 1991). Note that compound symmetry is a sufficient but not a necessary condition for circularity because there exist VCV matrices without compound symmetry yet for which $\sigma^2_{(y_u - y_w)} = c$. Therefore, circularity is a less severe requirement of a VCV matrix than compound symmetry. Circularity only assumes equality of the variances of difference scores, and as ANOVA is concerned with testing *differences* between waves, it is sufficient that the measurements of the waves meet this circularity requirement.

However, the circularity requirement can be relaxed even further. In general, we are testing *linear contrasts* of the waves, not just simple differences. Therefore, instead of assuming circularity it suffices to require a more general condition of which circularity is a special case: *sphericity*. A general formulation of the sphericity condition is

$$\mathbf{H}'\Sigma_Y\mathbf{H} = \lambda\mathbf{I} \tag{3.2}$$

where $\mathbf{H}$ is a $T(T-1)$ matrix of orthonormal vectors that define contrasts among the variables. In all columns of $\mathbf{H}$ the elements sum to zero, have unit sums of squares, and have cross products that equal zero. Σ_Y is the population VCV of the variables (i.e. the waves). The symbol λ denotes a constant, and $\mathbf{I}$ is the identity matrix. If the sphericity condition is satisfied, this means that the population variances of all contrast vectors $\mathbf{Yh}_2$ through $\mathbf{Yh}_T$ have the same within-groups variance. In that case, these within-groups variances may be pooled in order to obtain one common estimate of the within-group variance against which all between-groups effects can be tested. This is exactly what is done in an SPF-ANOVA of repeated measures data.

A measure of the sphericity of a VCV matrix is the so-called ε parameter developed by Box (1954). If the sphericity condition is satisfied, the ε parameter equals 1; the lowest possible value of ε is $1/(T-1)$. Procedures for estimating ε for multiple group data were developed by Greenhouse and Geisser (Greenhouse & Geisser, 1959). Huyhn & Feldt (1976) developed a less conservative estimate of ε. As the latter estimate tends to overestimate ε, Stevens (1996) proposes to use the average of the Box–Greenhouse–Geisser and Huynh–Feldt estimates of ε.

A statistical test of the sphericity assumptions was proposed by Mauchly (1940). Another test of sphericity, based on work by Box and Bartlett, is presented in Bock (1975) and Timm (1975). These tests are routinely performed in the MANOVA programs of BMDP, SAS and SPSS. Tests for the more stringent requirement of compound symmetry are a χ^2-test developed by Box (1950), which is described in, for instance, Bock (1975), and the test of Rouanet & Lépine (1970) described in Crowder & Hand (1990). These tests are not included in the major statistical packages.

3.1.10 Practical recommendations

If the sphericity requirements are met, univariate SPF is a valid procedure that is more powerful for assessing within-subject effects, than,
for instance, MANOVA on the same data (Stevens, 1996; Kesselman,
Kesselman, & Lix, 1995). If, however, the sphericity requirements are
probably not satisfied[7] one can proceed in several different ways (see
for instance Kirk, 1995; Hays, 1988; Keppel, 1982; Winer et al., 1991).

1. One may perform an SPF ANOVA and use the most conservative
   criteria for deciding that a particular effect is significant. This
   approach consists of adapting the degrees of freedom of the F-
   test by multiplying them with the lowest possible value of ε, that
   is $\varepsilon = 1/(T-1)$. If the effect under consideration now turns out
   to be significant (that is, the null hypothesis of no effect can be
   rejected), we are certain that the actual probability of having made
   a Type I error is equal to or lower than the nominal significance
   level α. If the effect is not significant one can either stop (this
   is the conservative approach advocated by Greenhouse & Geisser
   (1959)) or one can proceed as described in (2) and (3) below.

2. One may perform an SPF ANOVA and use the criteria that would
   be appropriate if one were certain that the sphericity assumptions
   are not violated. If the effect under consideration is not significant
   (the null hypothesis of no effect can not be rejected), we are of
   course 100% certain that we have not made a Type I error. As
   we have used a larger region of rejection than might have been
   appropriate, we are also certain that our test – in principle – had
   more power than under the normal circumstances. If (some of)
   the null hypotheses have been rejected, however, one can proceed
   in one of the manners described below.

3. If the null hypothesis cannot be rejected when the criteria are (possibly too) conservative, but can be rejected when the criteria are

---

[7]As Kirk (1981, p. 259) notes, it is not recommended to routinely use a statistical test of the
sphericity or compound symmetry assumptions. Not rejecting the null-hypothesis of sphericity
or compound symmetry does not guarantee that the assumptions are actually true, because our
statistical testing procedures are biased against rejecting a null hypothesis. If one doubts that the
assumptions are tenable, one should proceed in one of the ways described above. According
to the (too pessimistic?) view of Hand & Taylor (1987, p. 56) there is usually not sufficient
justification that the sphericity or compound symmetry requirements are met.

(possibly too) lenient, one way to solve the problem is to compute optimal approximations of the criteria that are appropriate for the situation. One may do so by using the Box–Greenhouse–Geisser estimates of ε or the adapted version of Huyhn & Feldt (1976) and derive the corresponding degrees of freedom that are appropriate for an SPF ANOVA of the data at hand.

4. One may do 'nothing' and proceed as if the sphericity require-ments are irrelevant. As Keppel (1982) notes *"The justification for this seemingly irresponsible recommendation is the fact that the positive bias in actual research applications ... is probably of the order of 2 to 3 percent and that most experimenters will still pay close attention to an F that is significant at α equal to 0.06 to 0.08, which is about what may be the case if decision rules are based on an uncorrected F nominally set at α = 0.05."* (p. 470)

5. One may refrain from adding the sums of squares of the separate ANOVAs of **Yh** and just interpret the results of these analyses one by one. One has to bear in mind, however, that this increases the number of statistical tests performed and thus could inflate the ac-tual level of significance. Therefore, one might consider using the Bonferroni approach in which the nominal level of significance is set at $\alpha/(T - 1)$. A slightly less conservative test would be the procedure based on a studentized maximum modulus (see Max-well & Delaney, 1990). Another problem of the one by one anal-ysis of **Yh** is that the results are restricted to the **h**-transformations chosen by the researcher. Finding that none of the effects is sig-nificant, does not necessarily mean that there is no effect at all. In principle, there could still exist another linear transformation of the data that would show one or more significant effects. This possibility could be inspected by also performing a multivariate test on the $T - 1$ transformed variables.

6. Finally, one may directly perform a truly multivariate analysis of the T original or $T - 1$ transformed variables. In doing so one is certain that the Type I error rate is set at the nominal level of α. On the other hand, the same holds for the approach described in (3).

When the sphericity assumption is not satisfied, the differences be-tween the univariate tests in SPF ANOVA and the multivariate tests in MANOVA thus concern the power and the interpretability of the two approaches. Unfortunately, it appears that none of these procedures is always or even most of the times more powerful than the other (Stevens, 1996; Kesselman et al., 1995). Unless the number of subjects in each group is small in comparison with the number of waves or variables (for example if $N_g < T + 10$), in which case he would not advocate MANOVA at all, Stevens (1992) recommends that *"given an exploratory study,* both *the adjusted univariate and multivariate tests be routinely used because they may differ in the treatment effects they will discern. In such a study half the experimentwise level of significance may be set for each test. Thus, if we wish overall alpha to be 0.05, do each test at the 0.025 level of significance."* (p. 456)

Then, a null-hypothesis can be rejected if either of the two tests reaches significance (Kesselman et al., 1995). Tabachnik & Fidell (1989), however, tend to prefer the approach outlined in (5). They argue that *"the best solution is often to perform trend analysis (or some other set of single df contrasts) instead of either profile analysis or repeated-measures ANOVA if that makes conceptual sense within the context of the research design. Many longitudinal, follow-up, and other time-related studies lend themselves beautifully to interpretation in terms of trends. Because statistical tests of trends and other contrasts use single degrees of freedom ... there is no possibility of violation of homogeneity of covariance. Furthermore none of the assumptions of the multivariate approach are relevant."* (pp. 471–472)

3.2   One-group/one-variable/two-waves designs

An example of a one-group/one-variable/two-waves design is given in Table 3.5, which shows the scores of twelve subjects on one variable on two occasions. How can those data be analysed, particularly with regard to the question of change? In other words is there a difference between the population means of the two waves? Below, we will consider several methods for answering this question.

3.2.1   *t*-test for dependent samples

The simplest answer to the above question can be obtained by performing a *t*-test for two dependent samples (also called the *t*-test for matched or paired observations). If we denote the score of subject i on occasion t by Y_{it} we can compute the wave means $\bar{Y}_{.1}$ and $\bar{Y}_{.2}$, the within-wave variances S_1^2 and S_2^2 and the correlation r_{12} between the measures at the two occasions. The t-test for $H_0 : \mu_1 = \mu_2$ is given by

$$t = \frac{\bar{Y}_{.2} - \bar{Y}_{.1}}{\sqrt{\frac{1}{N}\left(S_1^2 + S_2^2 - 2S_1 S_2 r_{12}\right)}} \tag{3.3}$$

with $N - 1$ degrees of freedom. In the present example $t = 2.50/0.597 = 4.19$. This t-value can be evaluated in a two-tailed or in a one-tailed manner; the two-tailed probability associated with $t = 4.19$ equals $p = 0.002$. Therefore, we can conclude that a significant positive change has occurred from Wave 1 to Wave 2.

Table 3.5: *Example of a One-Group/One-Variable/Two-Waves Data Matrix*

Subjects	Wave 1 Y_{i1}	Wave 2 Y_{i2}	Sum $Y_{i1} + Y_{i2}$	Difference $Y_{i2} - Y_{i1}$	
1	1	1	2	0	
2	3	5	8	2	$\bar{Y}_{.1} = 2.50$
3	1	3	4	2	$\bar{Y}_{.2} = 5.00$
4	2	1	3	-1	
5	1	3	4	2	$S_{21} = 1.364$
6	4	5	9	1	$S_{22} = 7.274$
7	2	6	8	4	
8	3	4	7	1	$r_{12} = 0.693$
9	3	8	11	5	
10	4	8	12	4	$S_D^2 =$
11	4	9	13	5	$(122 - 900/12)/11 =$
12	2	7	9	5	4.273
Sum	30	60	90	30	

3.2.2 t-test using difference scores

A computationally more practical way of performing the above t-test consists of computing the difference scores $D_i = Y_{i2} - Y_{i1}$, their mean

$\bar{D}_. = \sum_i D_i/N$ and their estimated population standard deviation S_D. The t-test for paired observations then becomes

$$t = \frac{\bar{D}_.}{\sqrt{\frac{1}{N}S_D^2}}$$

with $N-1$ degrees of freedom. In this example $t = 2.50/(4.273/12)^{\frac{1}{2}} = 4.19$. Thus, as always with two dependent sets of measurements, the analysis of difference scores and the t-test for paired observations are completely identical.

3.2.3 ANOVA

A third method to analyse the data of Table 3.5 is by means of ANOVA. The data can be regarded as a Repeated Measures Design, also called a Randomized Blocks (RB 2) design (see Kirk, 1995) in which each subject corresponds to a block. The ANOVA decomposes the total sum of squares

$$SS_{\text{total}} = \sum_{i=1}^{N} \sum_{t=1}^{T} (Y_{it} - \bar{Y}_{..})^2$$

into a between-subjects sum of squares

$$SS_{\text{subjects}} = T \sum_{i=1}^{N} (\bar{Y}_{i.} - \bar{Y}_{..})^2$$

with $df = N-1$, a within-subjects sum of squares for the waves

$$SS_{\text{waves}} = N \sum_{t=1}^{T} (\bar{Y}_{.t} - \bar{Y}_{..})^2$$

with $df = T-1 = 1$, and a residual sum of squares ($SS_{\text{residual}} = SS_{\text{total}} - SS_{\text{subjects}} - SS_{\text{waves}}$) with $df = (T-1)(N-1)$. The waves effect is tested by means of

$$F = \frac{SS_{\text{waves}}/1}{SS_{\text{residual}}/(N-1)}.$$

The ANOVA-results for the present example are displayed in Table 3.6. In our example $F = 37.50/2.136 = 17.556$. This F-value has 1 and $N - 1$ degrees of freedom, and is numerically identical to the square of the t-values of the earlier analyses.

Table 3.6 also lists the F-value and its corresponding probability under the null hypothesis for the between-subjects effect. This F-test is only appropriate in the following two cases: (a) if the variance due to interaction between waves and subjects is zero, or (b) if the waves are a random factor. If neither of these conditions holds, the F-test for subjects printed above is negatively biased, that is, one will reject too few false null hypotheses. The reason is that $MS_{residual}$ is expected to contain a subjects $\times$ waves interaction component. If the waves are fixed, such a component is not expected in $MS_{subjects}$. If the subjects are a fixed factor as well, the F-test of the waves effect is also negatively biased (see for instance Kirk, 1995).

Table 3.6: *ANOVA of One-Group/One-Variable/Two-Waves Data as an RB-2 Design*

Source	SS	df	MS	F	p
Between subjects	71.50	11	6.500	3.043	0.039
Waves	37.50	1	37.500	17.556	0.002
Residual	23.50	11	2.136		
Total	132.50	23			

3.2.4 MANOVA

Identical results can be obtained by performing a structured MANOVA on the data of Table 3.5 in matrix form. A structured MANOVA amounts here to computing two linear combinations $\mathbf{Yh}_1$ and $\mathbf{Yh}_2$ with $\mathbf{h}'_1 = \{0.707, 0.707\}$ and $\mathbf{h}'_2 = \{0.707, -0.707\}$ and performing univariate ANOVAs on the resulting scores. Note that $\mathbf{h}_1$ amounts to summing per subject over the waves; the sum of squares of these scores is an estimate of the between-subjects effect. The contrast vector $\mathbf{h}_2$, on the other hand, computes the differences between the two waves for each subject. The $SS_{\text{within cells}}$ in the MANOVA of $\mathbf{Yh_1}$ equals the $SS_{\text{between subjects}}$ of the univariate ANOVA. The SS_{total} of the MANOVA of $\mathbf{Yh_2}$ equals $SS_{\text{within subjects}}$ which can be decomposed into $SS_{\text{subjects} \times \text{waves}}$ (also called $SS_{\text{within cells}}$) and SS_{waves}. The latter sum of squares is obtained by squaring the sum of $\mathbf{Yh_2}$ and dividing by N. This sum of squares could also be labelled SS_{constant}.

The advantage of using a standard MANOVA-computer program such as in SPSS or SAS, is that, generally, such programs give information about the tenability of the homogeneity and sphericity assumptions of the data. In the simple one-group/two-waves example, however, such information is not relevant.

3.2.5   Analysis of covariance

With regard to one-group/one-variable/two-waves data, the last method of analysis to be discussed here is an analysis of covariance (ANCOVA) in which the measurements of the first wave are used as the covariate by which we can adjust the values of the second wave. In this simple one-group/one-variable/two-waves case, we act *as if* we have only one measure of the dependent variable, and since we also have only one group of subjects there are no within-subjects or between-groups effects that can be adjusted. The only entities that can be adjusted here, are the between-subjects variation and the mean of the measures of Wave 2. Thus we could test whether the population mean of Wave 2 equals zero after correction for the Wave 1 measurements. This amounts to testing the null hypothesis that the intercept a of the regression equation $\hat{Y}_{i2} = a + bY_{i1}$ equals zero. From standard regression theory it follows that $\hat{a} = \bar{Y}_{.2} - \hat{b}\bar{Y}_{.1}$, whose standard error, denoted by σ_a, is estimated by

$$\hat{\sigma}_a = \left[\left(\frac{1}{N} + \frac{\sum_i^N Y_{i1}^2}{\sum_i^N (Y_{i1} - \bar{Y}_{.1})^2} \right) (MS_{\text{subjects-adjusted}}) \right]^{\frac{1}{2}} \qquad (3.4)$$

where $MS_{\text{subjects-adjusted}}$ is the residual mean square of the scores on Wave 2 after being regressed on those of Wave 1 (see Draper & Smith, 1981). The t-test for testing the null hypothesis that the adjusted population wave means are equal, is

$$t = \hat{a}/\hat{\sigma}_a. \qquad (3.5)$$

Table 3.7 displays the results of this test on the data of Table 3.5, and it is clear that the intercept does not differ significantly from zero. This finding is in contrast with our earlier results, in which we found evidence of a significant amount of change from Wave 1 to Wave 2. So where has all this change gone? What is the nature of this paradoxical situation, which is known as Lord's paradox? The answer is: partially in the regression coefficient b which in our example equals 1.60. This can be clarified as follows.

That the ANCOVA results differ from the results of the earlier analyses, stems from the fact that the RB ANOVA and the ANCOVA basically investigate two different aspects of change. The ANOVA approach simply tests whether the average change between the two waves is equal to zero. This is called an *unconditional inference problem* (Bock, 1975; see also Chapter 1). The ANCOVA approach, on the other hand, solves a *conditional inference problem*. It tests whether the average change is zero *after* the individual differences among the observations of the second wave have corrected for individual differences on the first wave. ANCOVA thus tests whether there is any change at all after we have made the scores on the second wave as similar as possible to those on the first wave. Thus RB ANOVA and ANCOVA test two different models of change. The change model implied in the ANOVA is $Y_{i2} = Y_{i1} + (\bar{Y}_{.2} - \bar{Y}_{.1})$, whereas that of the ANCOVA is $Y_{i2} = bY_{i1} + b(\bar{Y}_{.2} - \bar{Y}_{.1})$. In the ANCOVA b and $b(\bar{Y}_{.2} - \bar{Y}_{.1})$ are, respectively, the slope and intercept of the regression equation $\hat{Y}_{i2} = a + bY_{i1}$. If there were no change at all, we would expect that the scores of each subject on Wave 1 and Wave 2 would be identical within the margins of measurement error. Therefore we would expect a regression slope coefficient of approximately 1.00 *and* an intercept of approximately zero. However, if any change does occur, it could show itself in two ways: by means of a non-zero intercept (which shows the gain as an additive component to be added to all subjects' Wave 1 scores) and by means of a regression coefficient that differs from unity. This coefficient shows to what extent the changes of the subjects are a function of their Wave 1 scores, that is, to what extent subjects with lower scores on Wave 1 gain or lose less (depending on the sign of the regression coefficient!) than subjects with higher scores. In other words, the amount of change has been decomposed in two parts: a component that is constant for all subjects and a component that varies with the initial score of a particular subject. In the present example we see that subjects with higher Wave 1 scores gain more than subjects with lower scores.

The difference between ANCOVA and ANOVA thus is that in the latter case it is *a priori* assumed that *b* equals one. One could compare the two models by testing whether *b* is significantly different from 1.0, for instance, by comparing the residual sum of squares of the ANCOVA with the sum of squares of the difference scores.

Table 3.7: *ANCOVA via Regression Analysis of One-Group/One-Variable/ Two-Waves data*

Source	SS	df		MS	F	p
Regression	38.40	1		38.40	9.231	0.0125
Residual	41.60	10		4.16		
Slope:	1.60	standard error:		0.527	$t = 3.038$	$p = 0.0125$
Intercept:	1.00	standard error:		1.442	$t = 0.693$	$p = 0.504$

3.2.6   Comparison of approaches

The *t*-test for correlated groups, the *t*-test for difference scores, the RBF ANOVA and the MANOVA all give identical results. This is of course not a mere coincidence, but rests on the mathematical equivalence of the three procedures. Therefore, the use of difference scores for testing differences between the mean scores of two waves is a completely valid procedure. It should be noted, however, that there is a lot of controversy in the literature about the use of difference scores (see the discussion in Section 3.3.5, which mainly concerns the validity, reliability and other measurement characteristics of the *difference scores of individual subjects*; see for instance Cronbach & Furby, 1970; Huck & McLean, 1975). In this light (provided that the fundamental assumptions are satisfied), many authors prefer ANCOVA as the most suitable method of analysis. This would certainly be the case if the Wave 1 scores are so called *pretest* measures, which precede some experimental intervention whose effects are observed by the *posttest* measures of Wave 2. In that case the best approach would be to assess overall change in terms of the intercept of the regression equation that enables us to establish to what extent the posttest values can be predicted from the pretest scores. At the same time, extreme values of b would still be of substantive interest.

Table 3.8: *Example of a Two-Group/One-Variable/Two-Waves Data Matrix[a]*

Group	Subj.	Wave 1 Y_{i1}	Wave 2 Y_{i2}	Sum $Y_{i1} + Y_{i2}$	Difference $Y_{i2} - Y_{i1}$
1	1	1	1	2	0
1	2	3	5	8	2
1	3	1	3	4	2
1	4	2	1	3	-1
1	5	1	3	4	2
1	6	4	5	9	1
Group total		12	18	30	6
2	7	2	6	8	4
2	8	3	4	7	1
2	9	3	8	11	5
2	10	4	8	12	4
2	11	4	9	13	5
2	12	2	7	9	5
Group total		18	42	60	24
Sum		30	60	90	30

[a]Note that the actual data in this table are identical to those in Table 3.5

3.3 Multiple-groups/one-variable/two-waves designs

3.3.1 Repeated measures ANOVA

In the simplest case, the multiple-group/one-variable/two-waves design has two groups of subjects, measured on one variable at two different points in time. An example is the well-known pretest–posttest control group design (see Campbell & Stanley, 1966). An example of this type of design is displayed in Table 3.8. Since there are only two measurement occasions in this data matrix, the sphericity assumption is no problem. Therefore, this split plot factorial (SPF 2.2) design could straightforwardly be analysed in a univariate manner, either by using the computational formulas to be found in for instance Kirk (1995) and Winer et al. (1991), or by using the 'average' results of a MANOVA computer program. The results of such an SPF analysis are displayed in Table 3.9. The most important result of this analysis is that the groups × waves interaction is significant. This means that one of the groups has changed more than the other. Inspection of the group averages on the two waves shows that Group 2 has changed much more than Group 1. The significant Wave effect shows that both groups have changed, and the significant Group effect shows that the groups differ from each other in terms of their mean scores averaged over Wave 1 and 2.

Table 3.9: *ANOVA of Two-Group/One-Variable/Two-Waves Data as an SPF 2.2 Design*

Source	SS	df	MS	F	p
Between subjects	71.50	11			
Groups	37.50	1	37.50	11.03	0.008
Subjects within groups	34.00	10	3.40		
Within subjects	61.00	12			
Waves	37.50	1	37.50	37.50	< 0.001
Groups × Waves	13.50	1	13.50	13.50	0.004
Subj.w.Gr. × Waves	10.00	10	1.00	1.00	
Total	132.50	23			

3.3.2   MANOVA

As there are only two waves, a structured MANOVA of the data of Table 3.8 amounts to two ANOVAs of $\mathbf{Yh_1}$ and $\mathbf{Yh_2}$ ($\mathbf{h'_1} =$

$\{0.707, 0.707\}$; $\mathbf{h}_2' = \{0.707, -0.707\}$) where the first analysis yields the between-subjects part of Table 3.9, and the second analysis yields the within-subjects sums of squares. As said before, it is not relevant to test the sphericity or compound symmetry assumptions, because there are only two variables (the two waves). However, as there are two groups, we have to worry about the assumption of equal within-group VCVs. In order to check this assumption, one usually performs univariate tests (for instance Bartlett–Box and Cochran C) concerning the homogeneity of the variances of Y_1 and Y_2 (the measurements on Wave 1 and Wave 2, respectively). In addition, one executes Box's multivariate test for the homogeneity of the dispersion matrices. However, the Box test should be used only if the within-group distributions of the data are multivariate normal. The results are listed in Table 3.10; the p-values of these tests show that there is no compelling reason to reject the null hypothesis of homogeneity of the within-group VCVs.

Table 3.10: *Tests of the Homogeneity of the Within-groups Variances and Covariances*

Name of test	Type of test	Test of	Value	df_1, df_2	p
Cochran's C	univariate	Y_1	0.667	2, 5	0.465
Bartlett–Box	univariate	Y_1	0.534	1, 300	0.465
Cochran's C	univariate	Y_2	0.500	2, 5	1.000
Bartlett–Box	univariate	Y_2	0.000	1, 300	1.000
Box's M	multivariate	$VCV(Y)$	3.289		
	F-approximation		0.365	6, 724	0.901
	χ^2-approximation		2.220	6	0.898

3.3.3 ANOVA on difference scores

Another way to analyse the data of Table 3.8 is to compute difference scores, which changes the SPF 2.2 design into a one-way or *completely randomized* (CR-2) design, and submit those to the corresponding ANOVA. The results of such an analysis are given in Table 3.11.

Note that the sums of squares in this analysis are proportional by a factor $0.707^2 (= 0.500)$ to the sums of squares of the within-subjects part of the SPF ANOVA. After all, when analysing difference scores we construct a transformed variable $\mathbf{Yk}$ with $\mathbf{k'} = \{-1,1\}$, whereas in the SPF ANOVA the within-subjects part is based on $\mathbf{Yh_2}$ with $\mathbf{h'_2} = \{-0.707, 0.707\}$. The SPF SS_{waves} that is lacking in Table 3.11 is equal to the product of 0.707^2 and $SS_{constant}$ of the difference scores. The group effect in the difference scores now actually is an estimate of the Group $\times$ Wave interaction effect.

Table 3.11: *ANOVA of Two-Group/Two-Wave Difference Scores as a CRF 2 Design*

Source	SS	df	MS	F	p
Groups	27.00	1	27.00	13.50	0.004
Residual	20.00	10	2.00		
Total	47.00	11			
Constant	75.00	1	75.00	37.50	< 0.001

3.3.4 Analysis of covariance

The fourth type of analysis that can be performed on the data of Table 3.8 is an ANCOVA in which the Wave 1 measures are used as the covariate. This type of analysis tests whether the change between the two waves is zero, *conditional* on the initial values of the groups on Wave 1 (Bock, 1975; see also Chapter 1 and Section 3.2.5). The results of this analysis are depicted in Table 3.12. They show that within each group the scores on Wave 2 can be predicted reasonably well on the basis of the respective Wave 1 scores. In the first group the regression equation equals $\hat{Y}_{i2} = (1.0)Y_{i1} + 1.0$, in the second one $\hat{Y}_{i2} = (1.0)Y_{i1} + 4.0$ (for both groups, the pooled squared correlation is $R^2 = 38.4/80.0 = 0.48$). Secondly, there is a significant group difference on the residuals that are obtained by subtracting the predicted values within each group from the observed ones. By computing these residuals, the researcher adjusts the Wave 2 group means for initial differences between the groups, and simultaneously adjusts the within-group variation on the assumption that each subject's score on Wave 2 should be linearly related to his or her initial deviation from the Wave 1 mean. Introduction of a covariate (in principle) reduces the total sum of squares to be explained and may change the between-groups versus within-groups ratio. In the example of Table 3.12 such changes have indeed occurred. The results show a significant group effect, which means that one group has changed more than the other group. A ne-

Table 3.12: *ANCOVA of Two-Group/One-Variable/Two-Waves Data as a CR 2 Design*

Source	SS	df	MS	F	p
Covariate Y_1	38.40	1	38.40	17.280	0.002
Groups	21.60	1	21.60	9.720	0.012
Residual	20.00	9	2.22		
Total	80.00	11			

Pooled within-groups regression coefficient (b) = 1.00

cessary condition of this ANCOVA is that the regression coefficients in both groups are homogeneous. The researcher can test this assumption of *parallel regression lines* by means of the following computational steps (see Edwards, 1985).

1. Perform an ANCOVA with Y_2 as the dependent variable, Groups as the independent variable and Wave 1 as the covariate. The residual sum of squares of this analysis corresponds to the residual that belongs to one common regression line (here $SS_{residual} = 20.00$).

2. Compute new variables which contain the interaction between Groups and Y_1, that is, express the group variable in terms of one or more dummy variables and compute the products of these dummy variables with the scores on Y_1. In our example we have only two groups, so one dummy variable suffices to code the group difference and one product variable is needed to code the Group × Wave 1 interaction.

3. Run an ANCOVA on Y_2 with Group as the independent variable and Y_1 and the product vector as covariates. The residual sum of squares of this analysis corresponds to the residuals around two separate regression lines in each group. (Here $SS_{residual} = 20.00$.) The unique contribution to the prediction of Y_2 by the interaction covariate(s) is equal to $SS_{residual}$ of Step 1 minus $SS_{residual}$ of Step 3. The degrees of freedom corresponding to this difference equal the number of interaction covariates. In our example the difference of residual SSs is zero; $df = 1$.

4. Test whether the contribution of the interaction covariate is significant: divide the difference between the residual SSs by its degrees of freedom. Divide the resulting mean square by $MS_{residual}$ of Step 3 (that is, $SS_{residual}$ of Step 3 divided by the corresponding df). Check if the resulting F-value is significant or not. If this F-value is significant, it means that each group has a different population regression coefficient. If the group regression coefficients are not equal, the whole idea of performing an ANCOVA should be dropped. If, on the other hand, the homogeneity assumption is not rejected, one should report the ANCOVA of Step 1 (in our example Table 3.12). In the present example, the sum of squares attributable to the interaction covariate is zero. Regression analyses of the data within each group also show that the regression coefficients in each group are both equal to 1.00.

3.3.5   Comparison of approaches

As we have seen in this example, MANOVA, SPF ANOVA and AN-OVA of difference scores yield identical sums of squares for the effects. Again, this is not a coincidence but follows necessarily from the mathematical equivalence of the procedures we have used. That this equivalence exists, is far from common knowledge (see Games, 1990; Huck & McLean, 1975). On the other hand, these methods may not be equivalent in a statistical or strategic sense. This point will be clarified below.

What is important in this example, is whether the Wave 1 values are *pretest* measures that precede the introduction of a between-group treatment (such as in the pretest–posttest control group design) or are measured after some intervention was administered to one or both of the groups. If in a pretest–posttest control group design, subjects are randomly assigned to the experimental and the control group, then we would usually expect a group difference on Wave 2 but no difference between the groups on Wave 1. In such a case, a test of the treatment variable could just as well be made by just comparing the group means on Wave 2 (see Cronbach & Furby, 1970). Under random assignment of subjects, the group means on Wave 1 are irrelevant for the treatment effect. As Huck & McLean (1975) demonstrate, SPF ANOVA using pretest and posttest scores as repeated measures may in this situation even be misleading because the Mean Square of the between-group effect underestimates the actual treatment effect. Hence the corresponding test is less powerful. The actual change brought about by the treatment variable now is divided among the between-groups main effect and the Group × Wave interaction. This makes interpretation sometimes more difficult. Difference scores, however, do not suffer from the above problems.

The most important reason to use pretest measures in a randomized experiment is to statistically control (that is, decrease) the within-group variance and thus obtain a greater *precision* of the test. This could be achieved to some extent by using difference scores, but the generally preferred method is ANCOVA because ANCOVA yields greater precision in adjusting the within-group variance and also statistically equates the groups with regard to initial pretest differences. This latter advantage is, of course, essential for non-randomized studies.

3.4 One-group/one-variable/multiple-waves designs

The one-group/one-variable/multiple-waves design is a relatively simple extension of the one-group/one-variable/two-waves case. An example of such data is given in Table 3.13. These data may be analysed as an RB-3 design if the requirement of sphericity is satisfied. Therefore, it would be advisable to use the procedure outlined in Section 3.1.10 and start by performing an RB ANOVA.

3.4.1   RB ANOVA

The results of an RB ANOVA are given in Table 3.14. The sums of squares, degrees of freedom, mean squares and F-values are computed as usual (that is to say, as if the sphericity assumption is satisfied). Next, the probability of obtaining those F-values under the null hypotheses must be evaluated. First we use the conservative approach proposed by Greenhouse & Geisser (1959) by assuming that the value of ε is at its lowest value, that is $\varepsilon = 1/(T-1)$. In that case, the F-value for Waves would be distributed with $(T-1)\varepsilon = 1$ and $(N-1)(T-1)\varepsilon = N-1$ degrees of freedom. The corresponding probability of the obtained F-value is smaller than 0.05, which means that the waves effect is significant, even now that we use the most conservative estimate of ε. If the F-test of the subjects effect is appropriate at all (see Section 3.2.3), a conservative test would use $(N-1)$ and $(N-1)(T-1)\varepsilon = N-1$ degrees of freedom.

In this example, both the conservative and the ordinary F-tests show a significant waves effect. Let us, however, for the sake of argument, assume that only the ordinary test leads to rejecting the null hypothesis. Then, one of the things we could do, is compute a sample estimate of ε, and estimate the appropriate degrees of freedom for the F-test. Formulas for computing ε are given, among others, by Kirk (1995). More conveniently, an estimate of ε is obtained from a MANOVA computer program. In the present case, the Greenhouse–Geisser $\varepsilon = 0.80$ and the p-value of Mauchly's test is 0.237. Thus the sphericity assumption need not be rejected. On the other hand, this relatively low p-value and the Greenhouse–Geisser ε of 0.80 (the lower bound of ε is 0.50) suggest that some deviation from sphericity may exist, albeit not statistically significant. If we use the ε correction, the adjusted degrees of freedom for F_{waves} thus become 1.6 and 17.6, and the corresponding p-value is still smaller than 0.01.

Table 3.13: *Example of a One-Group/One-Variable/Three-Waves Data Matrix*

Subjects	Wave 1 Y_{i1}	Wave 2 Y_{i2}	Wave 3 Y_{i3}	Sum $Y_{i1} + Y_{i2} + Y_{i3}$
1	1	1	5	7
2	3	5	6	14
3	1	3	2	6
4	2	1	4	7
5	1	3	2	6
6	4	5	5	14
7	2	6	8	16
8	3	4	9	16
9	3	8	10	21
10	4	8	11	23
11	4	9	10	23
12	2	7	12	21
Sum	30	60	84	174

Table 3.14: *ANOVA of One-Group/One-Variable/Three-Waves Data as an RB-3 Design*

Source	SS	df	MS	F	$p_{ordinary}$	$p_{conservative}$
Between subjects	163.667	11	14.879	5.168	0.001	$< 0.01 \; (df = 11)$
Waves	122.000	2	61.000	21.189	< 0.001	$< 0.01 \; (df = 1)$
Residual	63.333	22	2.879			$(df = 11)$
Total	349.000	35				

3.4.2 MANOVA

One of the many possible sets of linear combinations of the Y variables is obtained by the orthonormalized transformation matrix

$$\mathbf{H} = \left\{ \begin{array}{ccc} 0.577 & 0.707 & -0.408 \\ 0.577 & 0.000 & 0.816 \\ 0.577 & -0.707 & -0.408 \end{array} \right\}$$

whose last two columns are contrasts that correspond to the linear and quadratic components of a set of orthogonal polynomials. If the three waves are equidistant in time, these components can be interpreted as a linear and quadratic function of time. If the three waves are not equidistant in time, $\mathbf{h}_2$ is nothing more than just a comparison between the first and the third waves; $\mathbf{h}_3$ is a comparison of the middle wave and the mean of the first and third waves. The first linear combination $\mathbf{Yh}_1$ measures the between-subjects effects. In the present one-group case, MANOVA amounts to a decomposition of $SS_{\mathbf{Yh}_1}$ in a within-cells (= between-subjects) SS and an SS for the constant. The latter SS can be used to test whether the population mean of $\mathbf{Yh}_1$ equals zero.

Computer programs for MANOVA usually calculate several multivariate test statistics (Pillais, Hotelling, Wilks, and Roy) of the within-subjects effects. These statistics test the null hypothesis that the means of both $\mathbf{Yh}_2$ and $\mathbf{Yh}_3$ are simultaneously zero. Here, all four tests lead to the same result: the null hypothesis of no waves effect can be rejected at the 0.002 significance level.

In general the four test statistics may be regarded as equivalent. In some cases, Roy's statistic may be biased somewhat towards falsely rejecting the null hypothesis. Of the other tests, Wilks's statistic may be preferred slightly because it gives exact F-values instead of the approximations given by the Pillais and Hotelling procedures (see Games, 1990). All four tests are equally robust with regard to the effect of heterogeneity of the VCV matrices on Type I error (no problem in this example, as there is only one group!), although Hand & Crowder (1996) concluded that the Pillais statistic is the most robust one when VCV matrices differ because of occasional outliers. According to Stevens (1996), these multivariate test statistics have only small differences in power, although the relative power of the four tests depends on the nature of the departures from the null hypothesis of equal means. For instance, if the main differences are confined to one dimension, Roy's largest root criterion is the most powerful test (see Tatsuoka, 1988; Stevens, 1996).

In order to interpret the multivariate results, very often the univariate ANOVAs of $\mathbf{Yh_2}$ and $\mathbf{Yh_3}$ are inspected. In these analyses, the SS_{total} of each transformed variable is broken down into an $SS_{within-cells}$ and an $SS_{constant}$. For $\mathbf{Yh_2}$, the constant is significant; this means that the means of Wave 1 and Wave 3 are different (inspection of the means shows that they increase over time). The constant of $\mathbf{Yh_3}$ is not significantly different from zero; so there is no evidence of a curvilinear relationship of the wave means with time.

Since in our example the sphericity assumption was found to be tenable, one may sum the ANOVA SSs of $\mathbf{Yh_2}$ and $\mathbf{Yh_3}$, which leads to the well-known table of an RB ANOVA. In this summed analysis, the waves effect is still significant, but we know now that this due to $\mathbf{Yh_2}$.

3.4.3 Difference scores

If one wanted to use difference scores one could use three approaches: (a) subtract the scores on the first wave from the scores on all the other waves, (b) subtract the scores of the first wave from those of the second wave, those of the second wave from those of the third wave, and so on, or (c) define specific contrasts that correspond to differences between two (adjacent or nonadjacent) means at a time. Option (a) and option (b) reduce the number of waves by one, so that we have to analyse data on $T - 1$ measurements.

In principle, all the methods that were discussed so far, could be applied. However, it should be obvious that (M)ANOVA of difference scores leads to interpretations that are substantially different from those obtained from (M)ANOVA on raw scores.

Note that subtracting one vector of data from all the others introduces a certain amount of correlation among the remaining vectors. This could lead to problems with sphericity. Option (c) may lead to additional problems (notably, singularity of the VCV matrix) when the number of contrast vectors is larger than T and/or when these vectors are correlated.

3.4.4 Analysis of covariance

If the first wave is a pretest, which is followed by some sort of intervention variable, one could employ ANCOVA in this setting by using the data of the first wave as the covariate to adjust the measurements on the later waves. If the intervention comes after the second or third, or even a later wave, one would preferably use all pre-intervention waves as covariates. As there is only one group here, there are no group means to adjust for initial differences. The only function ANCOVA performs in this case, is to adjust the scores on the remaining variables for initial differences among the subjects and obtain greater precision (power) of the F-test.

3.5   Multiple-groups/one-variable/multiple-waves designs

This is a rather straightforward generalization of the designs discussed in Sections 3.3 and 3.4. The fact that there are two or more groups brings the equality of the within-groups VCVs to the fore. If homogeneity of the VCVs is not rejected, one can pool the VCV-matrices into one and subsequently test whether this matrix satisfies the sphericity assumption (for preliminary tests of multisample sphericity, see for instance Kesselman & Kesselman, 1993). If this assumption need not be rejected, these data could best be analysed as an SPF ANOVA problem. In that case, the statistical tests have maximum power. If the sphericity condition is not met, one could follow the procedure of Section 3.1.10, or one might want to do a MANOVA.

An example of this design is obtained by assigning the first six subjects of Table 3.13 to Group 1 and the remaining six subjects to Group 2. Cochran and Bartlett tests for the (univariate) homogeneity of the variances of Y_1, Y_2 and Y_3 all yield results that are far from significance at the 0.05 level ($p > 0.465$). Box's multivariate test for the homogeneity of the two within-group VCV matrices is not significant either ($p \approx 0.90$).

Again, linear combinations of the original Y variables are formed by applying the same orthonormal transformation matrix that was used in Section 3.4. This is followed by an ANOVA for $\mathbf{Yh}_1$, the between-subjects variable (see Table 3.15). The group difference on this transformed variable is found to be significant ($p < 0.001$).

With regard to the within-subjects components, first we have to check the sphericity of the data. As Mauchly's sphericity test is not significant ($p = 0.416$) and the Greenhouse–Geisser ε is 0.849, we need not reject the assumption of sphericity.

The multivariate tests of the Group $\times$ Waves effect is significant (all test statistics: $p < 0.001$). The univariate tests, however, only show a significant Group $\times$ Waves interaction on $\mathbf{Yh}_2$ ($p < 0.001$) and not on $\mathbf{Yh}_3$. This means that in Group 1 the values of the waves have a different relationship with time than in Group 2. In Group 1 the wave values increase over time whereas they decrease in Group 2.

The multivariate tests of the waves effect are significant (all statistics: $p < 0.001$). Of the corresponding univariate tests, only $\mathbf{Yh}_2$ shows a significant waves effect, which suggests an increasing monotone relationship of the wave means as a function of time.

As the sphericity assumption was found to be tenable, we can combine the univariate results of the within-subjects components in the traditional SPF ANOVA table presented in the bottom of Table 3.15.

3.6 Multiple-variables/multiple-waves designs

Data that consist of multiple variables measured in multiple waves are called doubly multivariate designs. An example of such a design is presented in Table 3.16. The MANOVA analysis of these data is presented in Tables 3.17 and 3.18.

Repeated measures MANOVA of a multiple-variables/multiple-waves design proceeds by constructing linear transformations of the waves for each variable separately. Thus, with T waves and M variables, we construct TM transformed variables, that is T transformations for each of the M variables. M of these transformations concern the between-subject differences on the variables. The remaining $M(T-1)$ transformations describe the within-subject effects. As an example, consider the data of Table 3.16, which represent a two-groups/three-variables/three-waves design. For ease of presentation, let us denote variable Y_1 measured at Wave 1 by $Y1W1$ and variable Y_3 measured at Wave 3 by $Y1W3$. The resulting analysis hinges on the 9×9 orthonormal transformation matrix $\mathbf{H}$ whose columns contain the coefficients by which the values of $Y1W1, Y1W2, \ldots, Y2W3$, and $Y1W3$ are multiplied

Table 3.15: *MANOVA of Two-Groups/One-Variable/Three-Waves Data*

Source	SS	df	MS	F	p
Yh₁ *(between-subjects)*					
Groups	121.000	1	121.000	28.36	< 0.001
Subj.-w-groups	42.667	10	4.267		
Total	163.000	11			
Constant	841.000	1	841.000	197.11	< 0.001
Yh₂ and **Yh₃** *(multivariate)*					
Groups × Waves *(all tests)*		2,9		21.14	< 0.001
Yh₂ *(univariate)*					
Groups × Waves	37.500	1	37.500	37.50	< 0.001
S.-w-groups × waves	10.000	10	1.000		
Yh₃ *(univariate)*					
Groups × Waves	0.500	1	0.500	0.33	0.581
S.-w-groups × waves	15.333	10	1.533		
Yh₂ and **Yh₃** *(multivariate)*					
Waves (all tests)		2,9		66.14	< 0.001
Yh₂ *(univariate)*					
Waves	121.500	1	121.500	121.50	< 0.001
S.-w-groups × waves	10.000	10	1.000		
Yh₃ *(univariate)*					
Waves	0.500	1	0.500	0.33	0.581
S.-w-groups × waves	15.333	10	1.533		
Combined *(within-subjects SPF)*					
Waves	122.000	2	61.000	48.16	< 0.001
Groups × Waves	38.000	2	19.000	15.00	< 0.001
S.-w-groups × waves	25.33	20	1.270		

Table 3.16: *Data Matrix of Two-Groups/Three-Variables/Three-Waves Design*

Subject	Group	Wave 1 Y_1	Y_2	Y_3	Wave 2 Y_1	Y_2	Y_3	Wave 3 Y_1	Y_2	Y_3
1	1	1	1	5	2	6	8	2	3	3
2	1	3	5	6	3	4	9	4	4	2
3	1	1	3	2	3	8	10	6	4	8
4	1	2	1	4	4	8	11	8	9	7
5	1	1	3	2	4	9	10	8	9	10
6	1	4	5	5	2	7	12	11	10	12
7	2	2	6	8	1	1	5	1	3	1
8	2	3	4	9	3	5	6	2	1	4
9	2	3	8	10	1	3	2	1	5	3
10	2	4	8	11	2	1	4	1	3	5
11	2	4	9	10	1	3	2	5	6	2
12	2	2	7	12	4	5	5	4	2	5

in order to obtain the transformed variables $\mathbf{Yh}_1$ through $\mathbf{Yh}_9$. This matrix of coefficients is depicted in Table 3.17.

Thus, the first transformation $\mathbf{Yh}_1$ 'sums' each subject's Y_1 values over the three occasions. $\mathbf{Yh}_2$ measures the differences between the Wave 1 and Wave 3 values on Y_1, and $\mathbf{Yh}_3$ is the contrast between Wave 2 and the mean of Waves 1 and 3. If the time points are equidistant, $\mathbf{Yh}_2$ and $\mathbf{Yh}_3$ measure, respectively, the linear and quadratic relationship of Y_1 with time. $\mathbf{Yh}_4$, $\mathbf{Yh}_5$, and $\mathbf{Yh}_6$ are the corresponding transformations of the Y_2 measures, and $\mathbf{Yh}_7$, $\mathbf{Yh}_8$, and $\mathbf{Yh}_9$ are their analogues with respect to Y_3.

MANOVA of $\mathbf{Yh}_1$ through $\mathbf{Yh}_9$ proceeds in a manner analogous to the MANOVAs described above. First, the homogeneity of the VCV matrices of the different groups is inspected. The Cochran and Bartlett tests of the univariate homogeneity of $Y1W1$ through $Y1W3$ are not significant, only $Y1W3$ may be seriously suspected to have heterogeneous within-group variances ($p = 0.079$). In our example, a multivariate test of the homogeneity of the 9×9 within-groups VCVs is impossible, be-

Table 3.17: *Transformation Matrix for Three-Variables/Three-Waves Data Matrix*

Observed variable	h_1	h_2	h_3	h_4	h_5	h_6	h_7	h_8	h_9
$Y1W1$	0.577	0.707	−0.408	0.000	0.000	0.000	0.000	0.000	0.000
$Y1W2$	0.577	0.000	0.816	0.000	0.000	0.000	0.000	0.000	0.000
$Y1W3$	0.577	−0.707	−0.408	0.000	0.000	0.000	0.000	0.000	0.000
$Y2W1$	0.000	0.000	0.000	0.577	0.707	−0.408	0.000	0.000	0.000
$Y2W2$	0.000	0.000	0.000	0.577	0.000	0.816	0.000	0.000	0.000
$Y2W3$	0.000	0.000	0.000	0.577	−0.707	−0.408	0.000	0.000	0.000
$Y3W1$	0.000	0.000	0.000	0.000	0.000	0.000	0.577	0.707	−0.408
$Y3W2$	0.000	0.000	0.000	0.000	0.000	0.000	0.577	0.000	0.816
$Y3W3$	0.000	0.000	0.000	0.000	0.000	0.000	0.577	−0.707	−0.408

cause we have inadvertently constructed the data in such a way that the VCV matrices are singular.

MANOVA of the between-subjects part of the design yields the results of the multivariate tests (that is Pillais', Hotelling's, Wilk's and Roy's) of the group effect using Yh_1, Yh_4, and Yh_7 as dependent variables. All criteria show that the group difference on Yh_1, Yh_4, and Yh_7 simultaneously, is not significant ($p = 0.349$). In the univariate tests that follow, it is shown that only Yh_1 approximates significance ($p = 0.061$). The between-subjects analysis is completed by multivariate and univariate tests of the constant (i.e. tests of the null hypothesis that the overall means of Yh_1, Yh_4, and Yh_7 are simultaneously and separately equal to zero). In the present case this null hypothesis should be rejected ($p < 0.001$).

MANOVA of the within-subjects part of the data uses the transformed variables Yh_2, Yh_3, Yh_5, Yh_6, Yh_8, and Yh_9. Firstly, these variables are tested for sphericity. In this example, Mauchly's test (here $p = 0.214$), the Greenhouse–Geisser ε (here 0.500; lower bound 0.167), and the Huynh–Feldt ε (here 0.810) suggest that for all practical purposes the sphericity assumption is tenable.

The multivariate tests of the groups × waves interaction all show a significant ($p = 0.021$) interaction effect. Of the univariate tests that

Table 3.18: *MANOVA of Two-Groups/Three-Variable/Three-Waves Data*

Between subjects; multivariate
Yh$_1$ Yh$_4$ Yh$_7$

Groups:		Wilks' Λ = 0.678;	F =	1.268;	df =	3,8;	p =	0.349
Constant:		Wilks' Λ = 0.021;	F =	122.355;	df =	3,8;	p <	0.001

Between subjects; univariate

Yh$_1$:	SS_{groups} =	17.361;	SS_{within} =	38.944;	F =	4.458;	df =	1,10;	p =	0.061
Yh$_4$:	SS_{groups} =	10.028;	SS_{within} =	54.278;	F =	1.847;	df =	1,10;	p =	0.204
Yh$_7$:	SS_{groups} =	13.444;	SS_{within} =	55.778;	F =	2.410;	df =	1,10;	p =	0.152

Within subjects:
Groups × Waves; multivariate
Yh$_2$, Yh$_3$, Yh$_5$, Yh$_6$, Yh$_8$, Yh$_9$

	Wilks' Λ = 0.099;	F =	7.575;	df =	6,5;	p =	0.021

Groups × Waves; univariate

Yh$_2$:	$SS_{g \times w}$ =	40.042;	SS_{error} =	28.417;	F =	14.091;	df =	1,10;	p =	0.004
Yh$_3$:	$SS_{g \times w}$ =	0.681;	SS_{error} =	23.472;	F =	0.290;	df =	1,10;	p =	0.602
Yh$_5$:	$SS_{g \times w}$ =	77.042;	SS_{error} =	31.417;	F =	24.523;	df =	1,10;	p =	0.001
Yh$_6$:	$SS_{g \times w}$ =	39.014;	SS_{error} =	45.139;	F =	8.643;	df =	1,10;	p =	0.015
Yh$_8$:	$SS_{g \times w}$ =	140.167;	SS_{error} =	64.667;	F =	21.675;	df =	1,10;	p =	0.001
Yh$_9$:	$SS_{g \times w}$ =	102.722;	SS_{error} =	16.889;	F =	60.822;	df =	1,10;	p <	0.001

Waves; multivariate
Yh$_2$, Yh$_3$, Yh$_5$, Yh$_6$, Yh$_8$, Yh$_9$

	Wilks' Λ = 0.167;	F =	4.152;	df =	6,5;	p =	0.070

Waves; univariate

Yh$_2$:	SS_{waves} =	22.042;	SS_{error} =	28.417;	F =	7.757;	df =	1,10;	p =	0.019
Yh$_3$:	SS_{waves} =	7.347;	SS_{error} =	23.472;	F =	3.130;	df =	1,10;	p =	0.107
Yh$_5$:	SS_{waves} =	0.042;	SS_{error} =	31.417;	F =	0.013;	df =	1,10;	p =	0.911
Yh$_6$:	SS_{waves} =	0.014;	SS_{error} =	45.139;	F =	0.003;	df =	1,10;	p =	0.957
Yh$_8$:	SS_{waves} =	20.167;	SS_{error} =	64.667;	F =	3.119;	df =	1,10;	p =	0.108
Yh$_9$:	SS_{waves} =	6.722;	SS_{error} =	16.889;	F =	3.980;	df =	1,10;	p =	0.074

Y$_1$, Y$_2$, and Y$_3$ combined;
Groups × Waves; multivariate

	Wilks' Λ = 0.121;	F =	11.277;	df =	6,36;	p <	0.001

Univariate

Y$_1$:	$SS_{g \times w}$ =	40.722;	SS_{error} =	51.889;	F =	7.848;	df =	2,20;	p =	0.003
Y$_2$:	$SS_{g \times w}$ =	116.056;	SS_{error} =	76.556;	F =	15.160;	df =	2,20;	p <	0.001
Y$_3$:	$SS_{g \times w}$ =	242.889;	SS_{error} =	81.556;	F =	29.782;	df =	2,20;	p <	0.000

Waves; multivariate

	Wilks' Λ = 0.304;	F =	4.890;	df =	6,36;	p =	0.001

Univariate

Y$_1$:	$SS_{g \times w}$ =	29.389;	SS_{error} =	51.889;	F =	5.664;	df =	2,20;	p =	0.011
Y$_2$:	$SS_{g \times w}$ =	0.056;	SS_{error} =	76.556;	F =	0.007;	df =	2,20;	p =	0.993
Y$_3$:	$SS_{g \times w}$ =	26.889;	SS_{error} =	81.556;	F =	3.297;	df =	2,20;	p =	0.058

Mauchly's Sphericity test: W = 0.042; χ^2 = 24.671; df = 20; p = 0.214
Greenhouse–Geisser ε = 0.500; Huynh–Feldt ε = 0.810; lower bound ε = 0.167

follow, all variables, except $\mathbf{Yh}_3$, show significant ($p < 0.02$) interaction effects. The multivariate test statistics of the waves effect all have p-values of 0.07; thus, there is no genuinely significant waves effect on all variables simultaneously. The univariate tests show a significant wave effect only for $\mathbf{Yh}_2$, the 'linear component' of Y_1. Tendencies to significance are found for $\mathbf{Yh}_3$ and $\mathbf{Yh}_9$.

Depending on whether the sphericity assumption is tenable or not, one may combine the results of the analyses of the within-subjects transformed variables. This leads to multivariate tests of the waves effect and the Group $\times$ Wave interaction in terms of the three variables Y_1, Y_2 and Y_3. The multivariate tests of the Group $\times$ Wave interaction are significant ($p < 0.001$), as well as the univariate tests for the separate variables ($p < 0.003$). Also, the multivariate main effect of the waves is significant (Wilks: $p = 0.001$), but the univariate tests show no effect at all for Y_2 ($p = 0.993$) and only a marginally significant effect for Y_3 ($p = 0.058$). Only Y_2 shows a strong waves effect ($p = 0.011$).

So far, we have seen which effects are present in the data after the original measures have been transformed into contrasts that describe the differences among the waves for each dependent variable. The univariate tests of $\mathbf{Yh}_1$ through $\mathbf{Yh}_9$ thus give some insight into the relative contributions of the original variables. In the multivariate tests of the (subsets of) $\mathbf{Yh}$ variables, however, the role of the original Ys is obscured. This can be remedied by performing a discriminant analysis to clarify the nature of each multivariate effect. Discriminant analysis looks for optimal combinations of the dependent variables: in this case, the $\mathbf{Yh}$s obtained by transforming the original Ys. For each multivariate effect we obtain (raw and standardized) coefficients for transforming the $\mathbf{Yh}$ variables into one or more *canonical variates* that optimally discriminate among the conditions of the design. If we collect these coefficients in the matrix $\mathbf{G}$, the canonical variates are equal to $\mathbf{YHG}$, which means that the columns of $\mathbf{Hg}$ contain the weights that are applied to the original Ys. For instance, the largest interaction effect of Group $\times$ Waves is found for a canonical variate obtained by using $\mathbf{g}' = \{-0.004, -0.156, -0.105, 0.040, -0.125, 0.663\}$ as the coefficients for linearly combining $\mathbf{Yh}_2$, $\mathbf{Yh}_3$, $\mathbf{Yh}_5$, $\mathbf{Yh}_6$, $\mathbf{Yh}_8$, and $\mathbf{Yh}_9$. This particular $\mathbf{Hg}$ thus equals $\{0.061, -0.127, 0.066, -0.091, 0.033, 0.058, -0.359, 0.541, -0.182\}$ which are the raw coefficients for combining $Y1W1$ through $Y1W3$. As interpretation of such raw coefficients is hazardous, one could use the standard deviations of the Ys to obtain standardized coefficients, which are comparable to β-coefficients in regression analysis. In addition, one could compute **YHG** and calculate the correlations (the so-called structure coefficients) between these transformed variables and the original Ys. Both sets of coefficients are valuable tools for interpretation. The structure coefficients indicate which substantive construct is measured by the canonical variates; the standardized coefficients show which variables have unique contributions to these constructs and which ones are redundant (see Stevens, 1996).

3.7 Relations with other techniques

3.7.1 Relations with multilevel analysis

One of the terms used for the analysis of repeated measures data is *profile analysis*. The underlying thought is that each subject's data form a profile, whose shape we want to investigate. If we assume that the waves are equidistant in time, we can do a trend analysis by using a transformation matrix **h** with the appropriate orthogonal polynomials. What we are doing then, is also known under the term *curve fitting*. Such an analysis enables us to test which components (i.e. powers of the time variable) are present in the profiles. If there are more groups, we can test whether the same components play an identical role in the profiles of each group. If different groups have different profiles, then we want to estimate the parameters of the polynomial function of each group, and test – through ANOVA procedures – whether these parameters are different. As we have seen (in Section 3.1.3), ANOVA amounts to regression analysis of a continuous dependent variable on a set of dummy variables that describe one or more categorical independent variables. ANCOVA, then, is a simple extension of ANOVA, obtained through adding one or more continuous independent variables to the predictor matrix. Thus, basically, we use regression analysis to test the null hypothesis of equal group profiles.

In many social and behavioural science investigations, groups of subjects are nested within larger categories, which themselves may be nested within still larger entities (for instance, patients nested in wards, nested in hospitals, nested in cities, nested in countries). The profile parameters of the various groups, may then be regressed on all kinds of variables that describe the groups at the various levels. In fact, this is essentially what is aimed for in *multilevel analysis* (see Chapter 5). The most important difference is that (M)ANOVA procedures for analysing repeated measures do not estimate profile parameters for the lowest level, the individual subject. In multilevel analysis, one could also compute the profile parameters of the subjects and test to what extent these parameters can be explained by characteristics of the groups and the individuals. In order to do so, one needs additional subject information (such as age, sex, IQ), and a far more general MANOVA program (see also Section 5.6).

3.7.2   Relations with structural equation models

As we have seen, ANOVA, ANCOVA, and MANOVA belong to the family of the *general linear model*, with AN(C)OVA and MANOVA being special cases of regression analysis and canonical analysis, respectively. The models underlying these techniques can all be represented as *structural equations models* (SEQ-models). However, SEQ-models are more general because (a) they allow the inclusion of unmeasured, so-called *latent* variables, (b) they allow various patterns of correlations among the error components of the data, and (c) they make it possible to study specific hypotheses with regard to causal relationships among the variables. (M)AN(C)OVA models, as such, do not have the possibility to postulate latent variables and/or to test causal hypotheses; moreover, it is always assumed that error components are uncorrelated. The use of structural equation models for the analysis of longitudinal data is discussed in Chapter 4.

3.8   Missing data

Throughout this chapter it has been tacitly assumed that all measures of all subjects are available on all waves. In practical research situations such an assumption is highly unrealistic. Especially in research that stretches over long periods of time it would be very exceptional not to lose data on increasing numbers of subjects as time goes by. Of course, such 'subject mortality' need not occur if the repeated measures are procured in one session. In that case, however, we might loose data because of apparatus malfunctioning, fatigue or lack of concentration of the subjects. Even then subjects might drop out because they do not have the time to go on with their tasks until the study is finished. (Note that in all these instances, we implicitly assume that data loss is unrelated to the nature of the treatments and unrelated to the scores of the subjects on the variables. In other words: the missing data are assumed to be missing *completely at random*. In longitudinal research, this assumption is often very unrealistic. See for instance Kromrey & Hines, 1994, and Chapter 1 of the present book.)

The problem with repeated measures ANOVA and MANOVA is that for these procedures to be technically possible, it is necessary to have data for all subjects on all waves. The only way in which these procedures can handle incomplete data is by *listwise deletion*, that is, all subjects with missing data are deleted from the analysis, even though they might have only missing observation. Given that incomplete data are the rule rather than the exception, we need to consider possible solutions to this problem.

Firstly, the solution of listwise deletion might be appropriate if there are many subjects in all groups, if the number of subjects with missing data is only quite small, and if the missing data are random. Secondly, one could try to substitute missing observations by values that probably would have been obtained if the observation had not been missing. Methods for estimating such substitute values range from relatively crude to very sophisticated. An example of the former would be to substitute all missing values by the overall mean. More advanced would be to use subject and wave means to compute substitute values (see Kirk, 1968, p. 281) or to use adjacent values of the data matrix (see Winer et al., 1991, p. 480). Finally one could use some iterative EM algorithm (see Little & Schenker, 1995; Rovine & Von Eye, 1991) to impute the most likely values that could have been observed.

The question is whether such imputation methods, especially the more advanced ones, are really worth the trouble. If we have so few subjects that we cannot afford to lose a few by listwise deletion, we would not put much faith in (M)ANOVA results of data that consist of a relatively large number of imputed values. Therefore, we would like to consider another, more practical, solution.

Given a number of waves and/or a number of variables, one could define a set of *theoretically interesting a priori* transformation vectors **Yh** and perform separate (M)ANOVAs on subsets of only those waves and variables that are involved in a particular **Yh**. Subjects with missing data can then be deleted listwise. The result is that, in general, we have to discard fewer subjects in the separate (M)ANOVAs than in one over-all (multivariate) analysis of all waves and variables simultaneously. In case of a substantial amount of missing data, this could diminish the problem considerably.

3.9   Discussion

In this chapter we discussed several techniques for the analysis of lon-gitudinal data. With one-variable/two-waves data, it is not difficult to decide which method to choose: RB or SPF ANOVA are the obvious choices, because (a) they are more general than the analysis of differ-ence scores, and (b) give a clearer picture of the change between Wave 1 and Wave 2 than either the analysis of difference scores or analysis of covariance. Analysis of covariance, however, is to be preferred if the Wave 1 measures are a pretest variable, which should be used to de-crease the error variance and to equate different groups on the Wave 1 measures. ANCOVA is also appropriate if there are additional measure-ments available on the subjects that can be used as covariates.

In the case of one-variable/multiple-waves data, the discussion hinges on the problem of sphericity. If the sphericity assumption is sat-isfied, RB and SPF ANOVA are the preferred analyses. If not, one can follow the procedures outlined in Section 3.1.10 or perform a so-called structured multivariate analysis. Using a MANOVA computer program is advantageous because (a) we obtain information about the sphericity, and (b) the program also performs multivariate and univariate tests of the transformations of the waves. By choosing an appropriate set of orthogonal transformation vectors (not necessarily the default ones of the computer program), one obtains tests of particular contrasts of the waves. Thus there is no need to do multiple comparison tests *after* the ANOVA has been performed. The topic of choosing the correct error term for *a posteriori* multiple comparisons of repeated measures data is not discussed in this chapter. The reader is referred to, for instance, Games (1990), Kirk (1995), or Winer et al. (1991).

With multiple-variable/multiple-waves data, there are three alternat-ives to choose from. The first one is to compute transformations of the waves for each variable and perform separate tests on these transformations. This is a basically univariate procedure. The second option is to perform multivariate tests on the same transformations of the different variables simultaneously. Finally, if sphericity holds, the former method's results can be combined ('averaged') into the multivariate equivalent of RBF and SPF designs. One cannot but perform a MAN-OVA on such data.

The problem with textbooks and computer manuals of MANOVA is that they usually stop after the multivariate and univariate tests have been performed, that is, after the null hypothesis has been tested for all variables simultaneously and separately. Significance of a multivariate test only informs the researcher that there exist one or more optimal linear combinations of the dependent variables on which a significant effect occurs. From a substantive point of view, one would want to know which combinations of the variables are responsible for these effects. Therefore, it is almost inconceivable that researchers perform a MAN-OVA without investigating (and reporting!) the canonical coefficients of the dependent variables and/or their correlations with the canonical variate, thereby missing the opportunity to draw graphs of the groups and variables in a canonical space. Examples of such graphs can be found in Chapter 2.

3.10 Further reading

There exists an enormous literature on ANOVA, both at an introductory and at a very advanced level. The more sophisticated texts fall into two categories: those which treat ANOVA as a univariate method, and those which treat ANOVA in a multivariate way. Some of the latter require knowledge of matrix algebra and a relatively advanced appetite for statistics. Excellent, and detailed textbooks of univariate ANOVA are the classics by Kirk (1968, 1981, 1995), Winer (1962, 1971), Winer et al. (1991) and Stevens (1990). A clear and rather complete introduction to ANOVA as a special case of multiple regression analysis is given by Draper & Smith (1981) and Edwards (1985). A mathematically and statistically advanced textbook on ANOVA is Scheffé (1959). Stevens (1992) and Tabachnik & Fidell (1989) give detailed accounts of the theoretical and practical issues of (M)ANOVA in the context of multivariate analysis in general. Very sophisticated discussions of (M)ANOVA, both with regard to mathematics and multivariate statistics can be found in Bock (1975), Morrison (1990), Timm (1975), or many others. A rather verbal introduction to MANOVA and analysis of repeated measures is given by Hand & Taylor (1987). Their approach in terms of contrast vectors is similar to the one adopted in this chapter. A variety of methods for analysing repeated measures is discussed in a statistically quite advanced monograph by Crowder & Hand (1990); (M)ANOVA is described in a very compact chapter of their book. Focusing on the same problems as we have done here, is a chapter by Games (1990), whose discussion of MANOVA uses SAS output. Moreover, Games gives detailed information on testing multiple comparisons and simple effects with repeated measures.

Chapter 4

Structural equation models for longitudinal data

Catrien C. J. H. Bijleveld
Ab Mooijaart
Leo J. Th. van der Kamp
Willem A. van der Kloot

4.1 Introduction

Since the 1920s, the pursuit of questions of causality and causal inference with nonexperimental data has been a major issue of research in disciplines such as biometrics, econometrics, psychometrics and sociology. In this long tradition, Wright (1918, 1934, 1960) was the first to study causal schemes in terms of path coefficients. Tukey (1954) stressed the relevance of this work on causation, regression and path analysis for disciplines other than biometrics. Gradually, the developments of path analysis and causal inference in the various disciplines no longer took place independently, but converged. In the 1950s and the early 1960s, sociological methodologists became aware of the possibility of utilizing path analysis for causal modelling in sociology (Blalock, 1964; Duncan, 1966; Simon, 1954). In psychometrics, Campbell & Stanley (1966) attacked the problems of causal inference in quasi- and non-experimental data, while Werts & Linn (1970) introduced a number of psychological examples of path analysis. All this, and more, led to a proliferation of research on causal modelling and structural equation models or covariance structure analysis. The latter two terms were mainly used in psychometrics and econometrics, while sociologists seemed to prefer the term causal modelling (see for a discussion Goldberger & Duncan, 1975). This research on causal modelling in the broad sense of the word, renewed philosophers' interest in problems of causality (see for instance Bunge, 1959, 1979 and Mackie, 1974). Behavioural scientists became involved as well in the causation and causal inference debate, as exemplified by the publications of Cliff (1983), Bullock, Harlow, & Mulaik (1994), Holland (1988), Kenny (1979), Sobel (1994, 1995) and White (1990), amongst others.

The main breakthrough in structural equation modelling (or SEM) in terms of the development of statistical theory as well as of applications in the social and behavioural sciences came from Karl G. Jöreskog. Especially the development of computer programs led to a wide use of these techniques. Following for instance Bock & Bargmann (1966), Jöreskog called his technique the analysis of covariance structures. ACOVS was the computer program for model parameter estimation and hypothesis testing (Jöreskog, Gruvaeus, & Van Thillo, 1970). Later on, the model was extended with structured means (the computer program ACOVSM). Jöreskog's present computer program for structural equation modelling is LISREL, an acronym for LInear Structural RELations.

Structural equation modelling is a branch of multivariate analysis with latent variables, or to be more specific, linear structural equation models with latent – that is, unobserved or unmeasured – variables. Latent variables are conceived of as hypothetical constructs or as constructs that are hypothesized to constitute a nomological network or a theory. Latent variables, however, are not the only variables in structural equation modelling: not only are the latent variables related to each other in a certain way, latent variables are also related to observed variables. The manner in which the latent and the manifest variables are related is specified by the researcher's theory, or may be hypothesized by a researcher based upon earlier empirical findings. That is, it is formulated in terms of a statistical model having a certain structural form (for instance a linear regression equation) with unknown parameters. Often, the primary aim is the estimation of the parameters of the model in question, as well as testing the goodness-of-fit of the model to the data. If there is no acceptable (in terms of some standards) model to data fit, the proposed model is rejected. Then the researcher may formulate an alternative model and investigate whether the latter model is an acceptable one for representing the (relations in the) data. In structural equation modelling, a model comparison approach to data analysis is thus typically followed (see e.g. Judd, McClelland, & Cutharie, 1995). Once a model is found that need not be rejected, then 'a plausible representation of the causal structure' of the measured and unmeasured variables is found (Bentler, 1980, p. 420). Causal structure refers to the manner in which latent and observed variables are presumed to be related to each other.

To be sure, much more can be said on the methodological status of the terms latent variable and causal modelling. It is beyond the scope of this chapter, however, to go into details. More on latent variables can be found in Sobel (1994, 1995), and the references mentioned. Typically, Cohen, Cohen, Teresi, Marchi, & Velez (1990) discuss problems in the measurement of latent variables in structural equation causal models. In structural equation modelling for longitudinal data, time is obviously an important factor: the temporal ordering implies certain causal paths and excludes others. For instance, a child's reading ability at eight years of age is presumed to be influenced by the child's reading ability at age seven, and not the other way around. Thus, structural equation model specification for longitudinal data is to a certain extent facilitated by the temporal ordering in the data.

Although we are dealing with longitudinal data, this chapter does not focus explicitly on models in which generalizations over time are made. We are thus not interested in forecasting per se. In the social sciences, we mostly have just a few time points, in practice five or six at the most. Thus, stability of the parameters can not come from the number of time points, but must come from the number of sample units. Indeed, the models discussed in this chapter are designed in such a way that stability of the parameter estimates is derived from sufficient replications in the person mode. Therefore, we will not apply structural equation modelling to ARIMA or related models, as in these models a great number of replications over time are present. In this chapter we limit ourselves to models in which the structural relationships between variables, connected through just a few time points, are of interest.

Before going into the application of structural equation modelling for longitudinal data a brief, non-technical, introduction will be given of the most important features of structural equation modelling and its application. Structural equation modelling will be represented graphically, using diagrams to visualize the models. Each diagram then implies structural equations with 'structural' parameters. Once the form is specified, parameters are estimated from the data, and suitable hypotheses with respect to certain parameters can be tested using goodness-of-fit statistics of the model with respect to the sample data. To do so, a number of computer programs are available (see for more comments on the software Bentler 1995; Bentler & Dudgeon 1996; Bentler & Wu 1995a,b; Browne & Arminger 1995).

In this chapter the EQS program has been used for analysing the examples of Bentler (1995). The basic model representation used in EQS (EQuationS) is the Bentler–Weeks model (Bentler & Weeks, 1980). This type of representation does not explicitly distinguish the structural part from the measurement part as is done in the Jöreskog LISREL formulation (see e.g. Jöreskog & Sörbom, 1993). EQS only represents the relationships between independent or predictor and dependent or criterion variables (latent or observed). The model specification in EQS is traditionally equation-oriented, and the equations, including the operation signs and error variables, have to be specified by the user. In addition to the references given earlier, we mention Byrne (1994) as a user-friendly introduction to this material.

The organization of this chapter is as follows. In Section 4.2 model specification, fitting and interpretation will be introduced. Types of variables and the relations between them are described. In the context of model fitting the following issues will be discussed: estimation, identification, fit and model modification. The application of structural equation modelling to longitudinal data is the subject of Section 4.3. In this context autoregressive and growth-curve modelling will be given attention. Recent developments in structural equation modelling are presented in Section 4.4. Although in Chapter 1 the general problem of missing data in the analysis of longitudinal data has been treated, special attention has to be given to this problem in the context of structural equation modelling. This is the subject of Section 4.5. A discussion in Section 4.6 and a summary of references (Section 4.7) useful for further reading close the chapter.

4.2 Linear structural equation models

The main purpose of structural equation modelling is to test specific statistical hypotheses with respect to the relations between a number of observed and unobserved variables. If the relations between the variables have been specified, the variances and covariances can be written as functions of the variables and the coefficients that specify these relations. The basic idea then is that the variance–covariance matrix of the variables can be decomposed into components attributable to the various relations in the models.

Given sufficient observations, estimates for the parameters that specify these relations, and for the variances and covariances of the variables, can be found. By testing the difference between the observed variance–covariance matrix and the variance–covariance matrix we expect to observe if our estimated model holds, we can assess to what extent the model fits the data.

Before going into details of the confirmation procedure, we will briefly introduce a number of relevant aspects in the types of models that can be analysed using structural equation modelling. Our treatment of the subject matter does not pretend to be, and is by no means, exhaustive. A wealth of literature is available to which the reader is referred for further details on particular topics. Our discussion of the practicalities of running structural equation models is comprehensive. The reader is referred to textbooks such as Dunn, Everitt, & Pickles (1993), Byrne (1994), Maruyama (1998), Hayduk (1987) and the classic by Bollen (1989) for a more in-depth introduction to structural equation modelling.

Structural equation modelling can very well be understood graphically, that is by using diagrams showing the relations of the variables involved. Each graphical representation corresponds to a structural equation or to a set of them. An additional reason for relying on graphics for illustration is that EQS can also be run from such graphical representations (see for instance Byrne, 1994).

4.2.1 Assumptions

For testing the difference between the observed variance–covariance matrix and the predicted variance–covariance matrix, it is assumed that all variables are continuous measures, and, in addition, that all variables are distributed multivariate normally. Most programs for structural equation modelling provide tests of the assumption of multivariate normality. For instance, in EQS Mardia's kappa gives an indication of multivariate normality (see for instance Dunn et al., 1993, or other textbooks mentioned above).

4.2.2   Structural equation and path diagrams for various models

Structural equation models consist of variables and relations between variables. We will briefly discuss several types of variables that may be employed in these models. We will also discuss various types of relationships that can be specified. Next, we show how the types of variables and types of relations can be used to distinguish between certain classes of models. We start with a number of examples of the graphical representations used.

Perhaps the simplest relationship between two variables is the well-known classical regression model. Suppose therefore that we have measured an independent variable and a dependent variable. Independent variables are often referred to as input or exogenous or explanatory variables, or as the predictors. Dependent variables are also often referred to as the output or endogenous variables, or as the criterion variables. However, in EQS, any variable that is regressed on another variable (whether that variable is exogenous or endogenous) is considered dependent in a technical sense. Also, any variable that is not predicted by another variable (whether that variable is a predictor variable, or a residual term), is considered independent in a technical sense. Therefore, we will in the remainder of this chapter in order to clearly delineate the role of variables in the model, always refer to independent variables as *predictor variables* and refer to dependent variables as *criterion variables*.

We wish to predict the criterion variable, which we call Y, from the predictor variable, which we call X. We will not be able to do so perfectly, so we have to assume that some *prediction error* is made. In other words: if Y is the criterion variable, if X is the predictor variable, and if E is the variable of prediction errors, then the model equation is:

$$Y = bX + E. \tag{4.1}$$

The graphical representation of the model given by the regression equation (4.1) is given in Figure 4.1.

Figure 4.1: *Simple Regression Model*

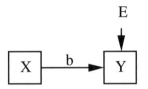

The predictor variable influences the criterion variable, as indicated by the arrow which points from X to Y. The regression coefficient b has been indicated close to this arrow. As both X and Y are measured or *manifest* variables they are represented as a square. An error term captures that part of Y which cannot be predicted from X:

$$E = Y - bX.$$

In Figure 4.1, the arrow pointing from E to Y shows how part of Y is attributable to E. The error term has not been measured. It is a convention that error terms are not represented in a square. Essentially, the error terms reflect the discrepancy between the observed data and the hypothetical model, that is:

$$\text{Data} - \text{Model} = \text{Error}.$$

Instead of using the term error, the discrepancy between data and model is also termed residual. Minimizing errors or residuals is a major purpose of statistical data analysis. The primary task in structural equation modelling as a model-testing procedure is to determine the goodness-of-fit of the hypothesized model to the sample data. In other words, residuals are sought that give an acceptable model to data fit.

Figure 4.2 gives an illustration of an extension of the regression model to the situation with three predictors: X_1, X_2 and X_3. Regression coefficients or regression weights b_1, b_2 and b_3 have been indicated for each of these variables.

The equation for this model is:

$$Y = b_1 X_1 + b_2 X_2 + b_3 X_3 + E. \tag{4.2}$$

Figure 4.2: *Multiple Regression Model*

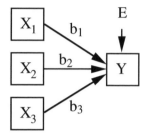

One of the most attractive features of structural equation models is that not only relations between manifest variables, but also between manifest and unobserved hypothetical, or *latent*, variables can be modelled. A latent variable is a variable that can not be measured directly, but only through one or more indicators. A generally adopted more formal definition is that a latent variable is a variable that can not be written as a linear combination of the observed or manifest variables (Bentler, 1982). For instance, the hypothetical construct intelligence is measured through several intelligence tests. As such, also error variables may be conceived of as independent unobserved variables. However, because the error terms are not hypothetical constructs, they play a very different role in the model. It is therefore useful to distinguish them from the latent variables. Perhaps the oldest and best known example of such a model with latent variables is the factor analysis model.

Figure 4.3 gives a representation of a factor analysis model with six manifest and two latent variables. The latent variables have been indicated as circles. For reasons of overview, the regression weights have not been indicated in the figure. The regression weights are commonly referred to as factor loadings in the context of factor analysis, so that we will also use this term here. The factor loadings are denoted by h_{jk} for the loading of variable j on factor k. (In statistical texts on factor analysis, factor loadings are usually indicated by the symbol λ; however, for reasons of comparability with the other chapters in this book, we indicate them by h). The equations for the model depicted in Figure 4.3

Figure 4.3: *Exploratory Factor Analysis Model*

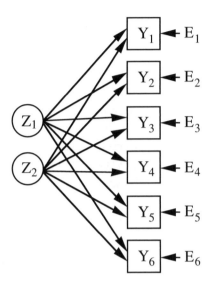

are:

$$Y_1 = h_{11}Z_1 + h_{12}Z_2 + E_1,$$
$$Y_2 = h_{21}Z_1 + h_{22}Z_2 + E_2,$$

$$\ldots$$

$$Y_6 = h_{61}Z_1 + h_{62}Z_2 + E_6.$$

$$(4.3)$$

For the situation in which the links between the latent variables and manifest variables are unknown, *exploratory factor analysis* is used to investigate how the observed or manifest variables are related to their underlying factors (that is, the latent variables). The model (4.3) is a model for exploratory factor analysis because all paths between the variables have been specified.

It may well be, however, that we have a well-developed theory on the relations between manifest and latent variables. For instance, our theory tells us that a number of manifest variables are predicted only by certain latent constructs and other manifest variables are predicted by other latent constructs. Suppose that we investigate to what extent advertising skills of business personnel can be predicted from two hypothetical constructs, linguistic ability and sociability. We have a battery of tests to measure advertising skills, consisting of the following six scales: 'well-spoken', 'theatrical', 'persuasive', 'tactful', 'sympathetic' and 'likeable'. We presume that the first two scales depend on linguistic skills only, that the next two depend on linguistic skills as well as sociability, and that the last two depend on sociability only. Structural equation modelling enables us to specify only those dependencies or paths that exist according to our theory, and subsequently test whether the model specified in this way is tenable for our sample data. The researcher can then test the hypothesis that a particular linkage between manifest variables and their underlying factors exists. A confirmation is sought of the researcher's theory, hence this model is coined the *confirmatory factor analysis* model. See Figure 4.4, in which the first and

Figure 4.4: *Confirmatory Factor Analysis Model*

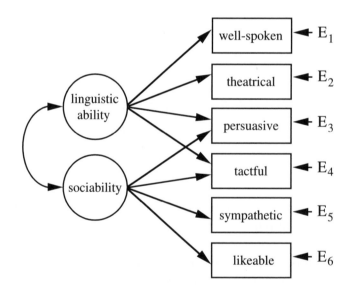

second criterion variables are explained exclusively from the first latent factor, and the fifth and sixth criterion variables are explained exclusively from the second latent factor; the third and fourth criterion variables are explained from both latent variables. The latent variables are correlated, as indicated by the curved bi-directional arrow between the two.

It is also possible to formulate a model with latent as well as manifest predictors for the association between the variables. In an example
similar to the one above, we may investigate to what extent the hypothetical constructs themselves depend on extraneous influences, such
as level of schooling, socio-economic status, attitudinal measures and
the like. Figure 4.5 gives a representation of the well-known multiple
causes multiple indicators or MIMIC model (Jöreskog & Goldberger,
1975) for one latent variable Z, six predictors $(X_1, \ldots, X_6)$ and four criterion variables $(Y_1, \ldots, Y_4)$.

Figure 4.5: *MIMIC Model*

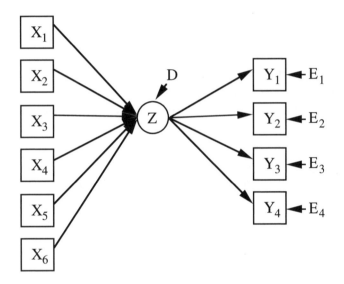

Note how the latent variable is now – strictly speaking – not anymore
an independent variable: the variables X predict the variable Z, which
in turn predicts the variables Y. There may be imperfect fit in predicting
the latent variable Z from the predictor variables X_l, so a residual term
D has been added. The terms named D are commonly referred to as the
disturbances; they are always linked to the latent variables. The E_j are
commonly referred to as the errors, these are always linked to observed

variables. The equations for this model are:

$$Z = g_1X_1 + g_2X_2 + g_3X_3 + g_4X_4 + g_5X_5 + g_6X_6 + D,$$
$$Y_1 = h_1Z + E_1,$$
$$Y_2 = h_2Z + E_2, \tag{4.4}$$
$$\ldots$$
$$Y_4 = h_4Z + E_4.$$

The h_j are again the loadings for criterion variable j on the latent factor; the g_l are the regression parameters for predictor variable X_l.

4.2.3   Model specification

Certain types of relations can be distinguished in structural equation modelling. We discuss a number of these, aided by another graphical representation (see Figure 4.6). Suppose that we are investigating linguistic and arithmetic skills in primary school children. We are particularly interested to know to what extent arithmetic skill is influenced by a mathematics training programme, in which children participated for varying numbers of hours. Arithmetic skills depend on intelligence, which is a hypothetical construct. Arithmetic skills are simultaneously influenced by reading ability, which is a hypothetical construct as well. To make matters more complicated, we know that intelligence influences reading ability (intelligent children are better readers) and vice versa (children with higher reading proficiency score higher in general intelligence – not just the verbal components of intelligence). Reading ability may be positively or negatively influenced by high exposure to television. We have tests that measure arithmetic skills and linguistic skills, respectively. The scores on either test depend on both hypothetical constructs. See Figure 4.6.

Note how both the latent constructs as well as the criterion variables appear as dependent variables, and are thus susceptible to disturbance and error respectively. Various causal effects can be distinguished here. The simplest and most direct relation is between exposure to the mathematics training programme and score on the arithmetic test; this is called a *direct causal effect*. The relation between television exposure and score on the linguistic test (or, for that matter, score on the arithmetic test) gives rise to an *indirect causal effect*: television exposure

Figure 4.6: *Hypothetical Model*

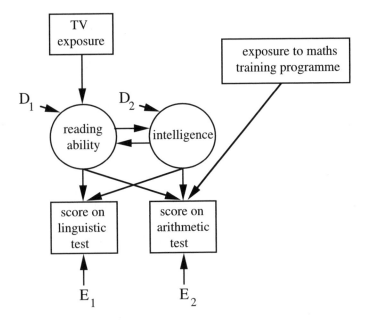

influences reading ability, which in turn influences the score on the linguistic test (or the score on the arithmetic test). A *reciprocal effect* occurs between the two latent constructs: either influences the other (we
should note here that the specification of the reciprocal effect for this
example is for illustrative purposes only; in practice, such reciprocity
is indistinguishable from a correlation between the two factors, which
would also be the most efficient formulation for the interrelations between the two latent variables).

The types of variables and the paths existing between them specify
certain classes of models. The part of the model in which the relations between the latent variables, and in which the relations between
dependent latent variables and independent predictors are specified is
called a *structural model* or the *structural part* of the model. Thus,
television exposure, reading ability, intelligence and the reciprocal relations between the latter constitute the structural part of the model. The
scores on the linguistic test, on the arithmetic test, reading ability and
intelligence constitute the measurement part of the model, or the *measurement model*. Note the parallelism with the formulation for linear

dynamic systems given in Section 2.4.2, where the temporal relation between the latent variables and the predictors is specified in the system equation, and where the relation between the latent variables and the criterion variables is specified in the measurement equation.

Whenever only manifest variables are present, we speak of a *path model* (see for instance Saris & Stronkhorst, 1984). The part of the model in which the relation between the mathematics training programme and scores on the arithmetic test is described, is thus strictly speaking a path model (albeit a tiny one).

Parameters   The confirmatory factor analysis model described above (represented graphically in Figure 4.4) was the first example in this chapter of a confirmatory model in the sense that a particular linkage between observed variables and latent factors is specified. In this model, no relations were specified between the first latent factor and the fifth and sixth criterion variable, and no relations were specified between the second latent factor and the first and second criterion variable.

Another way to view this is by saying that all relations are specified but that certain parameters are fixed to be zero. Fixing certain parameters, or imposing constraints on them, we define a model. (In the statistical literature, sometimes a distinction is made between constraints and restrictions; in this chapter we prefer to use the term constraint, in line with EQS formulation.) Whenever we *fix* a parameter, we set its value at some pre-determined value: for instance, $h_1 = 0$. When we *constrain* parameters, we equate their values to those of other parameters: for instance, $h_1 = h_2$. If we do not impose any constraints upon a parameter, this parameter may assume any value in the estimation process. Such a parameter is labelled *free*. Thus, we have three ways to treat parameters: free, constrained and fixed.

The confirmatory factor analysis model of Figure 4.4 is attained by fixing some of the parameters h_{jk} (the loadings of manifest variable j on latent variable k) to zero, or, specifically: by fixing the parameters h_{12}, h_{22}, h_{51} and h_{61} at zero. Imposing more constraints gives more parsimonious models. But for the arrow between linguistic ability and sociability, the model depicted in Figure 4.4 is a simplified version – or a submodel – of the model in Figure 4.3; the model in Figure 4.4 is then *nested* within the model in Figure 4.3.

Other constraints are possible. It is possible to fix parameters at certain theoretically viable values: for instance, $h_{51} = h_{61} = 0.5$. The possibility to constrain parameters is a particularly useful tool in longitudinal data analysis as we will see later. In the example given here it would be possible to set for instance $h_{31} = h_{41}$, or $h_{32} = h_{42} = h_{52} = h_{62}$. A further refinement, of which we will give no examples in the following, is to constrain certain parameters to be equal across different samples of subjects; in the literature this is referred to as *multisample modelling* (see for instance Bollen, 1989).

In general, imposing constraints on parameters is technically useful as it yields a more parsimonious model with fewer parameters. Imposing constraints makes it possible to impose structure on the model, and thus to test specific substantive theories. Constraints should preferably be guided by theoretical considerations rather than technical ones. The structural equation software tests whether constraints are technically viable, that is, whether constraints should be added or may be dropped (we return to this subject below in Section 4.2.4 on model modification).

4.2.4 Model testing

Estimation As stated above, the main purpose of structural equation modelling is to test specific statistical hypotheses with respect to the relations between observed (and latent) variables. The variances and covariances between the variables serve as input to the estimation procedure. The elements of the variance–covariance matrix of the variables are decomposed into functions of the parameters and the variances of the variables. Given sufficient numbers of variances and covariances relative to the number of parameters and variances to be estimated, and given other conditions to which we will return below, the parameters and variances can in principle be estimated.

Structural equation models assume multivariate normality of the observed variables. As the normal distribution is characterized by the vector of means and variances and covariances, it follows from standard statistical theory that the model can be fitted by maximization of the likelihood using the variance–covariance matrix. It is also possible to use the correlation matrix (for instance when all variables have been standardized).

It is advisable to use covariances as input for the program whenever the scale of the variables has a meaningful interpretation (such as length or weight). When covariances are used, the parameter estimates are also meaningful, as they depend on the scaling of the variables (in fact, just like regression coefficients). In many instances of behavioural research, the scaling of variables is unknown or irrelevant. In such cases, variables are often standardized, and correlations are then used.

When using the covariance or correlation matrix as input for the structural equation modelling program, information on the original values of the variables is lost. When using the correlation matrix, information on the variances is lost as well. This may be a disadvantage especially in longitudinal research, where one is particularly interested in growth. If we have observed a variable measuring, for instance, arithmetic skill, at several timepoints, and if we want to investigate how arithmetic skill develops over time, standardization per time point of the arithmetic skill variable makes it impossible to assess whether any growth has occurred over the time points.

To be able to identify differences in mean value of the variables, it is common practice to use the covariances plus the means instead of only the covariance matrix. However, once we assume multivariate normality, the covariances and variances can be estimated independently from the means. Information about the mean values of variables can be incorporated in the model only if we impose a particular structure on these means. Structure can be imposed in several ways, for instance by requiring that the means on certain variables be equal across different samples. Or, in case of longitudinal measurements, by requiring that the means of variables follow a certain pre-specified trend. In the literature, this type of modelling is referred to as *structured means modelling* (Sörbom, 1982). We return to this subject matter in Section 4.3.2.

In most cases where we analyse longitudinal data, we presume that there will be growth or change on a number of variables. In those instances, we expect that the means of the variables change over time; as the means change, the variances quite likely change as well. This means that whenever we are analysing longitudinal data, we would throw away information if we were to standardize the variables at each time point. Therefore, in general, when analysing longitudinal data, covariances (and preferably also the means) should be used as input for the estimation procedure.

Estimation occurs through an iterative procedure, in which estimates are updated during consecutive estimation steps or iterations, the details of which are of little relevance here, and for which we refer the reader to the literature (see for instance Bentler, 1995; Bentler & Wu, 1995a,b; Browne & Arminger, 1995; Jöreskog & Sörbom, 1993).

Identification To illustrate the issue of identification, which is quite important in the analysis of data through structural equation modelling, we reiterate less superficially the basic idea of the estimation procedure in structural equation modelling. Suppose that we have two indicator variables of one latent construct (see Figure 4.7).

Figure 4.7: *Simple Measurement Model*

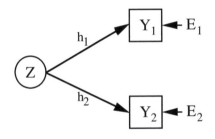

The equations of this model are:

$$Y_1 = h_1 Z + E_1,$$
$$Y_2 = h_2 Z + E_2.$$

We make the usual assumption that the error terms are uncorrelated, and that the correlations between the latent variable and either error term are zero as well. The variance–covariance matrix of the observed variables Y_1 and Y_2 from which we want to estimate the model parameters has three informative elements: $\text{Var}(Y_1)$, $\text{Var}(Y_2)$ and $\text{Cov}(Y_1, Y_2)$. If we formulate these three elements in terms of the model parameters we arrive at the following:

$$\text{Var}(Y_1) = h_1^2 \text{Var}(Z) + \text{Var}(E_1),$$
$$\text{Var}(Y_2) = h_2^2 \text{Var}(Z) + \text{Var}(E_2),$$
$$\text{Cov}(Y_1, Y_2) = h_1 h_2 \text{Var}(Z).$$

We can see from these equations that there are five unknowns: the factor loadings h_1 and h_2, and the variances $\text{Var}(Z)$, $\text{Var}(E_1)$ and $\text{Var}(E_2)$. However, we have only three equations for these five unknowns.

To illustrate the problem, suppose that we have found a solution for h_1, h_2, $\text{Var}(Z)$, $VAR(E_1)$ and $VAR(E_2)$ that fits the observed variances and covariances to a certain extent. If we multiply the solution for both h_1 and $\hat{h}_2$ by a factor 10, and divide the solution for $VAR(Z)$ by 100, the equalities hold as well:

$$\text{Var}(Y_1) = (10h_1)^2 \left(\frac{1}{100}\text{Var}(Z) \right) + \text{Var}(E_1),$$

$$\text{Var}(Y_2) = (10h_2)^2 \left(\frac{1}{100}\text{Var}(Z) \right) + \text{Var}(E_2),$$

$$\text{Cov}(Y_1, Y_2) = (10h_1)(10h_2) \left(\frac{1}{100}\text{Var}(Z) \right).$$

In this case, there is no unique solution for the unknown parameters.

The model is now said to be *unidentified*. A model is identified if *all* parameters of the model are identified. Usually this is not known in advance. Some parameters may be known to be identified as they can be estimated directly from the observed variances and covariances of the sample data. For other parameters, however, it is unknown whether they are identified. In order to be identified, it should be shown that the latter parameters are "...*functions only of the identified parameters and that these functions lead to unique solutions. (...) Thus the goal is to solve for the unknown parameters in terms of the known-to-be-identified parameters*" (Bollen, 1989, pp. 88–89).

For a model to be identified, it is a necessary (but not a sufficient) condition that the number of parameters to be estimated be smaller than or equal to the number of informative elements in the observed variance–covariance matrix. If this is not the case, we are faced with an unidentified model. A first remedy is to fix some of the unknown parameters, that is, set their values equal to some *a priori* values. A second remedy is to constrain the values of some parameters to be equal to those of others. Both remedies reduce the number of free parameters.

In the above example, we could get rid of the indeterminacy by constraining or fixing two of the five parameters of the model. For example we could fix the variance of the latent variable Z to 1.00 and constrain the loadings h_1 and h_2 to be equal. If we fix the variance of the latent variable, we effectively constrain only the scale of the solution; the values of the parameters relative to one another (or: the ratio of the parameter values) are unaffected. Another possibility would be to fix h_1 at 1.00; also this affects only the scale of the solution. If we add the constraint that $\text{Var}(E_1) = \text{Var}(E_2)$ (effectively requiring that the two variables Y have equal reliability), we end up with an identified model in which the values for the remaining parameters can be found from the data.

Whenever a model has more free parameters than the number of observed variances and covariances, we know that it is unidentified. However, the opposite is not true: when a model has fewer free parameters than the number of observed variances and covariances, we do not know for sure that it is identified. Even when a model is identified in a mathematical sense, it may be unidentified empirically. Such *empirical unidentification* may occur because one or more of the estimated parameters take on values that make it impossible to estimate (some of) the other free parameters. See for example the model outlined in Figure 4.8. In this model, we have four criterion variables (Y_1 to Y_4), and two latent variables (Z_1 and Z_2). The loadings h_{11} and h_{32} have been fixed to one. All other parameters are free, that is, in fitting this model, we want to find estimates for $\text{Var}(Z_1), \text{Var}(Z_2), h_{21}, h_{42}$, the correlation f between Z_1 and Z_2, and $\text{Var}(E_1)$ to $\text{Var}(E_4)$. As we have four observed variables, the variance–covariance matrix has ten informative elements. We have 9 unknowns, so in principle we are able to find estimates for the unknowns from the data. However, suppose in fitting this model that we find that, for our data, f approaches zero, or is zero: the one model then in fact becomes two disjunct submodels. For each submodel, we have three informative elements and four unknowns. As each submodel is unidentified, so the total model is also unidentified. For more on empirical identification issues in structural equation modelling, see Rindskopf (1984a).

Depending on the type of model, several conditions can be delineated that have to be met for identification. Such conditions and their (fairly complex mathematical) verifications are discussed in a number of textbooks on structural equation modelling. Particularly Bollen (1989) gives many useful suggestions on this issue for various models.

Figure 4.8: *Simple Measurement Model*

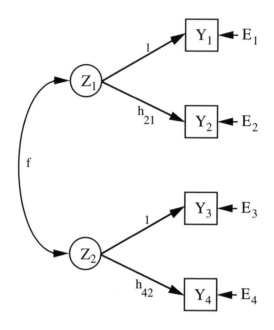

All programs for structural equation modelling print warnings when a model appears unidentified. These warnings are of basically two kinds. Either the program warns that the parameters are linear functions of one another, or the program warns that (some) standard errors can not be computed.

For many practical purposes (and for the purposes of this chapter), it is sufficient to note that whenever a model appears to be unidentified, one has to reduce the number of free parameters.

Sample size   In general, samples under roughly 100 subjects are considered too small for structural equation modelling. Samples towards 400 and above are considered desirable (Boomsma, 1983). Sample sizes in between these two numbers are in a grey area, where a lot depends on the empirical properties of the data. When the sample size is too small, the stability of the parameter estimates is affected. The argument for sufficient sample size is thus a statistical argument. The required sample size is related to the complexity of the problem to be analysed:

the more complex the model and the larger the number of variables, the larger the sample size required for fitting the model.

Optimization and fit indices In structural equation modelling, the observed covariance matrix S is compared with the covariance matrix Σ predicted from the model parameters. The null hypothesis is that the parameters are as predicted by the model. If the parameters are gathered in the vector θ, the predicted covariance matrix for a particular solution $\hat{\theta}$ may be written as $\Sigma\hat{\theta}$, with elements $\hat{\sigma}_{jl}$. The elements of S are s_{jl}. If the solution predicts the data well, the absolute values of the residuals $(s_{jl} - \hat{\sigma}_{jl})$ will be small. If the solution does not predict the data well, the absolute values of $(s_{jl} - \hat{\sigma}_{jl})$ will be large. Thus, we wish to minimize some function of $S - \Sigma(\hat{\theta})$, written as $F(S, \Sigma(\hat{\theta}))$. Most software programs for structural equation modelling provide a choice of several functions to be minimized. EQS provides ordinary least squares (OLS), in which the sum of the squared residuals $S - \Sigma(\hat{\theta})$ is minimized, generalized least squares (GLS) in which a weighted combination of the squared residuals is minimized, with weights depending on the observed variance–covariance matrix S, reweighted least squares (RLS) in which the weights are updated each iteration based on the current estimate of $\Sigma(\hat{\theta})$, and maximum likelihood (ML). In case of multivariate normality, RLS is equivalent to ML.

The tests in the maximum likelihood optimization procedure are based on covariances. The maximum likelihood method is much more complex when correlations are used (the technique then has to estimate the variances); see Hayduk (1987). In those cases other estimations methods are advisable. Maximum likelihood assumes multivariate normality. In principle, when one is unsure whether this condition is met, least squares methods should be used. However, many studies have shown maximum likelihood to be surprisingly robust against violations of normality: even though standard errors may change, the value of the goodness-of-fit statistic is generally unaffected. Thus, in practice researchers use maximum likelihood in nearly all situations.

For GLS and ML (or RLS), $F(S, \Sigma(\hat{\theta}))$ is asymptotically (that is: for sufficiently large samples) χ^2-distributed under the null hypothesis that the covariance matrix is as predicted by the model. The degrees of freedom are given by:

$$df = \frac{M(M+1)}{2} - \text{number of free parameters,}$$

with M the total number of manifest variables. Thus, given that the null hypothesis is the predicted model, the goodness-of-fit statistic should have a high p-value for the model to be assumed tenable. In practice, a value for the goodness-of-fit statistic around or somewhat below the number of degrees of freedom is considered adequate.

A number of indices is available for assessing model fit. We will briefly discuss the most frequently used. Hershberger, Molenaar, & Corneal (1996) give a concise summary of a number of indices. A thorough discussion of incremental fit indices is given in Marsh, Balla, & Hau (1996).

1. *Goodness-of-fit statistic.* To rely solely on the value of the X^2 goodness-of-fit statistic is hazardous. For the goodness-of-fit statistic to have any meaning, sample sizes should not be very large, as any statistic will then show the observed variance–covariance matrix to be significantly different from the variance–covariance matrix predicted under the null model, and thus non-fitting. Conversely, in case of very small sample sizes, no model will render a significant value for the goodness-of-fit statistic, so that for small sample sizes almost any model will fit. The test then lacks statistical power, so the result will be useless. In such cases, model specification should be guided by very strong theoretical considerations. A fundamental discussion of these matters can be found in Satorra & Saris (1985); see Dunn et al. (1993, pp. 187–191) for practical guidelines on sample size and power. In addition to the goodness-of-fit statistic, it is thus advisable to interpret other fit indices as well.

2. *Standardized residuals.* To assess the fit of the model, one should always inspect the absolute values of the standardized residuals. The standardized residuals are computed as the observed correlations between any pair of variables minus the predicted covariance divided by the product of the observed standard deviations: $r_{jl} - \hat{\sigma}_{jl}/s_{jj}s_{ll}$. Standardisation makes these residuals easier to inspect. The residuals should be small and preferably evenly spread

over the variables: high standardized residuals for certain variables are an indication of poor fit due to misspecification. The
standardized residuals are in the range $(-1, \ldots, 1)$, and the more
they are centred on zero, the better the solution is.

3. *Explained variance.* An indication of model performance can also
   be found in the value of the disturbances as displayed in the standardized solution; more particularly: the $1 - D_k^2$ give an indication
   of the variance explained by each k-th latent variable. The $1 - D_k^2$
   are thus indices for practical significance.

4. *Incremental fit indices.* Incremental fit indices evaluate model fit
   relative to the complexity of the model, that is, against the number
   of free parameters. Probably the best known incremental fit index
   is the Akaike Information Criterion (AIC) (Akaike, 1976). Both
   the AIC and its adapted version the consistent AIC (CAIC) are
   χ^2-distributed with a penalty for the number of parameters. Both
   the AIC and the CAIC can, however, never be used absolutely,
   but only comparatively: in comparing the AICs of several models, the model with the lowest AIC is considered preferable. A
   nice overview of five incremental fit indices for comparing various models (NFI, NNFI, AIC, Schwarz's Bayesian Information
   Criterion (SBIC) & Hannan–Quinn criterion (HQ)) is presented
   in Hershberger et al. (1996, p. 164). For a thorough discussion of
   these indices see Marsh et al. (1996).

5. *Other fit indices.* EQS also prints the Bentler Bonett normed
   fit index (BBNFI) and the so-called comparative fit index (CFI).
   Without going into the details of either, it can be stated that they
   should have values well above 0.9, and above 0.95 to be more on
   the safe side, before a model can be considered acceptable.

Model modification and reconfirmation   A model may have been specified inadequately. Most structural equation modelling programs give
guidelines for model improvement, both in terms of improvement of the
fit, as well as for improvement in terms of parsimony.

There are two ways for modifying causal models. The first is by
removing 'paths' in the path diagram, that is by deleting 'directed arrows', and thus creating a more parsimonious model. Parameters can
for instance be eliminated if their estimates are small relative to their

standard errors. After removing the parameters, the resulting model can be re-estimated. The second modification is by adding parameters. For this one can examine the residuals for indications of possible misspecification. If the residuals regarding certain variables are large, it is likely that some misspecification around these variables has occurred: for instance, a parameter has been fixed to a certain inappropriate value, or a path which has not been created should in fact be there.

EQS produces two useful statistics that can aid in model modification: one that indicates whether parameters could be dropped (that is: set equal to zero) without a substantial deterioration in model fit, and one that indicates whether parameters could be added to achieve a substantial improvement in model fit.

The Wald test assesses whether sets of parameters specified as free in the model, could in fact be simultaneously set to zero without substantial loss in model fit. The Wald test gives the increment in the value of the goodness-of-fit statistic caused by the deletion of certain paths, together with the associated *p*-value for this increase. A stepwise procedure is followed, in which after each deleted path, an additional path is deleted, and the increment is computed of the combined previous deletions (the multivariate increment), as well as of the last deletion (the univariate increment). The multivariate as well as univariate goodness-of-fit statistics and *p*-values are printed. If the *p*-values of these goodness-of-fit statistics are lower than a chosen level of significance, and in most instances 5% is chosen, one may rerun the model with the indicated paths deleted.

The Lagrange multiplier test assesses whether the addition of certain paths or parameters not present in the model would result in a substantial increase in model fit. Similarly to the Wald test, the Lagrange multiplier test gives multivariate and univariate tests for the change in the value of the goodness-of-fit statistic when certain constraints on the parameters are released. Again, if the *p*-values of the multivariate and univariate goodness-of-fit statistics are lower than a chosen level of significance (again in most instances 5% is chosen) it is advisable to rerun the model with the released constraints, and thus a certain number of added parameters. The Lagrange multiplier test may advise not only to release certain purposely imposed constraints (for instance to release a constraint $h_{11} = h_{21} = h_{31} = h_{41}$), but also to add certain paths. Examples are given below (Section 4.3.2).

Model comparison   Researchers often want to test not just one model, but investigate a set of possibly competing models. In such cases, it is possible to compare the statistical performance of these models. If two models are nested (see also Section 4.2.3) and both models are fitting, the difference between the values of the goodness-of-fit statistics X^2 is also χ^2-distributed with degrees of freedom equal to difference in degrees of freedom of the two models. It is then possible to test whether one model gives a significant improvement over the other model.

The performance of different models, applied on the same data set, can also be compared by analysing the various models, and comparing the Akaike information criteria for the various solutions: the model with the lowest information criterion is preferable. For this, it is not necessary that the models are nested.

4.2.5   Interpretation of results

Significance tests for the parameter values (which are distributed normally under the null hypothesis that the model is true) are provided in the unstandardized solution (which can be found in the measurement and so-called construct equations in EQS). As the magnitude of the coefficients depends on the scaling of the variables, it is also possible to attach a meaning to the coefficients (for instance, variable Y can be predicted as 2.5 times variables X_1 minus 1.8 times variable X_2). To assess the relative importance of the various parameters, it is easiest to inspect the standardized solution, in which both the latent variables and the errors and disturbances have been standardized to unit variance.

For interpretation, a two-stage procedure is thus generally followed. In the first step, the unstandardized solution is inspected, and parameter values which had emerged as statistically significant from zero are retained. In the second step, the standardized solution is inspected, referring only to those coefficients that were tested significantly different from zero in the unstandardized solution. Interpretation then is no different from the usual interpretation in regression models. Note, however, that in the standardisation process parameter constraints need not be preserved. In the examples below this will be illustrated.

4.3   Structural equation modelling of longitudinal data

In the previous sections, structural equation models were discussed in general terms. We discussed how the imposition of constraints on parameters is an important tool in model specification, as we can through the imposition of such constraints test whether certain relations as prescribed by the theory are supported by the data. We can for instance test whether certain paths exist between variables, or whether such paths do not exist. In that case, variables are not related directly; in graphical representations of such models we find no arrow between the corresponding variables.

Exactly this feature of constraining parameters makes structural equation modelling very useful for analysing longitudinal data. In longitudinal data analysis we want to take into account, and preferably model, the time dependence between the measurements. For instance, we assume that Y_4 depends on Y_3, which in turn depends on Y_2, which in turn depends on Y_1. The possibility of creating such paths between variables that are related in time – from a variable Y_i measured at time point t to the same variable measured at time point $t + 1$ – is an eminently useful feature of structural equation modelling for longitudinal model specification.

Temporal dependence can be viewed as merely one, fairly restrictive, type of dependence between variables. If we can specify the paths along which these dependencies stretch, we can specify a longitudinal model. There is more to specification of such models, however. As we will see below, it is conceptually viable to impose particular constraints on the parameters, reflecting the repeated observation of the variables. For instance, if we have measured several indicators of one construct variable repeatedly, it makes sense to assume that these criterion variables reflect the latent variable in the same manner at every time point (otherwise the latent variable has a different interpretation at each time point). This means that we must impose constraints on the *h*-coefficients.

In structural equation modelling, it is also possible to allow error terms to correlate: it is not necessary to assume uncorrelated errors as is usual in many other areas of statistical analysis. In Figure 4.9, for example, the time dependence between the measurements at time points 1, 2 and 3 is accommodated by assuming that the errors of the variables

Figure 4.9: *Longitudinal Model with Correlated Error Terms*

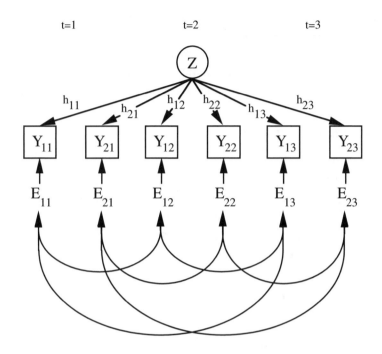

are correlated over time. The equations for this model are:

$$Y_{jt} = h_{jt}Z + E_{jt}, \qquad (4.5)$$

under the assumption $E\left(E_{it}'E_{jt}\right) = 0$ for $i \neq j$[1].

Note how the time dependence does not appear as such in the measurement model (4.5). It is accommodated only through the correlated errors. We will not use this type of specification for dealing with the longitudinal nature of the data, as it mainly serves as a drain for any serial dependence, without specifying a model for the dynamic dependence in the actual measures themselves. Instead, we prefer to formulate an explicit model for the shape of the time dependence between the temporal measurements.

Below we introduce two classes of longitudinal structural equation models. In both, a purposive model is specified for the temporal de-

---

[1]The model (4.5) is presented here for exemplary purposes only and should not be taken as state of the art: two indicators for one hypothetical construct is somewhat minimalistic, and the model (4.5) is by no means identified.

pendence in the observations. In the first class the data are analysed in a straightforward way, that is, the manner in which the variance–covariance matrix of the variables changes over time is analysed; these are the so-called autoregressive models. The second class consists of models in which it is assumed that the sample can be characterized by an average growth curve, which can be specified by means of an average intercept and average slope, around which individuals may vary.

4.3.1 Autoregressive models

Suppose we have measured a group of 6-year old children. We are interested in investigating the development of their reading ability, so we start to measure their reading ability at age 6 and continue to do so at ages 7, 8 and 9 years. To model the development of the test scores, called Y_1, Y_2, Y_3, and Y_4, we can use a model as displayed in Figure 4.10. The interpretation of this display is that there is a direct influence from

Figure 4.10: *Markov Model for Observed Variables*

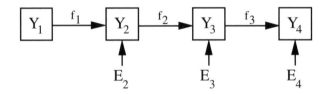

Y_1 to Y_2, from Y_2 to Y_3, and from Y_3 to Y_4, but not from Y_1 to Y_3, Y_1 to Y_4, nor from Y_2 to Y_4. A model like this is called a *first order autoregressive* or *first order Markov* model. Important in this model is that the influence of for instance Y_1 on Y_3 is indirect, or for our example, reading ability at age 8 is influenced directly only by reading ability at age 7, and not by reading ability at age 6. Of course, there is an influence of reading ability at age 6 on reading ability at age 8, but this influence is indirect: to predict reading ability at age 8 it is sufficient to know reading ability at age 7. Formulated differently, given reading ability at age 7, reading ability at age 6 and reading ability at age 8 are independent.

If we allow a direct influence from Y_1 to Y_3 and from Y_2 to Y_4, thus adding paths between these variables, we construct a second order autoregressive or second order Markov model. In the same way we can define *higher order autoregressive models* as well.

In order to analyse data with a Markov model, for instance by the computer program EQS, we have to specify the model equations. The model equations for the first order Markov model are:

$$Y_2 = f_1 Y_1 + E_2,$$
$$Y_3 = f_2 Y_2 + E_3, \quad\quad\quad (4.6)$$
$$Y_4 = f_3 Y_3 + E_4.$$

If all variables have been standardized at each time point, the correlation between the variables Y_1 and Y_2 is equal to f_1, the correlation between Y_2 and Y_3 is equal to f_2, etc. Furthermore, correlations between variables that are not contingent in time are equal to the product of the respective regression parameters: for instance, according to the Markov model, the correlation between Y_1 and Y_3 is $f_1 f_2$ and between Y_1 and Y_4 is $f_1 f_2 f_3$. A consequence of this property is that the absolute value of the correlation between two variables decreases with increasing time difference between the variables. A correlation matrix with such a feature is said to have a *simplex structure*.

Unfortunately, practice has taught that the Markov model is very restrictive, and seldom fits. One possible reason for this bad fit may be that the observed variables are measured with measurement error. For instance, in our example concerning reading ability, it is reasonable to assume that the test which measures the reading ability will not have perfect reliability. Therefore, an alternative to defining a Markov model with observed variables is to define a Markov model that includes unobserved or latent variables. A display of such a model is given in Figure 4.11, in which we see that the time dependence is accommodated by the relationships between the latent variables, and not by those between the observed variables. This can be reformulated into saying that the latent variables contain the true scores (that is, the observed scores minus the error scores) of the respondents. The Markov model is defined for the relationships between the true scores, of which the observed variables are a manifestation.

In order to analyse data with a Markov model for latent variables, for instance by the computer program EQS, we have to specify the model equations. The model equations for this first order Markov model de-

Figure 4.11: *Markov Model for Latent Variables*

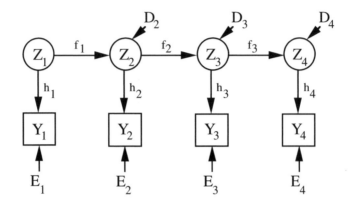

picted in Figure 4.11 are:

$$Y_1 = h_1 Z_1 + E_1,$$
$$Y_2 = h_2 Z_2 + E_2,$$
$$Y_3 = h_3 Z_3 + E_3,$$
$$Y_4 = h_4 Z_4 + E_4,$$

(4.7)

$$Z_2 = f_1 Z_1 + D_2,$$
$$Z_3 = f_2 Z_2 + D_3,$$
$$Z_4 = f_3 Z_3 + D_4.$$

The first four equations in (4.7) refer to the *measurement part* of the model: they specify the relations between the latent variables and the criterion variables. The last three equations in (4.7) refer to the *structural part* of the model: they specify the relations amongst the latent variables.

So far, we have presented examples where there was just one observed variable at each time point. It is also possible to have more observed variables at each time point. In that case we say that there are more indicators for the latent variable. If we assume more than one indicator for each latent variable, we have a *dynamic factor model*. In general, in a factor model, we have several observed variables or indicators, and one or more latent variables, called factors. If there are several indicators for a latent variable, then we have for each time point a factor model; if the latent factors are connected in time, a dynamic version of the well-known factor model emerges.

An extension of the dynamic factor model can be made if we assume that the latent variables themselves depend on one or more predictor variables. For instance, in the example of reading ability, we may assume that reading ability depends on the number of hours children spend on reading lessons in class. In that case the latent variable is regressed on the variable 'number of hours reading'. Let us name this variable X, then we can display this extension of the dynamic factor model as in Figure 4.12. The model in Figure 4.12 is also encountered under

Figure 4.12: *Dynamic Factor Model with Predictor Variables*

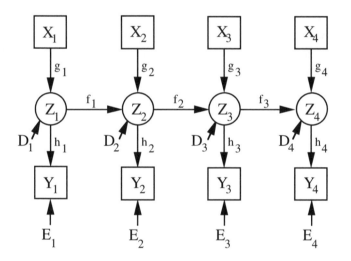

the name linear dynamic model, linear dynamic system or state space model, although the latter term is considered by some to be less appropriate, as the state space model stems from a branch of science where it is used in a different manner (see also Section 2.4.2). In the remainder of this chapter we will refer to this model mostly as the linear dynamic system.

The model equations for the linear dynamic system depicted in Figure 4.12 are:

$$Y_1 = h_1 Z_1 + E_1,$$
$$Y_2 = h_2 Z_2 + E_2,$$
$$Y_3 = h_3 Z_3 + E_3,$$
$$Y_4 = h_4 Z_4 + E_4,$$

$$(4.8)$$

$$Z_1 = g_1 X_1 + D_1,$$
$$Z_2 = f_1 Z_1 + g_2 X_2 + D_2,$$
$$Z_3 = f_2 Z_2 + g_3 X_3 + D_3,$$
$$Z_4 = f_3 Z_3 + g_4 X_4 + D_4.$$

Again, the first four equations in (4.8) refer to the *measurement part* of the model; note how this part is identical to the measurement part of (4.7). The last three equations in (4.8) refer to the structural part of the model, which now also encompasses the relations between input variables and latent variables. These latter equations have changed compared with (4.8): as they now specify not only the relations amongst the latent variables, but also between the latent variables and the predictor variables, to each equation a term $g_t X_t$ has been added. Note how model (4.8) resembles the MIMIC model discussed above in Section 4.2.2. At each time point, the relations between criterion variable(s), predictor variable(s) and the latent variable constitute a MIMIC model. The MIMIC models for the time points are linked through the latent variable. See also Jöreskog & Goldberger (1975) and Bijleveld & De Leeuw (1991).

Structural equation modelling of longitudinal data does have its complications. A first complication is that every time point adds M variables to the model, as new time points are implicitly treated as new variables (cf. Section 2.3.1). This can render models with more than a small number of time points complicated, and sometimes too complicated to handle. The model may be unidentified, or the number of subjects may become too small for the complexity of the problem, which may lead the technique to produce negative variances, or may lead to other degeneracies. Constraining parameters is then not only useful, but may be necessary to arrive at a solution. For this reason, in models such as model (4.8) above, one usually constrains the h-coefficients to be equal: $h_1 = h_2 = \cdots = h_T$. Apart from technical advantages, imposing this temporal or stationarity constraint has *conceptual* advantages as well: if we do not constrain the factor loadings to be time-unvarying, we cannot be sure that the variables have the same interpretation at each time point. In addition, one often constrains the values for the transition parameters from one latent state to the next to be time-invariant: $f_1 = f_2 = \cdots = f_{T-1}$. The *g*-coefficients can be constrained in the same manner as well. Of the three constraints, the constraint on the *h*-coefficients is the most important, because of the consequences for interpretation. Constraining parameters considerably reduces the complexity of the problem and the number of parameters to be estimated.

The next section gives an example of linear dynamic systems analysis of longitudinal data using structural equation modelling.

Example of linear dynamic systems analysis: depressive symptoms in relation to health and demographic characteristics We have at our disposal a data set on depression in the elderly (Beekman, Deeg, Smit, & Van Tilburg, 1995)[2]. Longitudinal data had been gathered on depression, health, and demographic characteristics. A random sample of older subjects from the population register of the small town of Sassenheim in the Netherlands had been submitted to a baseline measurement (t_0) and five successive time points or waves, at 12, 18, 30, 42 and 54 weeks from baseline.

Our research question focuses on the prediction of depressive symptoms at each of the five waves. This prediction is made from health indicators at each of the same time points. Baseline (stable) demographic characteristics such as marital status, limitations in daily functioning and living arrangements also served as predictors.

At each wave, depression had been measured with the Center for Epidemiologic Studies Depression Scale (CES-D). The CES-D is a 20-item self report scale which has been used widely in studies of the elderly, and has good psychometric properties (for references see Beekman

---

[2]The data had been collected in the context of the Longitudinal Aging Study Amsterdam (LASA), conducted at the Department of Psychiatry and the Department of Sociology and Social Gerontology of the Free University Amsterdam. The study is funded by the Netherlands Ministry of Welfare, Health and Sports. The authors acknowledge permission for use of these data

et al., 1995). The Dutch translation has also been shown to have good psychometric properties.

At each wave, subjects had reported, amongst others, their perceived health status, whether they had been ill and whether they had contacted a doctor the previous month. Marital status had been assessed at baseline, as well as whether subjects lived independently or were living in some kind of (sheltered) facility for elderly people. A scale referred to as 'instrumental limitations' (IADL) assessed to what extent subjects experienced difficulties in instrumental matters such as filling in forms, arranging money matters and the like.

We retained those subjects for whom depression had been assessed at two or more waves. Next, we selected those subjects who had at least one non-missing score on a demographic variable as well as at least one non-missing score on a health-related variable (such as doctor's visits). Two hundred and thirty nine subjects were retained in this manner.

Structural equation modelling of longitudinal data has as a starting point that all series are of equal length. As such it needs complete series. Our data set contained only 113 complete series (out of a total of 239 cases). This is quite a small number for fitting a model of our size (see Boomsma, 1983). In principle, when a number of series are incomplete, one solution is to fit the data on an estimated correlation or covariance matrix in which the missing have been deleted pairwise. However, as the correlations or covariances are then estimated on different samples, this in practice often leads to a matrix with a negative determinant, as the linear dependence need not be preserved in this way (see any statistical textbook on linear dependence in correlation matrices). Therefore, we imputed the missing variables and occasions using regression imputation (Little & Schenker, 1995). Regression imputation is possible when a variable is missing on not more than 50% of occasions. From simulations in which parts of a known data structure are omitted at random, it is known to reproduce the data quite well.

The variables illness and doctor's visits were highly correlated; in order to simplify the model, we therefore omitted illness and retained doctor's visits, which we presumed to be of the highest predictive value on depression. For 'marital status', which has four categories (unmarried, married, divorced, widowed) we constructed three dummy variables. We used effect coding so that the categories can be regarded as contrasts (for the respective dummy variables: unmarried versus married, unmarried versus divorced, and unmarried versus widowed). Table 4.1 lists the variables that were included in the analysis.

Table 4.1: *Depression Data: Variables in the Analysis*

criterion variable at $t_1, \ldots, t_5$	
DEPRESSION	(0 = not depressed,..., 98 = very depressed)
predictor variables at $t_1, \ldots, t_5$	
VISIT DOCTOR	(0=yes, 1=no)
GENERAL HEALTH	(0=healthy,..., 99=unhealthy)
at baseline t_0	
MARITAL STATUS	dummy 1 (unmarried (0)$\leftrightarrow$ married (1))
	dummy 2 (unmarried (0)$\leftrightarrow$ divorced (1))
	dummy 3 (unmarried (0)$\leftrightarrow$ widowed (1))
LIVING ARRANGEMENTS	(1=independent, 2=residential)
IADL	(0=severely limited,...,6=no limitations)
(instrumental limitations)	

We will attempt to predict depression at the five waves of measurement. We will do so in a longitudinal model that takes account of the time-dependence in the depression scores. Our model should thus be able to accommodate time-dependence. We will try to predict depression from time-varying predictor variables as well as from predictor variables that are stable over time, such as demographic characteristics. We assume that the depression scores are an imperfect realization of each subject's true psychological state. Therefore, we use a model with a latent variable.

The model is outlined in Figure 4.13. The baseline predictor variables flow into the model at Z_1, the latent variable at time point 1. We could also have chosen to let the baseline predictor variables predict each latent variable directly; however, the idea that the effect of the time-invariant variables is already there at time point 1, and that any impact of the background characteristics is passed on from time point to time point, is more in line with our ideas about the dynamics of the subject at hand. The time-varying predictor variables have an immediate impact on the latent variable of each respective time point. Note how the dummy variables for marital status appear in the figure, with separate regression coefficients for each dummy variable. The model we use is thus indeed essentially what is called a state space model or linear dynamic system.

Figure 4.13: *Depression Data: Linear Dynamic Model*

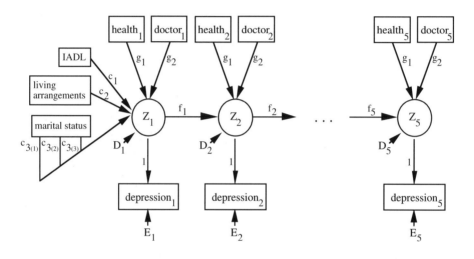

We constrained the factor loadings (the coefficients from the latent variable to the outcome variable 'depression') to be time-invariant. Without this constraint the latent variable could in principle have a different interpretation at each time point. We also fixed their values at 1. This causes no loss of generality, as the value of 1 changes only the scaling of the regression coefficients. Furthermore, we constrained the regression coefficients from the predictor variables to the latent variable to be time-invariant. A final, necessary, constraint is that the variances of the output variables be constrained to be time-invariant: $\text{Var}(E_1) = \text{Var}(E_2) = \text{Var}(E_3) = \text{Var}(E_4) = \text{Var}(E_5) = 1$; if these variances are left unconstrained, the model is unidentified. The constraint on the variances translates as requiring that the depression variable has the same reliability at each time point.

We did not constrain the transition parameters for the latent variables (f_t) to be time-invariant, even though this is generally done in this type of model to ensure that the latent variable is as comparable as possible across time points. However, leaving them unconstrained makes it possible to accommodate the unequal intervals between time points in our data set.

In principle, there would have been another possibility to accommodate unequal time intervals, by using so-called phantom variables. A phantom variable is a latent variable for which no indicators have been measured, and that is inserted at certain time points into the chain of latent variables, in order to accommodate unequal spacing of measurements. Our measurements were collected at 12, 18, 30, 42 and 54 weeks from baseline. Thus, t_1 and t_2 are 6 weeks apart, and the other time points are 12 weeks apart. For our example we could have accommodated these unequal intervals by using the model depicted in Figure 4.14. In the data set, every time point is 6 weeks apart, so if the first wave was at 12 weeks from baseline, the second at 18 weeks, we insert a third (for which we have only the phantom latent variable Z_3) 'phantom' occasion at 24 weeks; the third wave appears next at 30 weeks, after another interval of 6 weeks we insert again a phantom variable, and so on. In this way we construct a chain of equidistant measurement occasions. As this model is a lot more complicated (three phantom variables Z_3, Z_5 and Z_7 are needed for accommodating the one smaller interval) we deem it more efficient to simply allow the transition parameters to vary. For more on phantom variables, see Rindskopf (1984b).

We submitted the covariance matrix of the imputed data to EQS (Bentler, 1995). The algorithm converged to a model with a goodness-of-fit value of 171.243 ($p < 0.001$, $df = 73$). Thus the model does not fit. The Bentler–Bonett normed fit index was 0.937; the Akaike information criterion equalled 25.243. The absolute value of the largest standardized residual was 0.280, and the absolute average standardized residual 0.03. The explained variances $(1 - D_t^2)$ at the respective time points were 0.24, 0.72, 0.91, 0.81 and 0.89. None of the Wald tests for dropping parameters was significant; the Lagrange multiplier test recommended only that the equality constraint for the variances $\hat{\sigma}_E^2$ at time points 1 and 4 be dropped; however, as this constraint is necessary for the model to be identified, we did not follow this advice.

On the basis of the goodness-of-fit statistic, we must conclude that the model does not fit. The Bentler–Bonett normed fit index is in a grey area: not being higher than 0.95, it is certainly not good enough. How-

Figure 4.14: *Depression Data: Linear Dynamic Model with Phantom Variables*

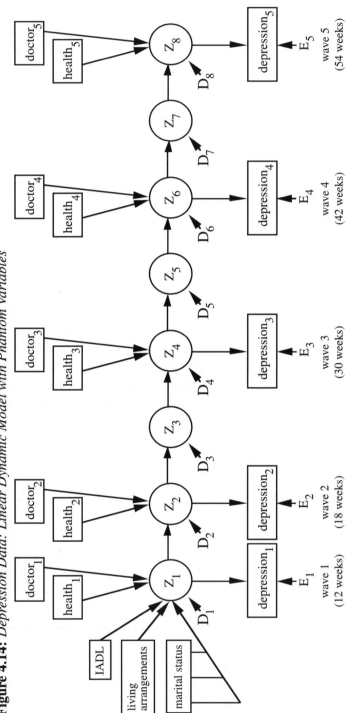

ever, not being below 0.9, it is also not so bad that we wholly discard the solution. In addition, the explained variances (apart from the first one at time point 1) are quite nice. Therefore, even though we should definitely seek for a better-fitting model, we will interpret the solution.

The standardized solution, in which both the latent variables and the residuals have been standardized to unit variance, is shown in Figure 4.15. Coefficients that were significantly different from zero, have been indicated bold face. The changed values for the h-coefficients, which had been constrained to 1, have been indicated between brackets (0.88, 0.89, 0.88, 0.90, 0.89); note how indeed the equality constraints are not preserved in the standardization process.

Interpreting the analysis results of this model, we arrive at the following conclusions. The depression measurements are strongly autoregressive; in fact, the parameters for the transition from one latent variable to the next are the highest of all. There is only a little fluctuation in the values of these parameters over the time points. Note that the loading from t_1 to t_2 is the lowest; this is surprising as the interval from t_1 to t_2 was the shortest of all. However, as we saw above, particularly the explained variance for the first wave is low; this is most likely because the baseline characteristics enter the model through the latent variable Z_1. Thus the latent variable Z_1 plays a different role than the other latent variables: it does not have an antecedent latent variable (in other words: the chain here does not have a starting point Z_0), but it does have the baseline characteristics as antecedents. This is maybe an explanation for the fact that the loading f_1 is lower than expected: Z_1 does not fit-in that well along with the other latent variables. The predictor variable health has a positive loading, implying that subjects who reported many health complaints are more likely to be depressed. The variable doctor has a negative loading, meaning that subjects who visit their doctor are also more likely to be depressed. The three dummy variables for marital status all had regression coefficients significantly different from zero. The first dummy has a negative sign, which can be interpreted as married subjects being less depressed than unmarried subjects. The second dummy variable has a positive sign, which must be interpreted as divorce also having a negative impact on depression (divorced subjects being more depressed than unmarried subjects). Finally, widowed subjects are less depressed than unmarried subjects. The parameter val-

Figure 4.15: *Depression Data: Results for Linear Dynamic Model*

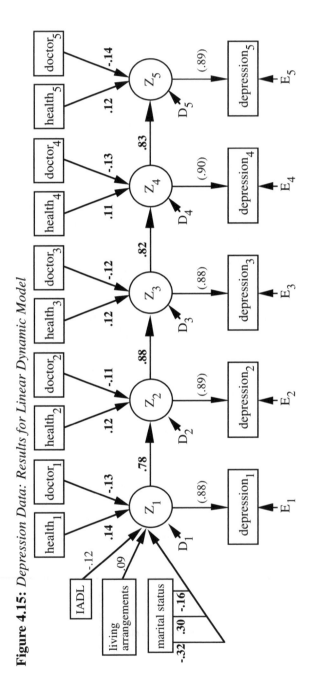

ues for instrumental limitations and living arrangements are not significantly different from zero; we will therefore not interpret them.

Thus, we may conclude that divorce is a risk factor for depression. Unmarried subjects are next in line, followed by widowers. Married subjects have the lowest risk of depression. The onset of depression may be characterized by decreased health and visits to the general practitioner. However, by far the most significant predictor of depression is subjects' previous condition. Depression levels at any time point are always best predicted from depression levels at the previous time point. This was underlined by a (non-significant) Lagrange multiplier test at the end of the output, which recommended the creation of a path between Z_1 and Z_5, indicating how we can in effect predict depression at the last time point from depression at baseline.

All significance levels reported here are derived from the solution in which multivariate normality was assumed. However, we know that quite a number of measures are skewed, such as depression, health status and limitations. Mardia's kappa coefficient, which gives an indication of non-normality, was 0.33, indicating that non-normality, though present, was not very serious. In addition, while platykurtosis is known to negatively affect the power of analyses (Stevens, 1996, p. 247), our data are leptokurtic, which makes the estimates of significance more conservative. Therefore, a pragmatic advice would be to leave the analysis as it is. Another approach would be to transform the skewed continuous variables such as depression and health. Unfortunately, for the dichotomous measures this is not possible. A better resort therefore seems to be to rerun the model using the ML,ROBUST option, which does not use the assumption of multivariate normality. For this example, ML,ROBUST produced a similar overall structure of parameter values. While significances were retained, overall significance levels were reduced. This is attributable to the relatively small number of cases in comparison to the size (in terms of the number of variables) of the model. Large variances increase errors of estimation, reducing any significances. All in all, the best approach in all likelihood is to search for another type of model that fits the data better.

Before moving on to such a model, we note that to analyse this kind of fairly complex model, it is important to start with good initial estimates of the parameters. This is best done by fitting simple parts of the model, assembling the parts to arrive at the full model. Secondly, as referred to above, the model fitted here is actually quite large given the number of observations. Each time point adds variables to the model (the attentive reader may have noted that structural equation modelling is done on what was called in Chapter 2.3 the BROAD matrix). Constraining parameters helps in the sense that fewer have to be estimated. A definitive solution for this problem can only be reached by working with much larger data sets.

4.3.2 Growth curve modelling

So far, we discussed a number of varieties of the autoregressive model, that explain the variance–covariance or correlation matrices of variables measured at different occasions. In this paragraph we will investigate a so-called *growth curve model*, in which not only the variances and covariances are explained, but also the means of the observed variables are modelled. In the literature such models are referred to as models with *structured means*. When we are investigating such models, we postulate a theoretical structure for the variances and covariances as well as for the means. Therefore, we have to analyse both the variance–covariance matrix and the vector of means. In technical terms we then analyse what is called the *augmented moment matrix*.

We discuss the growth curve model through an example on the development of reading ability. In this hypothetical example we assume that each subject starts with a certain ability at time point 1 and that this ability increases (or decreases) with the passage of time. Thus, if we plot the ability of an individual against time, we see a curve that starts at an intercept and develops over time either with constant slope (linear growth) or with slopes that vary over time as well (curvilinear growth). For a sample of individuals we can imagine a latent vector Z_1 containing the average score $\bar{Y}_1$ at t_1 (the intercept) and a latent variable Z_2 that represents the average difference between the scores at t_2 and t_1, that is: $\bar{Y}_2 - \bar{Y}_1$. This difference is also referred to as the slope.

In order to model these latent variables we define an observed variable V_{999}. The variable V_{999} contains ones only. It is connected to Z_1 and Z_2 by directed arrows with regression coefficients equal to the mean intercept and the mean slope respectively. As such a model would imply that all individuals have equal intercepts and equal slopes, we need two additional sources that represent the individual differences between the subjects. Those sources are the two disturbances D_1 and D_2. Because the disturbance D_1 is involved, the variance of Z_1 is equal to the variance of D_1. The same applies to Z_2 and D_2. A graphical representation of this model is given in Figure 4.16.

Figure 4.16: *Growth Curve Model of Latent Ability*

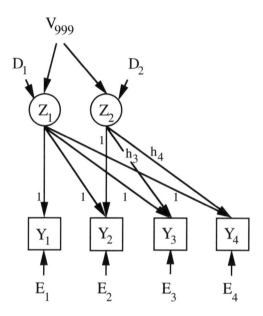

Suppose that the criterion variables Y_1, Y_2, Y_3 and Y_4 represent reading ability at time points 1, 2, 3 and 4 (for instance ages 6, 7, 8 and 9, respectively). The figure shows that the observed variable Y_1 is an indicator of Z_1. Because Z_1 is the only predictor of Y_1, Z_1 must therefore be identical to the latent ability scores at age 6. The regression parameter for the path from V_{999} to Z_1 is equal to the mean of these latent ability scores. Because the regression coefficient from Z_2 to Y_2 is also equal to 1, Z_2 explains the difference in scores between time point 1 and time point 2, and therefore embodies the slope.

In the figure the regression coefficients from Z_1 to Y_2, to Y_3 and to Y_4 are also fixed at 1. This means that the scores on the latter three Y-variables consist of the latent abilities Z_1 plus a contribution of latent variable Z_2, as well as error components E_2 through E_4.

To illustrate the specification of our model, note that according to our specification the prediction of Y_1, $\hat{Y}_1$, is set equal to Z_1:

$$\hat{Y}_1 = Z_1.$$

According to our specification it also applies that:

$$\hat{Y}_2 = Z_1 + Z_2 = \hat{Y}_1 + Z_2 \Longrightarrow Z_2 = \hat{Y}_2 - \hat{Y}_1.$$

In case of linear growth, we can write for time point 3:

$$\hat{Y}_3 = \hat{Y}_1 + 2(\hat{Y}_2 - \hat{Y}_1).$$

This generalizes to:

$$\hat{Y}_t = \hat{Y}_1 + (t-1)(\hat{Y}_2 - \hat{Y}_1)$$
$$= Z_1 + (t-1)Z_2.$$

Thus, when h_t equals $(t-1)$, we have linear growth. When other values for h_t are modelled, we have curvilinear growth.

The specification of the model and the parameters as outlined in Figure 4.16 thus ensures that the latent variable Z_1 represents the latent ability scores at age 6, and that the latent variable Z_2 represents the difference between the latent ability scores at age 6 and at age 7. From this it follows that the free parameters, labelled h_3 and h_4, can be interpreted as the proportion of the difference between age 6 and 7 which explains the scores at age 8 and 9.

One example of a research question which could be analysed using this model is whether the changes in ability between ages 7 and 8 or between ages 8 and 9 are equal to those between ages 6 and 7. In that case every subject's growth curve would be linear.

Other hypotheses can be tested using this growth curves approach to structural equation modelling. We can, for instance, test whether regression to the mean is present. To do so we create a path between Z_1 and Z_2: if subjects with high initial score tend to develop at a lower rate, and subjects with low initial score tend to develop faster, so that we have regression towards the mean, we would expect the coefficient for this path to be negative. The reverse effect can be investigated as well: if subjects with high initial score tend to grow faster (and vice versa) we would expect a positive value for the coefficient for the path between Z_1 and Z_2.

A vast literature on growth curve modelling exists. Important references are McArdle (1986), McArdle & Epstein (1987), Meredith & Tisak (1990), and Willett & Sayer (1996). In random effects growth models, that are discussed in Chapter 5, growth on one variable that has been measured at several time points, is summarized in a number of growth parameters. Then for each subject, T measurements are in principle reduced to a smaller number of k parameters. Usually, the intercept and slope are used to summarize growth, so that $k = 2$. In random effects models, properties of these individual growth parameters such as their variance, or the covariance between certain parameters are estimated.

In the following we discuss an empirical example of growth curve modelling.

Example of growth curve analysis: depressive symptoms in relation to health and demographic characteristics   We use the same data set on depression in the elderly (Beekman et al., 1995)[3] that was used above. Longitudinal data were available on depression, health, and demographic characteristics. Baseline data on instrumental limitations (IADL), as well as a number of demographic variables will serve as time-invariant predictors. Data had been collected at a baseline measurement (t_0) as well as at five successive waves. Again, our research question focuses on the prediction of depressive symptoms at each of the five waves, from health indicators and baseline (unvarying) demographic characteristics such as marital status and limitations. For reasons of comparability, we will use the same variables that were used in the first example.

In our example, we are interested in investigating growth in relation to time-varying predictors as well as in relation to baseline characteristics. These baseline characteristics are particularly interesting from a prevention point of view: if we could identify risk groups as early as the first measurement point, we could gear special prevention, monitoring and treatment programmes to the groups most at risk of developing

---

[3]The data had been collected in the context of the Longitudinal Aging Study Amsterdam (LASA), conducted at the Department of Psychiatry and the Department of Sociology and Social Gerontology of the Free University Amsterdam. The study is funded by the Netherlands Ministry of Welfare, Health and Sports.

depression. In the context of growth curve modelling, the slope parameters are thus of special interest.

Thus, we will use a growth curve model, and attempt to predict depression from two latent variables, one representing the intercept and the second representing growth, predicting intercept and growth from a number of background characteristics. For this, we use the same imputed data set that was used in the previous example, choosing the same time-invariant predictors (marital status, living arrangements and instrumental limitations). For an overview of the categories of the criterion and predictor variables we refer back to Table 4.1.

As explained above and in Dunn et al. (1993, pp. 125–130), to fit this type of model using EQS, a 'super'-independent variable – consisting of ones only – for estimating the means has to be included. This variable is labelled V_{999} in Figure 4.17, which graphically represents the model we are fitting. All parameters relating to the intercept have been given a subscript 'i'; all parameters relating to the slope have been given a subscript 's'. The latent variable representing the intercept is thus indicated as Z_i; the latent variable representing the slope is indicated as Z_s.

In Figure 4.17, arrows point not only from V_{999} to Z_i and Z_s, but also from V_{999} to the depression variable at time point 1: addition of this path had emerged as a recommendation from preliminary analyses.

In addition, arrows have been drawn from V_{999} to the predictors, that is: to the three dummy variables for marital status, to living arrangements and to instrumental limitations. This is necessary because we have to incorporate also the means of these variables into the model. The error variances ($VarE_t$) were again fixed to unity for all time points, for reasons outlined above.

Introduction of the one super-independent variable V_{999} has a number of consequences. Firstly, the model has many more paths. More importantly, introduction of the super-independent variable causes all previously independent variables such as living arrangements and marital status to become dependent variables technically speaking (see the corresponding arrows and coefficients in Figure 4.17), which makes estimation much more complicated. Because of this, the algorithm needs exceedingly good starting values to be able to analyse the model at all. To obtain these, it is advisable to fit the model in parts: each time, one part of the model is fitted to the data, and the parameter estimates de-

Figure 4.17: *Depression Data: Growth Curve Model with Demographic Predictors*

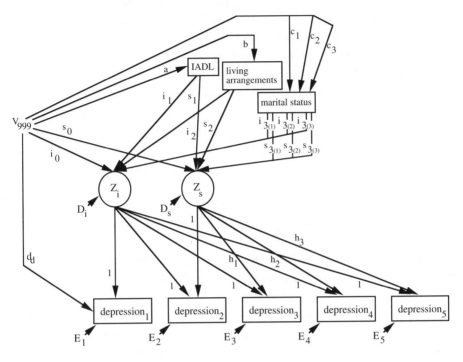

rived from these partial analyses can be used in the final, agglomerate, model.

The algorithm converged to a model with a goodness-of-fit value of 25.707. As the degrees of freedom for this model are 31, the value of the goodness-of-fit statistic is well below the degrees of freedom, and we can conclude that the model fits well. The Bentler–Bonett normed fit index was 0.976, the Akaike information criterion equalled -36.293. The absolute value of the largest standardized residual was 0.058, and the absolute average standardized residual 0.0153. Nevertheless, the explained variances $(1 - D_i^2)$ and $(1 - D_s^2)$ of the respective latent variables Z_i and Z_s were 0.19 and 0.19, indicating that there is a lot of individual variation around the mean intercept and slope values. None of the Wald tests for dropping parameters or Lagrange multiplier tests for adding parameters were significant, however. Thus, even though we have obtained a solution that is satisfactory from a statistical point of view, its practical significance is limited.

The standardized solution, in which both the latent variables and the residuals are standardized to unit variance, is represented in Figure 4.18. Coefficients that had been tested as significantly different from zero, have been indicated bold face. Note again how the equality constraints (for instance all factor loadings on Z_i) are not preserved in the stand-ardization process. As the solution presented here is the standardized solution (in which all means become zero), all coefficients for the paths from V_{999} to the predictor variables have also become zero. We have indicated between brackets, coefficients that had been fixed at a certain value but have been altered because of standardization. The significance of the parameter values for intercept, slope as well as for any deviations at time point 1 from the straight line have been tested, and the results of these tests have been represented in the figure as well (either as 'sign' or as 'not sign').

There are significant differences in scores on the intercept variable as well as in the initial depression score itself (indicated as 'sign' for the paths from V_{999} to Z_i and to depression at time point 1). Differences in intercept appear to be related to differences in instrumental limitation as well as to differences in marital status. Combining information from the sign of coefficients with the category values (see Table 4.1), we infer how subjects with high scores on the variable instrumental limitations (i.e. no limitations) generally have lower scores on the intercept variable and vice versa. Subjects with high scores on the first dummy variable for marital status (that is: the married subjects) have lower scores on the intercept variable than those with low scores (that is: the unmarried subjects), subjects with high scores on the second dummy variable for marital status (that is: the divorced subjects) have higher scores on the intercept variable than the unmarried subjects, and subjects with high scores on the third dummy variable for marital status (that is: the wid-owed subjects) have lower scores on the intercept variable than the un-married subjects. (Note the regression-towards-the-mean type of effect in the coefficients for marital status: categories with positive coefficient values for the intercepts have negative coefficient values for the slopes, and vice versa.)

For differences in the level of depression during all five measure-ment occasions, we thus find more or less the same pattern as in the

Figure 4.18: *Depression Data: Growth Curve Results with Demographic*
Predictors

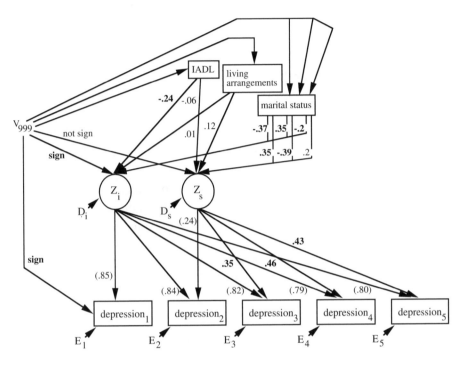

previous example: least depressed are the married subjects; next in line
are the widowed subjects, then the unmarried subjects, and divorced
subjects are again most depressed. While instrumental limitations was
not significant in the previous example, it appears as a significant predictor of intercept differences here.

No significant differences in slope were found. The significance of
the coefficients h_3, h_4 and h_5 is thus of little relevance: even though
the slope predicts the depression scores at time points 3, 4 and 5, the
slope itself is not significantly different from zero. The same applies
qualitate qua to those coefficients for marital status to slope that are
significantly different from zero: while differences in marital status are
related to slope differences, the slope differences themselves are again
not significantly different from zero.

All in all, the analysis – though technically sound – is not entirely
satisfactory. As an overall conclusion, one could even state that as no

differences in slope can be found, it is not necessary to investigate depression longitudinally. On the other hand, the explained variances of the two latent variables are very low, so it is perhaps more valid to conclude that a model in which longitudinal development of depression is predicted from an overall intercept and growth curve, that are in turn predicted from demographic risk factors, is too restrictive. A logical next step would be to search for a more flexible model, that includes not only static, demographic predictors of growth, but time-varying predictors as well.

Therefore, we extended the model with the predictor variables of the previous example, that is, with the variables for health and doctor's visits at each of the successive waves. We now again use all the variables given in Table 4.1. The model we arrive at in this fashion is graphically represented in Figure 4.19. The time-varying predictors have been added in the bottom part of the figure. Arrows have to be drawn from V_{999} to these predictors as well, to incorporate the means of these variables into the model. An arrow has been drawn from V_{999} to depression not only at the first time point, but to the second time point as well, as the Lagrange tests from preliminary analyses had indicated that this would give a significant improvement of model fit. The error variances ($VarE_t$) were again fixed to unity for all time points, to ensure equal reliability at all time points – and because otherwise the model would not be identified. Note how the previous model depicted in Figure 4.17 is nested within the model in Figure 4.19 (see Section 4.2.3).

Also for this model it applies that the presence of the one super-independent variable V_{999} makes estimation complicated. To obtain good starting values, also here we fitted the model in parts: each time, one part of the model was fitted, and the parameter estimates derived from these parts of the model were used in the final model.

The algorithm converged to a model with a goodness-of-fit value of 114.220. As the degrees of freedom for this model are 185, also here the value of the goodness-of-fit statistic is well below the degrees of freedom, and we may conclude that the model fits well. The value of the Akaike information criterion equalled −255.078. The Bentler–Bonett normed fit index was 0.958, the absolute value of the largest standardized residual was 0.260, and the average absolute standardized residual 0.038. The explained variances $(1 - D_i^2)$ and $(1 - D_s^2)$ of the respective latent variables Z_i and Z_s were 0.19 and 0.13, however, indicating how

Figure 4.19: *Depression Data: Growth Curve Model with Demographic and Time-Varying Predictors*

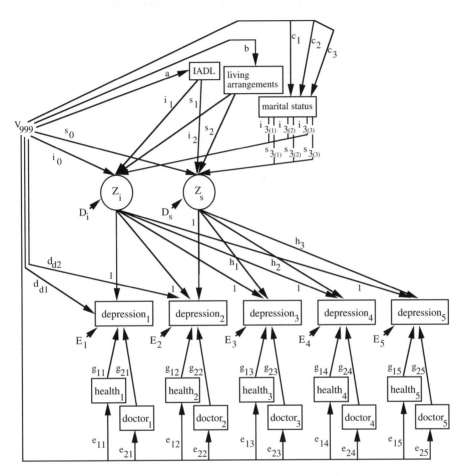

the second latent variable is capturing even less of the dynamic process under investigation than in the previous analysis. None of the Wald tests for dropping parameters or Lagrange multiplier tests for adding parameters was significant, however.

The standardized solution, in which both the latent variables and the residuals have been standardized to unit variance, is represented in Figure 4.20. Note again how the equality constraints are not preserved in the standardization process; we have indicated between brackets, coefficients that had been fixed at a certain value but have been altered because of standardization. Coefficients that had been tested as significantly different from zero, have been indicated bold face. The significance of the parameter values for intercept, slope, as well as for any deviations at time point 1 and time point 2 from the straight line, have been tested, and the results of these have been represented in the figure. As the solution presented here is the standardized solution (in which all means become zero), all coefficients for V_{999} have also become zero.

Figure 4.20: *Depression Data: Growth Curve Results with Demographic and Time-Varying Predictors*

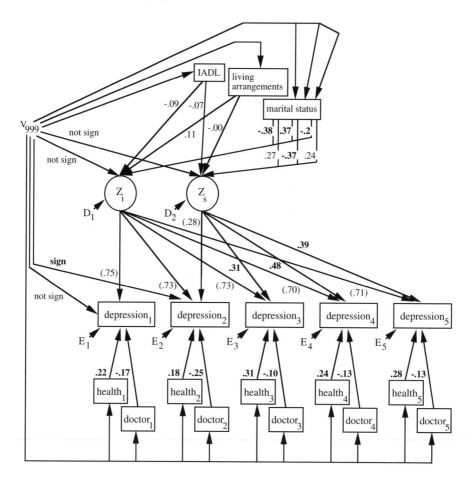

From Figure 4.20 we see how the coefficients of both time-varying predictors are significantly different from zero at all time points. High scores on health (that is: feeling unhealthy) are related to high scores on depression, and vice versa. High scores on doctor's visits (that is: no visits to the doctor) are related to low scores on depression, and vice versa. Neither the intercepts nor the slopes were significantly different from zero. This means that, even though a number of predictors of intercept and slope were significant, the intercepts and slopes themselves were not. (Note the regression-towards-the-mean type of effect in the coefficients for marital status: categories with positive coefficient values for the intercepts have negative coefficient values for the slopes, and vice versa.) The same applies to the significance of intercept and slope as predictors of depression. The significance of the coefficient from V_{999} to depression at time point 2 shows that there is some discontinuity at this wave. The discontinuity is furthermore reflected in the magnitude of the coefficients for health and doctor's visits: for all other time points, health is the more important predictor; for time point 2, doctor's visits is the more important. It is unclear to what this effect can be attributed. It might be due to the relatively short interval between the first and second measurement point, or it might be a period effect.

From this last analysis, it appears as if depression scores are perhaps better predicted by time-varying indicators such as health and doctor's visits, than by the fairly stringent growth curves represented by Z_i and Z_s. Health and doctor's visits more or less usurp most of the temporal variation in depression, leaving little for the two factors used in our growth curve model.

We are now left with two growth curve models for this data set, which both fit the data well. To decide which model is the better model, we first compare the two models using the respective goodness-of-fit statistics. If two models are fitting, we can compare their statistical performance by testing the significance of the difference of the goodness-of-fit statistics, with degrees of freedom equal to the difference of the respective degrees of freedom. For our example we then find a goodness-of-fit statistic equalling $(114.220 - 25.707 =)88.513$, with degrees of freedom equalling $(185 - 31 =)154$. As also here the value of the goodness-of-fit statistic is well below the degrees of freedom, we must conclude that there is no statistically significant difference between the two models. To choose between the two, we can resort to either the Bentler–Bonett normed fit index (which is 0.976 for the first growth curve model and 0.958 in the second), or to the Akaike information criterion, which is a better indicator as it incorporates aspects of parsimony. Not surprisingly, the information criterion of the second growth curve model (that had the highest degrees of freedom) has the lowest value (-255.778), meaning that the second growth curve model should be preferred over the first.

As an overall conclusion, we may state that it appears that the development of depression generally can not be forecasted on the basis of a classification into risk groups, such as defined by marital status. There is a lot of individual variation around the general growth curve. It thus appears that depression does not follow a predictable universal course, and is perhaps better additionally monitored using signal variables such as health and doctor's visits.

It may be that, through other structural equation models or other types of analysis (with as a most likely candidate the latent mixed Markov models described in Section 6.3.4), subgroups of subjects can be found for whom predictable, simple courses can be identified. It is likely that time-varying indicators for the onset of depression fine-tune the predictive strength of all such models.

4.4   Recent developments in structural equation modelling of longitudinal data

So far in this chapter we have been dealing with a sample from a population. We tried to generalize from the sample characteristics to the characteristics in the population. In order to do so, we made a number of assumptions. For instance, we assumed that the variables are multivariate normally distributed and that the sample elements are independent of each other. This latter assumption means that the scores of a sample element, usually an individual, do not depend on the scores of any other sample element. Thus, we have many individuals which are independent of each other. In such cases we can develop statistical tests for testing our hypotheses.

However, a not uncommon occurrence in the context of longitudinal modelling is the analysis of single series. In that case, we want to analyse the data for just one sample element. For instance, during one complete year we measure each week the mood states of a subject undergoing therapy and we want to describe the development of the mood states in terms of a parsimonious model. At first sight, it might appear as if it is impossible to analyse such a single series using structural equation modelling. Single series can nevertheless be analysed if we use lagged versions of the measurements. This can be envisaged as follows.

Suppose, in the example above, that mood state is measured through two indicators at 52 occasions, so that $T = 52$. We can then construct a 52×2 data matrix, where the rows refer to the occasions and the columns to the variables. For this data matrix we can compute the covariance matrix. This covariance matrix is called the zero-order lagged covariance matrix. We now add a third and fourth column to the data matrix, which are the same as columns 1, and 2 respectively, but shifted one step (compare Chapter 2, Section 2.3.3). In that case the covariance matrix of column 1 and 2 with column 3 and 4 can be defined as the first-order lagged covariance matrix. Shifting 2, 3, and more rows we can define second-, third-, and higher order lagged covariance matrices. In this manner we have defined covariance matrices for the lagged relations between variables. Using the first order lagged covariance matrix we can analyse the relations between variables one time point apart, and thus AR(1) models; using higher order lagged covariance matrices we can analyse higher order autoregressive models. Though the basic idea behind this kind of analysis is not that hard to grasp, things are not as easy in practice.

The main difference between structural equation modelling as discussed in the previous sections and structural equation modelling for lagged variables is of course that the rows in the data matrix are now not sample elements, but occasions. However, a fundamental assumption in structural equation modelling is that the rows in the data matrix are independent. With lagged variables (where the occasions constitute the rows in the data matrix) this assumption is not met (we are even explicitly interested in the dependence between the rows). This means that well-known statistical theory does not apply.

As this chapter focuses mainly on those applications of structural equation modelling where generalizations over subjects are made (and not over occasions) we will not go into the statistical details of structural equation modelling for lagged variables. The main references for further information are Molenaar (1985), MacCallum & Ashby (1986), Molenaar, De Gooijer, & Schmitz (1992), Browne (1992), Wood & Brown (1994), Hershberger et al. (1996) and Van Buuren (1997a).

In Section 4.3 we discussed an autoregressive model which resulted in a so-called simplex structure of the correlation matrix. If a sample correlation matrix has a simplex structure it may seem rational to analyse the data with an autoregressive model. However, as Rogosa has argued many times (see for instance Rogosa & Willett, 1985), there may be other models as well which can describe such correlation matrices and, more importantly, these alternative models may be much more appropriate because the parameters have a much nicer interpretation than the regression coefficients in a structural equation model. More particularly, Rogosa suggested the use of individual growth curve models for analysing such data. Browne & Du Toit (1991) give a number of nice examples in which they used growth curve models for learning data. They proposed three models in which they specified a nonlinear model for the relationship between the means and the time variable. These nonlinear models are functions of certain parameters, and these parameters have interesting interpretations: for instance, one parameter may represent the asymptote of individual scores, and another the rate of growth. Such growth curve models, though quite interesting in an area such as psychology, unfortunately make use of nonlinear model equations, so that standard computer programs (like LISREL and EQS) can not estimate the parameters routinely. For this reason we will not discuss these models further, but refer to the literature (Browne & Du Toit, 1991; McArdle, 1988; Meredith & Tisak, 1990; Du Toit, 1979).

Another interesting recent development is the use of Kalman filtering (Kalman 1960; for a short description see Chapter 2, Section 2.4.2). Kalman filtering is a least squares optimal procedure for estimating the scores on one or more latent variables. It can be used when the transition matrices in a state space model or linear dynamic system (that is: **F**, **G** and **H**) are known and when information on the uncertainty captured in the errors and disturbances is available. In social and behavioural research, such information is generally unavailable. Estimates can, however, be found from structural equation modelling, after which estimates for the scores on the latent variables can be computed using the Kalman filter. Using the property that the Kalman filter becomes independent of the initial state very quickly, such Kalman filtering can very well be used for short series as well. Extending structural equation modelling with Kalman filtering is useful in those areas of behavioural and social research where the researcher is not only interested in the structural equation parameters (like regression coefficients or factor loadings), but also in the individual latent growth curves. Obviously, this will be the case in many areas of behavioural research. The computer program LISKAL can carry out such structural equation modelling with subsequent Kalman filtering; see Oud, Van den Bercken, & Essers (1990). It has been applied especially in educational research (for instance, prediction of test results for primary school children on the basis of their previous performance). More on structural equation modelling with Kalman filtering can be found in Jansen & Oud (1995) and Oud & Jansen (1996).

4.5 Missing data

Missing data constitute a problem in structural equation modelling. Little & Rubin (1987, 1989) distinguish three types of missing data: missing completely at random (MCAR), missing at random (MAR), and non-ignorable missing. When data are missing completely at random, the likelihood of an observation being missing does not depend on the values of the observed or of the latent variables. When data are missing at random, the likelihood of an observation being missing may depend on the values of the observed variables, but does not depend on the values of the latent variables. When data are non-ignorable missing, none of this applies. For more information, see Section 1.6.3.

When data can be assumed to be missing completely at random, a pragmatic approach is to just run computations with the nonmissing part of the data and generalize the results to the population from which the sample was drawn. However, MCAR is a very strong assumption, which is hardly ever met. In most cases data are not missing completely at random, and not even missing at random. Usually, those who drop out during the course of the study deviate from those who remain throughout the study, either on background variables, or on one or more of variables that are of specific interest in the study. Dropouts are generally: more criminal, more depressed, less adaptable, etc. Thus, simply leaving out these subjects altogether may seriously invalidate the findings.

There are basically four approaches to the missing data problem in structural equation modelling. When data can be assumed to be missing completely at random, a first approach is to delete all subjects with any missing values from the data, equivalent to listwise deletion. When the data are missing at random, listwise deletion gives biased, though consistent estimates (Arbuckle, 1996). In practice, it will leave the researcher with a much smaller sample size, which may present technical problems. As explained above, it also leaves the researcher with a biased sample. Thus, in general, this is too drastic an option to be feasible.

A second possibility is pairwise deletion: (co)variances or correlations are then computed on the basis of the available data for each (pair of) variable(s). While this gives a covariance matrix for all subjects, there is no guarantee that the covariance matrix has the proper structure: each element of this matrix is computed from, in principle, a different sample, and the elements of the matrix may not be well structured (see any statistical textbook on linear dependence in correlation matrices). Even if the analysis produces a solution, pairwise deletion gives biased estimates for data missing at random; it also lacks a method to estimate standard errors as well as a method to test hypotheses (Arbuckle, 1996). Thus, while worthwhile trying out, especially in case of small numbers of missing values well spread over subjects, it is by no means a guaranteed or satisfactory method.

A third possibility is applicable when we have series of unequal length. We can then apply multisample modelling. For this, we divide the sample into subsamples: the first sample consists of all subjects who have complete series, the second sample consists of all subjects who have complete series up to time point $T - 1$, the third series consists of all subjects who have complete series up to time point $T - 2$, etc. Next, we perform a multisample analysis in which we constrain the parameters to be equal across samples. Although in principle viable, this method may become difficult to perform when the various samples become very small.

A fourth possibility is to impute the missing data. A number of techniques have been developed for such imputations, the basic ideas can be found in Little & Rubin (1987, 1989). In general, the missing data are estimated on the basis of the available data, from some assumed structure. Possibilities for doing so range from simple interpolation (for example, if a variable is missing at the second wave, the average of its value of the first and third wave is substituted) to quite sophisticated methods, whose merits have not always been conclusively demonstrated. A number of fairly equivalent methods have been proposed to impute the missing data using structural equation programs themselves (Allison, 1987; Bentler, 1989; Muthén, Kaplan, & Hollis, 1987). In the EQS manual (Bentler, 1989, pp. 197–200) an example illustrates how imputation can be done using a two-group design, one group constituting the group with no missings at all, and one group constituting the group with missings. From the two covariance matrices, a new covariance matrix for the total group is then estimated, which can be analysed once more using structural equation modelling. A disadvantage of these methods is that they can be used only when not too many distinct patterns of missing observations are present in the data (Arbuckle, 1996). They are also not easy to apply. Arbuckle (1995, 1996) has developed a structural equation modelling program (Amos) that has a more user-friendly option for ML estimation of missing data. Mx (Neale, 1994) offers basically the same possibilities. Neither program limits the number of missing data patterns. Arbuckle reports (1996) how, for data missing at random, ML imputation gives results that are superior by a wide margin to pairwise deletion. Another option for imputation is regression imputation, which we used in our examples above. For details see Little & Schenker (1995).

For more details on the missing data problem in structural equation modelling see Muthén et al. (1987), Bentler (1990), Brown (1994) and Rovine (1994).

4.6 Discussion

Structural equation modelling is a potentially useful class of techniques in longitudinal data analysis. This usefulness comes from the versatility in specifying models, where many types of paths between variables can be created and errors can be allowed to correlate. At the same time, this versatility in itself constitutes a risk. In fact, structural equation modelling has acquired something of a bad name because of the deceptively easy way in which superficially sophisticated models could be tested, and presented as 'true' and 'causal' without the necessary theoretical support.

In general, one should always heed that model formulation is theory driven rather than fit driven, and that parsimonious models (with possibly lower fit) are always preferable over more complicated models (in spite of their possibly higher fit). In this context, we would like to cite Fergusson & Horwood (1988, p. 351): *"...the major contribution of current SEM methods to the social sciences may not be in the area of developing substantive models but rather in the area of sensitizing research workers to the theoretical, formal and empirical problems which must be confronted when causal account of correlational evidence are offered."*

Another caution in the use of structural equation modelling is the possible existence of equivalent models, that is, models that are equally plausible as the hypothesized model to fit the data. Equivalent models, though fitting the data equally well, imply very different theoretical conceptualizations of the data. At the theoretical level, there is more often than not no demarcation criterion for deciding which conceptual model to choose, while researchers differ in opinion about what an adequate theoretical framework to base a model specification on should look like. At the statistical level, the question emerges which of the equivalent models is the true model. More on the specification of equivalent models before data collection can be found in Hershberger (1994). The importance of the problem, and some remedies for it, are discussed by MacCallum, Wegener, Uchino, & Fabrigar (1993), while Bekker, Merckens, & Wansbeek (1994) have more on equivalent models and the identification problem.

Indeed, there has been a lot of debate about the usefulness of structural equation modelling for longitudinal data. Rogosa & Willett (1985) have argued that different structural equation models may fit a particular longitudinal data set equally well, and that the parameters from structural equation modelling that describe the relationship between the variables often lack substantial interpretation. Instead, they suggest using individual growth curve models. We discussed mean growth curve models, but did not discuss individual growth curve models in this chapter, as they are strongly related to the multilevel models which will be discussed in Chapter 5. In this context, Stoolmiller & Bank (1995) argue that autoregressive models are often less adequate for uncovering the causal mechanisms underlying many phenomena.

The practicalities of structural equation modelling may not be without problems either. In running our examples we found how fitting a model (especially the growth curve models) can be quite an art in itself and enormously time consuming, as a lot may depend on finding the right starting values. In such cases, one should start by fitting small parts of the model, and assemble the results until satisfactory results are obtained. The models presented here had only a 'limited' number of time points, however. When the length of series increases, the model fitting process may become increasingly complicated or even impossible, as the algorithms are more likely to arrive at improper solutions when the number of subjects becomes too small for the complexity of the problem at hand. In such cases, structural equation models cease to be a feasible data analytic option, and other models (such as the type of linear dynamic systems discussed in Chapter 2, or models in which the data matrix is flattened discussed in the same chapter) may become more appropriate. In general, one may state that structural equation models are suitable when a theoretical model with a high degree of specificity needs to be tested, in which a large number of subjects have been measured at a small number of occasions.

Simulation studies have shown the structural equation models to be surprisingly robust against violations of the assumption of multivariate normality. Parameter estimates are generally consistent, although the standard errors are affected. If possible, non-normal data may be transformed to normality (using for instance the square root or a logarithmic transformation), after which analysis may proceed with the transformed data. In some cases such transformations are not feasible, for instance because the scale has some 'natural' interpretation which we do not want to lose. In such cases, it is also possible to arrive at statistical tests through different procedures. A first possibility is to use jackknife or bootstrap methods, but both can be very time consuming. EQS has the 'ML, ROBUST' option for such resampling methods. An option for bootstrap resampling is present as well. Another possibility is to use methods that incorporate information on the higher order moments of the distribution. EQS has the arbitrary distribution generalized least squares or AGLS option for this. Such methods need substantially larger samples than usual, and will thus be generally impracticable in longitudinal situations in which sample size tends to be smaller. See Dunn et al. (1993, pp. 167–170 ff.) for practical matters.

Another complication may arise when the data are not continuous but categorical. In the examples above we showed how a nominal input variable with four categories could be accommodated using three dummy variables. When data are dichotomous, we can compute the correlations as if the variables were continuous, or we can use polychoric correlation coefficients. Simulations have shown that in both cases standard errors are underestimated and test statistics inflated. Conclusions from these should thus be presented with caution. Muthén's program for structural equation modelling, LISCOMP, can handle dichotomous data (Muthén, 1987).

4.7   Further reading

A lot of literature is available on structural equation modelling. Bollen (1989) is an excellent reference. The introduction by Dunn et al. (1993) is very user-friendly and software oriented. More on EQS can be found in Bentler & Wu (1995a,b), Bentler & Dudgeon (1996) and Browne & Arminger (1995). Other readable textbooks are Byrne (1994) and Hayduk (1987). There are many introductions to LISREL, the structural equation program by Karl Jöreskog; see for instance Jöreskog & Sörbom (1993).

More on longitudinal modelling through structural equation models can be found in McArdle (1986), McArdle & Epstein (1987), Meredith & Tisak (1990), and Willett & Sayer (1996), as well as in a number of textbooks mentioned above.

References for more advanced, recent developments were mentioned above in Section 4.4.

Chapter 5

Multilevel analysis of longitudinal data

Rien van der Leeden

5.1   Introduction

Hierarchically structured data are common in social and behavioural research. Social, and in particular educational systems, are frequently characterized by a structure in which the units of observation at one level are grouped within units at a higher level of organization. Repeated measures data may be regarded as having a hierarchical structure as well. In this chapter we will examine the multilevel approach and discuss the analysis of repeated measurements viewed as hierarchical data.

5.1.1   Multilevel data

In social and behavioural research one often encounters hierarchically structured data. For instance, employees are grouped into departments, sportsmen are grouped into teams, or people are grouped into clans and clans into tribes. Classical examples of hierarchical data can be found in educational research. Students are grouped or 'nested' within classes, and classes in turn are nested within schools, schools within districts, and so on. In the latter situation, districts form the highest level (here level-4, or the fourth level) and students the lowest level (level-1). The term *multilevel* is used to refer to such data structures and to analysis techniques that take these structures, that is, the interrelatedness of the levels in view of the variation within a level, into account. The designation multilevel points out that nested membership relations among the units of observation constitute the explicit object of study. The different levels refer to the different groupings that can be distinguished within the data.

Often the groupings themselves are of interest and not viewed merely as giving a specific structure to the data. Higher level units, for instance classes, can be considered sample elements themselves, being elements of a random sample drawn from some population of classes. Often, especially in educational research, this is also the way in which the data are collected: a sample of schools is taken, and within schools, classes and individuals are sampled. In that way, we can imagine having a sample consisting of a large number of randomly drawn students from a smaller number of randomly drawn classes, from a smaller number of randomly drawn schools. Usually, there are variables measured at different levels of the hierarchy. For instance, we could have the variable 'reading achievement' measured at the student level, the variable 'style of leadership of the teacher' measured at the class level, and the variable 'schoolsize' measured at the school level.

An example from social and behavioural science research in which a multilevel modelling framework is used, is given by Mason, Wong, & Entwisle (1984). Mason et al. studied the effects of maternal education and urban versus rural residence on fertility rates in 15 countries. From earlier studies on fertility it is known that in many countries high levels of education and urban residence for women predict low fertility rates. These effects, however, may well depend upon the characteristics of the countries, for instance on the level of economic development (as expressed in the Gross National Product) and the effect of family planning measures. Mason et al. (1984) indeed found differential effects on fertility rates. In their study, the levels involved were women nested within countries.

Hierarchical, or multilevel data may also be described in terms of *clusters* of observational units. In a certain sense, talking about the hierarchical structure refers more to the design, while the term clustered data refers more to the sampling procedure, that is, to clustered sampling. For instance, we could have clusters of students within a class, clusters of classes within a school, etc. Hence, in the literature one can find the terms *clustered population* and *cluster* or *multistage sample* as well.

5.1.2 Multilevel analysis

Multilevel analysis is used as the name for a class of methods employing hierarchical linear regression models. Over the past 15 years, much progress has been made in the development of multilevel analysis. Not surprisingly, this has occurred mainly within the field of educational statistics (see e.g. Bock, 1989; Burstein, Linn, & Capell, 1978; De Leeuw & Kreft, 1986; Raudenbush, 1988; Tate & Wongbundit, 1983). Today however, these methods are increasingly being used in numerous other research settings too. Well-known textbooks covering a wide range of theory and applications of multilevel analysis include Bryk & Raudenbush (1992), Longford (1993) and Goldstein (1995). A nontechnical and easily accessible introduction to multilevel analysis is given by Hox (1994) and by Kreft & De Leeuw (1998).

According to Raudenbush (1988), the failure of traditional 'single level' models to attend to the hierarchical nature of research data was shown very clearly for the field of educational research. This is not strange, because traditional regression models rely on the assumption of a random sample consisting of independent observations drawn from a homogeneous population. The 'nested' structure of multilevel data, however, produces dependency among the observations within units at each level of the hierarchy. For instance, students within a class are more alike than students from different classes. One aim of educational research is therefore to study the effects of group properties on individual student characteristics. Utilizing traditional regression analysis brings up the unit of analysis problem. This problem amounts to the question whether the effect of group level variables should be studied using students, classes or even schools as the unit of analysis. A regression analysis on the class level, for instance, usually includes student level variables that have been aggregated to the class level. The regression coefficients resulting from these analyses, however, tend to be different from equivalent coefficients resulting from a regression on the student level (see Knapp, 1977). This complication is called 'aggregation bias'. The problem is that the choice for different levels of analysis may lead to different conclusions about the effects of particular variables (see Cheung, Keeves, & Sellin, 1990, for a further elaboration on this topic).

Ignoring the hierarchy in the data leads to misestimated precision. When ordinary least squares estimation is applied to nested data, standard error estimates fail to include (co)variance components that are attributable to the effects of grouping in the data (see Aitkin, Anderson, & Hinde, 1981, for an example).

Thus, if the hierarchy in the data is not taken into account, the problems of aggregation bias and misestimated precision will threaten standard hypothesis testing. Moreover, Raudenbush (1988) argues that single level models encourage poor conceptualization when applied to hierarchical data, stressing the need to formulate models that explicitly take into account this special feature. So, modelling hierarchically structured data in terms of multilevel models is not only more precise from a model estimation point of view, but also conceptually more adequate than using classical regression models.

Multilevel analysis provides researchers with a very flexible and powerful set of tools to handle hierarchical data, both with respect to model formulation and with respect to hypothesis testing. Aggregation bias is dealt with by formulating models and hypotheses for processes and relations that take place within and between units at a certain level. Variables are allowed to have different effects at different levels of aggregation. Effects may vary between units and there may be 'cross-level effects', that is, interactions between effects at different levels. In multilevel analysis one can model this variation and these interactions by combining the information from units at different levels. Furthermore, precision problems are tackled by a variety of ways to specify error structures, that is, random components, in these models. As such, multilevel models may account for (co)variance parts emerging from the grouping in the data. As a result, differences between groups concerning an effect, are modelled as different distributions within each group, and not only by revealing a difference in means. In fact, when using a multilevel model one is actually modelling a hierarchical distribution.

In the literature, multilevel models go under various names. One may find the terms *random coefficient regression models* (De Leeuw & Kreft, 1986; Prosser, Rasbash, & Goldstein, 1991), *contextual effects models* (Blalock, 1984), *multilevel mixed effects models* (Goldstein, 1986b), *random parameter models* (Aitkin & Longford, 1986), *full contextual models* (Kreft & De Leeuw, 1991), *variance components models* (Aitkin & Longford, 1986), *multilevel linear models* (Goldstein, 1995; Mason et al., 1984) and *hierarchical linear models* (Bryk & Raudenbush, 1992). Although there are minor differences, all these models are basically versions of the hierarchical linear regression model. In the late seventies as a forerunner, or rather a similar approach to multilevel analysis, Boyd & Iversen (1979) proposed *contextual analysis*. A more extensive review of terminology is provided by Longford (1995, p. 530).

Multilevel modelling can be applied in a variety of research settings, not limited to the field of educational statistics. In every situation where the notion of a hierarchical data structure makes sense, the methodology will or may have a surplus value above 'normal' single level regression analysis. It is therefore not amazing that in recent years a number of more or less specific multilevel models have been developed. For example, Strenio, Weisberg, & Bryk (1983) study the analysis of growth curve data using a two-level approach, Mislevy & Bock (1989) present a hierarchical item-response model, Muthén & Satorra (1989) discuss multilevel aspects of varying parameters in structural relations models, Hox, Kreft, & Hermkens (1990) discuss multilevel models for factorial designs for survey data, and Longford & Muthén (1991) study factor analysis for clustered observations. The developments in this field have been very fast (see e.g. McArdle & Hamagami, 1996; Muthén, 1997; Willett & Sayer, 1996).

5.1.3 Multilevel analysis of longitudinal data

One important extension of the multilevel model is the application of two- and more-level models for the analysis of longitudinal data, that is, repeated measures on a group of individuals. Useful references include Laird & Ware (1982), Goldstein (1986a,b, 1995), Bryk & Raudenbush (1987, 1992), Raudenbush (1989), Bock (1989) and Goldstein, Healy, & Rasbash (1994). Models of this kind have already been around for some time, and constitute in fact one of the most natural extensions of multilevel methodology. This may be explained by the fact that the application of multilevel models to the analysis of repeated measures data is rather straightforward. The key idea is that longitudinal data are treated as having a hierarchical structure as well: the repeated measures can be conceived as structured within an individual. The repeated measures, viz. the time-points at which the observations are collected, are subsumed under individuals. The measurements at the different points in time are regarded as 'nested' within individuals. Here individuals are at the top of the hierarchy and time-points are at the bottom.

The multilevel treatment of repeated measures data is attractive. In this chapter we will elaborate on this topic. First, in Section 5.2, we will briefly discuss the basic two-level model. In Section 5.3, this model will be extended to and interpreted as a model for the analysis of repeated measures data. Section 5.5 emphasizes several relevant aspects that make multilevel methodology attractive for longitudinal data. In Section 5.4, some special topics are treated. Next in Section 5.6, the relations of this approach with MANOVA are discussed.

5.1.4   Software for multilevel analysis

In recent years, several computer programs have become available by which multilevel models can be fitted. Three major packages are MLn, a program able to fit multilevel models to data with up to 15 levels (Rasbash, Yang, Woodhouse, & Goldstein, 1995), HLM, a program for two- or three-level analysis (Bryk & Raudenbush, 1988) and VARCL, which consists of VARCL3, a program for two- or three-level analysis, and VARCL9, designed to analyse data with up to nine levels (restricted to simple models however) (Longford, 1987a,b). Additional software for multilevel analysis is MIXOR/MIXREG (Hedeker & Gibbons, 1994), BUGS (Best, Spiegelhalter, Thomas, & Brayne, 1996) and MLA (Busing, Meijer, & Van der Leeden, 1994, 1995). Multilevel models can also be estimated with SAS (SAS MIXED procedure, SAS Institute, 1992) and with BMDP (BMDP5V procedure, Dixon, 1988; Schluchter, 1988).

The procedure BMDP5V, part of the BMDP statistical software package, has been designed by Jennrich & Schluchter (Jennrich & Schluchter, 1986) as a general MANOVA procedure for the analysis of repeated measures. Special characteristics of the program include structured covariance matrices and the treatment of unbalanced data sets. Although BMDP5V was not developed with the purpose of fitting hierarchical models, it has special features that make it suited to handling versions of these models. It is highly likely that new generations of statistical software systems, such as SPSS or BMDP, will implement dedicated subprograms for multilevel analysis.

An extensive discussion and comparison of HLM, ML3 (the predecessor to MLn), VARCL, BMDP5V and GENMOD (Mason, Anderson, & Hayat, 1988, this program is no longer generally available) is given in Kreft, De Leeuw, & Van der Leeden (1994). Van der Leeden, Vrijburg, & De Leeuw (1996) compare HLM, ML3 and BMDP5V with special emphasis on the modelling of repeated measures data.

5.2 A Two-Level Model

In this section we will briefly discuss a simple two-level model for hierarchical data, structured in a 'normal' way, that is, non-longitudinally. These data could be collected, for instance, in an educational setting. We will formulate the model equations and discuss the corresponding assumptions. The idea of a within-unit and between-unit model will be explained, as well as the concept of a mixed model consisting of random and fixed parts. We will end the section with a paragraph on estimation.

5.2.1 Two levels: a within-unit and a between-unit model

In multilevel analysis, individuals are usually considered the first level, and the grouping of individuals constitutes the second level. Clearly, when groupings of groups are involved, we need a third level, and so on. A simple two-level situation can be clarified as follows. Suppose we have data collected in J classes, each consisting of N_j students. Suppose further that these data are scores on the (student-level) variables 'reading achievement' (RA) and 'total income of parents' (TIP), the latter variable taken as an indicator for 'social-economic status' (SES). If a researcher is interested in the relation between RA and SES, indicated by TIP, one could use a linear regression model in which RA is the dependent variable, and TIP is the predictor variable. That is, one could formulate the following level-1, or *within-unit model*,

$$Y_{ij} = \beta_{0j} + \beta_{1j}X_{ij} + e_{ij}. \tag{5.1}$$

In Equation (5.1), Y_{ij} and X_{ij} are the scores on the variables RA and TIP, respectively, for student i in class j. If X_{ij} is scaled such that a score of 0 represents the average total income, then the intercept β_{0j} is equal to the expected level of RA of a student of which the parents have an average total income. In the same way, the slope β_{1j} represents the average change in RA for each unit of change in TIP. The random term e_{ij} is assumed to have zero mean; it stands for the error in the prediction of Y_{ij}, that is, the effects of all other variables that may influence RA, other than TIP, including measurement error.

Now the multilevel treatment of these data means that we allow the coefficients β_{0j} and β_{1j} to vary across classes. Hence, the hierarchical nature of the data is incorporated in the model by treating β_{0j} and β_{1j} as random variables at the class level, that is, at level-2. The most simple level-2, or *between-unit model*, is one in which we are only modelling simple random variation. This is expressed as

$$
\begin{aligned}
\beta_{0j} &= \gamma_{00} + u_{0j}, \\
\beta_{1j} &= \gamma_{10} + u_{1j},
\end{aligned}
\tag{5.2}
$$

in which γ_{00} corresponds to the mean RA of students of which the parents have average total income, γ_{10} represents the average effect of TIP on RA, and the u_{0j} and u_{1j} are random terms representing the fluctuation of β_{0j} and β_{1j} around these γ_{00} and γ_{10} coefficients, that is, across the J classes. More specifically, we could call model (5.2) a between-class model, whereas (5.1) could be called the within-class model.

Not surprisingly, the model consisting of the combination of (5.1) and (5.2) is referred to as a *random coefficient model*. There are, however, many ways to specify other between-unit, that is, between-class models. For instance, one of the more general cases is a model in which we try to explain (a part of) the variation of β_{0j} and β_{1j} using a class-level variable Z, say 'class size' (SIZE), with Z_j denoting the number of students in class j. Such a model could be written as:

$$
\begin{aligned}
\beta_{0j} &= \gamma_{00} + \gamma_{01}Z_j + u_{0j}, \\
\beta_{1j} &= \gamma_{10} + \gamma_{11}Z_j + u_{1j}.
\end{aligned}
\tag{5.3}
$$

In (5.3), γ_{01} can be interpreted as the average effect of SIZE on mean RA of students of which the parents have average total income. The coefficient γ_{11} in (5.3), stands for the average increase of the slope β_{1j} that is accounted for by differences in SIZE. Clearly, model (5.3) is more informative than (5.2) for practical research situations. A researcher might be particularly interested in situations where the variability in the coefficients of within-class models is a function of differences between classes, indicated by some feature Z.

A more general formulation of model (5.1) is given by

$$Y_{ij} = \beta_{0j} + \beta_{1j}X_{1ij} + \beta_{2j}X_{2ij} + \ldots + \beta_{Qj}X_{Qij} + e_{ij}, \qquad (5.4)$$

where the $X_{qij}(q = 1, \ldots, Q)$ are individual characteristics, that is, a set of predictor variables. In the terminology of Bryk & Raudenbush (1992), the level-1 model, that is, model (5.1) or (5.4), is called the *person-level model*, and the level-2 model is called the *organization-level model*. The regression coefficients β_{qj} represent the 'distribution effects', because they indicate how the outcomes Y_{ij} are distributed in 'organization' j, as a function of person characteristics. Clearly, we need a total number of $Q + 1$ equations, similar to those in (5.2) and (5.3) or consisting of combinations of both, to be able to specify the organization-level model in which the variation of the coefficients β_{qj} is modelled.

Organization-level models can be specified in more than one way. Not for all level-1 variables may one wish to include a random effect. Theoretical considerations, for instance, may lead to treating some β_{qj} coefficients as fixed coefficients, and others as random coefficients. A random effect may also be dropped from the model because the corresponding coefficient does not show significant variation. Furthermore, one may wish to attribute the variance of the different β_{qj} coefficients to different level-2 predictor variables. An example of an organization-level model, in which the coefficients are modelled somewhat differently, is given by

$$\begin{aligned}
\beta_{0j} &= \gamma_{00} + u_{0j}, \\
\beta_{1j} &= \gamma_{10} + \gamma_{11}Z_j + u_{1j}, \\
\beta_{2j} &= \gamma_{20}, \\
\ldots &= \ldots \\
\beta_{Qj} &= \gamma_{Q0} + u_{Qj}.
\end{aligned} \qquad (5.5)$$

In (5.5), simple random variation is modelled for the coefficients β_{0j} and β_{Qj}. The variance of β_{1j} is partly accounted for by the variable Z_j. The coefficient β_{2j} is treated as fixed.

5.2.2 Single equation version: a mixed linear model

One may gain a better understanding of the models presented above by combining the within-unit and between-unit models, that is, the person-level and the organization-level models, into one single equation. For model (5.1) and (5.3), this single equation is given by

$$Y_{ij} = \underbrace{\gamma_{00} + \gamma_{01}Z_j + \gamma_{10}X_{ij} + \gamma_{11}Z_jX_{ij}}_{\text{fixed}} + \underbrace{u_{0j} + u_{1j}X_{ij} + e_{ij}}_{\text{random}}. \qquad (5.6)$$

Model (5.6) shows that one can distinguish between a fixed part and a random part. The fixed part consists of those terms associated with the γ-coefficients, of which the interpretation was explained in the previous section. The random part contains the level-1 and level-2 error terms. Accordingly, the model parameters can be divided into a set of fixed parameters and a set of random parameters. The fixed parameters consist of the γ-coefficients and are correspondingly called fixed effects. The random parameters consist of the (co)variance components associated with the level-1 and level-2 error terms. These (co)variance components emerge if we express the variance of $R_{ij} = Y_{ij} - \hat{Y}_{ij} = Y_{ij} - (\gamma_{00} + \gamma_{01}Z_j + \gamma_{10}X_{ij} + \gamma_{11}Z_jX_{ij})$, as

$$\text{Var}(R_{ij}) = \text{Var}(u_{0j} + u_{1j}X_{ij} + e_{ij}) = \sigma_0^2 + 2\sigma_{01}X_{ij} + \sigma_1^2X_{ij}^2 + \sigma_e^2, \qquad (5.7)$$

where $\sigma_0^2 = \text{Var}(u_{0j})$, $\sigma_1^2 = \text{Var}(u_{1j})$, $\sigma_{01} = \text{Cov}(u_{0j}, u_{1j})$ and $\sigma_e^2 = \text{Var}(e_{ij})$.

The (co)variance terms in (5.7) can be used for purposes of interpretation. If we return to the example variables from the previous section, then σ_0^2 is the variance of the intercept β_{0j} as far as it can not be explained by X_{ij} and Z_j; this equals the remaining variance of reading achievement between classes, after the variables total income and class size have been fitted. In the same way, σ_1^2 is the remaining variance of the slope β_{1j}, and σ_{01} is the remaining covariance between intercept and slope after X_{ij} and Z_j have been fitted. The term σ_e^2 is the final unexplained, residual variance in the variable reading achievement.

The fixed effects and the (co)variance components are the two usual sets of parameters in the multilevel model. This is reflected by Equation (5.6) from which the β_{qj} coefficients (cf. Equations (5.2), (5.3) and (5.5)) seem to have vanished. However, these β_{qj}s do constitute an additional, third set of parameters (which are random), called *random level-1 coefficients* (Bryk & Raudenbush, 1992) or *random regression coefficients*. These parameters specify the regression models within each level-2 unit. It depends on the purpose of the analysis whether the focus is upon estimates of their variances and covariances only (the level-2 variance components), or upon separate estimates of these parameters as well.

In Equation (5.6) the term $\gamma_{11}Z_jX_{ij}$ specifies an interaction between level-1 and level-2. Therefore this term is often called cross-level interaction. For some researchers, this interaction term provides a major source of attraction to multilevel analysis. The cross-level interaction term leads to the interpretation of 'slopes-as-outcomes' (as specified in the second parts of Equations (5.2) and (5.3)) (see Aitkin & Longford, 1986). Equations (5.2) and (5.3) may also lead to the interpretation of 'intercepts-as-outcomes'. Both ways of interpretation reflect that the level-1 regression coefficients can be viewed as outcome variables of a regression analysis on the second level.

Equation (5.6) shows that the two-level model presented here can be considered as a *mixed linear model* (Harville, 1977), which can be characterized by a fixed and a random part. As illustrated by the model descriptions in the previous section, we can have varieties of both within- and between-unit models. Consequently, the mixed linear model formulation reflects the very flexible approach that multilevel modelling offers to the analysis of hierarchical data.

5.2.3 Assumptions

For the multilevel model defined by Equation (5.6), the following assumptions are usually made. The predictor variables X_{ij} and Z_j are assumed to be known, fixed variables. For the (level-1) random terms e_{ij} in class/group j it is assumed that they are independently, normally distributed with zero expectation and variance σ_e^2. This assumption defines the level-1 covariance matrix $\Sigma_{(1)}$ to be equal to $\sigma_e^2\mathbf{I}$. The class-level (level-2) random terms u_{0j} and u_{1j} are assumed to have a joint normal distribution with zero expectation and covariance matrix $\Sigma_{(2)}$. It is further assumed that the random terms of the different levels are distributed independently of each other.

5.2.4 Estimation

Estimating a multilevel model amounts to estimating the parameters of a combined model, such as given in Equation (5.6), instead of separate models for each level. It is the translation of the idea that, although separate models for each level may be formulated (cf. Equations (5.4) and (5.5)), they are connected statistically. Generally, two sets of parameters have to be estimated: the fixed and the random parameters, but the estimation of one set of parameters depends on the other set. When the (co)variance components are known, straightforward solutions exist for the estimation of the fixed effects. Usually in practice, however, the (co)variance components are unknown so that these parameters have to be estimated from the data.

To obtain estimates for the two sets of model parameters, several numerical procedures are available. In one way or another, these procedures are all versions of the maximum likelihood approach. Maximum likelihood estimators have several attractive properties, such as consistency and efficiency. Both full information maximum likelihood (FIML) and restricted maximum likelihood (REML) methods have been developed. A drawback of these methods, however, is their relative complexity so that they generally require iterative procedures.

Computational procedures that apply maximum likelihood include the EM algorithm (see Dempster, Rubin, & Tsutakawa, 1981) and the Fisher scoring method (Longford, 1987a, 1993). Goldstein (1986b) developed an iterative generalized least squares (IGLS) method to obtain efficient parameter estimates for a general multilevel model. He shows that if the random terms follow a multivariate normal distribution, these IGLS estimates are identical to FIML estimates. A restricted version of IGLS, RIGLS, is available as well (Goldstein, 1989). This procedure is shown to be equivalent to REML. RIGLS and REML claim to provide unbiased estimates of the variance components, which makes them more attractive in, for instance, small sample situations (for an extensive discussion of these topics see Searle, Casella, & McCulloch, 1992, Chapter 6).

Another method to estimate the (co)variance components is Bayes estimation (Lindley & Smith, 1972; Strenio, 1981). Seltzer (1990) has developed this approach for a general hierarchical linear model. However, a disadvantage of Bayes estimation here is that with large data sets and complex models the method requires heavy computational effort.

The procedure to obtain the 'best' estimates for the third set of parameters, the random level-1 coefficients or random regression coefficients, can be illustrated by an example. Suppose, in educational research, that schools are to be ranked in terms of effectiveness, using their estimated slope coefficients as indicator (Kreft & De Leeuw, 1991). The first thing that comes to mind is to simply estimate them by an ordinary least squares regression for each school separately. However, this procedure has the serious disadvantage that the coefficients will not be estimated with the same precision for each school. For instance, in one school, we could have, say, 45 students, whereas in another school we only have 7 students. This will definitely influence the accuracy of results. A more attractive approach, available within the framework of multilevel analysis, is provided by a method called *shrinkage* estimation.

The underlying idea of shrinkage estimation is that there are basically two sources of information: the separate estimates from each school (level-2 unit) and the estimates that could be obtained from the total sample, ignoring any grouping. Shrinkage estimation consists of a weighted combination of these two sources. The more reliable the estimates within the separate level-2 units, the more weight is put on them. Vice versa, the less reliable these estimates are, that is, the less precise, the more weight is put on the estimates obtained from the total sample. The result is that estimates are 'shrunken' towards the mean of the estimates over all level-2 units. The amount of shrinkage depends on the reliability of the estimates from the separate level-2 units. The less precise the estimates are, the more they are shrunken towards the overall mean.

More details concerning shrinkage estimation can be found, for instance, in Goldstein (1995, pp. 24–25). Extensive treatment of the various estimation procedures can be found in the textbooks on multilevel analysis, mentioned in Section 5.1.2.

5.3 The multilevel treatment of longitudinal data

In this section we will discuss the way in which repeated measures data can be analysed using multilevel methodology. We will extend the basic two-level model discussed in the previous sections in an appropriate way. When repeated measures data are interpreted as hierarchical data, within-unit and between-unit models are viewed as within-subject and between-subject models. We will discuss the emphasis on the modelling of individual growth trajectories and the possibility of modelling complex, for instance time dependent, within-subject covariance structures. We end the section with an illustrative example.

5.3.1   The hierarchical interpretation of repeated measures

As discussed in Chapter 1, the main goal of longitudinal research is the assessment of change. In social and behavioural research, this change often concerns some kind of growth: for instance, physical growth, learning achievement, and so on. When individuals are measured repeatedly over a period of time, their repeated measurements could be called growth data. More specifically, growth data can be considered as measurements on one variable for the same (groups of) individuals on a number of consecutive points in time.

In multilevel model building, individuals are generally considered as the lowest level (level-1) units. Above we used the example that students are members of classes, and classes (level-2) are nested within schools, and so on. Repeated measures data, or growth data, can be interpreted as having a hierarchical structure too. Data from individuals that are measured at a number of consecutive points in time can be understood as having a two-level structure: individuals are considered as level-2 units and the repeated observations as level-1 units, so that the longitudinal measurements are nested within the individuals.

This two-level approach implies that each individual is allowed to have his/her own growth curve or growth trajectory, just as each class of students was allowed to have its own regression equation in the cross-sectional hierarchical model. And just as the within-class regression coefficients were allowed to vary across classes, the individual growth parameters may vary across individuals. In that way the longitudinal application of a multilevel model allows for the estimation of the mean growth trajectory (for a group) and for the estimation of individual variation around this mean. Grouping, or other background variables may be used as explaining variables to account for the between-subject variation in individual growth parameters. As such, systematic variation in growth trajectories can be studied as a function of background variables and experimental treatments. In longitudinal multilevel models, differences between groups of individuals concerning initial growth status and growth rate will be modelled as different distributions of these parameters within each group, and not only by modelling the mean levels.

5.3.2 Two levels: a within-subject and between-subject model

Because repeated measures or growth data may be viewed as reflecting a developmental process as a function of time, one suitable method to model them is by describing the expected values of the observations as functions of time. Individual growth may often be modelled as a polynomial function of time and it has become very common to use such functions for this purpose. The results can be presented in the form of (growth) curves.

In the two-level approach to the analysis of growth data, the model for an individual growth trajectory constitutes the first level. The basic *within-subject model* to fit the responses of a single individual as a polynomial function is given by

$$Y_{ti} = \beta_{0i} + \beta_{1i}T_{ti} + \beta_{2i}T_{ti}^2 + \ldots + \beta_{pi}T_{ti}^p + e_{ti}. \qquad (5.8)$$

In model (5.8), Y_{ti} is the measurement on the dependent or outcome variable for individual i on occasion t. The βs are the coefficients of a polynomial function of degree p and the e_{ti}s are random error terms. The variable T_{ti} could represent, for instance, the age of individual i at time t. The powers $\beta_{gi}T_{ti}^g, (g = 1, \ldots, p)$, represent transformations of this variable, specifying a quadratic, cubic or higher order polynomial growth function.

Analogously to Equations (5.2) or (5.3), we could write for a simple *between-subject model*,

$$\begin{aligned}
\beta_{0i} &= \gamma_{00} + u_{0i}, \\
\beta_{1i} &= \gamma_{10} + u_{1i}, \\
\beta_{2i} &= \gamma_{20} + u_{2i}, \qquad (5.9) \\
\ldots &= \ldots, \\
\beta_{pi} &= \gamma_{p0} + u_{pi}.
\end{aligned}$$

This level-2 model accounts for simple variation of the individual growth parameters across the total group. Clearly, each person has its own set of growth parameters, which implies that each person's

growth curve is unique. In longitudinal applications, Bryk & Raudenbush (1992) call the level-1 model the *repeated-observations model* and
the level-2 model the *person-level model*. This terminology is in accordance with the presentation in Section 5.2.1 and just facilitates the
introduction of, for instance a level-3 model, which is then called the
organization-level model.

Using more convenient matrix notation, the within-subject model
(5.8) is written as

$$\mathbf{y}_i = \mathbf{T}\boldsymbol{\beta}_i + \mathbf{e}_i, \tag{5.10}$$

where $\mathbf{y}_i$ is the $(T \times 1)$ response vector containing the repeated measurements for subject i, $\mathbf{T}$ is a $(T \times r, r \leq T)$ matrix of known, constant
variables (e.g. age in years, number of months, etc.) and (quadratic,
cubic, etc.) transformations of these variables, $\boldsymbol{\beta}_i$ is an $(r \times 1)$ vector
of individual parameters specifying the shape of the growth curve for
person i, and $\mathbf{e}_i$ is a $(T \times 1)$ vector of random error components. Matrix
$\mathbf{T}$ can be defined as

$$\mathbf{T} = \begin{bmatrix} 1 & T_1 & T_1^2 & \cdots & T_1^p \\ 1 & T_2 & T_2^2 & \cdots & T_2^p \\ \cdot & \cdot & \cdot & \cdots & \cdot \\ 1 & T_T & T_T^2 & \cdots & T_T^p \end{bmatrix}. \tag{5.11}$$

Since $\mathbf{T}$ is of order $(T \times r, r \leq T)$ (and $r = p + 1$), the degree of the
polynomial fitted for person i is p, and is $T - 1$ maximally. Note that in
this formulation, it is not necessary for all individuals to have the same
T measurements. Apart from explanatory variables, such as weight or
age, and powers of those variables, the matrix $\mathbf{T}$ may also contain a set
of standard polynomial vectors (see for instance De Lury, 1950).

Analogously, a more general between-subject model is given by

$$\boldsymbol{\beta}_i = \mathbf{Z}_i\boldsymbol{\gamma} + \mathbf{u}_i. \tag{5.12}$$

In Equation (5.12), $\mathbf{Z}_i$ is an $(r \times q)$ between-subject design matrix with
known, fixed elements, $\boldsymbol{\gamma}$ is a $(q \times 1)$ vector of fixed coefficients and $\mathbf{u}_i$
is an $(r \times 1)$ vector of random error components. The between-subject
model (5.12) is formulated in a general way. For instance, if $\mathbf{Z}_i = \mathbf{I}$, we
have a model of simple variation in which $\boldsymbol{\gamma}$ is a vector containing parameters indicating the mean growth curve over all individuals, with the

elements of $\mathbf{u}_i$ denoting the departure(s) from this mean curve for each individual i. More elaborate models emerge if $\mathbf{Z}_i$ contains (dummy) variables coding subgroups of individuals and/or other explanatory variables that could account for the variation of the β_is. In that way it is possible to study the variability of the growth curve coefficients as a function of the differences between the individuals on some characteristic that remains fixed across occasions (e.g. sex). Another extension to the model would be to include time-varying covariates to matrix $\mathbf{T}$.

Again, the within- and between-subject models can be combined into one single equation model that is written as

$$\mathbf{y}_i = \underbrace{\mathbf{TZ}_i\gamma}_{\text{fixed}} + \underbrace{\mathbf{Tu}_i + \mathbf{e}_i}_{\text{random}}, \tag{5.13}$$

assuming that the elements of $\mathbf{e}_i$ are independently distributed as $\mathbf{e}_i \sim N(0, \Sigma_{(1)})$ with $\Sigma_{(1)} = \sigma^2\mathbf{I}$, that the level-2 random terms in $\mathbf{u}_i$ are independently distributed as $\mathbf{u}_i \sim N(0, \Sigma_{(2)})$, and that the level-1 random terms, the elements of $\mathbf{e}_i$, are distributed independently from the level-2 random terms in $\mathbf{u}_i$. Analogously to the formulation regarding (5.6), in the combined model (5.13) the term $\mathbf{TZ}_i\gamma$ is called the fixed part and the terms $\mathbf{Tu}_i + \mathbf{e}_i$ the random part.

5.3.3 A hypothetical example

Suppose we have obtained data consisting of measurements on an arithmetic skills test for a group of students entering a special arithmetic instruction programme, after 2, 4, 6, 8 and 10 months of classroom instruction. We are interested to investigate the effect of continuance of classroom instruction on the development of students' arithmetic skills (SKIL). Also, we believe that students' growth in arithmetic skills may be related to their initial level. A linear growth model by which this research question can be studied, is given by

$$(\text{SKIL})_{ti} = \beta_{0i} + \beta_{1i}(\text{MONTH})_{ti} + e_{ti}, \tag{5.14}$$

for the within-subject or repeated-observation part of the model, where MONTH denotes the number of months of instruction. Random variation of the individual growth trajectories is provided by the between-subject or person-level model

$$\beta_{0i} = \gamma_{00} + u_{0i},$$
$$\beta_{1i} = \gamma_{10} + u_{1i}.$$

(5.15)

In model (5.15), the fixed parameters γ_{00} and γ_{10} denote the estimated mean intercept and mean slope respectively. These parameters represent the mean initial status and mean growth rate of arithmetic skills over the total group. The estimated variances of the individual growth parameters β_{0i} and β_{1i} provide us with information about the deviations of the individual growth trajectories from the mean growth curve. These variance estimates are given by $\sigma_0^2 (= \text{Var}(u_{0i}))$ and $\sigma_1^2 (= \text{Var}(u_{1i}))$. A possible interaction between initial status and growth rate is indicated by $\sigma_{01} (= \text{Cov}(u_{0i}, u_{1i}))$. The variance of e_{ti}, the level-1 residual variance denoted by σ_e^2, represents the remaining part of the variance in SKIL which can not be accounted for by the growth function.

Applying this model, various hypothesis tests concerning its parameters can be performed. For instance, using a χ^2-statistic, we could test whether there is true variation in individual growth parameters or not. That is, we could answer the question whether students vary significantly in their initial level of arithmetic skills at entry into the special programme and if students vary significantly in their learning rate during the programme. Another possibility is to test whether the initial level of arithmetic skills influences the learning rate during the programme; this is done by testing whether the covariance parameter σ_{01} differs significantly from zero. Note that the tests mentioned so far are all tests concerning random effects. Hypotheses about the fixed parameters can be tested using t-ratios. We will return to the topic of hypothesis tests in a later section.

Model (5.14) combined with (5.15) can be called an *unconditional model*, since no person-level predictor variables are involved. Fitting an unconditional model will often be the first step in a multilevel analysis. After examining the results of such an analysis, one may proceed by adding level-2 or, in this case, person-level variables to the model, trying to explain part of the remaining variability of the level-1 coefficients. An example of a person-level model for the hypothetical example described above, that accounts for differences in development between boys and girls, is given by

$$\beta_{0i} = \gamma_{00} + \gamma_{01}(\text{SEX})_i + u_{0i},$$
$$\beta_{1i} = \gamma_{10} + \gamma_{11}(\text{SEX})_i + u_{1i}, \qquad (5.16)$$

where SEX is an effects coded variable with values $+1$ and -1 for boys and girls respectively. Thus, in model (5.16), part of the variation in individual growth trajectories can be explained by sex differences. Applying this model we could, for instance, test if the mean initial level of arithmetic skills and the mean learning rate is significantly different for boys and girls.

5.3.4 The within-subject covariance structure

The variance of the random part $\mathbf{Tu}_i + \mathbf{e}_i$ in model (5.13), that is, the (co)variances among the elements of $\mathbf{y}_i$ not accounted for by the fixed part, is given by

$$\text{Var}(\mathbf{y}_i|\mathbf{TZ}_i\gamma) = \text{Var}(\mathbf{Tu}_i + \mathbf{e}_i) = \Sigma_i = \mathbf{T}\Sigma_{(2)}\mathbf{T}' + \sigma_e^2\mathbf{I}. \qquad (5.17)$$

Equation (5.17) shows that the assumptions described in Section 5.3.2, especially the assumption that $\mathbf{e}_i \sim N(0, \Sigma_{(1)})$ with $\Sigma_{(1)} = \sigma_e^2\mathbf{I}$, lead to a relatively simple covariance structure on the first (individual) level: the error terms are equal and uncorrelated between the time points. Bryk & Raudenbush (1992) argue that it is defensible to assume this simple error covariance structure when there is a limited number of time points. In such cases with short time series, the assumption is very practical and unlikely to corrupt the results of the analysis.

   However, it is possible to formulate a more general model incorporating a more complex level-1 covariance structure, which can take on a variety of forms. In many longitudinal situations it may be most adequate to model some form of time dependent or autocorrelation structure, especially when there are many time points per individual (see e.g. Ware, 1985). Goldstein et al. (1994) discuss multilevel time series models. Other instances include studies where the measurements take place close together in time, or situations in which the error terms are dependent on measured variables, such as age or time (see, e.g. Goldstein, 1995, pp. 47–54). Error variance may also be group or person specific (Strenio, 1981). A model that is able to handle a variety of error covariance structures is derived when Equation (5.13) is extended to

$$\mathbf{y}_i = \underbrace{\mathbf{TZ}_i\boldsymbol{\gamma}}_{\text{fixed}} + \underbrace{\mathbf{Tu}_i + \mathbf{X}_{(1)i}\mathbf{e}_i}_{\text{random}}, \tag{5.18}$$

where $\mathbf{X}_{(1)i}$ is a $(T \times M)$ matrix of explanatory variables whose coefficients are random at level-1. In practice, the matrices $\mathbf{Z}_i, \mathbf{T}$ and $\mathbf{X}_{(1)i}$ will often contain versions of the same variables. Model (5.18) is less restrictive than (5.13) because, firstly, explanatory variables can have random coefficients at level-1 and, secondly, explanatory variables in the random part of the model have not necessarily been included in the fixed part. Hence, model (5.18) is the most general and flexible version of the longitudinal mixed linear model.

The covariance structure of the error part of model (5.18), that is, the (co)variances among the elements of $\mathbf{y}_i$ not accounted for by the fixed part, is given by

$$\text{Var}(\mathbf{Tu}_i + \mathbf{X}_{(1)i}\mathbf{e}_i) = \Sigma_i = \underbrace{\mathbf{T}\Sigma_{(2)}\mathbf{T}'}_{\text{level-2}} + \underbrace{\mathbf{X}_{(1)i}\Sigma_{(1)}\mathbf{X}'_{(1)i}}_{\text{level-1}}. \tag{5.19}$$

As can be understood from (5.19), time dependent or autocorrelation covariance structures can be modelled through particular specifications of the level-1 part of the total covariance structure of the error terms.

5.3.5 Hypothesis testing

In Section 5.3.3, in our discussion of the hypothetical example, we made a few remarks concerning the testing of hypotheses. In this section, we will elaborate on this topic. To provide a frame of reference, we consider the general multilevel growth model defined by Equations (5.10) and (5.12), which is, in short,

$$\begin{aligned} \mathbf{y}_i &= \mathbf{T}\boldsymbol{\beta}_i + \mathbf{e}_i, \\ \boldsymbol{\beta}_i &= \mathbf{Z}_i\boldsymbol{\gamma} + \mathbf{u}_i, \end{aligned} \tag{5.20}$$

with corresponding assumptions and notation. We will treat the formulation and testing of hypotheses about the fixed effects (the γ_{pq}s), the random level-1 coefficients (the β_{pi}s), and the (co)variance components (the elements of $\Sigma_{(1)}$ and $\Sigma_{(2)}$). Single-parameter tests will be discussed, referring to single hypotheses. The discussion on so-called multi-parameter tests, which refer to composite hypotheses, will be restricted to likelihood-ratio tests. For a more elaborate discussion on hypothesis tests, we refer to Bryk & Raudenbush (1992).

Fixed effects The usual null hypothesis for a fixed parameter γ is given by

$$H_0 : \gamma_{pq} = 0, \tag{5.21}$$

which means that we test the null hypothesis that a specific person-level predictor variable (in $\mathbf{Z}_i$) has no effect on a corresponding growth parameter in the person-level model. H_0 may be tested using a z statistic defined as

$$z = \frac{\hat{\gamma}_{pq}}{\sqrt{\hat{V}_{\hat{\gamma}_{pq}}}}. \tag{5.22}$$

In (5.22), $\hat{\gamma}_{pq}$ is the maximum likelihood estimate of γ_{pq}, and $\hat{V}_{\hat{\gamma}_{pq}}$ is the estimated sampling variance of $\hat{\gamma}_{pq}$ (see Bryk & Raudenbush, 1992, p. 47). However, Bryk & Raudenbush (1992) argue that in practice a t statistic will give a more accurate result. One t statistic is defined as the ratio of the parameter estimate to its estimated standard error, with degrees of freedom equal to $(N - q - 1)$, where N is the number of individuals and q is the number of person-level (level-2) predictors (except for the unit variable associated with the intercept). In most cases this t-ratio is used as a test for fixed effects. It is not explicitly given in all computer output, but standard errors always are, so it can easily be calculated.

Random level-1 coefficients A hypothesis about random level-1 coefficients could be, for instance, the null hypothesis that for a particular individual the linear growth rate is zero. This hypothesis can be expressed as

$$H_0 : \beta_{pi} = 0. \tag{5.23}$$

Analogously to the fixed parameter tests, this hypothesis can be tested using a t-ratio computed as the ratio of the parameter estimate to its estimated standard error. A problem with this test is that one needs to have estimates for the β_{pi}s, which are not routinely provided in most output. One has to choose either between computing shrinkage estimates or ordinary least squares estimates (see also paragraphs 5.2.2 and 5.2.4). The testing of random level-1 coefficients is a more complex problem than the testing of fixed effects. However, in longitudinal applications we will not frequently be concerned with hypotheses regarding single (or multiple) individual growth parameters. Instead, in most cases the focus will be on their (co)variances. Therefore we will not treat this topic in more detail here.

(Co)variance components   The testing of (co)variance components can be of great use in most multilevel applications. A hypothesis of this kind could be, for instance, the null hypothesis that there is no variation in the slope-parameter across individuals. Testing this hypothesis, we could answer the question whether individuals vary significantly in their (linear) growth rate. Such a hypothesis can be written as

$$H_0 : \sigma_p^2 = 0, \tag{5.24}$$

where $\sigma_p^2 = \mathrm{Var}(\beta_{pi})$. If (5.24) is rejected, one may conclude that the variance of the corresponding β_{pi} differs significantly from zero. In general, if the level-2 groups are large enough to compute the ordinary least squares estimates (for the separate within-group regression models) – that is, here, if the number of measurements per individual is sufficient – we compute the following statistic. Let $\hat{d}_{pi}$ denote the pth diagonal element of $\hat{\mathbf{D}}_i = \hat{\sigma}_e^2 \, (\mathbf{T}'\mathbf{T})^{-1}$. Then the statistic

$$\sum_i \left(\hat{\beta}_{pi} - \hat{\gamma}_{p0} - \hat{\gamma}_{p1} Z_{1i} - \cdots - \hat{\gamma}_{pq} Z_{qi} \right)^2 / \hat{d}_{pi} \tag{5.25}$$

will be approximately χ^2 distributed with degrees of freedom equal to $(N - q - 1)$ (see Bryk & Raudenbush, 1992, p. 55).

Another test of hypothesis (5.24) is derived from the estimated standard error of $\hat{\sigma}_p^2$, computed from the inverse of the information matrix (see Longford, 1987a). We may compute the z-ratio

$$z = \frac{\hat{\sigma}_p^2}{\sqrt{\mathrm{Var}(\hat{\sigma}_p^2)}}. \tag{5.26}$$

For large samples, this z-ratio is approximately normally distributed. However, according to Bryk & Raudenbush (1992), in many instances the normality approximation will be very bad, so that the use of this z-ratio may be misleading.

Multi-parameter tests   Multi-parameter tests for fixed parameters and for random level-1 coefficients are formulated using contrast vectors. They are based upon χ^2 distributions. When using a full information maximum likelihood procedure, an alternative approach to multi-parameter tests for fixed effects is a *likelihood-ratio test*. Multi-parameter tests for (co)variance components are generally based on likelihood-ratio tests too.

The use of likelihood-ratio tests applies to the topic of *nested* models as well. We consider, for instance, a certain model I to be nested within another model II if the set of parameters for model I is a subset of the set of parameters for model II. This concept can be used to formulate and test hypotheses and construct a so-called model hierarchy. In such a hierarchy, models are nested within other models, which are again nested within other models, and so on. Applying the principles of maximum likelihood, we can obtain the optimal value of the likelihood function for each separate model k, say L_k. Following standard statistical theory, the $-2\log L_k$ value is defined as the *deviance* of model k ($D_k = -2\log L_k$). The deviance can be considered as a measure of model fit and can be used to compute likelihood-ratio tests for comparing nested models. More formally, we may construct hypotheses like

$$\begin{aligned} H_0 &: \theta = \theta_k, \\ H_1 &: \theta = \theta_l, \end{aligned} \tag{5.27}$$

where θ_k and θ_l are the sets of parameters for models k and l, respectively, and where θ_k is a subset of θ_l (or vice versa). For instance, think of θ_k as the set of parameters of a growth model in which only the slopes β_{1i} are randomly varying across individuals, whereas θ_l corresponds to the same model, except that it also incorporates random variation of the intercepts β_{1i}. To test whether the addition of the random intercept parameter is appropriate, we can compute the test statistic

$$\lambda = D_k - D_l. \tag{5.28}$$

From standard literature it is well known that λ follows a χ^2 distribution with degrees of freedom equal to the difference between the number of independent parameters for model k and model l. Hence, to test the hypothesis concerning the random intercept formulated above, we should refer to a χ^2 distribution having 2 degrees of freedom, because the addition of a random intercept introduces a person-level variance and a covariance component, and thus two additional parameters.

5.3.6 Empirical examples

In this section we will discuss three examples that serve to illustrate multilevel analysis of repeated measures data. For these examples, models are fitted in which the growth parameters vary randomly across the level-2 units (mostly individuals) and in which this variation is (partially) explained by variables at the group level. In the first example (Dental data) there are two groups of individuals. The second example (Rat data) deals with a covariate. The third example (School data) mainly serves to illustrate the modelling of the within-subject covariances.

Dental data   The Dental data are taken from Potthoff & Roy (1964). They were collected at the University of North Carolina Dental School and concern the measurements of the distance (DIST), in millimetres, from the centre of the pituitary to the pteryomaxillary fissure for eleven girls and sixteen boys, at ages of 8, 10, 12 and 14. In the literature, these data have been used several times to illustrate different approaches to growth curve modelling. Probably, as is the case here as well, without much intimacy with their practical significance. Apparently, the relation between measured distance and age is interesting in the field of dental research.

The results presented by Potthoff and Roy suggest that the best approach probably is by fitting linear growth curves for these data found as a regression of distance on age. In the multilevel framework the repeated measurements are considered nested within the subjects. Thus, at level-1 the individual growth curves are modelled, while at level-2 the coefficients of these curves are treated as random variables. Also at the second level, SEX, defined as an effects coded variable with values -1 for girls and 1 for boys, is used as an explanatory variable accounting

for part of the random variation across the individual growth trajectories.

The within-subject model can be written as

$$(\text{DIST})_{ti} = \beta_{0i} + \beta_{1i}(\text{AGE})_{ti} + e_{ti}, \tag{5.29}$$

and the between-subject model as

$$\beta_{0i} = \gamma_{00} + \gamma_{01}(\text{SEX})_i + u_{0i},$$
$$\beta_{1i} = \gamma_{10} + \gamma_{11}(\text{SEX})_i + u_{1i}. \tag{5.30}$$

The single-equation version of the model is written as

$$(\text{DIST})_{ti} = \gamma_{00} + \gamma_{01}(\text{SEX})_i + \gamma_{10}(\text{AGE})_{ti} + \gamma_{11}(\text{AGE})_{ti}(\text{SEX})_i +$$
$$+ u_{0i} + u_{1i}(\text{AGE})_{ti} + e_{ti}. \tag{5.31}$$

Parameter estimates for this model were obtained with ML3, using the
RIGLS method. Results are presented in Table 5.1.

Table 5.1: *Dental Data, Fixed Parameter and Variance Component
Estimates, Standard Errors and t-ratios for Linear Growth Model*

Fixed parameter	Estimate	SE	t-ratio
γ_{00}	16.860	0.798	21.128
γ_{10}	0.632	0.067	9.433
γ_{01}	−0.516	0.798	−0.647
γ_{11}	0.152	0.067	2.269
Variance component	Estimate	SE	
σ_e^2	1.716	0.330	
σ_0^2	5.786	4.973	
σ_{01}	−0.290	0.403	
σ_1^2	0.033	0.036	
Deviance	427.96		

Referring to Equation (5.31), we find the following entries in
Table 5.1. First we have the fixed parameters, the gammas; γ_{00} and
γ_{10} denote the fixed intercept and slope of the average growth curve for

the entire group. Deviations from this average intercept and slope for the group of girls and for the group of boys, are given by γ_{01} and γ_{11}, respectively. Hence, the fixed intercept and slope of the average growth curve for the girls are given by $(\gamma_{00} - \gamma_{01})$ and $(\gamma_{10} - \gamma_{11})$, respectively. Equivalently, the fixed intercept and slope of the average growth curve for the boys are given by $(\gamma_{00} + \gamma_{01})$ and $(\gamma_{10} + \gamma_{11})$, respectively.

The variance components constitute the second set of parameters in Table 5.1. The terms σ_0^2 and σ_1^2 denote the variances, across individuals, of the random (within-subject) intercept and slope, respectively, not accounted for by SEX. The term σ_{01} gives the covariance between both random coefficients (conditional on the variable SEX). The variance of the first level disturbances is contained in σ_e^2. It is the variance in the observed distances that remains unexplained, that is, which is not accounted for by the 'time variable' AGE, the person-level explanatory variable SEX, and the variable specifying the interaction between AGE and SEX. Note that the random coefficient model discussed here does not include a special covariance structure for the error components, despite the fact that the measurements are time related here. As discussed earlier, the relatively simple covariance structure which is modelled here, is usually appropriate with a short time series.

Table 5.1 shows that the linear term for the (average) growth curve (γ_{10}) is significant, which corroborates earlier findings of Potthoff and Roy. Clearly, DIST is linearly related to AGE. The fixed parameter associated with SEX (γ_{01}) is not significant. This indicates that, on average, neither boys nor girls differ significantly concerning their initial 'dental distance'. However, the 'interaction' parameter γ_{11} is significant, showing that, on average, boys' dental distance $(\gamma_{10} + \gamma_{11})$ increases faster over time than girls' dental distance $(\gamma_{10} - \gamma_{11})$. Thus, it seems useful to model DIST for each group with a separate growth curve. These findings are reflected in Figure 5.1, where the predicted average growth curves for both groups are plotted, as well as the predicted average growth curve for the entire group. Because in this example sample size is very small, z-ratios and χ^2 tests are questionable for testing hypotheses concerning the variance components. However, likelihood-ratio tests, based on the results of additional analyses not reported here, show that inclusion of the variance component parameters significantly improves model fit. Thus, inclusion of these parameters results in a more appropriate modelling of the disturbances.

Figure 5.1: *Dental Data, Predicted Growth Curves*

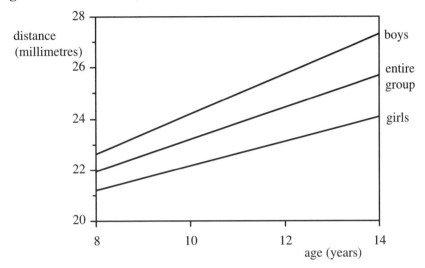

In principle, the level-2 variance components can be interpreted in terms of individual differences. Although not really suited to computation of statistical tests, the standard errors indicate that the estimated values of these parameters are not substantial: estimates and standard errors are roughly of the same size. Other results, not reported here, show that this is partly due to adding the variable SEX to the model. Apparently, SEX accounts for most of the variation in the individual growth trajectories.

Finally, note that the estimate of the covariance term σ_{01} has a negative value. Sometimes, in applications to growth data, a negative covariance between initial status and growth rate is interpreted as an indication that subjects who start at a low level tend to grow faster than those who start at higher levels.

Rat data   For a second example we use a set of data on the growth of rats, which was originally presented and analysed by Box (1950), and afterwards by several others (Hills, 1974; Rao, 1965; Strenio et al., 1983). The Rat data analysed here are taken from Strenio et al. (1983). These authors used only a part of the original set, and because their purpose was to provide an illustrative analysis as well, they added

some random error and constructed a covariate. The data consist of
the weights of 10 rats (WEIGHT), measured initially and after each of
four consecutive weeks. The covariate is mother's weight (MW).

As in the first example, results from the literature (mentioned above)
indicate a linear growth model. The variable WEEK has values 0, 1, 2,
3 and 4. The within-rat (level-1) model can be written as

$$(\text{WEIGHT})_{ti} = \beta_{0i} + \beta_{1i}(\text{WEEK})_{ti} + e_{ti}, \tag{5.32}$$

and the between-rat (level-2) model is

$$\begin{aligned}
\beta_{0i} &= \gamma_{00} + \gamma_{01}(\text{MW})_i + u_{0i}, \\
\beta_{1i} &= \gamma_{10} + \gamma_{11}(\text{MW})_i + u_{1i}.
\end{aligned} \tag{5.33}$$

The single-equation specification of the model is

$$(\text{WEIGHT})_{ti} = \gamma_{00} + \gamma_{01}(\text{MW})_i + \gamma_{10}(\text{WEEK})_{ti} + \gamma_{11}(\text{WEEK})_{ti}(\text{MW})_i +$$
$$+ u_{0i} + u_{1i}(\text{WEEK})_{ti} + e_{ti}. \tag{5.34}$$

Model (5.34) was estimated by ML3, using the RIGLS method. The
results are given in Table 5.2.

Table 5.2: *Rat Data, Fixed Parameter and Variance Component Estimates,*
Standard Errors and t-ratios for Linear Growth Model

Fixed parameter	Estimate	SE	*t* ratio
γ_{00}	12.940	36.300	0.356
γ_{10}	0.251	0.223	1.126
γ_{01}	2.967	11.850	0.250
γ_{11}	0.147	0.073	2.014

Variance component	Estimate	SE
σ_e^2	91.750	23.690
σ_0^2	82.840	63.210
σ_{01}	-19.270	19.120
σ_1^2	5.514	6.975

Deviance	376.72	

The model fitted to this data is very similar to the model used in the first example, except that now the level-2 explanatory variable Mw is a continuous variable that varies across level-2 units, instead of an effects coded variable defining different groups of level-2 units. Thus, Table 5.2 and Table 5.1 correspond to a great extent in appearance. Again, σ_0^2 and σ_1^2 denote the variance of the intercepts (initial growth status) and the variance of the slopes (growth rate), respectively, that is, the variance not accounted for by Mw, whereas σ_{01}^2 denotes the covariance between both growth parameters.

Standard errors and *t*-ratios indicate that, except for the 'interaction' parameter γ_{11}, none of the fixed parameters is significantly different from zero. Results from fitting a random coefficient growth model without Mw (not reported here) show that this is attributable to the presence of the covariate in the model: when Mw was left out of the analysis, several fixed parameters became significant. Clearly, Mw has a strong effect on the growth trajectories: the variable appears to explain a substantial amount of the level-2 variance, that is, the variance of the initial weights and growth rates.

Neglecting the *t*-ratios for the sake of our illustrative purposes (because of the extremely small sample size one could argue the usefulness of these significance tests here) provides the following interpretation of the fixed parameters. Despite the insignificance of the fixed intercept and slope parameters in the model, a linear trend (γ_{10}) is present. The fixed parameters further show that Mw has a positive effect on initial rat weight (γ_{01}), as well as on the growth rate (γ_{11}). This means that rats with a stout mother have a higher initial weight and gain weight faster.

As in the previous example, we have negative covariance between initial status and growth rate. This might be interpreted in the same way: rats that start at a low level tend to develop faster than rats that start at a higher level. Other interpretation of the variance components is similar to that in the previous example: Mw accounts for a considerable amount of the variation in the within-rat growth trajectories.

To illustrate the estimation of the within-rat growth parameters (the β_{0i}s and β_{1i}s), additional 'shrinkage' estimates (see Sections 5.2.2 and 5.2.4) were computed. These are used to plot the predicted growth curves for each rat in Figure 5.2.

Figure 5.2: *Rat Data, Predicted Growth Curves for 10 Rats*

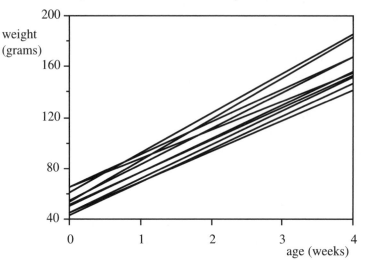

School data   Because growth data can be expected to be serially dependent, it is interesting to consider the modelling of the within-subject
or level-1 covariance matrix by a characteristic structure: for instance,
an autocorrelation structure (see also Section 5.3.4).

   To illustrate the modelling of these special covariance structures, we
use part of the results from a longitudinal educational study. The data
are taken from Voeten (1991) who studied the individual development
of technical reading (TR). Technical reading is measured as a score on
a so-called 'One-Minute Test'. This test measures the speed at which
a pupil can decode words. Scores of 384 pupils on 25 Dutch Primary
Schools are used which are measured after respectively 1, 8, 11, 18 and
22 months (the values of the variable TIME) (for further details, see
Guldenmund, 1991).

   We fit a random coefficient model to these data in which TR is regressed on TIME by a quadratic function. At the person-level, SEX is
used as an explanatory variable. The within-subject model is

$$(\text{TR})_{ti} = \beta_{0i} + \beta_{1i}(\text{TIME})_{ti} + \beta_{2i}(\text{TIME})_{ti}^2 + e_{ti}, \qquad (5.35)$$

and the between-subject model is

$$\beta_{0i} = \gamma_{00} + \gamma_{01}(\text{SEX})_i + u_{0i},$$
$$\beta_{1i} = \gamma_{10} + \gamma_{11}(\text{SEX})_i + u_{1i}, \qquad (5.36)$$
$$\beta_{2i} = \gamma_{20} + \gamma_{21}(\text{SEX})_i + u_{2i}.$$

The single-equation version of this model is given by

$$(\text{TR})_{ti} = \gamma_{00} + \gamma_{01}(\text{SEX})_i + \gamma_{10}(\text{TIME})_{ti} + \gamma_{20}(\text{TIME})_{ti}^2 +$$
$$+ \gamma_{11}(\text{SEX})_i(\text{TIME})_{ti} + \gamma_{21}(\text{SEX})_i(\text{TIME})_{ti}^2 + \qquad (5.37)$$
$$+ u_{0i} + u_{1i}(\text{TIME})_{ti} + u_{2i}(\text{TIME})_{ti}^2 + e_{ti}.$$

Again, model 5.37 is very similar to the model discussed in the Dental data example, except that we have a much larger sample now and we fit a quadratic, instead of a linear growth curve. Note that adding a quadratic term to the growth curve (γ_{20}) yields a second (fixed) 'interaction' parameter to the model (γ_{21}), as well as an additional random term (u_{2i}). For the relatively simple random coefficient structure, this results in one additional variance component σ_2^2 and two covariance parameters σ_{02} and σ_{12}.

The procedure `BMDP5V` (see Section 5.1.4) was used to obtain parameter estimates. Contrary to the commonly available multilevel programs, this procedure explicitly provides several possibilities to model the within-subject covariance structure. A set of frequently encountered special structures are built into the program, including autocorrelation or autoregressive structures. For this example, four different covariance structures have been combined with the quadratic growth curve model (5.37): general autoregressive, first order autoregressive, completely unconstrained (unstructured) and the already familiar random coefficient structure.

The results for these four models are presented in Table 5.3. Estimates of the fixed parameters γ_{pq} are listed just for completeness; standard error estimates have been omitted. We will not pay further attention to the significance and interpretation of the fixed parameters, because model (5.37) so strongly conforms to the model discussed in the Dental data example (one may, however, notice some remarkable differences in magnitude of the estimated values for corresponding parameters across the different models, especially for the linear term γ_{10} of the growth

Table 5.3: *School Data, Results for Quadratic Growth Model with Four*
Different Structures for Σ

	Structure for Σ			
	Model I	Model II	Model III	Model IV
Fixed parameter	Σ Unconstrained	$\Sigma =$ $\mathbf{T}_F \Omega \mathbf{T}'_F + \sigma^2 \mathbf{I}$	$\sigma_{ij} = \theta_k$ $k = \lvert i - j \rvert + 1$	$\sigma_{ij} = \sigma \rho^{\lvert i-j \rvert}$
γ_{00}	49.549	46.260	44.733	48.116
γ_{10}	0.834	0.688	1.041	0.568
γ_{20}	0.016	0.031	0.015	0.030
γ_{01}	−1.033	−0.949	−1.055	−0.965
γ_{11}	−0.031	−0.046	−0.020	−0.035
γ_{21}	0.002	0.003	0.002	0.002
Number of parameters	15	7	5	2
Deviance	13270.10	13412.62	13431.50	13859.86

curves). Instead we focus attention upon the different covariance structures.

Because the two models applying autoregressive covariance structures (Model III and IV), as well as the model with the random coefficient structure (Model II), are nested within the model with unconstrained covariance matrix (Model I), likelihood-ratio tests can be computed to decide which model is the most appropriate. Differences between particular deviance values are χ^2 distributed with degrees of freedom equal to the difference between the number of independent parameters in the corresponding models. From Table 5.3 it must be concluded that neither of the models applying autoregressive covariance structures is to be preferred over the random coefficient model ($\chi^2 = 447.2$, $df = 5$ for the first order autoregressive model, and $\chi^2 = 18.9$, $df = 2$ for the general autoregressive model), nor can they be preferred over the unconstrained model ($\chi^2 = 589.8$, $df = 13$ for the first order autoregressive model, and $\chi^2 = 161.4$, $df = 10$ for the general autoregressive model). In fact, Table 5.3 shows that the random coefficient model is even less appropriate than the completely unconstrained model ($\chi^2 = 142.5$, $df = 8$). Apparently, in this case, despite possible serial dependencies in the data, all of the 'characteristic' structures for the within-subject covariances, including the random coefficient structure, are too restrictive. The quadratic growth curve model with unconstrained within-subject covariance matrix seems the most satisfactory model for these data.

5.4 Further issues in longitudinal multilevel analysis

In this section we will discuss a number of further issues relevant for the application of multilevel methodology in the analysis of longitudinal data. These issues are the use of time-varying covariates, possible choices for the location (centring) of the explanatory variables and a brief presentation of two other types of growth models, other than the polynomial models discussed in this chapter.

5.4.1 Time-varying covariates

The hierarchical treatment of repeated measures data makes it easy to incorporate time-varying covariates in the model. In general, a covariate can be considered a variable for which one wishes to adjust the response variable. Most interesting for the study of individual growth are covariates that change over the different time points. For example, reconsider the hypothetical example discussed in Section 5.3.3, where the number of months of classroom instruction within a special arithmetic training programme was used to model the development of students' arithmetic skills over time. Now suppose that part of this programme consisted of a voluntary computer-assisted training. In that case one could use the number of hours spent between two measurement occasions at this computer training as a covariate in the repeated-observations model. This means that the arithmetic skills test scores would be adjusted for the extra training, and we would get a clearer modelling of the individual growth trajectories as a function of the amount of classroom instruction only.

The way to include time-varying covariates in the longitudinal multilevel model is to treat such variables as additional predictor variables in the level-1 or repeated-observations model. Formally, such a model can be written as

$$Y_{ti} = \beta_{0i} + \alpha_i G_{ti} + \beta_{1i} T_{ti} + \beta_{2i} T_{ti}^2 + \cdots + \beta_{pi} T_{ti}^p + e_{ti}, \qquad (5.38)$$

where G_{ti} are the values of covariate G for individual i at occasion t. In our hypothetical example (see Section 5.3.3), the repeated-observations model would look like

$$(\text{SKIL})_{ti} = \beta_{0i} + \alpha_i(\text{COMP})_{ti} + \beta_{1i}(\text{MONTH})_{ti} + e_{ti}. \qquad (5.39)$$

where COMP obviously stands for the extra hours of computer training, causing the additional temporal variation one wishes to adjust for.

By nature, covariates will normally be treated as fixed in the person-level model (e.g. $\alpha_i = \gamma_i$). If necessary, however, a covariate can also be specified as random.

5.4.2   Centring of explanatory variables

In the application of multilevel modelling, as in all quantitative model-ling, we encounter the problem of *centring*. This problem means that we are looking for an *appropriate location* for the variables in a model. One could say that choosing the right location will determine if a model makes sense. In particular, the choice of a location will determine the way in which the coefficients of a model should be interpreted. This can best be illustrated considering the simple level-1 model

$$Y_{ij} = \beta_{0j} + \beta_{1j}X_{ij} + e_{ij}. \qquad (5.40)$$

In model (5.40) it holds that $\beta_{0j} = E(Y_{ij}|X_{ij} = 0)$, that is, the intercept β_{0j} is defined as the expected outcome for an individual i in group j, who has a score of zero on variable X. It implies that the meaning of $X_{ij} = 0$ should be clear in a model that accounts for the variation in β_{0j}, because it determines the interpretation of β_{0j}. Hence, the level-1 in-tercept can only be understood in relation to the location of the level-1 predictor variables. There is also a technical reason why centring is important, as there are cases in which the choice of a location also in-fluences the numerical stability of the estimation procedure (Bryk & Raudenbush, 1992).

Analogously, the interpretation of level-2 intercepts is determined by the location of the level-2 predictor variables. Bryk & Raudenbush (1992) argue that numerical stability of estimation is not affected by the location of level-2 predictors, however. A suitable choice for a location will nevertheless simplify the interpretation of results.

Thus, in a two-level (longitudinal) model we have to consider the location of the X (or T) variables at level-1, and the location of the Z variables at level-2.

Level-1

Assuming X to be measured on an interval scale, several possibilities for the location of X exist. These include:

Natural metric In some applications it may be sufficient to leave X in its original metric, which means that we do not centre X at all. Again, the most important thing to keep in mind is the meaning of $X_{ij} = 0$. For instance, in cases where the minimum score of X is larger than zero, the β_{0j} parameter will be without a proper meaning. Such a model could lead to peculiar results, such as a correlation between intercept and slope almost equal to -1.0. In other cases, however, the meaning of $X_{ij} = 0$ will be perfectly clear and usable.

Centring on the grand mean Very often, it is useful to centre the variable X on the grand mean. This is, for instance, the standard location for X_{ij} in the traditional analysis of covariance (ANCOVA) model (see Kirk, 1982, p. 715). The result of this centring is that the intercept β_{0j} equals the expected outcome for an individual who has a score on variable X_{ij} equal to the grand mean. This intercept can be interpreted as an adjusted mean for group j, consisting of the group mean and a part dependent on the difference between the group mean and the grand mean. The variance of the β_{0j}s is the variance of these adjusted means among the level-2 units.

Centring on the level-2 mean This option implies that for each level-2 unit, the variable X is centred on its level-2 unit mean. Now the intercept β_{0j} equals the mean of group j, and the variance of the β_{0j}s is just the variance of the group means among all groups (the level-2 units).

Special locations Depending upon the purpose of the study, several special choices for the location of X may be intelligent. For instance, if the population mean for a predictor is known, one may wish to use this value for centring. In that case the intercept becomes the expected outcome in group j for the 'average person in the population' (Willms, 1986). For longitudinal applications, it may be of interest to centre the level-1 predictors in such a way that the intercept equals the expected outcome for person i at a specific point in time, for instance, at the start of the training programme. Note that for longitudinal applications, where $X_i\ (= T_i)$ may consist of a set of equal values for each individual, centring on the grand mean, as well as centring on the level-2 (person) means, will give the same results.

If X contains an effects coded variable, indicating sex for instance, we may centre this variable as well. The interpretation in this case is similar to the interval scale case described above, except that we make use of proportions now. Note that in our examples we used the values -1 and $+1$ to code girls and boys, respectively. Dummy coding, using values 0 and 1, could be used as well but it would change the interpretation of the model parameters.

Level-2

We can be short about the choice for the location of the Z variables at level-2. In general, this choice is not problematic, because the γ coefficients can be easily interpreted no matter what choice we have made for the level-2 predictors. It will often just be convenient, particularly for reasons of overall interpretation, to centre all level-2 predictors on their grand means.

Metric of the outcome variable

We conclude this section on the metric of the explanatory variables with a remark concerning the dependent or outcome variable. It may sound a bit superfluous, but it should be noted that it is essential to the modelling of growth that the dependent variable, which we want to model as a function of time, at each point in time, is measured on a common scale. This is to ensure that changes over time reflect growth or development and not changes in the measurement scale.

5.4.3 Other growth models

The bulk of this chapter concerns the application of longitudinal multilevel models in which a polynomial of degree p is used to model the outcome variable as a function of time. The reason for focusing upon this type of growth curve model is that in various research settings, polynomial functions have been proven to be very suitable for modelling individual growth, and that the use of these functions and their corresponding curves have become a common routine. However, to complement this chapter on growth curve modelling using multilevel methodology, we will briefly discuss two other, related approaches to analysing growth trajectories. First, we will discuss *fixed occasion models*, and second, we will discuss *piecewise linear growth models*.

Fixed occasion models   In fixed occasion models, the outcome variable is modelled as a function of dummy variables or indicator vectors denoting the different time points. The T scores for an individual i, measured on variable Y on occasion t can be expressed as

$$
\begin{aligned}
Y_{1i} &= \beta_{1i}1 + \beta_{2i}0 + \cdots + \beta_{Ti}0, \\
Y_{2i} &= \beta_{1i}0 + \beta_{2i}1 + \cdots + \beta_{Ti}0, \\
\ldots &= \ldots \\
Y_{Ti} &= \beta_{1i}0 + \beta_{2i}0 + \cdots + \beta_{Ti}1.
\end{aligned}
\tag{5.41}
$$

Now, for individual i, the effect of occasion q, β_{qi}, can be modelled as a mean value γ, adjusted by a deviation u, for each time point for that individual. This can be expressed as

$$
\begin{aligned}
\beta_{1i} &= \gamma_{10} + u_{1i}, \\
\beta_{2i} &= \gamma_{20} + u_{2i}, \\
\ldots &= \ldots \\
\beta_{Ti} &= \gamma_{T0} + u_{Ti},
\end{aligned}
\tag{5.42}
$$

under the usual assumptions. It means that in model (5.41) and (5.42), the effect of occasion q, γ_{q0}, is estimated as the mean of the outcome variable at occasion q over all individuals. Hence, in model (5.41) and (5.42), we have to estimate the fixed parameters γ_{q0}, and the (co)variances among the individual deviations at the consecutive time points, $\sigma_1^2, \sigma_{12}, \sigma_2^2, \ldots, \sigma_T^2$. Thus, rather than representing growth by means of curves, we are modelling the development of the mean outcome over time, together with the (co)variances among the occasion effects.

Piecewise linear growth models When repeated measures data have a structure such that nonlinear growth curves should be applied, another option is to break up the nonlinear growth trajectory into several linear parts. This alternative can be interesting, for instance, when we want to compare growth rates during two separate periods. Suppose one wishes to specify a three-piece linear growth model, that is, we want to model a different growth rate for Periods 1, 2 and 3, respectively. Then, a suitable repeated-observations model would be

$$Y_{ti} = \beta_{0i} + \beta_{1i}T_{1ti} + \beta_{2i}T_{2ti} + \beta_{3i}T_{3ti} + e_{ti}. \qquad (5.43)$$

In Equation (5.43), the variables T_{1ti}, T_{2ti} and T_{3ti} are coded in such way that they represent a piecewise regression, in which β_{1t}, β_{2t} and β_{3t} are the growth rates during Periods 1, 2 and 3, respectively. Obviously, at the person-level, one has a variety of choices for a model that accounts for the variation of intercept and growth rates across all individuals (see for details, Bryk & Raudenbush, 1992).

5.5   Properties of longitudinal multilevel analysis

In this section we will remark on a number of useful properties of multilevel methodology for the analysis of longitudinal data. First, we will discuss two characteristics of growth that are captured in all longitudinal multilevel models. Second, we will follow Bryk & Raudenbush (1992) in their presentation of five major topics that are useful for characterizing longitudinal multilevel methodology and for distinguishing it from more traditional MANOVA repeated measures methods. These topics are: the emphasis on individual growth, the flexibility of the multilevel approach to longitudinal data, the possible modelling of the within-subject covariance structure, the correspondence between MANOVA repeated measures methods and appropriately specified multilevel models, and the application of models with more than two levels. In Section 5.6, we will return to the relation between longitudinal multilevel analysis and MANOVA repeated measures methods once more, and treat the subject more formally.

5.5.1 Characteristics of growth

Even the most simple longitudinal multilevel model as defined by (5.8) – (5.9), in which polynomial growth curves of degree p are fitted, captures two important characteristics of growth or development. First, the (co)variances among the observations, or the between-subject (co)variation, is a function of time. This can easily be seen from Equation (5.17), which expresses the (co)variances among the elements of $\mathbf{y}_i$, not accounted for by the fixed part, for both model (5.8) – (5.9) and for the more general model (5.13). These (co)variances are contained in the $(T \times T)$ matrix Σ_i given by

$$\Sigma_i = \mathbf{T}\Sigma_{(2)}\mathbf{T}' + \sigma_e^2\mathbf{I}. \tag{5.44}$$

For example, consider a simple linear growth model with random coefficients

$$\begin{aligned}
Y_{ti} &= \beta_{0i} + \beta_{1i}T_{ti} + e_{ti}, \\
\beta_{0i} &= \gamma_{00} + u_{0i}, \\
\beta_{1i} &= \gamma_{10} + u_{1i},
\end{aligned} \tag{5.45}$$

of which the single equation version is written as

$$Y_{ti} = \underbrace{\gamma_{00} + \gamma_{10}T_{ti}}_{\text{fixed}} + \underbrace{u_{0i} + u_{1i}T_{ti} + e_{ti}}_{\text{random}}. \tag{5.46}$$

Now define $r_{ti} = u_{0i} + u_{1i}T_{ti} + e_{ti}$, the random part of model (5.46). Then, for any individual i, the (co)variances among the elements of $\mathbf{y}_i$, are given by

$$\text{Var}(r_{ti}) = \sigma_0^2 + 2\sigma_{01}T_{ti} + \sigma_1^2 T_{ti}^2 + \sigma_e^2. \tag{5.47}$$

Hence, both the variances of the observations and the covariances among them are functions of time. The fact that the between-subject variation is a function of time (or age) makes sense because we expect individuals to grow at different rates.

Second, the responses of an individual on different occasions are correlated, that is, every two observations for a single subject are correlated. Clearly, this characteristic corresponds to the serial dependence in repeated measurements. It can be shown by expressing the covariance between the observations of individual i at occasions t and t' as

$$\text{Cov}(r_{ti}, r_{t'i}) = \sigma_0^2 + (T_{ti} + T_{t'i})\sigma_{01} + T_{ti}T_{t'i}\sigma_1^2. \tag{5.48}$$

Note that Equation (5.48) shows that the correlation between every two responses depends on the spacing of the observations, on the relative size of the variances of both the intercepts and the slopes, and on the covariance between them. Equations (5.46) – (5.48) make clear that the (co)variances among the observations depend both on the specification of the repeated-observations model (the assumptions for, or modelling of the error terms e_{ti}) and on the (co)variances among the parameters of the person-level model (the individual growth coefficients). Particularly the specification of the error terms e_{ti} in the repeated-observations model, allow for the modelling of a variety of covariance structures (see also Section 5.3.4, Equations (5.18) and (5.19)).

5.5.2   Emphasis on individual growth

The longitudinal multilevel model explicitly takes into account individual growth. Clearly, the starting point of the model is the repeated-observations model (for instance Equation (5.8)), which represents the individual growth trajectory. In traditional MANOVA repeated measures methods, the modelling of individual variation in growth trajectories emerges only from the interaction of repeated measures by individuals and is not modelled directly. One could say that the hierarchical approach is therefore conceptually better suited for growth-curve modelling (see also Willett, 1988).

5.5.3   Flexibility of approach

The longitudinal multilevel model is more flexible than the MANOVA repeated measures model. Within the multilevel framework, it is possible to formulate a variety of growth models. For instance, the polynomial growth curves can be of any degree, and we have maximal freedom to chose variables for each growth parameter separately to act as predictors in the person-level model. The use of time-varying covariates in the repeated-observations model, that is, the incorporation of predictor variables other than time or age, which themselves vary over the different time points, is rather straightforward (we elaborate on this topic in Section 5.4). The time or age variable does not need to be a set of fixed points, but may also be continuous. Especially noteworthy is the possibility for both the number of observations per individual, and the spacing of these observations in time, to vary. This kind of unbalancedness can only be dealt with in highly generalized MANOVA repeated measures procedures, such as the approach of Jennrich & Schluchter (1986).

5.5.4 Modelling of the within-subject covariance structure

The longitudinal multilevel model allows for the modelling of the within-subject covariance structure. This is accomplished by the specification of a structure for the (co)variances among the random (or error) terms of the model (see also Section 5.3.4). It is possible to include explanatory variables that (partially) account for these (co)variances, and to model specific structures, such as autocorrelation structures. Using MANOVA repeated measures methods it is usually impossible to model the within-subject covariance structure. The generalized MANOVA procedure of Jennrich & Schluchter (1986) mentioned above was the first repeated measures approach in which (specific) covariance structures could be modelled directly.

5.5.5 Correspondence in results

Conventional MANOVA repeated measures methods are more restrictive than longitudinal multilevel models concerning data requirements (such as balancedness) and assumptions (for instance about the within-subject covariance structure). In situations in which these MANOVA requirements are satisfied, the longitudinal multilevel model gives the same estimates for fixed effects and the same *t*-ratios as a MANOVA repeated measures procedure. Hence, the conventional MANOVA repeated measures model can be derived as a special case of the longitudinal multilevel model.

5.5.6 Models with more than two levels

The hierarchical approach to data permits the formulation not only of two-level models, but also of higher-level models. Analogous to the person-level and organization-level terminology, longitudinal models incorporating a third level give the opportunity to study the effect of organization on growth, for instance the effect of a certain grouping of the individuals. In that way, we have a combination of individuals nested within organizations and of repeated measures nested within individuals. In educational research we can think of studying the development of students who are nested within schools. An example of this kind is given by Bryk & Raudenbush (1988). In their model the individual growth trajectories are captured in the level-1 model, the between-subject variation in growth parameters among students within a school is contained in the level-2 model and the variation between schools is captured in the level-3 model.

5.6   Relations with (generalized) MANOVA

Longitudinal multilevel models in a MANOVA repeated measures context   A huge amount of literature exists concerning MANOVA and MANOVA repeated measures models. They are discussed extensively in many textbooks on multivariate data analysis, such as Timm (1975) or Bock (1975) (see also Chapter 3 of this book). Relevant for our present discussion is the following. Typically, MANOVA models focus upon the *between-group/subject* side of the analysis. The total variance to be explained in the dependent variables, is accounted for by differences in group membership as much as possible. Main effects as well as interaction effects are estimated by looking at differences between the overall mean and the group means. Usually, this takes place under fairly simple assumptions for the *within-group/subject* covariances.

MANOVA models therefore typically emphasize the fixed part of the model. A model that explains the structure of the means is estimated and the *within-group/subject* covariances are considered as random error, that is, they are the remaining part of the variance in the dependent variables that can not be explained by group membership.

In repeated measures applications of MANOVA, the fixed part of the model is expanded. To fit polynomial growth curves of a certain degree, the set of explanatory variables, first indicating group membership alone, is supplemented with within-subject variables (and powers of those variables) corresponding to the different time points, such as age. On the individual level, we can write such a model as

$$\mathbf{y}_i = \mathbf{X}\boldsymbol{\beta} + \mathbf{v}_i. \tag{5.49}$$

Again, $\mathbf{y}_i$ contains the T repeated measurements for a single subject i, $\mathbf{X}$ is a known $(T \times q)$ design matrix and $\boldsymbol{\beta}$ is a $(q \times 1)$ vector of regression coefficients. The $\mathbf{v}_i$ are vectors of random error components. Because the repeated measures are likely to be dependent (they are measures obtained from the same individual; see also Section 5.3.4), it is assumed that the $\mathbf{v}_i$ are independently distributed as $N(0, \Sigma_i)$. Hence, the matrix Σ_i contains the (co)variances among the elements of $\mathbf{v}_i$. It should be noted that in MANOVA it is usually assumed that Σ_i has a relatively simple structure, such as $\Sigma_i = \sigma^2 \mathbf{I}$. The columns of $\mathbf{X}$ correspond to the different terms in the model, that is, the elements of β. Normally the first column is a vector of ones, necessary to specify the intercept. Further columns code (between-subject) grouping variables and (within-subject) explaining variables (and powers of those variables). The fixed parameters in β can be combined so that we find the parameters of a mean growth curve for the whole group and of separate (mean) curves for the subgroups, specified as deviations from this mean curve.

Clearly, model (5.49) is not aimed at conceptualizing individual growth. Only if $\mathbf{X}$ were specified in such a way that each individual forms a subgroup, could we estimate individual growth curves. However, this option is not very attractive from a statistical point of view, because there will not be much variation in groups where $N = 1$. Moreover, we would be confronted with the problem of incidental parameters, which means that each new individual adds another set of parameters to the model. The result of this process is a dramatic increase in the number of model parameters, which may introduce 'too much freedom' in a model (see e.g. Kendall & Stuart, 1979; Van der Leeden, 1990).

Thus, even though the fixed part of the repeated measures model contains both between- and within-subject elements, it still remains fixed. To include random variation of the individual growth parameters in model (5.49), we have to give the random part (the error components) of the model a more complex structure. This can be accomplished by specifying

$$\mathbf{v}_i = \mathbf{Z}\mathbf{b}_i + \mathbf{r}_i, \tag{5.50}$$

where $\mathbf{v}_i$ is as before and $\mathbf{Z}$ is a known $(T \times r)$ matrix. The $(r \times 1)$ $\mathbf{b}_i$ and $(T \times 1)$ $\mathbf{r}_i$ are independent random vectors. It is assumed that the $\mathbf{b}_i$ and $\mathbf{r}_i$ are independently, identically distributed as $\mathbf{b}_i \sim N(0, \Psi)$ and $\mathbf{r}_i \sim N(0, \sigma^2 \mathbf{I})$, respectively. If $\mathbf{Z}$ is specified accordingly, $\mathbf{b}_i$ contains the (random) growth parameters for subject i. This holds if the columns of $\mathbf{Z}$ contain the same (within-subject) explaining variables (and powers of those variables). The $\mathbf{r}_i$ contain the remaining random error which can not be accounted for by the fixed part modelled with $\mathbf{X}$ and the random part modelled with $\mathbf{Z}$. As we have shown in previous sections, both models (5.49) and (5.50) can be combined into one single equation model,

$$\mathbf{y}_i = \underbrace{\mathbf{X}\boldsymbol{\beta}}_{\text{fixed}} + \underbrace{\mathbf{Zb}_i + \mathbf{r}_i}_{\text{random}}. \qquad (5.51)$$

Again, this model can be split into a fixed part and a random part. The variance of the random part in (5.51) is given by

$$\text{Var}(\mathbf{Zb}_i + \mathbf{r}_i) = \text{Var}(\mathbf{y}_i|\mathbf{X}\boldsymbol{\beta}) = \Sigma_i = \mathbf{Z}\boldsymbol{\Psi}\mathbf{Z}' + \sigma^2\mathbf{I}. \qquad (5.52)$$

Equations (5.49) and (5.50) define the very general MANOVA model, that Jennrich & Schluchter (1986) presented. Their model is formulated at the level of the individual response vectors. It may be considered the most encompassing repeated measures model as it includes all other previously suggested approaches as special cases, such as the univariate mixed-model ANOVA and (versions of) MANOVA (for details see Jennrich & Schluchter, 1986). In the model of Jennrich & Schluchter, the within-subject (co)variances can be modelled as arbitrary functions of a set of unknown (co)variance parameters. The mean structure is specified by a set of regression parameters defined by a (fixed) between-subject design matrix. The general parametrization of the within-subject covariance matrix makes it possible to fit a number of different structures, among which, from our point of view, random effects and time series structures are the most interesting for the analysis of growth data. The model is implemented in the BMDP software package, as the procedure BMDP5V. This program is documented extensively in Dixon (1988).

A comparison of Equations (5.13) and (5.17) with (5.51) and (5.52) respectively, shows that both approaches, that is the multilevel and the MANOVA repeated measures framework, if specified accordingly, lead to the same longitudinal mixed linear model (see also Van der Leeden et al. (1996) for a comprehensive discussion on this comparison). If we let $\mathbf{X} = \mathbf{X}_F$, $\boldsymbol{\beta} = \boldsymbol{\gamma}$, $\mathbf{Z} = \mathbf{T}_R$, $\mathbf{b}_i = \mathbf{u}_i$ and $\mathbf{r}_i = \mathbf{e}_i$ in (5.51), if we let $\mathbf{TZ} = \mathbf{X}_F$ and $\mathbf{T} = \mathbf{T}_R$ in (5.13) (with the subscripts $_F$ and $_R$ indicating fixed and random, respectively) and if we let $\boldsymbol{\Psi} = \Sigma_{(2)}$ and $\sigma^2 = \sigma_e^2$ in

(5.52), we can write this longitudinal mixed linear model as

$$\mathbf{y}_i = \mathbf{X}_F \gamma + \mathbf{T}_R \mathbf{u}_i + \mathbf{e}_i, \tag{5.53}$$

where the $\mathbf{u}_i$ and $\mathbf{e}_i$ are independently, identically distributed as $\mathbf{u}_i \sim N(0, \Sigma_{(2)})$ and $\mathbf{e}_i \sim N(0, \sigma_e^2 \mathbf{I})$, respectively. The variance of the random part, $\text{Var}(\mathbf{T}_R \mathbf{u}_i + \mathbf{e}_i)$, is then written as $\mathbf{T}_R \Sigma_{(2)} \mathbf{T}_R' + \sigma_e^2 \mathbf{I}$. From previous sections, we know that models employing this relatively simple within-subject covariance structure generally go under the name of 'random coefficient models' (De Leeuw & Kreft, 1986; Prosser et al., 1991; Potthoff & Roy, 1964).

Concluding, one could say that when the error covariance structure of a MANOVA model is specified in an appropriate way, the model approaches or becomes identical to a random coefficient model. This indicates that MANOVA models can be derived as special cases of a multilevel model. Then, modelling hierarchically-structured data provides a common framework for studying the interrelations among both approaches.

5.7 Relations with structural equation modelling

Structural equation models can be extended to clustered data, and Muthén (1989) should receive credit for having developed latent variable modelling in heterogeneous populations. McDonald & Goldstein (1989) gave the modelling framework and the computational procedures to do so. Structural equation modelling of clustered data started with factor analysis. The basic idea is that the total variance is decomposed into person- and group-level components, or within-subject and between-subject components. This connects Sections 5.2 and 5.3 of the present chapter with Section 4.2 of Chapter 4. (In the latter chapter a path diagram framework has been used for the visualization of structural equation models. This can be extended to latent variable modelling of clustered data, and to other models as well. This is exemplified by McArdle & Hamagami (1996), among others.)

It is no surprise that the latent variable framework unites the modelling of longitudinal data with longitudinal multilevel modelling. Longitudinal multilevel models with latent variables provide analytic models that deal with hierarchically structured data (longitudinally structured and clustered otherwise) in terms of unmeasured or latent variables.

The same framework includes e.g. latent growth modelling (cf. Section 4.3.2 as well). Eminent in this field of causal modelling of longitudinal and multilevel data is the work by Muthén (Muthén, 1997). This development of more general latent variable multilevel models (and software for estimation and testing) is the main direction for future research.

5.8   Missing data

In principle, missing values of the *dependent* variable in longitudinal multilevel models do not pose any particular problem, since it is not necessary for each individual to have the same number of observations. Missing data of *explanatory* variables on the other hand can not be handled in the same natural way. A distinction must be made between randomly missing data and missing data resulting from some sort of 'missing data mechanism'.

Randomly missing data may be handled by procedures that predict the values which are missing from the available measurements. Subsequently, model parameter estimates are obtained from the resulting 'supplemented' data set. The best way to deal with non-random missing data depends on what is known about the missing data mechanism. This could result in another but similar prediction approach, recoding, forms of deletion, and so on. A more detailed discussion of missing data procedures in the context of multilevel analysis is given by Goldstein (1995, pp. 155–159).

The EM algorithm provides a satisfactory, more or less standard estimation approach for handling missing values of the dependent variable (see Little & Rubin, 1987, Ch. 7). This could occur, for instance when we do have a score on a time-varying covariate (see also Section 5.4.1) at occasion t, whereas the score on the dependent variable at the same occasion (and for the same individual) is missing.

If there are relatively few missing data, either at random or non-random, a few standard ad hoc approaches can be applied, such as listwise deletion (deletion of entire cases with one or more missing values), pairwise deletion (for instance, computation of a covariance on the basis of the available scores on the relevant variables), or substitution methods, such as mean substitution (substitution of the mean of the observed variable for each missing score on that variable). An advantage of these approaches is that they are easy to apply. None of them is fully satisfactory, of course, but they may solve the problem if one has nothing better.

5.9 Discussion

In this chapter we discussed how multilevel modelling can be applied in a longitudinal context. Longitudinal multilevel models accommodate two important characteristics of growth or development. The first of these is that the responses of an individual on different occasions are correlated. The second of these is that the covariances among the observations, that is, the between-subject variations, are a function of time. Particularly in comparison with repeated measures MANOVA, multilevel models are conceptually attractive. As we showed, they are well-suited for growth-curve modelling because the individual growth trajectory is the explicit starting point of the model.

We also showed how the multilevel approach is flexible, and how a variety of models can be formulated. This variation emerges firstly because polynomials can be of any degree. Secondly, the inclusion of covariates is easy and straightforward, and these covariates can be predictor variables at the individual level, fixed over time points, or covariates that vary over time. Thirdly, time or age can be included as a continuous variable. We showed how the number of observations per individual as well as spacing of these observations in time may vary. Lastly, a within-subject (Level-1) covariance structure can be modelled, for instance some autocorrelation structure. Moreover, multilevel models may have more than the usual two levels (within- and between-subjects). For instance, in a model with a third level such as 'organizations' (with individuals nested within organizations), it is possible to study the effect of organizational characteristics on growth.

Multilevel modelling has some less attractive features as well. Usually, maximum likelihood methods are applied for model estimation. It is well known that these methods are less feasible in small samples. In such cases, the variance component estimators are negatively biased (see e.g. Searle et al., 1992) and the reported standard errors can be quite different from the true ones. In part, these complications can be overcome by using restricted maximum likelihood methods, but limitations in hypothesis testing still remain. Problems of this kind may in principle be circumvented by bootstrap and/or jackknife estimation (see e.g. Busing, Meijer, & Van der Leeden, 1997; Van der Leeden, Busing, & Meijer, 1995).

Fitting complex level-1 covariance structures allows for multilevel time series models (Goldstein et al., 1994). However, longitudinal multilevel models appear unsuitable for long single series for one subject. Few replications per individual pose no special problems, although of course the order of the polynomials is bounded by the number of time points per individual.

In principle, longitudinal multilevel models can not handle categorical variables. However, when categorical predictor variables are measured, it is possible to use dummy-coding. Categorical outcome variables can be dealt with through logistic versions of the model. Optimal scaling versions of the multilevel model would be an asset and would widely increase the scope for applications, as of course hierarchical data can be continuous, but may just as well be categorical. Some progress has been made in this area by Michailides (1996) who presents a multilevel version of homogeneity analysis for categorical data.

In this chapter, longitudinal multilevel models were formulated as univariate models. In principle, multivariate (longitudinal) multilevel models can be specified (see e.g. Goldstein, 1995), but the generalization is not straightforward for general users.

In general, multilevel modelling, and particularly the hands-on proficiency in handling multilevel modelling software in particular, has a relatively steep learning curve. In part, this may be solved by the use of specialized macros or tailored user interfaces. The MLn program, for instance, is accompanied by an extensive set of macros which facilitate the fitting of a number of specialized models. A recent development is MLwiN, the latest release of the MLn program. MLwiN is a Windows95 application that provides a visual interface for multilevel modelling. In general, however, longitudinal multilevel models, like ordinary multilevel models, have to be built step by step. Some effort is therefore required, and novices should be prepared to invest some time and energy in this respect.

5.10 Further reading

Most of the important references have already been mentioned in passing. We repeat and group the basic references here. Comprehensive textbooks covering a wide range of theory and applications of multilevel analysis are Goldstein (1995), Bryk & Raudenbush (1992) and Longford (1993). A basic and nontechnical introduction is given by Hox (1994). Kreft & De Leeuw (1998) provide an easily accessible introduction to multilevel analysis, especially aimed at practical application of the technique. This book has a minimum number of equations and a lot of examples.

Generalizations of multilevel analysis to other techniques and other recent developments can be found in the following references. Mislevy & Bock (1989) present hierarchical item-response models. Muthén (1989, 1997), McDonald & Goldstein (1989), Muthén & Satorra (1989), and McArdle & Hamagami (1996) discuss extensions of structural relations models to multilevel modelling (see also Chapter 4). In Longford & Muthén (1991) factor analysis of clustered data can be found. Hox et al. (1990) discuss multilevel models for complex factorial designs for survey data. Michailides (1996) presents a multilevel version of homogeneity analysis.

Longitudinal multilevel modelling can be found in Laird & Ware (1982), Strenio et al. (1983), Bryk & Raudenbush (1987), Raudenbush (1989), Bock (1989), Goldstein (1986a, 1995) and Goldstein et al. (1994).

Chapter 6

Log-linear and Markov modelling of categorical longitudinal data

Ab Mooijaart

6.1 Introduction

Categorical data arise when the variables of interest assume a limited number of values. The measurement scale thus consists of a set of categories. Such data occur frequently in many areas of research: psychology, sociology, political science, education. Whenever we have categorical data, we have discrete measurements, and the responses to our variables can be grouped into a small number of values. The data in this chapter are generally either nominal or ordered categorical. This chapter does not present techniques particularly suited to the analysis of interval variables.

Categorical longitudinal data can be analysed by two broad classes of analytical methods: exploratory techniques and confirmatory techniques. Exploratory techniques for the analysis of categorical longitudinal data were discussed in Chapter 2: these techniques are based on the principle of optimal scaling, that is, a transformation of the data is sought that optimizes a well-defined criterion. Among confirmatory techniques for the analysis of categorical longitudinal data, log-linear models and Markov models are most prominent and most often used. These models are the subject of this chapter.

Log-linear models loom large in so-called multiway frequency analysis or the analysis of cross-classified frequencies, also known as the analysis of contingency tables. The origin of log-linear models for categorical data was in sociology by a technique called elaboration procedure (see Hyman, 1955; Lazarsfeld, 1955). However, because these elaboration procedures were quite complex, log-linear models became quite popular in the seventies, mainly through the work of Goodman (1972, 1973). Since then, several good text books on log-linear models have appeared, e.g. Bishop, Fienberg, & Holland (1975), Goodman (1978), Haberman (1978, 1979), Fienberg (1980) and Agresti (1984, 1990). We will use log-linear models to analyse data with manifest variables. We will apply log-linear models for the analysis of so-called transition tables, where a transition table is a table with frequencies in the cells which denote how many people change or do not change from categories of a certain variable over time.

As a concise enumeration of the (statistical) literature on categorical data analysis, including the analysis of contingency tables and log-linear models, we give the following references. Sloane & Morgan (1996) provide an introduction to categorical data analysis, paying attention to its origins as well. The analysis of contingency data is explicitly treated in Agresti (1984, 1990), Bishop et al. (1975), Everitt (1992), Fienberg (1980) and Sobel (1995). Regression models for (longitudinal) categorical data are given by Liang, Zeger, & Qaqish (1992) and Fitzmaurice, Laird, & Rotnitsky (1993). Hagenaars (1990, 1993, 1994), Gilula & Haberman (1994), Clogg (1995) and Vermunt (1996, 1997) pay attention to general as well as specific topics in log-linear models.

A more recent development in the analysis of longitudinal categorical data is Markov modelling (Markov models were introduced in Section 2.4.1). In Markov models, transitions from one point in time to another point in time are investigated. Markov models may vary from simple to highly complex. In the simplest model it is assumed that there is a single Markov chain. In more complex models it is assumed that there is more than one Markov chain, where each subject, or sample unit, belongs to one chain. The idea then is that each Markov chain may have its own dynamics.

Even more complex models are possible if we introduce latent variables. In these models we assume that the observed categorical variables are indicators of one or more *categorical* latent variables, and a model is defined for the unobserved latent variables and for the relation between the observed variables and the latent variables. As the observed variables are indicators of the latent variable(s), they are not perfectly related to the latent variable. We also can state that the observed variables have some 'measurement error'. Now a model for changes in the latent variables can be conceived of as a model for 'true change' because the 'measurement error' has been removed from the observed changes.

There are two possible generalizations of the Markov models. The first of these is that we can define models for several subpopulations, just as for the models with observed variables only. For instance, we can define a different model for men and women, or for people with low and high educational background. A disadvantage of using models for several subpopulations or groups may be that the number of parameters to be estimated may become very large; also, group membership must be constant over time. To overcome this disadvantage a second generalization is to define models in which the latent variables are regressed on predictor variables. These predictors can be either time-constant or time-varying predictors. An example of a time-constant predictor is 'gender' and an example of a time-varying predictor is 'use of some specific drug'. In Chapter 2 such predictors were encountered under the name of input variables. The models we discuss in this chapter are indeed closely related to the state space model or linear dynamic system described in Chapter 2. Here we also have input variables (also called predictors, independent or explanatory variables, and often confusingly referred to as covariates or concomitant variables), output variables (called here indicators) and state variables (called here latent variables). The difference between Chapter 2 and the present chapter is that in Chapter 2 we used optimal scaling and minimized a loss function, whereas here we assume a probabilistic model and optimize the likelihood function. Another difference between the two chapters is that by assuming a probabilistic model, it is possible to test specific hypotheses, or to test whether the model fits the data. Relevant references for Markov models are: Wiggins (1973), Poulsen (1982), Van de Pol & De Leeuw (1986), Langeheine (1988), Van de Pol & Langeheine (1989,

1990), Langeheine & Van de Pol (1990), Vermunt (1996) and Yamaguchi (1996).

We will not discuss Markov models with predictors or input variables here. For dealing with input variables in Markov models see Dayton & Macready (1988a,b). Another way to deal with input variables is through so-called causal log-linear models, see Hagenaars (1990, 1993, 1994) and Heinen (1993).

A number of computer programs is available for log-linear and Markov modelling. SPSS and other software packages feature log-linear analysis. The computer program which is related strongly to the book by Hagenaars is LCAG (see Hagenaars & Luijkx, 1990). For other ways of dealing with predictors, see Formann (1992, 1994) and Spiel (1994). Two computer programs through which Markov models for observed and latent variables can be analysed are PANMARK (see Van de Pol, Langeheine, & De Jong, 1989) and LEM (see Vermunt, 1993, 1997). LEM is the most general computer program, through which many different types of models can be analysed, in particular models with input variables. Models with input variables cannot be handled by PANMARK; on the other hand, PANMARK can analyse the more complicated class of so-called mixed Markov models (see definition below).

In principle a distinction can be made between continuous time models and discrete time models. In continuous time models, a variable representing the time axis is related to the rate of change on a variable over the measurement waves. In discrete time models we observe at a limited number of time points whether there is a change of position or not and with what probability change occurs. This chapter is restricted to discrete time models.

We will discuss log-linear analysis in Section 6.2. Markov models are discussed in Section 6.3. In Section 6.4, we elaborate on the similarities and differences between the two classes of models. The chapter closes with sections on missing data (Section 6.5), a discussion (Section 6.6), and suggestions for further reading, including a brief overview of a number of related methodologies (Section 6.7).

6.1.1 Assumptions

The models that will be discussed in this chapter can be used under fairly mild assumptions. The only relevant assumption for log-linear and Markov modelling is that the data follow a multinomial distribution. This assumption is rather weak and has turned out to be quite appropriate in practice.

6.2   Log-linear models

In this section we discuss log-linear models. We will not treat the models in full detail, but refer for complete information to textbooks that deal with log-linear models extensively (for instance Agresti, 1984; Bishop et al., 1975; Fienberg, 1980). As there are computer programs for log-linear analysis, also we will not discuss how to estimate the model parameters, what the standard errors of the estimates are and how to test a special model. Instead we will give the main ideas of log-linear analysis as far as we need them for our purposes.

6.2.1   Notation and an example

We start with an example on panel data, introducing notation in the meanwhile. We assume there is one variable, called Y, and just two time points. In general the variable Y may have I categories, but suppose that Y_1 and Y_2 are the measures of a dichotomous variable Y at time 1 and 2, respectively. So, variable Y has two categories, i.e. $I = 2$. The frequencies for a sample of size N can be collected in a 2×2 contingency table and will be denoted by f_{ij}, with i and j denoting the categories of the row and column variable respectively, and $i, j = 1, 2$. This table is encountered under several names in the literature: mobility table, turnover table, transition table, or contingency table, although this last label is not generally associated with longitudinal data. An example of such a mobility table is given in Table 6.1.

In the table we can see how $f_{11} = 348$, $f_{12} = 183$, $f_{21} = 174$ and $f_{22} = 1379$. Thus: 348 subjects remained in category 1, 183 subjects moved from category 1 to category 2, and so on. If category 1 is unemployed, and category 2 is employed, a possibly interesting hypothesis can be formulated as: is the number of people who are employed in 1985 after being unemployed in 1984 equal to the number of people who are not employed in 1985 after being employed in 1984? Formally, the null hypothesis is: $H_0 : F_{12} = F_{21}$, where F_{12} and F_{21} are the expected frequencies. Testing this hypothesis, also called the quasi-symmetry

Table 6.1: *Example Data: Employment Status 1984 and 1985*

		1985 ($t = 2$) Status		
		Not employed	Employed	Total
1984	Not employed	348	183	531
($t = 1$)	Employed	174	1379	1553
Status	Total	522	1562	2084

model, results in a X^2-statistic of 0.18 with one degree of freedom (how this test can be performed will be discussed later on). This result suggests that there is no difference in frequency of people who are first unemployed and become employed and people who are first employed and become unemployed.

A disadvantage of the hypothesis above is that the frequencies f_{11} and f_{22} do not play any role. To show that these frequencies may be important we present the same frequencies in a different way; see Table 6.2.

Table 6.2: *Example Data: Employment Status 1984 and Mobility 1985*

		1985 ($t = 2$) Status		
		Same	Different	Total
1984	Not employed	348	183	531
($t = 1$)	Employed	1379	174	1553
Status	Total	1727	357	2084

In Table 6.2 the variable at time 2 is different from the variable at time 2 in Table 6.1: in Table 6.2 the variable at time point 2 has categories 'same' and 'different'. The variable at time point 2 now reflects 'mobility'. The Tables 6.1 and 6.2 contain the same information. However, because they differ in their representation of the data, we can test different hypotheses. For instance, testing the independence of the two variables of Table 6.2, gives a X^2-statistic of 622.2 with one degree of freedom. This result suggests that previous employment status and mobility are related: there are many more people who are first unemployed who become employed, than there are people who are first employed and who become unemployed. Reformulating the data thus makes it possible to test different, possibly more interesting hypotheses.

The two tests on the same data give quite different results. This is not surprising, as the two tests stand for different hypotheses. From this example we learn that the diagonal elements in Table 6.1 may play an important role for measuring change over time. We also learn that we have to specify the appropriate tests for our specific hypotheses.

6.2.2   Model specification

The basic idea of log-linear analysis is that a linear model is formulated for the *logarithms* of the frequencies instead of for the frequencies themselves. This linear model is completely analogous to the linear model in analysis of variance. Let F_{ij} be the expected frequency under some model, and $\hat{F}_{ij}$ the sample estimate of F_{ij} under the same model. Furthermore, we define F_{i+} as $\sum_j F_{ij}$. Analogously, F_{+j} is defined. Because we are analysing turnover tables, the two variables – in fact one variable but measured twice – have the same number of categories. This number will be denoted by I; so $i, j = 1, \ldots, I$. The log-linear model we are going to present is a log-linear model for a two-dimensional square table. This is of course not the general case, but generalizations to larger tables can easily be deduced. The log-linear model can be written as

$$\log F_{ij} = u + u_{1(i)} + u_{2(j)} + u_{12(ij)}. \tag{6.1}$$

The indices 1 and 2 refer to the variables Y_1 and Y_2, and the indices between brackets refer to the categories of these two variables. The parameters in (6.1) can be interpreted as follows: the 'u' parameter is a general effect parameter, the '$u_{1(i)}$' and '$u_{2(j)}$' parameters denote the main effects for the categories of the variables Y_1 and Y_2, and '$u_{12(ij)}$' denotes the interaction between the variables Y_1 and Y_2. Note the analogy with analysis of variance. If we count the number of parameters, we get for the u parameters: one for the general effect parameter, I for the $u_{1(i)}$ parameters, I for the $u_{2(i)}$ parameters, and I^2 for the $u_{12(ij)}$ parameters. The total number of parameters is therefore $1 + 2I + I^2$. The total number of observed frequencies is equal to I^2. So we do not have a model with estimable parameters because there are more un-known parameters than observed frequencies. Such a model is called overparametrized. To get rid of this overparametrization, we have to introduce restrictions to identify the parameters. (Again, note the ana-logy to the situation in analysis of variance). As restrictions, we choose: $\sum_i u_{1(i)} = \sum_j u_{2(j)} = \sum_i u_{12(ij)} = \sum_j u_{12(ij)} = 0$.

The model in (6.1) is represented in abbreviated form as [12], signi-fying that there is an interaction between variable Y_1 and Y_2 denoted by $u_{12(ij)}$. Such a model without an interaction term is generally referred to as [1][2].

6.2.3   Log-linear analysis for a 2×2 contingency table

Let us, briefly, discuss the case $I = 2$. The model equations can be written as

$$\log F_{11} = u + u_{1(1)} + u_{2(1)} + u_{12(11)}, \tag{6.2a}$$

$$\log F_{12} = u + u_{1(1)} + u_{2(2)} + u_{12(12)}, \tag{6.2b}$$

$$\log F_{21} = u + u_{1(2)} + u_{2(1)} + u_{12(21)}, \tag{6.2c}$$

$$\log F_{22} = u + u_{1(2)} + u_{2(2)} + u_{12(22)}. \tag{6.2d}$$

As we have seen before, this is an overparametrized system and we impose a number of restrictions. In this case, with $I = 2$, we choose $u_{1(2)} = -u_{1(1)}, u_{2(2)} = -u_{2(1)}, u_{12(12)} = -u_{12(11)} = -u_{12(21)} = u_{12(22)}$. So there are, in fact, 4 unknown independent parameters: $u, u_{1(1)}, u_{2(1)}$ and $u_{12(11)}$, and all other parameters are simple functions of these para-meters. On the other hand, in this case, we have just 4 frequencies in the contingency table. So the model is not a model in the sense that it sim-plifies things or is more parsimonious than the observed data. We call such a model a *saturated model*. Taking into account the restrictions mentioned above, we can write for the four expected frequencies

$$\log F_{11} = u + u_{1(1)} + u_{2(1)} + u_{12(11)}, \tag{6.2e}$$

$$\log F_{12} = u + u_{1(1)} - u_{2(1)} - u_{12(11)}, \tag{6.2f}$$

$$\log F_{21} = u - u_{1(1)} + u_{2(1)} - u_{12(11)}, \tag{6.2g}$$

$$\log F_{22} = u - u_{1(1)} - u_{2(1)} + u_{12(11)}. \tag{6.2h}$$

Because (6.2e) – (6.2h) are four linear equations with just four unknown parameters, it is possible to solve these four unknown parameters from this set of equations. For instance, it follows:

$$\log F_{11} + \log F_{22} - \log F_{12} - \log F_{21} = \log(F_{11}F_{22}/F_{12}F_{21}) = 4u_{12(11)}.$$

This gives:

$$u_{12(11)} = \frac{[\log(F_{11}F_{22}/F_{12}F_{21})]}{4}.$$

In the literature the term $F_{11}F_{22}/F_{12}F_{21}$ is called the odds ratio and is denoted by θ. So we have $u_{12(11)} = [\log(\theta)]/4$, which means that the term $u_{12(11)}$ in a log-linear model is a simple function of the odds ratio. It is easy to verify that if and only if the two variables Y_1 and Y_2 are independent of each other, θ is equal to one, in which case the interaction parameter $u_{12(11)} = 0$. Analogously as we have done for the interaction parameter, we can find expressions for the other parameters as well.

As said before, the model discussed here is not a parsimonious model because it does not reduce the data, it only transforms the data in a special way. A model can be formulated by imposing restrictions on the parameters. A well-known restriction is to put $u_{12(ij)} = 0$. In that case we have 4 frequencies and 3 parameters. Equating the interaction terms to zero means that we postulate an independence model for the two variables. Such a model can be estimated by some of the computer packages mentioned above (for instance SPSS). Two goodness-of-fit measures denote how well the model fits the data. These measures, the likelihood ratio G^2 and Pearson X^2, are, according to statistical theory, χ^2 distributed with certain respective degrees of freedom.

The Pearson chi-square statistic is defined as:

$$X^2 = \sum_{\substack{s \text{ over} \\ \text{all cells}}} \frac{\left(f_s - \hat{F}_s\right)^2}{\hat{F}_s}$$

where f_s is an observed frequency of cells, and $\hat{F}_s$ is an estimate of the frequency under some model for the expected frequency F_s. The likelihood-ratio statistic is defined as

$$G^2 = 2 \sum_{\substack{s \text{ over} \\ \text{all cells}}} f_s \log\left(\frac{f_s}{\hat{F}_s}\right).$$

The two statistics are asymptotically identical for large samples, and thus in most practical instances fairly similar. It is common practice to present both of the two statistics when presenting the results of any statistical test. In the following, we will generally, for ease of presentation, present just one of the two.

In the example given here we can therefore use these statistics to decide whether we have to reject a model, or not. For instance, for the data in Table 6.1, a X^2 value of 572.5 with 1 degree of freedom is found. With type-I error (α) at 5%, the critical value for a X^2-statistic with 1 degree of freedom is 3.84. So, the model must be rejected because we find a goodness-of-fit value which is much larger. The interpretation of this is that we have to reject the hypothesis that the two variables are independent. This result can not surprise us because we are measuring the same variable twice. In general, in longitudinal analysis, one can hardly expect that variables measured repeatedly will be independent of each other.

6.2.4   Log-linear analysis for more than one table

In the previous sections we discussed two-way contingency tables of order 2×2. We will discuss two illustrative examples of generalization to more-dimensional tables now.

In the analysis of a turnover table it may be interesting to know if for several groups of people the same turnover characteristics hold. For instance, is switching from one political party to another the same for men as for women, or the same for young people as for the elderly? In fact, we introduce here a grouping variable and have one response variable measured twice. This types of hypothesis can be investigated easily with log-linear models.

Let us discuss a more complex example. Assume we have for two groups of subjects a mobility table. For instance we have a mobility table for Denmark and one for Britain. Table 6.3 gives the data, which is in fact a reduced table from the table of mobility in Denmark and Britain as given by Bishop et al. (1975). The variables in Table 6.3 are Father's status (FATHER), Son's status (SON) and Nationality (NATIONALITY). The categories of the variable status are labelled 1 to 3, where '1' refers to high status and '3' to low status; socio-economic status now refers to a broader concept than just employment. Strictly speaking, such a mo-

Table 6.3: *Danish and British Social Mobility Data*

		Denmark Son's status			Britain Son's status		
		1	2	3	1	2	3
Father's	1	164	188	23	297	264	63
status	2	164	1029	293	253	1232	543
	3	14	270	246	45	392	411

bility table does not contain longitudinal data: we have not measured one variable at two (dependent) time points, but we have measured one variable for two 'dependent' persons. However, such a table can well be conceived of as a longitudinal table, and thus serves our purposes adequately. We thus have one variable (status) measured twice (for father and son) and one grouping variable (NATIONALITY). (In fact, the grouping variable functions as a covariate here, as we perform the analyses separately per category of the grouping variable.) The explanatory variables will be denoted by FATHER, SON and NATIONALITY, respectively. So in fact we have a $3 \times 3 \times 2$ table. The expected frequencies are F_{ijk} with $i, j = 1, 2, 3$ and $k = 1, 2$. The general log-linear model for this table can be written as

$$\log F_{ijk} = u + u_{1(i)} + u_{2(j)} + u_{3(k)} +$$
$$u_{12(ij)} + u_{13(ik)} + u_{23(jk)} + u_{123(ijk)}. \quad (6.3)$$

The equation above is a simple generalization of the model equation for the two-dimensional case: see (6.1). The indices 1, 2 and 3 in expression (6.3) refer to the variables FATHER, SON and NATIONALITY, respectively. Assume that the number of categories for FATHER, SON and NATIONALITY, are I, J and K, respectively, then the number of parameters to be estimated can be computed easily. For instance, the number of parameters $u_{3(k)}$ is equal to K, and the number of parameters $u_{13(ik)}$ is equal to IK. So the total number of unknown parameters is equal to $1 + I + J + K + IJ + IK + JK + IJK$. This can easily be verified. However, the number of observed frequencies in the three-way table is IJK, so the total number of unknown parameters is larger than the number of observed frequencies. Therefore, we have to impose restrictions on the parameters, just as we did for the two-dimensional case. Here we choose, in analogy to the two-dimensional case: $\sum_i u_{1(i)} = \sum_j u_{2(j)} = \sum_k u_{3(k)} = \sum_i u_{12(ij)} = \sum_j u_{12(ij)} = \sum_i u_{13(ik)} = \sum_k u_{13(ik)} = \sum_j u_{23(jk)} = \sum_k u_{23(jk)} = \sum_i u_{123(ijk)} = \sum_j u_{123(ijk)} = \sum_k u_{123(ijk)} = 0$.

Should we now estimate all the unknown parameters, with the restrictions given above, then there are as many unknown parameters as observed frequencies. In fact in such a case we do not have an estimable model, because the parameters are just transformations of the observed frequencies. As above, we call such a model a saturated model.

Suppose that in the example we discuss here, we are interested in the interaction term FATHER × SON, that is in the terms $u_{12(ij)}$. If we want to investigate if these terms are the same for the Danish and the British subjects, we want to investigate whether the relation between father's status and son's status is the same for Britain and Denmark. In terms of the model this can be formulated as: are the $u_{12(ij)}$ equal, conditional on the categories of the third variable? In model terms, we test whether there is no interaction between FATHER and NATIONALITY, between SON and NATIONALITY, and between the combination of FATHER, SON and NATIONALITY. This can be tested by a model in which all elements of $u_{13(ik)}$, $u_{23(jk)}$, $u_{123(ijk)}$ are zero. A model in which these terms are zero is called a *non-saturated* model. It is a parsimonious model because there are fewer unknown parameters than observed frequencies. So we test the model in which the following terms are not zero: $u_{1(i)}$, $u_{2(j)}$, $u_{3(k)}$, and $u_{12(ij)}$. This model is denoted by [12][3].

The notation [12] means that the interaction term between variable 1 and 2 is estimated as well as the main effects of variables 1 and 2. Such a model is called a *hierarchical* model in the sense that the higher-order interactions imply presence of the lower-order main effects and interactions (note the difference from the definition of hierarchical in the chapter on multilevel models). In the context of log-linear analysis, hierarchical models are defined as follows: if a higher order interaction term has to be estimated then all lower order terms which appear in this higher order term, will also be estimated. Conversely, if an interaction term is restricted to be zero, then all higher order interaction will be zero too. For instance, in a model with four variables where we want to estimate the interaction terms $u_{123(ijk)}$, the following terms will by necessity be estimated as well: $u_{1(i)}$, $u_{2(j)}$, $u_{3(k)}$, $u_{12(ij)}$, $u_{13(ik)}$, $u_{23(jk)}$.

Conversely, if we restrict the interaction terms $u_{12(ij)}$ to be equal to zero, then the following interaction terms are restricted to zero as well: $u_{123(ijk)}$, $u_{124(ijl)}$, $u_{1234(ijkl)}$.

In our example here, we estimate a hierarchical model [12][3]. This notation defines the model completely, because from it we can infer that we estimate the interaction terms $u_{12(ij)}$, and therefore also the main effects $u_{1(i)}$, $u_{2(j)}$; furthermore, by the notation [3] we indicate that we also estimate the main effects $u_{3(k)}$. Thus, in a hierarchical model [12][3] the terms $u_{1(i)}$, $u_{2(j)}$, $u_{3(k)}$, $u_{12(ij)}$ will be estimated and the terms $u_{13(ik)}$, $u_{23(jk)}$, $u_{123(ijk)}$ are restricted to be zero.

A consequence of the fact that the terms $u_{3(k)}$ are estimated is that the marginals of the third variable, i.e., in Table 6.3 the variable NATIONALITY, are fitted perfectly by the model (for proof we refer to standard text books). For that reason, we choose not to analyse the absolute frequencies, but the relative frequencies, that is, the frequencies divided by the sample sizes of the two nations. This is a natural thing to do here, because in our example the sample sizes in the two nations are unequal and so we have to correct for the sample size. In an analogous way, in the model [12][3] the marginals of the cross-table of variables FATHER and SON are fitted perfectly, too. Testing the model [12][3] gives a goodness-of-fit value of 56.0 which is χ^2 distributed with 8 degrees of freedom; see Model 1 in Table 6.4. The interpretation is that model [12][3] does not fit. This indicates that the interactions between the variables FATHER and SON are not equal in Denmark and Britain. We therefore conclude that the mobility patterns in the two nations are different.

An explanation for this result may be that the frequency distribution of father's status is different for the two nations. This can be investigated by the model [12][13], because then we fit the interaction [13] and so we fit the marginals for the first variable (FATHER) for each category of the third variable (NATIONALITY) perfectly. So, in this model the data are corrected for different frequencies in father's status in the two nations. Testing this model gives a goodness-of-fit value of 45.3 which is χ^2 distributed with 6 degrees of freedom; see Model 2 in Table 6.4. Also this model does not fit the data.

Another explanation for this may be that the marginals of the second variable (SON) are different for different categories of the third variable (NATIONALITY). Such a model can be tested by fitting the model

[12][23]. This results in a goodness-of-fit value of 16.1 which is χ^2 distributed with 6 degrees of freedom; see Model 3 in Table 6.4. This model is better than the second model, because the X^2 value is substantially lower than that of the second model with the same number of degrees of freedom. However, also the third model still does not fit properly.

Therefore, we combine Model 2 and 3 into Model 4: [12][13][23]. In this model we thus test equality of the relation between father's and son's status for the two categories of nationality, while simultaneously taking into account the relation between nationality and father's as well as son's status. Table 6.4 gives a summary of the results of testing the

Table 6.4: *Danish and British Social Mobility Data: Summary of Test Results*

Model	Likelihood ratio	Pearson	*d.f.*
Model 1: [12][3]	56.0	55.1	8
Model 2: [12][13]	45.3	44.5	6
Model 3: [12][23]	16.1	15.7	6
Model 4: [12][13][23]	10.8	10.5	4

different hypotheses. The test statistics are the likelihood ratio statistic and the Pearson X^2-statistic. For large sample sizes these two statistics should be about equal, and we see that here that is indeed the case. From this table we see that none of the models holds although Model 4 does not fit that badly if we take into account that we have a rather large sample. Thus, we must conclude that mobility patterns in Denmark and Britain are different, also if we correct for the different distribution of the status of fathers and sons in the two nations.

Testing an even less restricted model does not make sense because then we arrive at the model [123] which is the saturated model and so does not reduce the data in any sense.

In addition to testing models by means of the likelihood ratio G^2-statistic or the Pearson X^2-statistic, additional interesting information can be obtained by inspecting the residuals, as these give an indication to what part of the table misfit can be attributed to and are thus useful for interpretation. In Table 6.5 we give the standardized residuals of model [12][13][23]. These standardized residuals are equal to

$$(f_{ij} - \hat{F}_{ij})/\sqrt{\hat{F}_{ij}},$$

where f_{ij} are the observed frequencies and $\hat{F}_{ij}$ are the estimated frequencies according to a special model, here the model [12][13][23]. Each standardized residual can be conceived of as a z-score, so that only standardized residuals lower than -1.96 or higher than 1.96 may be considered as statistically significant ($\alpha = 5\%$). Inspecting these residuals can show us where the model fits and where the model does not fit. The sum of squares of the standardized residuals is in fact the Pearson X^2-statistic. This statistic is also χ^2 distributed with the same degrees of freedom as the likelihood ratio test.

Table 6.5: *Danish and British Social Mobility Data: Standardized Residuals*

		Denmark Son's status			Britain Son's status		
		1	2	3	1	2	3
Father's	1	0.3	0.1	−1.0	−0.2	−0.1	0.7
status	2	0.3	0.3	−0.8	−0.2	−0.3	0.6
	3	−1.6	−0.7	1.3	1.2	0.6	−0.9

If model [12][13][23] fitted the data perfectly, all the residuals in Table 6.5 would be zero. So it is informative to interpret the deviations from zero. A positive residual means that the observed frequency is larger than the expected frequency. As said above, all residuals can be interpreted as z-scores under a standard normal distribution. Thus it follows from Table 6.5 that none of the residuals is by itself significantly different from zero, although the total fit of the model is significant by a narrow margin. The sum of squares of the standardized residuals is 10.5, which equals the Pearson X^2 value. Interpreting the residuals in the table, we see that in Denmark relatively fewer people than in Britain move from low to high status, also fewer people in Denmark than in Britain move from high to low. In addition, people in Denmark with low status are less mobile. All in all, we may conclude that there is less social mobility in Denmark than in Britain.

6.2.5 Log-linear analysis for an I × I contingency table: testing various hypotheses on change

We will now discuss the log-linear model for an $I \times I$ contingency table. The log-linear model is the same as given in (6.1), but now i and j vary from $1, \ldots, I$. Taking into account the usual restrictions for the u-parameters, we have the following number of unknown parameters: 1 parameter for 'u', $I - 1$ parameters for 'u_1', $I - 1$ parameters for 'u_2', and $(I - 1)^2$ parameters for 'u_{12}', which gives in total I^2 unknown parameters. Because an $I \times I$ contingency table contains I^2 frequencies, we again do not have a restrictive model if we estimate all the unknown parameters.

Table 6.6: *Danish Social Mobility Data*

		Son's status				
		1	2	3	4	5
	1	18	17	16	4	2
Father's	2	24	105	109	59	21
status	3	23	84	289	217	95
	4	8	49	175	348	198
	5	6	8	69	201	246

The data in Table 6.6 serve to illustrate log-linear analysis of panel data collected in an $I \times I$ contingency table. We will test a series of specific models useful for studying change. The data are taken from Svalastoga (1959); see also Bishop et al. (1975). The data are on intergenerational mobility in Denmark. Note again that we are not analysing longitudinal data in a strict sense. However, the examples generalize immediately to the longitudinal case by replacing father's status with $t = 1$ and son's status by $t = 2$. The variables are concerned with the socio-economic status of fathers and sons. The categories of the variable are labelled 1 to 5, where '1' refers to high status and '5' to low status. A number of hypotheses may be of importance. We shall discuss these hypotheses separately.

The specific models we want to discuss arise by introducing specific restrictions to the saturated log-linear model discussed earlier.

The independence model (Model A)   In the independence model we test whether the two variables (or waves in the longitudinal analogue) are independent. The independence model is specified by setting the terms $u_{12(ij)}$ equal to zero, and the model is denoted as [1][2]. The independence model is formulated as:

$$\log F_{ij} = u + u_{1(i)} + u_{2(j)}.$$

Testing this model gives a goodness-of-fit value which is χ^2 distributed with $(I-1)^2$ degrees of freedom. We find a goodness-of-fit statistic of 654.2 with 16 degrees of freedom. As expected the independence assumption has to be rejected.

Table 6.7: *Danish Social Mobility Data: Standardized Residuals for the Independence Model*

		Son's status				
		1	2	3	4	5
	1	11.7	4.3	0.1	−3.6	−3.1
Father's	2	4.2	11.8	2.3	−4.9	−6.2
status	3	−0.1	0.7	6.8	−1.8	−5.5
	4	−3.5	−4.0	−2.7	4.8	1.1
	5	−2.8	−6.6	−6.4	1.3	10.9

Table 6.7 presents the standardized residuals of the independence model. In the table we see that the residuals on the main diagonal are large. This means that many more sons have the same status as the father than would be expected from the independence model. So clearly, there is some dependence between the two variables. As said before, the independence assumption can hardly be expected to hold in longitudinal research.

The quasi-independence model (Model B)   Particularly in mobility tables we often see that the diagonal frequencies are large compared with the off-diagonal frequencies. The reason for this is that no change in status occurs much more often than change of status. In longitudinal terms: over the course of a longitudinal study most subjects remain stable. Therefore, an interesting hypothesis is: is the new status independent of the old status for the movers, that is for those who do not stay in the same status. So we formulate a model only for those pairs of fathers and sons whose statuses differ. This is a formulation of the so-called 'quasi-independence' assumption. This term was introduced by Goodman (1968) in dealing with the so-called mover–stayer model in social mobility tables. See also Caussinus (1965). In log-linear analysis the quasi-independence model can be formulated as:

$$\log F_{ij} = u + u_{1(i)} + u_{2(j)}. \qquad \text{for } i \neq j$$

The difference with the independence model is the specification $i \neq j$. So in the quasi-independence model, the diagonal frequencies do not play any role, that is, independence of the variables is investigated for the off-diagonal cells only. Because we do not have a model for the diagonal frequencies, we have to fit them perfectly. Then, $\hat{F}_{ii} = f_{ii}$. Note the difference with the independence model in which it holds $\hat{F}_{ii} = f_{i+}f_{+i}/N$. The quasi-independence model can be analysed by fitting only the off-diagonal elements. If we test the hypothesis of quasi-independence we find a goodness-of-fit value which is χ^2 distributed with degrees of freedom $(I-1)^2 - I$. For the Danish mobility table this gives a goodness-of-fit value of 248.7 with 11 degrees of freedom. Although the reduction in χ^2, if we compare this quasi-independence model with the independence model, is enormous for just 5 degrees of freedom, also the quasi-independence model does not fit the data.

Table 6.8: *Danish Social Mobility Data: Standardized Residuals for the Quasi-Independence Model*

		Son's status				
		1	2	3	4	5
	1	0.0	6.8	1.5	−3.0	−2.1
Father's	2	5.9	0.0	5.5	−3.6	−3.8
status	3	1.0	4.1	0.0	−0.8	−2.0
	4	−3.1	−2.2	−1.5	0.0	4.5
	5	−1.6	−4.4	−2.9	5.0	0.0

In Table 6.8 the standardized residuals are given. Comparing Table 6.7 and 6.8, we find that the standardized residuals for the quasi-independence model are generally smaller than the residuals for the independence model. Note that in Table 6.8, the residuals for the diagonal elements are zero. Because the diagonal elements do not play any role in the quasi-independence analysis, these parameters are fitted perfectly (i.e. have zero residuals).

The interpretation of the result above is that, for people who move from one status to another, the new status is not independent of the old status. In particular, if we inspect Table 6.8 we see that close to the diagonal, the residuals are generally quite large. This means that the data show that if there is a change in status from father to son, the change tends to be small.

In this case only the diagonal elements are left out the analysis. However, in the same way it is possible also to drop other elements from the analysis. In all those cases we speak of quasi-independence, as we test the independence of parts of the turnover table.

Marginal homogeneity model (Model C) If we want to investigate whether the distribution of a certain categorical variable changes over time, this question is phrased in terms of the contingency table as: are the marginal frequencies of the contingency table equal. In our example this becomes: are the frequencies of the categories of the variables Y_1 and Y_2 equal for fathers and sons? This is called the marginal homogeneity hypothesis and can be written as

$$F_{i+} = F_{+i}, \qquad\qquad \text{for } i = 1, \dots, I.$$

Unfortunately, this hypothesis can not be tested directly with log-linear models. The reason is simple: in the hypothesis we do have a linear model for the frequencies but not a linear model for the logarithm of the frequencies, as is the case in log-linear models (see (6.2)). After discussing the next two hypotheses, we will show how to test for marginal homogeneity in an indirect way.

Symmetry model (Model D) Another interesting question in the context of longitudinal research may be: is the contingency table symmetric? In other words: are there as many people who move from status i to status j as there are people who move from status j to status i. Then the table has to be symmetric, implying $F_{ij} = F_{ji}$, which can be formulated as a log-linear model by

$$\log F_{ij} = u + u_{1(i)} + u_{1(j)} + u_{12(ij)}, \qquad \text{with } u_{12(ij)} = u_{12(ji)}.$$

Note that, in contrast to the standard log-linear model, the u_2 parameters are here set equal to the u_1 parameters, or, to put it differently, the row effects are set equal to the column effects because this is what we want to test. Log-linear analysis of this model gives a goodness-of-fit statistic which is χ^2 distributed with $I(I-1)/2$ degrees of freedom. Furthermore the maximum likelihood estimates are formed in the following way:

$$\hat{F}_{ij} = (f_{ij} + f_{ji})/2, \qquad \text{for } i \neq j,$$
$$\hat{F}_{ii} = f_{ii}.$$

For the Danish mobility table we find, under the symmetry assumption, a goodness-of-fit value of 24.80 and 10 degrees of freedom. So the assumption of symmetry must be rejected.

In Table 6.9 we give the standardized residuals for the symmetry model. From this table we see that the standardized residuals are much lower than the residuals of the independence and the quasi-independence model, which means that the symmetry model fits better than the other two models. However, the goodness-of-fit statistic shows that the model does not fit well enough.

Table 6.9: *Danish Social Mobility Data: Standardized Residuals for the Symmetry Model*

			Son's status			
		1	2	3	4	5
	1	0.0	−0.8	−0.8	−0.8	−1.0
Father's	2	0.8	0.0	1.3	0.7	1.7
status	3	0.8	−1.3	0.0	1.5	1.4
	4	0.8	−0.7	−1.5	0.0	−0.1
	5	1.0	−1.7	−1.4	0.1	0.0

Quasi-symmetry model (Model E)   We saw above that symmetry does not hold for the Danish mobility table. Looking at the problem from the opposite angle, it is obvious that if symmetry holds then the marginal distributions must be equal. So it is still possible that the table would be symmetric after taking into account the heterogeneity of the marginal distributions. Or to put it differently: symmetry may hold if we 'correct' for the heterogeneity of the marginal distributions. Testing this assumption can be done by the so-called quasi-symmetry hypothesis. In log-linear terms this hypothesis can be written as

$$\log F_{ij} = u + u_{1(i)} + u_{2(j)} + u_{12(ij)}, \qquad \text{with } u_{12(ij)} = u_{12(ji)}.$$

Note that here, contrary to the symmetry model (model D), the row and column effects may be unequal. This implies that we correct for the hetrogeneity of the marginal distributions. Log-linear analysis gives a goodness-of-fit index which as usual is χ^2 distributed with $(I-1)(I-2)/2$ degrees of freedom. For our example this gives a goodness-of-fit value of 6.47 with 6 degrees of freedom, which is not significant (at 5% level).

Table 6.10: *Danish Social Mobility Data: Standardized Residuals for the Quasi-Symmetry Model*

		\multicolumn{5}{c}{Son's status}
		1	2	3	4	5
	1	0.0	0.6	0.1	−0.6	−0.9
Father's	2	−0.5	0.0	0.4	−0.6	0.8
status	3	−0.1	−0.4	0.0	0.1	0.3
	4	0.5	0.8	−0.1	0.0	−0.4
	5	0.8	−1.0	−0.4	0.4	0.0

In Table 6.10 the standardized residuals of the quasi-symmetry model are given. We see from this table that all standardized residuals are indeed low. As the quasi-symmetry model fits the data, the result can be interpreted as: the Danish mobility table is symmetric, taking into account the differences of the marginal distributions.

Table 6.11: *Danish Social Mobility Data: Summary Table of Goodness-of-Fit Tests for Respective Models*

Model	Goodness-of-fit	*d.f.*
Model A: Independence	654.2	16
Model B: Quasi-Independence	248.7	11
Model C: Marginal Homogeneity	18.3	4
Model D: Symmetry	24.8	10
Model E: Quasi-Symmetry	6.5	6

We now return to the marginal homogeneity model, (Model C above). In discussing the quasi-symmetry model we stated that if we have symmetry, the marginal distributions must be equal. Unfortunately, if we do not have symmetry, we cannot be sure that the marginal distributions are therefore unequal, so there is no unequivocal link between symmetry and marginal homogeneity. However, we defined quasi-symmetry as: symmetry with any heterogeneity in the marginal distributions removed or corrected for. Thus, if we have quasi-symmetry, and if we have marginal homogeneity as well, we achieve symmetry. Formulated somewhat intuitively: the difference between symmetry and quasi-symmetry is marginal homogeneity.

Now denote H_S, H_{QS} and H_{MH} as the three hypotheses for symmetry, quasi-symmetry and marginal homogeneity, then the following expression therefore holds:

$$H_S \equiv H_{QS} \cap H_{MH}.$$

Translated in terms of testing this can be formulated as: if we have a test for the hypotheses H_S and H_{QS} we also have indirectly a (conditional) test for the hypothesis H_{MH}. This means that we can use an indirect way to test the hypothesis H_{MH}, namely by using the hypothesis H_S in combination with H_{QS}. We thus have to apply a conditional test, because we investigate whether there is symmetry conditional to quasi-symmetry. As the test is conditional, it can only be applied if the quasi-symmetry hypothesis has not been rejected. The difference between the tests for symmetry and quasi-symmetry then constitutes the test for marginal homogeneity.

For the Danish mobility table, we recall that the test for quasi-symmetry was not significant. Thus, we may apply the conditional test for marginal homogeneity. The difference between the tests for symmetry and quasi-symmetry gives a goodness-of-fit value of $(24.8 - 6.5 =)$ 18.3 with $(10 - 6 =)$ 4 degrees of freedom. As 18.4 is above the critical value for 4 degrees of freedom, we conclude that the null hypothesis of marginal homogeneity may be rejected, so that we can conclude that indeed the distributions of the marginals are different.

In Table 6.11 we summarize the results for models A – E.

6.3   Markov models

In the previous sections, we discussed models for the relation between two variables. As the variables may just as well be perceived as the same variable measured at two time points, these models are applicable in a longitudinal context. However, in none of these models is time or the time-dependence between measurements explicitly accommodated. In the forthcoming sections, we will introduce models that do specify particular dependencies between the variables at the consecutive time points. To discuss these models, we will formulate (mathematical) models for change over time, using the so-called class of Markov models.

As was discussed in Chapter 2 and Chapter 4, latent variables may be quite a useful addition to models for the relation between observed variables. In the behavioural sciences it is frequently assumed that these latent variables correspond to theoretical constructs. Such a construct may for instance be an attitude. Instead of dealing with observed variables, we assume that the observed variables are (imperfect) indicators of latent variables and we are mainly interested in the relationship between the latent variables. The same approach is used in linear structural equation modelling and in linear dynamic systems analysis, where the model is viewed as consisting of two parts: a measurement part that contains the observed variables and their relation to the latent variables, and a structural part that contains the latent variables and the interrelations between these. Also here we therefore distinguish between these two parts in the model: in the measurement part it is assumed that the scores on the observed variables are measured with some measurement error, and the relations between the latent and observed variables are investigated. In the structural part the relationship between the latent variables is investigated.

In Markov models, transitions from one point in time to another point in time are investigated. Markov models can vary from simple to highly complex. In the most simple Markov model (to which we will refer as *the simple Markov model*) it is assumed that there is a single Markov chain where only the most recent occasion is important for predicting the present state. In this single Markov chain model the population is homogeneous, which means that all subjects have the same transition probabilities, that is: all subjects have the same probability of moving from category i at time point 1 to category j at time point $t+1$ (for instance at time point 1 all employed subjects have the same probability to be unemployed at time point 2). In more complex Markov models it is assumed that there is more than one Markov chain, where each Markov chain corresponds to a homogeneous subpopulation; these models are referred to as *mixed Markov models*. In this case it is possible to investigate a heterogeneous population by assuming several homogeneous subpopulations. Even more complex models are possible if we introduce latent variables. In these models we assume that the observed categorical variables are indicators of one or more latent variables and the Markov chain model is defined not for the observed variables, but for the unobserved latent variables. In case of one chain these models are named *latent Markov models*, in case of more chains they are called *latent mixed Markov models*. In that case we can have models consisting of more than one chain defined for the latent variables, where the observed variables are indicators of the latent variables.

The relationships between these models is displayed in Figure 6.1. This figure shows that the simple Markov model is a special case of both the mixed Markov model and the latent Markov model. Below, we will also discuss the so-called latent class model. This model has not been indicated in the figure as it is a different special case of the mixed Markov model and the latent Markov model. In the latent class model, subjects do not change their latent class over time: the scores on the latent variable are unchanging. Thus: each subject belongs to one latent class and stays in that class over time[1]. Note that the simple Markov

---

[1]The term 'latent class' is also often used to designate the entire class of latent Markov models; we will, however, use this term only for the one special case of the latent Markov

Figure 6.1: *Overview of Markov Models*

	manifest variables	manifest and latent variables
one chain	simple Markov models	latent Markov models
several chains	mixed Markov models	latent mixed Markov models

model is not a special case of the latent class model. We will return to the relationships between these models in the next sections.

We must remark that in all the models we discuss in this section the Markov model is always a first order Markov model, that is, transitions are defined only from time point t to time point $t + 1$; see also Section 2.4.1. These models are quite adequate for most longitudinal applications in behavioural research, and they have nice conceptual properties. For the handling of second order Markov models as an extension of first order Markov models, see Appendix A of Van de Pol & Langeheine (1990).

In Section 6.3.1 we discuss the simple Markov model for observed variables. In Section 6.3.2 we expand these models by introducing latent variables, we then attain the latent Markov model; in that section we also give an example of the latent class model. In Section 6.3.3 we expand the one chain Markov model for observed variables to the more than one chain model, that is, to the so-called mixed Markov model. In Section 6.3.4 the latent mixed Markov model, which is a combination of the latent Markov model and the mixed Markov model, as it has latent variables as well as several chains, is discussed.

As an illustration of all these models we analyse a small data set. These data stem from a Los Angeles panel with 752 respondents recording their depression state at four consecutive time points. The score

---

model, that is, for the latent Markov model in which subjects remain in the same class over time.

'0' refers to 'not depressed' and the score '1' to 'depressed'. For more information see Morgan, Aneshensel, & Clark (1983). These data were also analysed by Langeheine & Van de Pol (1990) for several Markov models, in particular the mover–stayer model. All analyses were carried out with the computer program PANMARK. The data are given in Table 6.12.

Table 6.12: *Los Angeles Panel Data for State of Depression at Four Consecutive Time Points*

$t = 1$	$t = 2$	$t = 3$	$t = 4$	Frequencies
0	0	0	0	487
0	0	0	1	35
0	0	1	0	27
0	0	1	1	6
0	1	0	0	39
0	1	0	1	11
0	1	1	0	9
0	1	1	1	7
1	0	0	0	50
1	0	0	1	11
1	0	1	0	9
1	0	1	1	9
1	1	0	0	16
1	1	0	1	9
1	1	1	0	8
1	1	1	1	19

6.3.1 Simple Markov models

Suppose there are three time points and that at each time point we have observed a variable Y. We can display this situation as in Figure 6.2. In this Figure, Y_1, Y_2 and Y_3 stand for the measurements at time points 1, 2 and 3. A so-called transition matrix $\mathbf{F}$ specifies the probabilities of subjects' scores at a certain time point $t + 1$, given their scores at the previous time point t.

Figure 6.2: *Simple Markov Model for Three Time Points*

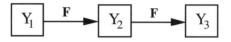

Remember that in this chapter we discuss the situation with categorical observed variables only. So the Y variables are categorical variables. For instance, let the Y variable be 'political preference', with categories 'Democrat' and 'Republican'. In a longitudinal study, we might be interested to investigate how party preference changes over time. In terms of the dichotomous outcome variable Y, we could find that people either change their political preference over time from one party to another, or stick to their political preference. Now, a transition matrix $\mathbf{F}$ can be defined such that the elements denote the proportions of people sticking to their political preference, and the proportions changing their political preference. An example of a transition matrix is given in Figure 6.3.

(Note that we assume that transition matrices are equal across time points: $\mathbf{F}_t = \mathbf{F}$. We call such models *time-invariant* Markov models. However, it is also possible to relax this assumption and to assume that the transition matrices $\mathbf{F}$ vary over time; we then define a *time-varying* Markov model.)

We see in this example that 70% of Democrats remain Democrats and that 80% of Republicans remain Republicans. Furthermore, we see that 30% of the Democrats at time point 1 have switched to Republican at time point 2, and that 20% of the Republicans at time point 1 have switched to Democrat at time point 2. Obviously, for each row, the proportions must add to one, so we are dealing here with conditional probabilities. This will also hold in situations where we have more than two categories for the Y variables.

Several remarks must be made about the model discussed above. As we investigate only simple Markov models, the prediction of the category a subject belongs to at a certain moment depends only on the category to which the subject belonged at the immediately preceding point in time, i.e. Y_t depends directly only on Y_{t-1}, and there is no direct

Figure 6.3: *Example of a Transition Matrix* **F**

$$T = t+1$$

	Democrat	Republican
Democrat	$f_{11} = 0.7$	$f_{12} = 0.3$
Republican	$f_{21} = 0.2$	$f_{22} = 0.8$

$T = t$

connection between Y_t and Y_{t-2}, or Y_{t-3}, Y_{t-4}, etc. Such a chain is called a first order Markov chain. Models that have only a first order Markov chain are called first order Markov models. More complicated models can be formulated: if we allow the measurements at time point t to depend not only on those at time point $t-1$, but also on those at time point $t-2$, we have formulated a second order Markov model. In the same manner, higher order Markov models can be formulated. However, as we said previously, for most longitudinal behavioural applications, a first order model is quite appropriate. See also Section 2.4.1. Secondly, we remark that the population is called homogeneous, because everybody in a certain category at time point t has the same probability of being in the same (or a different) category at time point $t+1$.

Thus, in the model above, the unknown model parameters which have to be estimated are the elements in the matrix **F**. To estimate these parameters, we first have to write down the model equations, and to do so we need notation. Suppose that there are three time points, so that the Y variable is measured three times. We can reformulate this by saying that there are three Y variables called Y_1, Y_2, Y_3. For the scores at the three time points we write a, b, c, meaning that a is the score at time point 1, b is the score at time point 2 and c is the score at time point 3. The data matrix then is in fact a three-dimensional cross table. This data matrix will be denoted by $p[Y_1, Y_2, Y_3]$, which is a matrix of proportions denoting how many people are in the respective categories at time points 1, 2 and 3. In the population, we do not have proportions but probabilities and these will be denoted by $P[Y_1, Y_2, Y_3]$. For the model equations we therefore need a formulation in terms of model parameters for $P[Y_1, Y_2, Y_3]$. We will show that we have all the ingredients for doing this.

In general it holds:

$$P[Y_1, Y_2, Y_3] = P[Y_2, Y_3|Y_1]P[Y_1]. \tag{6.4}$$

This is nothing new, but just standard probability theory. But, according to the same standard theory, we can write

$$P[Y_2, Y_3|Y_1] = P[Y_3|Y_1, Y_2]P[Y_2|Y_1]. \tag{6.5}$$

Now we introduce the specified first order Markov model. In a first order Markov model it holds that Y_3 does not depend directly on Y_1, so we can write

$$P[Y_3|Y_1, Y_2] = P[Y_3|Y_2]. \tag{6.6}$$

Combining (6.4), (6.5) and (6.6) gives

$$P[Y_1, Y_2, Y_3] = P[Y_3|Y_2]P[Y_2|Y_1]P[Y_1], \tag{6.7}$$

which is the model equation for the first order Markov model for three time points. On the right hand side of the equation sign in (6.7) we have the elements of the transition matrices, because $P[Y_3|Y_2]$ and $P[Y_2|Y_1]$ denote the proportion of people (in the population) who change over time from one category to another. Furthermore, $P[Y_1]$ denotes the probabilities of subjects in the categories at time point 1; these are known from the proportions of subjects in the categories at time point 1.

Suppose for one group of subjects that they are in category a at time point 1, in category b at time point 2, and in category c at time point 3, then $Y_1 = a$, $Y_2 = b$ and $Y_3 = c$. Then we have

$$P[Y_1, Y_2, Y_3] = f_{bc}f_{ab}p_a = p_af_{ab}f_{bc}, \tag{6.8}$$

where $f_{bc} = P[Y_3|Y_2]$, $f_{ab} = P[Y_2|Y_1]$, $p_a = P[Y_1]$, and where the following restriction must hold:

$$\sum_{b=1}^{r} f_{ab} = 1,$$

with r the number of categories of variable Y. A similar condition holds for subsequent time points.

On the left hand side of the equality sign in (6.8) we have the probabilities of change over the three time points from one category to another. We can obtain estimates of these probabilities from the corresponding proportions in the sample. So we end up with a model of probabilities in terms of model parameters and we have to obtain sample estimates for these probabilities. These sample estimates can be computed easily from the proportions in the sample.

We will now give the results of the analysis of the Los Angeles panel data by the simple Markov model. Table 6.12 contains the data. In the example of the Los Angeles panel data there are four time points. There are two categories to which subjects can belong: '0' being not depressed, and '1' being depressed. In Table 6.13 the estimates of the parameters for the simple Markov model are given.

From the first two columns in Table 6.13 we see that the initial proportions are equal to 0.826 and 0.174. This means that at time point 1, 82.6% of the respondents are not depressed and so 17.4% are depressed. These percentages can be computed easily, immediately from the data in Table 6.12. The last two columns in Table 6.13 contain the three transition matrices F_1, F_2 and F_3. F_1 contains the proportions f_{ab} of people moving from one category at $t = 1$ to the same or a different category at $t = 2$. F_2 contains the proportions f_{bc} that describe transitions from $t = 2$ to $t = 3$, and F_3 contains the proportions f_{cd} that describe transitions from $t = 3$ to $t = 4$. We see that the transition matrices are not invariant over time, so we have different transition matrices for time point 1 to time point 2, for time point 2 to time point 3, and for time point 3 to time point 4. For instance, 89.4% of the respondents who are not depressed at time point 1 will also be not depressed at time point 2, whereas 10.6% of the respondents who are not depressed at time point 1 are depressed at time point 2. Over the four time points, around 90% of the respondents who are not depressed at some time point, will also be not depressed at the next time point (see the values 89.4%, 92.0%

Table 6.13: *Los Angeles Panel Data: Results for the Simple Markov Model*

Initial proportions p_a		Transition probabilities f_{ab} Y_2		
			$b=0$	$b=1$
$a=0$	0.826	Y_1 $\quad a=0$	0.894	0.106
$a=1$	0.174	$a=1$	0.603	0.397
			$\mathbf{F_1}$	

		Transition probabilities f_{bc} Y_3		
			$c=0$	$c=1$
Y_2	$b=0$		0.920	0.080
	$b=1$		0.636	0.364
			$\mathbf{F_2}$	

		Transition probabilities f_{cd} Y_4		
			$d=0$	$d=1$
Y_3	$c=0$		0.900	0.100
	$c=1$		0.564	0.436
			$\mathbf{F_3}$	

Degrees of freedom	8
Likelihood ratio	76.23
Probability level	0.00

and 90.0%). On the other hand about 60% of the respondents who are depressed at some time point, are not depressed at the next time point (see the values 60.3%, 63.6% and 56.6%). Approximately 10% of subjects who are not depressed at some time point, will be depressed at the next time point. For depressed subjects, approximately 40% remain depressed from one time point to the next. Thus, interpretation of the results is straightforward.

The value of the goodness-of-fit statistic is 76.23. The number of degrees of freedom is equal to the number of possible patterns in the data minus 1 (so 16 patterns – see Table 6.12 – minus 1, which is 15), minus the number of free parameters (in this case 7: 1 for the initial proportions and 1 for every row of every $\mathbf{F}$ matrix; as every row must sum to 1, only one element is free). Therefore, the statistic is χ^2 distributed with 8 degrees of freedom and so the model must be rejected. Note that in the model we analyse here, the transition matrices are not invariant over time. If we were to take the model to be invariant over time (after all, the transition matrices are fairly similar), that is, all three transition matrices constrained to be equal, the model would be even worse fitting than the model we used here, because a model with time-invariant transition matrices is more restricted than a model in which these may vary over time, and so the χ^2 value will be larger. The conclusion is that it does not make sense to reanalyse the data with invariant transition matrices.

In the next sections we will discuss models that are less restrictive than the simple Markov model, and that thus probably fit the data better.

Before doing so, it should be said that there are several interesting types of simple Markov models. Each of these models specifies some hypothesis about the transition matrix, and it can be tested whether such a model fits the data or not.

For instance, if each subject has at each time point the same score on the Y variable, then there are no changes of state. In such a model it holds $f_{aa} = 1$, and so $f_{ab} = 0$ for $a \neq b$. So the transition matrix $\mathbf{F}$ is the identity matrix. This model is called the 'stayer' model. Obviously, this will seldom occur in practice, although it is possible that almost everyone has the same scores on the variable over time and only a small proportion of subjects have different scores over time. By testing such a model we can investigate whether this proportion differs statistically from zero or not.

6.3.2 Latent Markov models

The previous section discussed Markov models for observed variables only. However, as we said before, in many cases it is reasonable to assume that the observed variables are measured with some measurement error, because the reliability of the observed measures is not perfect. In such cases we may introduce latent variables and postulate a Markov model not for the observed variables, but for the latent variables. An example of such a model is given in Figure 6.4.

Figure 6.4: *Latent Markov Model for Three Time Points, One Observed Variable*

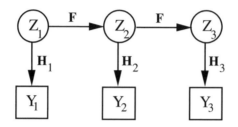

In Figure 6.4 the *Y* variables are observed variables (denoted by squares in the figure) and the *Z* variables are unobserved, or latent, variables (denoted by circles in the figure). The **F** in the figure refers to the transition matrix, just as in the previous section, but now for the latent variables. Note that this **F** matrix is invariant over time. The matrices H_t in the figure refer to the relationships between the latent and the measured or observed variables. Note that here it is assumed that there are three different matrices H_1, H_2, H_3, implying that **H** may vary over time. **H** is also encountered under the name *response probability matrix*. As an example, let us assume that the variables *Z* reflect 'political preference' and that its indicators, i.e. the observed *Y* variables, refer to 'voting behaviour'. The response categories of both variables, *Y* and *Z*, are again 'Democrat' and 'Republican'. Then the model indicates that 'voting behaviour' is an indicator of 'political preference', but that the relationship between the two variables may not be perfect. As the matrix H_t is allowed to vary over time, the extent to which voting behaviour reflects political preference may also vary. If we were to assume that all H_t matrices are equal, we would define a special case of the model in Figure 6.4.

An example of an H_t matrix is given in Table 6.5. In this example it holds that 90% of people with preference for the Democratic party will also vote 'Democrat', and that 10% of these, for one reason or another, vote 'Republican'. On the other hand, 80% of people with

Figure 6.5: *Example of a Matrix* $\mathbf{H}_t$

$$Y_t$$

	Democrat	Republican
Democrat	$h_{11,t} = 0.9$	$h_{12,t} = 0.1$
Republican	$h_{21,t} = 0.2$	$h_{22,t} = 0.8$

Z_t

preference for the Republican party will vote 'Republican', and 20% of these vote 'Democrat'. Obviously, for $\mathbf{H}_t$ it holds – just as for the transition matrices $\mathbf{F}$ – that the rows of $\mathbf{H}_t$ sum to 1, as again we are dealing with conditional probabilities: the rows contain the probabilities for a certain category of Y_t given a certain category of Z_t. This also holds in situations in which the Y variable has more than two categories.

Note that in this example the relationship between the observed variable, 'voting behaviour', and the latent variable, 'political preference', is indeed not perfect. A perfect relation between the two variables would exist if $h_{11,t}$ and $h_{22,t}$ were equal to one, and so $h_{21,t}$ and $h_{12,t}$ were zero, because then all Democrats would vote 'Democrat', and all Republicans would vote 'Republican'. In that case $\mathbf{H}_t$ is the identity matrix $\mathbf{I}$. Thus, if the relationship between the variables is not perfect, we may say that the observed variable is measured with some measurement error. Obviously, this is a quite common situation in behavioural sciences.

Just as in the case with Markov models for observed variables only, we write down the model equation. Suppose again that there are three time points. Because we are dealing with probabilistic models, we will first write down the joint probabilities of all variables, the observed as well as the latent variables. So we write down the joint probabilities of the Y and the Z variables, i.e. $P[Y_1, Y_2, Y_3, Z_1, Z_2, Z_3]$ as a function of the model parameters.

In general it holds that

$$P[Y_1, Y_2, Y_3, Z_1, Z_2, Z_3] = P[Y_3 | Y_1, Y_2, Z_1, Z_2, Z_3] P[Y_1, Y_2, Z_1, Z_2, Z_3].$$

This equation holds regardless of the model we assume, because, from standard probability theory, it is a property which holds for all conditional probabilities. Because, in the model, Y_3 depends only on Z_3, we can write

$$P[Y_1, Y_2, Y_3, Z_1, Z_2, Z_3] = P[Y_3 | Z_3] P[Y_1, Y_2, Z_1, Z_2, Z_3].$$

Using the same standard probability theory, we can write

$$P[Y_1, Y_2, Z_1, Z_2, Z_3] = P[Z_3 | Y_1, Y_2, Z_1, Z_2] P[Y_1, Y_2, Z_1, Z_2].$$

Recursively, because Z_3 depends only on Z_2, we can write

$$P[Y_1, Y_2, Z_1, Z_2, Z_3] = P[Z_3 | Z_2] P[Y_1, Y_2, Z_1, Z_2].$$

So we find for the joint probability of all variables

$$P[Y_1, Y_2, Y_3, Z_1, Z_2, Z_3] = P[Y_3 | Z_3] P[Z_3 | Z_2] P[Y_1, Y_2, Z_1, Z_2].$$

Now, using the same procedure as before, we can formulate the probability $P[Y_1, Y_2, Z_1, Z_2]$ in terms of the conditional probabilities. Doing this, we end up with the equation

$$P[Y_1, Y_2, Y_3, Z_1, Z_2, Z_3] =$$
$$P[Y_3 | Z_3] P[Z_3 | Z_2] P[Y_2 | Z_2] P[Z_2 | Z_1] P[Y_1 | Z_1] P[Z_1].$$

Note that the model parameters collected in the matrices $\mathbf{F}$ and $\mathbf{H}_t$ correspond to the probabilities $P[Z_t | Z_{t-1}]$ and $P[Y_t | Z_t]$, respectively. If we define $Y_1 = i$, $Y_2 = j$, $Y_3 = k$, $Z_1 = a$, $Z_2 = b$, $Z_3 = c$, then we can write

$$P[Y_1, Y_2, Y_3, Z_1, Z_2, Z_3] = p_a h_{ai,1} f_{ab} h_{bj,2} f_{bc} h_{ck,3},$$

where $p_a = P[Z_1 = a]$ and the following must hold

$$\sum_{i=1}^{r} h_{ai,t} = 1,$$

for each a and each t, where r is the number of categories of Y. A parallel condition holds for the other time points. From the equation above, we can write down the model equations for the probabilities of the observed variables. Again, from standard probability theory, it follows that

$$P[Y_1, Y_2, Y_3] = \sum_a \sum_b \sum_c p_a h_{ai,1} f_{ab} h_{bj,2} f_{bc} h_{ck,3}. \qquad (6.9)$$

This is the basic model equation for the latent Markov model for three time points. Generalization to more time points is straightforward.

We have discussed the situation where there is just one Y variable at each time point; however, in many practical situations we have more than one Y variable at each time point. For instance, a model in which at each time point we measure two variables, can be displayed as in Figure 6.6.

Figure 6.6: *Latent Markov Model for Three Time Points, Two Observed Variables*

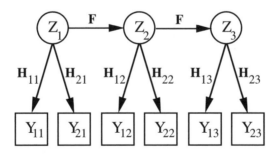

In the model displayed in Figure 6.6 we have implicitly introduced an assumption. In the figure we see that here is no arrow between, for instance, Y_{11} and Y_{21}. So there is no direct relationship between these two variables, but only an indirect relation between these two variables via the latent Z variable. This means that Y_{11} and Y_{21} are independent of each other, given a certain value of Z_1. This assumption is called the *local independence assumption*. The basic idea of this assumption is as follows: given the scores on the latent variable – in our case for those people who fall in a certain category of the latent variable Z – there is no relationship between the two observed variables Y (here: Y_{11} and Y_{21}). Any relation between the two Y variables is accounted for by the differences of the categories of the latent variable Z. The relationship between observed variables is thus explained from the differences of the categories of the latent variable. This idea holds not only for the models we discuss in this chapter, but is the basic assumption of a broad class of models, the *latent trait models*, which we will not discuss here (see for instance Embretson, 1991; Lord & Novick, 1968).

Also for these models with more than one observed variable per time point it is possible to write down the model equations, although the equations are considerably more complex. However, there is a fairly simple alternative method to deal with models with more than one observed variable. This method, which is used also in the PANMARK program, is illustrated by the display in Figure 6.7.

Figure 6.7: *Latent Markov Model for Three Time Points, Two Observed Variables and Two Latent Variables Set Equal*

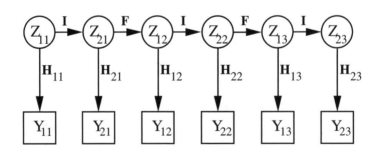

This figure contains six observed variables and six latent variables. However, in the figure we also see that the transition matrices between Z_{11} and Z_{21}, between Z_{12} and Z_{22}, and between Z_{13} and Z_{23} are all equal to the identity matrix, which means that the elements in these pairs of latent variables are thus identical. While it seems as if there are six latent variables, in fact there are just three latent variables, one for each time point. By equating Z_{1t} to Z_{2t}, we in effect do not add a second latent variable to the model at each time point. On the other hand, the (seemingly trivial) presence of the duplicate latent variable Z_{2t} enables us to specify a unique matrix $\mathbf{H}_{jt}$ for each observed variable j. In this way, i.e. by defining some transition matrices equal to the identity matrix, we can deal with more than one indicator (Y variable) at each time point.

In Section 6.3.1 we analysed the Los Angeles panel data using the simple Markov model, which contains observed variables only. We will now reanalyse the same data, using the latent Markov model. Table 6.14 presents the results.

Table 6.14: *Los Angeles Panel Data: Results for the Latent Markov Model*

Initial proportions		Transition probabilities f_{ab}			Response probabilities h_{ai}		
	p_a	Z_t	Z_{t+1}		Z_t	Y_t	
			$b=0$	$b=1$		$i=0$	$i=1$
$a=0$	0.805	$a=0$	1.000	0.000	$a=0$	0.941	0.059
$a=1$	0.195	$a=1$	0.128	0.872	$a=1$	0.372	0.628
			F			**H**	

Degrees of freedom	10
Likelihood ratio	8.32
Probability level	0.60

The first thing we have to remark is that we have restricted both the transition matrices and the response probability matrices to be invariant over time. This is a difference from the previous section, where the transition matrix varied over time. So here we have only one transition matrix, called **F**, and one response probability matrix, called **H**. As stated previously in Chapter 4, such restrictions are not only important from the point of view of parsimony, they are also conceptually important. If we do not constrain the elements of **H** to be invariant over time, we cannot be sure that the latent variable has the same interpretation at each time point.

Although this model might seem quite restrictive, we see that the model fits the data nicely. The likelihood ratio statistic is 8.32, and as it is χ^2 distributed with 10 degrees of freedom this results in a probability level of 0.60, so that we may conclude that the model fits the data well. If we compare the results of the simple Markov model and the latent Markov model, it is obvious that the latent Markov model fits much better than the simple Markov model. This illustrates how using latent variables may lead to a better fit than using observed variables only. To put it differently: in this example apparently it makes sense to assume that depression is not measured perfectly by the observed variables, but is measured with some measurement error. This is a nice demonstration of what we said in the introduction of this section: in many cases the reliability of the observed scores may not be perfect. As the model fit is quite good, we will not proceed to give the results for models which are less restrictive, because those models will also fit the model very well, but will be less parsimonious.

Interpretation of the results is as follows. The initial probability of the category 'not depressed' is 0.805, which means that at time point 1, 80.5% of the respondents fall within the latent category 'not depressed', and so 19.5% of the respondents fall in the latent category 'depressed'. This may seem an odd difference with the previous results (discussed in Section 6.3.1) where the initial proportions p_a were found to be 82.6% and 17.4% respectively. One should keep in mind, however, that, whereas in the first analysis we estimated the initial proportions of subjects in the categories of the observed variable Y_1 ($p_a = P(Y_1 = a)$), here we are estimating the initial proportions of subjects falling in the categories of the latent variable Z_1 ($p_a = P(Z_1 = a)$).

A striking result is that the transition probability f_{00} is equal to 1.000. This means that all respondents in the latent category 'not depressed' at time point 1 stay in the latent category 'not depressed' over time. Only respondents who are in the latent category 'depressed' at time point 1 exhibit change.

We see in this example that the latent variables are not equal to the manifest variables (which was the case in the simple Markov model presented above) because the matrix with response probabilities is not equal to the identity matrix. So the observed variables are indicators of the latent variables, but there is not a perfect relationship between these two variables, or to put it differently: the observed variables are imperfect realizations of the latent variables. Especially for depressed subjects there is quite a bit of measurement error: 37.2% are in fact observed as not depressed.

Because the model fits nicely, it does not make sense to assume a model which is less restrictive than the model with invariant transition matrix and response probabilities. However, what we could do is assume a more restrictive model. Such a model is the latent class model. In the latent class model it is assumed that all transition matrices are equal to the identity matrix. Then we have just one latent categorical variable for all time points, and all variables are independent of each other conditional on the latent scores, i.e. the local independence assumption holds. Substituting the restriction that **F** is the identity matrix into (6.9) gives the following model equation for the latent class model for three time points:

$$P[Y_1, Y_2, Y_3] = \sum_a p_a h_{ai,1} h_{aj,2} h_{ak,3}. \tag{6.10}$$

Note how the latent class model arrived at in this manner is thus indeed a special case of the latent Markov model. In the latent class model, the initial proportions from the Markov model are now called the 'class sizes', because they are not only 'initial': all respondents in a latent class remain in the same latent class.

Table 6.15: *Los Angeles Panel Data: Results for the Latent Class Model*

Class sizes		Response probabilities h_{ai}		
Z	p_a	Z	Y	
			$i = 0$	$i = 1$
$a = 0$	0.842	$a = 0$	0.934	0.066
$a = 1$	0.158	$a = 1$	0.404	0.596
			H	
Degrees of freedom			12	
Likelihood ratio			16.40	
Probability level			0.15	

The results of this analysis for the Los Angeles panel data are given in Table 6.15. The probability level being 0.15, the model seems to fit the data (though not very well). In this latent class model we assume, just as in the latent Markov model in Table 6.14, that all response probabilities are invariant over time. Thus we have analysed a model that is not at all longitudinal: apart from the fact that the response probabilities are invariant over time, also there is just one latent variable for all time points (all respondents in a latent class stay in the same latent class). We have therefore arrived at a remarkable result, where for these longitudinal data we have formulated a model that does not model time at all, but still fits the data.

There is another possible model to fit to the data, that is less restrictive than the latent class model with response probabilities invariant over time. This is the latent class model in which the response probabilities collected in **H** are allowed to vary over time. Then, instead of one matrix **H** we have t matrices $\mathbf{H}_t$: any temporal changes are then accommodated by the time-varying response probabilities. If we fit this model, we subtract six degrees of freedom, two for each time point (even though every matrix $\mathbf{H}_t$ has four elements, remember that rowwise they sum to one, so that of every four elements, two are free). Thus, instead of the two free parameters for the latent class model with **H** identical for each time point, we now have 8 parameters to estimate. The model is thus a lot less parsimonious. Testing this model will result in a χ^2 distribution with 6 degrees of freedom. Though we do not present the results here, we have tested this model, and found that it fits the data quite well. Thus, we have two models that fit the data well: the latent class model with time-varying response probabilities, and the latent Markov model. It would be nice to be able to compare the two models statistically, but this is not possible because the models are not nested. Thus, we have to compare their attractiveness on the basis of our own comparison of model fit against the light of the number of parameters. In that case, we first conclude that the two models are both well fitting. However, the latent Markov model has 10 degrees of freedom and is thus more parsimonious than the latent class model. Already for this reason we prefer the latent Markov model. In addition, and perhaps more importantly, where the latent class model fixes subjects in a certain category, the latent Markov model models dynamic development on latent variables, which is conceptually much more attractive in a longitudinal context.

6.3.3 Mixed Markov models

In the previous sections we were dealing with a homogeneous population in the sense that the transition and response probabilities were assumed to be equal for each individual. In practice this seems to be a rather strong assumption, in particular in the Markov models for observed variables only. So instead of generalizing the simple Markov model by introducing latent variables, we can also generalize the simple Markov model by assuming that the population is heterogeneous. For that, we define the population as consisting of several unknown groups of individuals. Each group has its own dynamics, for instance for each group a different Markov chain is postulated. Even though the chain itself is not a latent chain, there is uncertainty, as we do not know to what chain subjects belong. (If group membership had been known *a priori*, we could have performed a multisample analysis, or performed a separate analysis per subgroup.)

Again we need the model equation. It can be written down easily, as for each respective chain we know the respective model equation, so that we only have to generalize over the chains. For an example with three time points, we can then generalize (6.8) to:

$$P[Y_1, Y_2, Y_3] = \sum_s \delta_s p_{as} f_{abs} f_{bcs}, \qquad (6.11)$$

where the parameters f and p are the same as before, but now an index 's' has been added for each chain 's'. The parameter δ_s is the unknown relative size of each chain.

Several models go under the term mixed Markov models. These are the mover–stayer model (see Blumen, Kogan, & McCarthy, 1955), the black-and-white model (see Converse, 1964, 1970), the latent class model, and a number of models mentioned in Morgan et al. (1983).

(Note how in the previous section we formulated the latent class model as a special case of the latent Markov model. The model equations of the latent class model (see (6.11)) can also be derived from the model equations of the mixed Markov model by restricting $f_{abs} = f_{bs}$ for $a = b$ and $f_{bcs} = f_{cs}$ for $b = c$. The latent class model is therefore both a special case of the latent Markov model and a special case of the mixed Markov model.)

In this section we start by discussing the mover–stayer model for the Los Angeles panel data. In the mover–stayer model it is assumed that one chain consists of those people who stay in their initial category, with probability 1, over time, whereas other people may move from one category to another category over time. So for the 'stayers' the transition matrix is the identity matrix, whereas for the movers the transition matrix contains unknown parameters. This is a useful model to apply to our data, as a sizeable proportion of subjects ($N = 487$) in our sample are never depressed. Developing one model for this group in combination with those who move from one state to the other may make it much harder to model the dynamics of change. The results of applying this model to the data are given in Table 6.16.

Table 6.16: *Los Angeles Panel Data: Results for the Mixed Markov Model*

	Size chain δ_s	Initial proportions p_a	Transition probabilities f_{abs}		
			Y_1	Y_2	
				$b=0$	$b=1$
$s=1$	0.475	$a=0$ 0.678	$a=0$	0.764	0.236
		$a=1$ 0.322	$a=1$	0.701	0.299
				$\mathbf{F}_{\text{mover}}$	
$s=2$	0.525	$a=0$ 0.960	$a=0$	1.000	0.000
		$a=1$ 0.040	$a=1$	0.000	1.000
				$\mathbf{F}_{\text{stayer}}$	
Degrees of freedom		10			
Likelihood ratio		15.50			
Probability level		0.11			

It can be seen from the transition matrices and chain sizes that chain 1 consists of the movers (47.5%) and chain 2 consists of the stayers (52.5%). Of the stayers, 96% are continuously undepressed and 4% are continuously depressed. Of the movers, 67.8% are not depressed and 32.2% are depressed at time point 1. For the movers it further holds that 23.6% of the respondents who are not depressed at time point t, will be depressed at time point $t + 1$. On the other hand, 70.1% of the movers who are depressed at time point t, will be not depressed at time point $t + 1$. From the likelihood ratio test we see that the model fits the data adequately, through not very well, the probability level being 0.11.

If we compare these results with the results we obtained for the simple Markov model, we see that in this mixed Markov model, two different **F** matrices have been found: for the stayers this matrix is of course the identity matrix, the matrix for the movers is not very different from that found earlier for the entire group in the simple Markov model. Given the fact that the fit has improved considerably, we may conclude that, apparently, by separating the movers from the stayers, we are much better able to explain the changes over time, for each subgroup or chain separately.

Instead of the mover–stayer model we can try to fit other models as well. One alternative model that is appealing given the results for the model presented in Table 6.16 (with each pair of f_{0b1} and f_{1b1} fairly similar), is to fit the independence model for the movers. In this model the current state is independent of the previous state. The general formulation for this situation is: $f_{1b} = f_{2b} = f_{3b} \ldots$. In that case, all rows of the transition matrix $\mathbf{F}_{mover}$ are the same and equal to the marginal distribution at time $t + 1$. The interpretation of such a model is that, for the movers, the transition from time point t to time point $t + 1$ does not depend on the category to which the respondent belongs at time point t. If, besides the independence model, we assume that a next state is chosen randomly from the previous state, then all elements in the transition matrix are equal to $1/r$; see Converse (1964). All these models can be tested.

For the example presented in Table 6.16, another possibility is to assume that chain 2 does not consist of stayers, but that respondents belonging to this chain may also move from one state to another. In the latter case we have a different two chain mixed Markov model. Still another model is a model in which it is assumed that for one chain the transition from one state to another is completely random. This can be defined by restricting all the transitions for that chain to be equal to 0.5. All these models can be analysed with the computer program PANMARK, and for a more in-depth discussion of these extensions we refer to Langeheine & Van de Pol (1990).

6.3.4   Latent mixed Markov models

We can combine the mixed Markov model and the latent Markov model into the latent mixed Markov model. In this combined model observed variables may have measurement error and there may be more than one group, that is, there may be more than one latent Markov chain. Here again, we can write down the model equation by generalizing the latent Markov model equations to more than one chain. This gives

$$P[Y_1, Y_2, Y_3] = \sum_s \delta_s \sum_a \sum_b \sum_c p_{as} h_{ai,1s} f_{abs} h_{bj,2s} f_{bcs} h_{ck,3s}.$$

The parameters in this equation are analogous to the parameters in the latent Markov model, but now they have a subscript 's' for each latent chain.

We will illustrate this model by applying it to the Los Angeles panel data. We assume that there are two latent chains. The first chain consists of those respondents who move from one latent state to another over time, the second chain consists of respondents who remain in their latent state. So again we have a mover–stayer model. In chain 1 (the movers) the transition probabilities have to be estimated, and in chain 2 (the stayers) the transition matrix is, by definition, equal to the identity matrix. We add a number of assumptions. We assume that in the group of stayers, the second chain, the variables are measured without measurement error, so that we identify a subgroup of stayers in which there are no uncertainties. In the group of movers the variables may have measurement error. We also assume that the transition probabilities and response probabilities are invariant over time. The results are given in Table 6.17.

To start with, we observe that the fit of the model is quite nice, so this model fits the data very well. Interpretation of the results is as follows. From the first two columns we see that 36.6% of the respondents belong to chain 2, the stayer chain. All of them belong to the first category, $a = 0$, as the initial proportion p_a of subjects in this category is 1.000. Thus, all stayers are undepressed. Then, we see that 63.4% of the respondents belong to chain 1, the mover chain. Of these movers, 77.8% are undepressed at time point 1, and 22.2% are depressed at time point 2. If we look at the matrix $\mathbf{F}_{\text{mover}}$, we see that 17.7% of subjects who are depressed at time point t, are not depressed at the next time point $t + 1$. From the response probabilities in the matrix $\mathbf{H}_{\text{mover}}$ we see that

Table 6.17: *Los Angeles Panel Data: Results for the Latent Mixed Markov Model*

Size chain δ_s		Initial proportions p_a	Transition probabilities f_{ab} Z_t	Z_{t+1} $b=0$	$b=1$	Response probabilities f_{ia} Z_t	Y_t $i=0$	$i=1$
$s=1$	0.634	$a=0$ 0.778	$a=0$	0.996	0.004	$a=0$	0.866	0.134
		$a=1$ 0.222	$a=1$	0.177	0.823	$a=1$	0.273	0.727
				F$_{\mathrm{mover}}$			**H**$_{\mathrm{mover}}$	
$s=2$	0.366	$a=0$ 1.000	$a=0$	1.000	0.000	$a=0$	1.000	0.000
		$a=1$ 0.000	$a=1$	0.000	1.000	$a=1$	0.000	1.000
				F$_{\mathrm{stayer}}$			**H**$_{\mathrm{stayer}}$	

Degrees of freedom	9
Likelihood ratio	6.99
Probability level	0.64

86.6% of undepressed subjects are correctly measured as undepressed; 72.7% of depressed subjects are correctly measured as depressed. From the off-diagonal elements we see that 27.3% of depressed subjects are incorrectly observed as not depressed, and that 13.4% of undepressed subjects are observed as depressed.

If we compare the results from this latent mixed Markov model with those from the previous mixed Markov model, we see that, where the **F** matrix in the mixed Markov model had a high off-diagonal value for the movers (0.701) and subsequently a fairly low diagonal value as well, in the latent mixed Markov model the **F** matrix for the movers has high diagonal values and low off-diagonal values. So, in this latent mixed Markov model, the movers are fairly stable in the sense that in general they do not move from one category to another that much. This is also reflected in the increased δ_1: in the mixed Markov model 47.5% of subjects belonged to the mover chain; for the latent mixed Markov model this proportion has jumped to 63.4%. In all likelihood, a number of subjects who are actually stayers now belong to the mover chain (this is also an explanation for the increased diagonal elements and decreased off-diagonal elements). Lower off-diagonal elements in **F** could have been achieved by simply 'transferring' them to the **H** matrix: that is, by modelling some of the mobility as measurement error. From the table we can see that this has not occurred: also the **H** matrix has high (though somewhat lower) diagonal values. We may conclude that in this example introduction of latent variables (and thus allowing for measurement error) gave an improvement in the sense that nicer results were found and the fit improved.

6.4 Log-linear analysis and Markov models

In this section we compare the two main classes of models we discussed in this chapter. These are the class of log-linear models and the class of Markov models. In Markov models the transition matrices play a prominent role. For instance in Table 6.13 we saw a model in which the transition matrices were allowed to vary over time. The question could also have been raised whether the observed transitions (from time t to time $t + 1$) are stable over time. Such an hypothesis can be answered by Markov modelling if we simply set $\mathbf{F}_t = \mathbf{F}$, and test whether the model fits the data. The question can also be addressed with log-linear analysis. If we reformulate the Los Angeles Panel data displayed in Table 6.12, we can define three turnover tables: from $t = 1$ to $t = 2$, from $t = 2$ to $t = 3$, and from $t = 3$ to $t = 4$. These three turnover tables are given in Table 6.18.

Table 6.18: *Los Angeles Panel Data: Turnover Tables*

	t_2			t_3			t_4	
t_1	555	66	t_2	583	51	t_3	592	66
	79	52		75	43		53	41

The same data can also be written as transition matrices, with the observed transition proportions as given in Table 6.19. Note how the transition proportions in the three tables are quite similar.

Table 6.19: *Los Angeles Panel Data: Observed Transition Proportions*

	t_2			t_3			t_4	
t_1	0.894	0.106	t_2	0.920	0.080	t_3	0.900	0.100
	0.603	0.397		0.636	0.364		0.564	0.436

Let us now define a variable with three categories, 1, 2, and 3; we name this variable TIME. Furthermore we name the column variables of each turnover table matrix lag(0), and we name the row variable lag(1). This definition is according to the definitions used in Chapter 2: the variable containing measurements up to time t is called the lag(0) variable, the variable containing measurements up to time $t-1$ is called the lag(1) variable, and so forth. Then we can define the data as a three-dimensional table, constituted as the cross-tabulation of the variables LAG(1), LAG(0) and TIME.

In the Markov models, we were analysing transition proportions. In log-linear analysis we can in effect do the same if we fix the marginals of the TIME by LAG0 table. If we now fit the model [TIME × LAG1] [LAG1 × LAG0], we in fact fit a model with no interaction between the variable TIME and the transition matrices (there is no higher order interaction term for these three variables). This amounts to fitting a model where the transition matrices are invariant over time.

For this analysis, the likelihood ratio statistic was 3.856 and the Pearson test statistic was 3.797. Both are χ^2-distributed with 4 degrees of freedom, so both tests result in a nice fit, with p-values 0.426 and 0.434, respectively. This result can be interpreted as that, statistically speaking, the transition matrices are invariant over time.

This result is surprising, given our earlier results from the simple Markov model. In fitting the simple Markov model (see Section 6.3.1) to the same data, we imposed fewer restrictions as we left the transition matrices free to vary over time, and found that the model did not fit (see Table 6.13).

These different results can be explained as follows. In a Markov model we formulate a model that specifies the complete response patterns, i.e. for a variable with two categories and T time points, there are

2^T possible response patterns. In log-linear analysis as specified above we test specific hypotheses for particular response patterns (from $t = 1$ to $t = 2$, from $t = 2$ to $t = 3$, etc.), without a model, however, for all response patterns. In the Markov models, the model also specifies what the second order transition matrices are on the basis of the first order transition matrices: for instance, $f_{ac} = f_{ab}f_{bc}$. In log-linear analysis on the same turnover tables, the second order transition matrices are completely free. This means that the Markov model is a much more encompassing model than log-linear analysis given above; it is also more restrictive as we saw. However, it must be remarked that some Markov models can be analysed by log-linear models. This holds for the Markov models with one chain and without latent variables. For instance, in the example given above, one can specify the log-linear model as $[t_1 \times t_2][t_2 \times t_3][t_3 \times t_4]$. It can be proven that this model gives exactly the same parameters and goodness-of-fit statistics as, for instance, PANMARK. Furthermore, the estimates of the transition probabilities are equal to the observed transition proportions. Even second order Markov models can be specified in this way. In the example above a second order Markov model can be specified by $[t_1 \times t_2 \times t_3][t_2 \times t_3 \times t_4]$. Unfortunately, it is not possible to use log-linear models in situations with more than one chain and with latent variables. As we have discussed in this chapter, we think latent variables are important, because measurement error as well as imperfectly observed variables can be dealt with through latent variables. Therefore, log-linear analysis is of limited use for Markov modelling.

6.5   Missing data

Missing data constitute a problem in log-linear and (latent) Markov analysis, although some of the arising problems can be overcome.

When missing values occur, that is, when at a certain time point measurements on a number of variables are missing, the transition proportions can be computed for the group of subjects who have nonmissing values on the relevant variables (a procedure in fact comparable to pairwise deletion). This results in the different proportions being estimated for each time, different subsamples, of the main sample under investigation.

The EM algorithm (Dempster, Laird, & Rubin, 1977) is a natural algorithm for dealing with missing data. The EM algorithm maximizes the likelihood function of the so-called complete data matrix, where the complete data matrix is defined as a matrix consisting of all observed scores and all unobserved scores. Mostly, the unobserved scores are scores on the latent variables, but missing data may be viewed as unobserved scores in the observed variables. For our algorithms this means that the proportions are not based on the total sample size, but on a smaller sample size, depending on how many missing there are for any combination i, j and k.

It is unclear how many observations may be missing for the stability of the parameter estimates to remain unaffected. From a number of studies (see Collins, Fidler, Wugalter, & Long, 1993; Langeheine, Pannekoek, & Van de Pol, 1996) it appears that the models are relatively unaffected by missing data. However, it also appears that in situations with very sparse data, the G^2-statistics are not anymore χ^2 distributed, which has to be dealt with as well.

6.6 Discussion

This chapter discussed and illustrated two main classes of techniques for the analysis of longitudinal categorical data. The first class consists of models for log-linear analysis, the second class contains a variety of Markov models. The techniques in the two classes have in common that they are both performed on mobility tables.

Contrary to the techniques discussed in, for example, Chapter 4, where multivariate normality is assumed for the numerical variables, the techniques discussed in this chapter assume only that the categorical variables follow a multinomial distribution.

While we illustrated log-linear analysis for data sets in which there were only two time points, the technique can easily be applied to data with more time points. In practice, however, log-linear analysis is not often used for data containing more than 4 to 5 time points. The same applies to Markov models. One reason for this is that particularly Markov models need increasingly large samples as the number of time points increases. This is so, because every possible pattern has to have been observed a sufficient number of times. For instance, if we have a variable with only two categories that has been observed at 7 time points, we have already $2^7 = 128$ possible patterns. Thousands rather than hundreds of subjects are needed to enable application of these models then.

The techniques in both classes are confirmatory: the focus is on testing specific hypotheses on the relations between the variables. For log-linear analysis these hypotheses regard the frequencies in the mobility table. As no parameter estimates are involved, this means that log-linear models do not really specify an underlying model for the data. We merely investigate the association between two (or more) categorical variables, and in the longitudinal case these variables are generally the same variable measured at two time points.

While log-linear analysis investigates the relations between the temporal versions of the variables, in (latent) Markov analysis a dynamic model for change is proposed. In that sense, (latent) Markov analysis is more ambitious. The choice between log-linear analysis or latent Markov analysis is therefore generally guided by the researchers' ambitions, as well as by the extent of *a priori* knowledge that is available on the phenomenon of interest.

A disadvantage of particularly log-linear, but also Markov models is that the focus of these models is on aggregate change. It is not surprising that these models are indeed used most often for answering questions of a sociological nature. In both models, the formulation of hypotheses, viz. model specification, is flexible; the interpretation of results is straightforward.

6.7 Further reading

Log-linear and Markov models are widely used in many areas of social and behavioural research. We discussed the most important models, but our presentation was by no means exhaustive. Most of the useful books and papers for further reading were already given above. References on log-linear analysis we recommend are: Fienberg (1980), Agresti (1984, 1990), Everitt (1992), Hagenaars (1994), Gilula & Haberman (1994), Clogg (1990), Clogg (1995), Sobel (1995), and Vermunt (1996, 1997). On Markov modelling of frequency tables further reading is provided by Wiggins (1973), Poulsen (1982), Van de Pol & De Leeuw (1986), Langeheine (1988), Van de Pol & Langeheine (1989, 1990), Langeheine & Van de Pol (1990), Vermunt (1996, 1997) and Yamaguchi (1996).

Figure 6.8: *Example of Transition Matrix for Stage-Sequential Model*

$$T = t+1$$

	summation	subtraction	multiplication	division
summation	f_{11}	f_{12}	f_{13}	f_{14}
subtraction	0	f_{22}	f_{23}	f_{24}
multiplication	0	0	f_{33}	f_{34}
division	0	0	0	f_{44}

$T = t$ (left side label)

We did not discuss latent transition analysis. Latent transition analysis models are useful for investigating stage-transitional models for development. They can be derived as a special case of latent Markov models. For instance, suppose that we want to test a theory on the acquisition of cognitive skills, and that this theory states that children in acquiring arithmetic skills pass through stages in which they first master summation, then subtraction, then multiplication and lastly division. Each stage subsumes the previous stages: if a child masters division, it also masters multiplication, subtraction and summation, and so forth. We can test this theory by using a latent Markov model in which we impose structure on the **F** matrix (see Figure 6.8).

In Figure 6.8, the subdiagonal elements are all zero. This means that children cannot move from a more advanced stage to a less advanced stage from one time point to the next. Through this specification of the **F** matrix, a stage sequential model can be tested on the data, in which children progress in the theoretically prescribed sequence from one stage to the next, and cannot fall back from an advanced stage to a less advanced stage. For other types of stage-sequential hypotheses, structure can be imposed on the **H** matrix. For more on these models, see Collins & Wugalter (1992), Collins et al. (1993) and Collins, Fidler, & Wugalter (1996).

Another interesting application of log-linear models has been around for a number of years. It uses the same concepts illustrated in Section 2.3.3, and discussed in Section 4.4. The basic idea is that one analyses the lag(0) and lag(1) versions of the same (or different) variables that stretch over a considerable period of time, and that by analysing cross-tabulations of these lagged versions of variables, hypotheses about the sequencing of certain behavioural categories can be tested. For more information on this type of analysis, see Bishop et al. (1975) and Bakeman, Adamson, & Strisik (1995).

Van der Heijden's work on log-linear and correspondence analysis of longitudinal data was already mentioned in Chapter 2 (see Van der Heijden, 1987; Van der Heijden & De Leeuw, 1985). The relevant parts for our purposes can be summarized by saying that, after the elimination of certain effects by means of log-linear analysis, the residuals are investigated for structure (for instance for relations between a number of variables, or between temporal versions of variables). As such, these applications focus more on correspondence analysis than on log-linear analysis.

Input or explanatory variables constitute an obvious extension to the Markov models discussed above. A lot has already been done in this area. Langeheine (1994, p.375) defined a model with several populations as the most general model. Such models may have disadvantages, however, as the number of parameters may become very large. It is also possible to define as the most general model a model with input variables. The model with several populations can then be defined as a model with explanatory variables by coding population membership into dummy variables and using these dummy variables as explanatory variables. Useful references are Langeheine (1994), Vermunt (1996) and Mooijaart & Van Montfort (1997).

A number of authors have written on parameter estimation in Markov models, for which the EM-algorithm is a natural tool. See amongst others Dempster et al. (1977), Van de Pol & De Leeuw (1986), Van de Pol et al. (1989), Mooijaart & Van der Heijden (1992), and Mooijaart & Van Montfort (1997).

Chapter 7

Epilogue

Catrien C. J. H. Bijleveld
Ab Mooijaart
Leo J. Th. van der Kamp

Quite a number of data analytic and statistical techniques have been developed over the years for the analysis of data collected in behavioural and social research. Choosing among the available techniques is not an easy task. There are many relevant criteria upon which the choice of technique or method of analysis can be based. These criteria are: the purpose of the study (description, explanation or prediction), characteristics of the analysis question (and often this question is a consequence of theoretical considerations), characteristics of the data collection procedure or design, and characteristics of the data themselves. The data may be characterized by their empirical or conceptual status (manifest versus latent attributes), by the measurement level of the variables, the number of variables, distributional assumptions on the variables, and the presence or absence of a partitioning of the variables. Lastly, properties such as the number of subjects and the number of time points can be decisive factors as well.

The purpose of a longitudinal study may be mere description, that is, summarizing the data collected. In addition, exploration can be sought.

Usually this is not what is sought ultimately. Rather, the primary interest is explanation and/or prediction, or even forecasting of future behaviour.

If we consider the observation or the measurement of behaviour, then the question arises whether we deal with ostensive attributes such as age, sex, education, criminal record and the like, or with attributes not immediately observable, such as anxiety, social intelligence, emotional control, etc. This distinction in two types of attributes corresponds to the distinction between manifest and latent variables, or that between nonhypothetical and hypothetical variables. Observed variables are always present; whether latent or unobserved variables are supposed to be part of the model, is thus a criterion in choosing a certain technique.

As to the measurement level of the variables, an obvious division of variables is to distinguish between categorical variables and continuous variables. A distinction that is more appropriate at the analysis level is between nominal, ordinal and interval variables. For a definition see Chapter 2.1.

As to the number of variables, the distinction between one or more variables refers to the univariate versus multivariate situation. Not only can we have one or more variables in an investigation, we can also have one or more groups or sets of variables. And a common distinction in a case of two sets of variables is the one between dependent and independent variables. Both sets may contain one or more than one variable. Again, the possibility to distinguish variables or groups of variables is an important guideline in deciding on a certain technique.

If a researcher is interested in statistical hypothesis testing, then assumptions have to be made about the population distribution of scores on the variables. In this context a distinction can be made between parametric and distribution-free or non-parametric statistical methods. One can also refrain from considering distribution forms at all and take refuge in exploratory data analysis.

Even though seemingly of less relevance, the number of subjects as well as the number of time points are important guidelines for choosing a particular technique. Some techniques need a large number of time points, some can analyse only a few. Some techniques need a large number of subjects, and if that number is too small, one has to take refuge in other techniques, or adapt the model requirements to be able to choose among a wider set of possible techniques.

The important factors for selecting an appropriate method for the analysis of longitudinal data are thus not fundamentally different from those for the selection of analysis techniques in the general, cross-sectional situation. While it is important that an appropriate model and technique be sought for answering the research question at hand, it is also important to realize that many techniques are related in some way, if not mathematically, then at least conceptually. Before moving on to guidelines for the choice of a longitudinal analysis technique, we will therefore briefly outline the most pertinent (conceptual) similarities – and differences – between the longitudinal techniques that were discussed in the previous chapters.

7.1 Relations between longitudinal analysis techniques

In the previous chapters, a number of techniques for the analysis of longitudinal data were discussed. These techniques were (in order of appearance): homogeneity or multiple correspondence analysis, nonlinear generalized canonical analysis, dynamic systems analysis with optimal scaling, repeated measures (M)ANOVA, structural equation modelling, multilevel analysis, log-linear analysis and Markov modelling. We will briefly summarize the most pertinent characteristics of each. We will do this along the following properties: the presence of latent variables, measurement level of the observed variables, distributional assumptions, whether variables are partitioned or not (that is, whether variables are treated as symmetric or distinguished into sets (or into predictor and criterion variables). The number of subjects and the number of time points are considered as well. We indicate the required numbers of subjects and numbers of time points with fairly fuzzy epithets (small, medium and large). These labels should definitely be understood and treated as fuzzy, as these numbers depend on other factors as well, such as the number of variables, the number of categories, etc. In general, by small numbers of subjects we mean approximately 30–100 subjects, medium up to 300, large over 300, and very large towards 1000 and over. Small numbers of time points are understood to be 3 to 6, medium towards 20, and large over 20. The techniques and their properties are represented in a matrix in Table 7.1.

In Chapter 2, exploratory multivariate techniques were discussed for the analysis of categorical data. The techniques are exploratory, that

Table 7.1: *Characteristics of Longitudinal Analysis Techniques*

Longitudinal analysis technique	Latent variables	Measurement level	Distributional assumptions	Partitioning of variables	Number of subjects	Number of time points
Multiple Correspondence Analysis	yes	categorical	none	no	any	any
Nonlinear Generalized Canonical Analysis	yes	categorical	none	yes	any	any
Linear Dynamic Systems Analysis with Optimal Scaling for N=1	yes	categorical	none	yes	1	large
Linear Dynamic Systems Analysis with Optimal Scaling for N>1	yes	categorical	none	yes	any	medium to large
Repeated Measures (Multivariate) Analysis of Variance	no	continuous	normality	yes	small to large	small to medium
Structural Equation Modelling	yes	continuous	normality	yes	large	small
Multilevel Analysis	no	continuous	normality	yes	medium to large	small to medium
Log-linear Analysis	no	categorical	multinomial	no	large	small
Markov Modelling	yes	categorical	multinomial	yes	very large	small

is: no statistical confirmation is sought and therefore also no distributional assumptions are made. All techniques that were discussed in this chapter use optimal scaling to accommodate the various measurement restrictions on the nominal, ordinal and interval categorical variables. Optimal scaling implies that the categorical data are transformed into continuous data, such that the transformation is optimal in some well-defined sense (a goodness-of-fit function is optimized).

In *multiple correspondence analysis* the correspondence between categorical variables is maximized. Multiple correspondence analysis is a symmetrical technique in the sense that variables are not distinguished into sets such as predictors and criterion variables. The technique searches for directions that explain maximum variance. These directions constitute the dimensions of the solution. These dimensions or (in a broad sense) latent factors are useful in a longitudinal context for displaying subjects' scores at the various measurement occasions graphically. By connecting subjects' scores at the respective measurement occasions, change can be visualized and interpreted. As long as the number of rows in the flattened data matrix is in the usual ratio to the number of variables (often as a rule of thumb it is assumed that the number of rows should be 10 times the number of variables), multiple correspondence on the LONG matrix can handle any number of subjects and any number of time points. Just to give a number of examples, it may be applied with hundreds of subjects and just two time points, or with 5 subjects and 100 time points, or with one subject and 20 time points.

In *nonlinear generalized canonical analysis*, the correspondence between two or more sets of categorical variables is maximized. The variables can be rescaled according to their measurement level. Using nonlinear generalized canonical analysis on the flattened data box it is possible, just as in multiple correspondence analysis, to connect subjects' scores at the various time points, and thereby visualize change. Variables are distinguished into sets. Sets of variables can also be added to the data, for instance a set containing a variable representing (a categorical version of) the time axis. Correspondence can then be sought between the categorical data and the time axis, or between the categorical data and any monotone or categorical transformation of the time axis. In this way, it is possible to model a great many varieties of categorical longitudinal data analysis. For instance categorical versions of growth curve analysis can be approximated by inclusion of variables representing interindividual (intercept) as well as intraindividual (growth) differences. With regard to numbers of subjects and numbers of time points, the same applies for nonlinear generalized canonical analysis that applied for multiple correspondence analysis. As long as the number of rows in the flattened data matrix is in the usual ratio to the number of variables, any number of subjects and any number of time points can be dealt with.

In *linear dynamic systems analysis*, an autoregressive structure is modelled for one or more latent variables. These latent variables capture the time dependence in the sense that any temporal dependence is accommodated through these latent variables. Simultaneously, the dependence of criterion variables on predictor variables passes through the latent variables. Using optimal scaling, any categorical predictor or criterion variables can be rescaled. Linear dynamic systems analysis with optimal scaling can be used for one, or for many subjects. When it is used for one subject, sufficient replications over time are needed to attain stability. However, even when it is used for more than one subject or even for a reasonable large sample of subjects, the number of time points should be substantial, as the technique needs a certain number of time points for the dynamics of the process to be retrievable. The technique differs from the varieties of nonlinear generalized canonical analysis presented in the same chapter, although solutions often in the same manner stress interindividual and intraindividual differences. The model is conceptually quite close to the longitudinal MIMIC model presented in Chapter 4. In fact, the graphical representations of the two models are identical (except for a starting point at time point t_0). Differences are firstly that the structural equation models aim at statistical confirmation under fairly restrictive assumptions. Secondly, structural equation models are regression-oriented in the sense that models are evaluated on the basis of significance of the regression coefficients, whereas the exploratory dynamic techniques focus on interpretation of the actual latent state scores (which can not be found from structural equation modelling).

It should be stressed once more that the techniques discussed in Chapter 2 are useful not only for analysing variables of which the categories can not be ordered *a priori*, but also for analysing variables of which the categories can be considered ordered or even at interval level, but may are presumed to behave in a nonlinear fashion.

In Chapter 3 *(multivariate) analysis of variance* techniques for the analysis of longitudinal data was discussed. These techniques can be typified as inferential statistical techniques for continuous dependent variables. Multivariate normality of the criterion variables is assumed. Although there are no technical limitations to analysing a large number of time points, solutions tend to become harder to interpret with larger numbers of time points. Therefore, in practice, the number of time points is often limited. The techniques can be used with fairly small numbers of subjects. The time variable, that is, the occasion mode, is treated as a design variable. So we can distinguish between two- or more-wave data resulting from the corresponding designs. Difference scores can very well be used in an analysis of variance framework. The analysis of variance techniques do not have options for autoregressive modelling. The analysis of variance methods stand out here, as they are the only longitudinal data analysis techniques for experimental data discussed in this book.

Structural equation models in longitudinal research are the subject of Chapter 4. In structural equation models, relations between the latent and observed variables are specified. The variances and covariances can then be written as functions of the variables and the coefficients that specify these relations. Decomposing the variance–covariance matrix of the variables into components attributable to the various relations in the models, estimates for the parameters and for the variances and covariances of the variables are obtained. Multivariate normality is assumed.

These models are quite popular for multivariate statistical data analysis, for data in which a distinction can be made between manifest and latent variables, or where two or more data sets are involved. It is possible to test models with autoregressive as well as growth curve features. The bulk of structural equation models have to do with continuous variables. They need substantial numbers of subjects and can in practice handle only a limited number of time points. Structural equation models have also been proposed for the analysis of longitudinal data, including data from developmental studies (e.g. Alwin, 1988; Bentler, 1984; Fergusson & Horwood, 1988).

The usefulness of this approach in longitudinal research, however, is questioned by some researchers (see e.g. Rogosa 1995; see also Freedman, 1987, 1991. The first point of critique is that structural equation models have but limited potential in the confirmation of substantive theories. Many authors agree that these models should be used for testing of competing models, rather than for confirmation as such. A second point of critique has been worded by Stoolmiller & Bank (1995), who argue that many temporally dependent phenomena are strongly autoregressive, and that the type of autoregressive model often employed in longitudinal structural equation models is unfit for uncovering exogenous influences or causal mechanisms. Instead, they propose that growth curve models be used.

Growth curve models can indeed very well be investigated using structural equation modelling. In fact, in recent years a gap has been bridged between structural equation modelling and growth curve analysis through multilevel modelling. In a particular formulation employed by numerous authors (McArdle, 1986; Meredith & Tisak, 1990; Willett & Sayer, 1996) structural equation models are close to the multilevel models discussed in Chapter 5. However, when structural equation modelling is used for growth curve analysis, the number of time points is limited in practice. A further disadvantage is that the actual scores on the growth curves are not found from the analysis. In the examples we gave of growth curve analysis through structural modelling, interindividual differences as well as growth were modelled as latent variables. Again, just as in multilevel analysis, we showed how it is possible to relate either of these from background variables. However, multilevel analysis appears in a number of respects as more flexible, given the many additional features that can be incorporated in multilevel models (for instance, multilevel models can handle series of unequal length).

Multilevel analysis for longitudinal data was introduced in Chapter 5. Multilevel data are characterized by a hierarchical structure. An example of a hierarchical data structure is a study in which patients are observed who underwent several forms of therapy. Patients are nested within hospitals. In addition, if the patients are followed over time, a doubly-nested structure arises: time-points or measurement occasions are nested within patients, who in turn are nested within hospitals. Essentially, multilevel analysis aims at studying individual change while explicitly taking into account cross-level interactions, that is, the influence of time and grouping characteristics. Multivariate normality is assumed. Multilevel analysis can handle samples of medium to large size, and small to medium numbers of time points. Multilevel modelling has conceptual resemblances to repeated measures MANOVA as well as to some particular formulations of structural equation modelling.

These last three models are in fact not only conceptually, but also mathematically related, as they can each be written as special cases of one general model. However, they differ in their approach to the various elements in the model. MANOVA emphasizes the fixed part of the model. That is, in MANOVA, the between-group part is emphasized, implying that we focus on the manner in which groups (and thus generally treatments) differ. Within-group effects are basically regarded as noise. In longitudinal applications hypotheses are formulated both with regard to group differences and with regard to differences between the occasions on which the same subjects are measured. As such, MANOVA represents the classical, experimental approach to hypothesis testing.

Structural equation modelling on the other hand focuses on the structure of (or the patterning in) the variance–covariance matrix. As such, hypotheses regard the structure that best describes the observed covariances, that is, we test for a model that is optimal (or fitting sufficiently) against some statistical criterion. For instance, we test to what extent a first order, second order or third order autoregressive model describes the data. In principle, individual growth curves are not modelled; the emphasis is again on averages over subjects. Even though structural equation modelling resembles MANOVA in this respect, important differences are that many more less restrictive models than those in MANOVA may be tested, and that the emphasis is not just on group differences but on the structure, and the relations or paths between the variables, that is: on a model as may be predicted by substantive theory.

In multilevel analysis we can not only test for between-group differences and parameters, but also test for the variance of individual parameters. This is an important and essential distinction between multilevel analysis and the previous techniques. Individual growth trajectories are the explicit starting point of the model.

All in all, differences between MANOVA, structural equation modelling and multilevel analysis evolve around the type of questions that can be addressed. Although all three can be formulated as versions of one overall model, they differ in the attention they pay to its various parts. For instance, what is essentially nuisance in MANOVA (the subjects within groups variation) is one source of variation that is modelled in multilevel analysis. See also Jennrich & Schluchter (1986). Retrospectively, this is one reason why the three models are well suited to be discussed within one book.

The analysis of categorical longitudinal data is the subject of Chapter 6. The techniques discussed in this chapter stand out in the sense that they are frequency-oriented. At the same time, they assume an intermediate position in the sense that while no assumptions have to be made for the exploratory techniques, and while fairly stringent assumptions are needed for the analysis of variance, multilevel and structural modelling techniques, both the log-linear and Markov models are based on the much weaker multinomial assumption. Still, the goal of applying both log-linear as well as Markov models is statistical confirmation.

Log-linear models have conceptual resemblance to the multiple correspondence techniques discussed in Chapter 2 in the sense that they seek correspondence between variables, without imposing a lot of structure, that is, a model, on the data. They also resemble multiple correspondence analysis in a second respect, namely in the sense that the variables are treated in a symmetric manner. Conversely, in their statistical approach, they are closest to the analysis of variance techniques discussed in Chapter 3. Log-linear analysis can in fact (while not directly translating mathematically) be conceptualized as an analysis of variance on the logarithms of the frequencies. In practice only a few time points are generally analysed.

Markov models have many ties with other techniques. As can be seen from the many illustrations, they bear close resemblance to the dynamic models presented in Chapter 2, and to their counterparts presented in Chapter 4. (In fact, representations such as depicted in Figure 6.4 are very similar to the state space model as depicted in Figure 4.10, or to that in Figure 2.27 without the input variables.) While the linear dynamic models for categorical data rescale categorical data to continuous scores, after which an essentially linear model is fitted on the data, in the Markov models discussed in Chapter 6 the data are treated as inherently categorical. Accordingly, the dynamics of the process are modelled not in terms of the level of scores transferred autoregressively by means of some regression coefficient from one time point to the next, but in terms of the probability of observing a certain category given some category observed at a previous time point. This autoregressive process may be modelled for the observed variables or for a latent variable. Markov modelling as presented in this chapter needs fairly large data sets and can handle a relatively small number of time points. The larger the number of time points, the larger the sample size needed.

7.2 Choosing a longitudinal analysis method

Using the characteristics outlined in Figure 7.1, we will sketch a number of paths that can be followed in choosing among the analysis techniques presented in this book. A number of paths are possible, because the various characteristics can be phrased as questions at different points in time. The decision tree we outline in Figure 7.1 is thus by no means the only possible decision tree.

Perhaps the easiest starting point is to ask whether the aim of the analysis is exploration or statistical testing. Once it has been affirmed that the aim is exploration, we have to assess whether we want to explore an autoregressive structure or not. If we do (and if sufficient replications over time are available), we can perform an exploratory analysis using linear dynamic systems analysis with optimal scaling. If only one subject has been observed, we can perform an exploratory analysis using the $N = 1$ version of linear dynamic systems analysis with optimal scaling. It is then also possible to perform either nonlinear generalized canonical correlation analysis (with either a categorical time variable or lagged versions of the variables) or multiple correspondence analysis on the flattened data box, but the choice here depends on the model one has in mind for the relations between the data. When the number of time points becomes too small (as a rule of thumb, smaller than approximately 6 times the number of input and output variables), one has to resort to these latter two techniques. Nonlinear generalized canonical correlation analysis can be used when we have longitudinal data that can be partitioned into two or more sets: for instance, we have characteristics of the therapeutic process and we have psychological indicators. Again either a categorical time variable or lagged versions of the variables can be incorporated. Multiple correspondence analysis can be used for longitudinal data where no such partitioning is feasible.

If the aim is not exploration but confirmation, the next question to ask is whether the data are categorical. If they are categorical, we can choose log-linear analysis when the aim is merely the testing of par-

Figure 7.1: *Paths for Choice of Analysis Method*

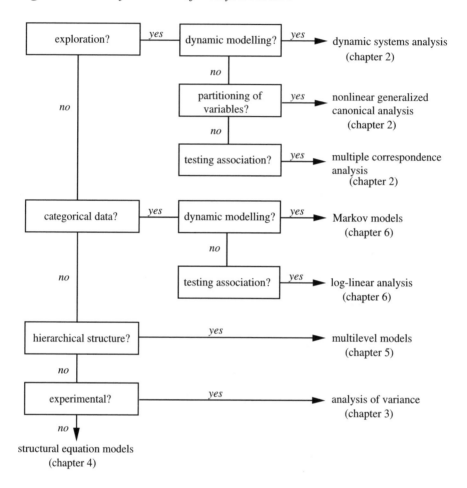

ticular hypotheses on associations between the variables. If we have a particular dynamic model we can choose an appropriate Markov model.

If the data are not categorical, the next question is whether there are hierarchies in the data, in the sense that certain observations can be regarded as nested within the categories of certain variables, implying that we presume that this nesting induces a certain association between variables. For instance, we may presume that the reading skills scores of pupils in one class are more alike than the reading skills of pupils in different classes. Whenever such hierarchies are present, and we explicitly want to take into account the hierarchical structure in the data, we may choose multilevel models.

A last question is whether we are interested in the testing of specific hypotheses on differences between the levels of the scores in groups of subjects (or points in time). In that case, we opt for MANOVA.

Finally, if none of the above applies, we end up with structural equation models, which are indeed very flexible in terms of model specification. Quasi-experimental as well as other questions on the data can be addressed using these models. We outlined a number of limitations in terms of measurement level, distributional assumptions, number of subjects and number of time points in Table 7.1.

The choice of analysis method depends to a great deal on the type of research question. Almost no technique is exclusively suited to addressing one question only. In fact, analysing the same data with various models should lead in most cases to approximately the same conclusion. However, differences may occur sooner when the model underlying a certain technique is less adequate given the research question at hand. Thus, asking the right question is important.

7.3 Longitudinal analysis techniques we did not discuss

A number of methods and techniques for longitudinal data analysis are not included in the present volume. The most prominently absent of these is event-history analysis or survival analysis. Event-history models analyse duration data, that is, data that register the timing until a certain event. They can be used, for example, for modelling job moves and for studying mobility or survival processes in general. The data can be obtained with a retrospective longitudinal panel design, and in this context one is interested in the stochastic process describing transitions between and durations in 'states' of a variable. In health psychology, changes in mental health can be modelled by event-history analysis. In criminology, recidivism is studied using these models. Singer & Willett (1991) and Willett & Singer (1991) list some applications in educational and psychological research. Blossfeld, Hamerle, & Mayer (1991) describe event-history models in social mobility research.

Event-history models for longitudinal research have been excluded from this volume mainly because of their statistical and conceptual idiosyncracies which are somewhat out of line with those of the other techniques in this volume. A thorough introduction to the statistical methodology of event-history analysis is given by Kalbfleisch & Prentice (1980) as well as Petersen (1995). A very readable introduction focusing on criminological research is provided by Schmidt & Wytte (1988).

A second technique which we do not discuss in this volume is item-response theory. Item-response theory has also been applied in the measurement of change. The theory typically uses responses on single items of a psychological test, and models change in terms of probability models, with person, item and change parameters. In Europe, the most popular probability models are the linear logistic models or Rasch models (see e.g. Fischer, 1976, 1977). Item-response models for longitudinal research have not been included in this volume because of their limited generality and applicability for longitudinal research in the social and behavioural sciences.

We also did not discuss dynamic factor analysis as such (although a number of fairly advanced extensions of these models have been proposed). Dynamic factor analysis can be subsumed under a number of techniques, such as the linear dynamic systems presented in Chapter 2 and the structural equation models that are the subject of Chapter 4. For more information on dynamic factor analysis we refer to Molenaar (1985) and Molenaar, De Gooijer, & Schmitz (1992).

Lastly, and certainly not least, we mentioned only superficially the immense field of time series techniques. Time series techniques, such as the family of AR(I)MA models, spectral analysis and the classical state space models, are not used widely in the behavioural sciences and have within the social and behavioural paradigm, in our view, but limited potential. This is so because these techniques aim strongly at exact high-dimensional forecasting, using series of data that need to be (often too) long given practical and financial constraints.

References

Agresti, A. (1984). *Analysis of categorical data*. New York: Wiley.

Agresti, A. (1990). *Categorical data analysis*. New York: Wiley.

Aitkin, M. A., Anderson, D., & Hinde, J. (1981). Statistical modelling of data on teaching styles. *Journal of the Royal Statistical Society, Series A, 144*, 419–461.

Aitkin, M. A., & Longford, N. T. (1986). Statistical modeling issues in school effectiveness studies. *Journal of the Royal Statistical Society, Series A, 149*, 1–43.

Akaike, H. (1976). Canonical correlation analysis of time series and the use of an information criterion. In R. Mehra, & D. G. Lainotis (Eds.), *Advances and case studies in system identification*, (pp. 27–96). New York: Academic Press.

Allison, P. D. (1987). Estimation of models with incomplete data. In C. C. Clogg (Ed.), *Sociological methodology*, (pp. 71–103). San Francisco: Jossey-Bass.

Alwin, D. F. (1988). Structural equation models in human development and aging. In K. W. Schaie, R. T. Campbell, W. Meredith, & S. C. Rawlings (Eds.), *Methodological issues in aging research*, (pp. 70–170). New York: Springer-Verlag.

Aoki, M. (1988). Personal communication.

Aoki, M. (1990). *State space modeling of time series*, 2nd edn. Berlin: Springer-Verlag.

Arbuckle, J. L. (1995). *Amos user's guide*. Chicago, IL: SmallWaters.

Arbuckle, J. L. (1996). Full information estimation in the presence of incomplete data. In G. A. Marcoulides, & R. E. Schumacker (Eds.), *Advanced structural equation modeling: Issues and techniques*, (pp. 245–277). Mahwah, NJ: Lawrence Erlbaum.

Arminger, G., Clogg, C. C., & Sobel, M. E. (Eds.) (1995). *Handbook of statistical modeling in the social sciences*. New York: Plenum.

Bakeman, R., Adamson, L. B., & Strisik, P. (1995). Lags and logs: statistical approaches to interaction (SPSS version). In J. M. Gottman (Ed.), *The analysis of change*, (pp. 279–308). Mahwah, NJ: Lawrence Erlbaum.

Baltes, P. B., Reese, H. W., & Nesselroade, J. R. (1977). *Life-span developmental psychology: Introduction to research methods*. Monterey, CA: Brooks/Cole.

Beekman, A. T. F., Deeg, D. J. H., Smit, J. H., & Van Tilburg, W. (1995). Predicting the course of depression in the older population: results from a community-based study in the Netherlands. *Journal of Affective Disorders, 34*, 41–49.

Bekker, P. A., Merckens, A., & Wansbeek, T. J. (1994). *Identification, equivalent models and computer algebra*. Boston, MA: Academic Press.

Bentler, P. M. (1973). Assessment of developmental factor change at the individual and group level. In J. R. Nesselroade, & H. W. Baltes (Eds.), *Life-span developmental psychology: Methodological issues*, chap. 7. New York: Academic Press.

Bentler, P. M. (1980). Multivariate analysis with latent variables: causal modeling. *Annual Review of Psychology, 31*, 419–456.

Bentler, P. M. (1982). Linear systems with multiple levels and types of latent variables. In K. G. Jöreskog, & H. Wold (Eds.), *Systems under indirect observation, Part 1*, (pp. 101–130). Amsterdam: North-Holland.

Bentler, P. M. (1984). Structural equation models in longitudinal research. In S. A. Mednick, M. Harway, & K. M. Finello (Eds.), *Handbook of longitudinal research. Volume One: Birth and childhood cohorts*, (pp. 88–105). New York: Praeger.

Bentler, P. M. (1989). *EQS Structural equations program manual*. Los Angeles: BMDP Statistical Software.

Bentler, P. M. (1990). EQS structural models with missing data. *BMDP Communications, 22*, 9–10.

Bentler, P. M. (1995). *EQS Structural equations program manual*. Encino, CA: Multivariate Software.

Bentler, P. M., & Dudgeon, P. (1996). Covariance structure analysis: statistical practice, theory, and directions. *Annual Review of Psychology, 47*, 563–592.

Bentler, P. M., & Weeks, D. G. (1980). Linear structural equations with latent variables. *Psychometrika, 45*, 289–308.

Bentler, P. M., & Wu, E. J. C. (1995a). *EQS for Macintosh user's guide*. Encino, CA: Multivariate Software.

Bentler, P. M., & Wu, E. J. C. (1995b). *EQS for Windows user's guide*. Encino, CA: Multivariate Software.

Benzécri, J. P. (1973). *l'Analyse des données [Data analysis]*. Paris: Dunod, (2 Vols).

Bergman, L. R., & Magnusson, D. (1990). General issues about data quality in longitudinal research. In D. Magnusson, & L. R. Bergman (Eds.), *Data quality in longitudinal research*, (pp. 1–31). Cambridge: Cambridge University Press.

Bergstrom, A. R. (1984). Continuous-time stochastic models and issues of aggregation over time. In Z. Griliches, & M. D. Intriligator (Eds.), *Handbook of econometrics*, (pp. 1145–1212). Amsterdam: North-Holland.

Berk, R. A. (1983). An introduction to sample selection bias in sociological data. *American Sociological Review, 48*, 386–398.

Best, N. G., Spiegelhalter, D. J., Thomas, A., & Brayne, C. E. G. (1996). Bayesian analysis of realistically complex models. *Journal of the Royal Statistical Society, Series A, 159*, 323–342.

Bijleveld, C. C. J. H. (1989). *Exploratory linear dynamic systems analysis*. Ph.D. thesis. Leiden, the Netherlands: DSWO Press.

Bijleveld, C. C. J. H. (1993). The evaluation of the impact of adult education on abolishing female circumcision in the northern Sudan. *Arab Medical Bulletin, 12*, 22–36.

Bijleveld, C. C. J. H., & Bijleveld, F. D. (1997). A comparison of the applicability of two approaches to linear dynamic systems analysis for N subjects. *Kwantitatieve Methoden, 55*, 37–56.

Bijleveld, C. C. J. H., & De Leeuw, J. (1991). Fitting longitudinal reduced-rank regression models by alternating least squares. *Psychometrika, 56*, 433–447.

Bijleveld, C. C. J. H., & Monkkonen, E. H. (1991). The dynamics of police behavior: a data re-analysis. *Historical Methods, 24*, 16–24.

Bijleveld, F. D., Bijleveld, C. C. J. H., & De Leeuw, J. (1994). *On least squares optimization of linear dynamic systems*. UCLA Statistics Series 145, UCLA.

Birren, J. E., & Schaie, K. W. (Eds.) (1985). *Handbook of the psychology of aging*, 2nd edn. New York: Van Nostrand Reinhold.

Bishop, Y. M. M., Fienberg, S. E., & Holland, P. W. (1975). *Discrete multivariate analysis: Theory and practice*. Cambridge, MA: MIT Press.

Blalock, H. M. (1964). *Causal inferences in nonexperimental research*. Chapel Hill, NC: University of North Carolina.

Blalock, H. M. (1984). Contextual-effects models: Theoretical and methodological issues. *Annual Review of Sociology, 10*, 353–372.

Blossfeld, H. P., Hamerle, A., & Mayer, K. U. (1991). Event-history models in social mobility research. In D. Magnusson, L. R. Bergman, G. Rudinger, & B. Törestad (Eds.), *Problems and methods in longitudinal research: Stability and change*, (pp. 212–235). Cambridge: Cambridge University Press.

Blumen, I. M., Kogan, M., & McCarthy, P. J. (1955). *The industrial mobility of Labor as a probability process*. Ithaca, NY: Cornell University Press.

Bock, R. D. (1975). *Multivariate statistical methods in behavioral research*. New York: McGraw-Hill.

Bock, R. D. (Ed.) (1989). *Multilevel analysis of educational data*, Vol. 1. San Diego, CA: Academic Press.

Bock, R. D., & Bargmann, R. E. (1966). Analysis of covariance structures. *Psychometrika, 31*, 507–534.

Bollen, K. A. (1989). *Structural equations with latent variables*. New York: Wiley.

Boomsma, A. (1983). *On the robustness of LISREL (maximum likelihood estimation) against small sample size and non normality*. Ph.D. thesis, Department of Statistics and Measurement, Groningen University, Groningen, the Netherlands.

Box, G. E. P. (1950). Problems in the analysis of growth and wear curves. *Biometrics, 6*, 362–389.

Box, G. E. P. (1954). Some theorems on quadratic forms applied in the study of analysis of variance problems. *Annals of Mathematical Statistics, 25*, 290–302, 484–498.

Box, G. E. P., & Jenkins, G. M. (1976). *Time series analysis, forecasting and control*. San Francisco: Holden-Day.

Box, G. E. P., & Tiao, G. C. (1977). A canonical analysis of multiple time series. *Biometrika, 64*, 355–365.

Boyd, L. H., & Iversen, G. R. (1979). *Contextual analysis: Concepts and statistical techniques*. Belmont, CA: Wadsworth.

Brillinger, D. R. (1981). *Time series*. San Francisco, CA: Holden Day.

Brown, R. L. (1994). Efficacy of the indirect approach for estimating structural equations with missing data: A comparison of five methods. *Structural Equation Modeling, 1*, 287–316.

Browne, M. W. (1992). Circumplex models for correlation matrices. *Psychometrika, 57*, 469–497.

Browne, M. W., & Arminger, G. (1995). Specification and estimation of mean – and covariance – structure models. In G. Arminger, C. C. Clogg, & M. E. Sobel (Eds.), *Handbook of statistical modeling in the social sciences*, (pp. 185–249). New York: Plenum.

Browne, M. W., & Du Toit, S. H. C. (1991). Models for learning data. In L. M. Collins, & J. L. Horn (Eds.), *Best methods for the analysis of change*, (pp. 47–68). Washington, DC: American Psychological Association.

Bryk, A. S., & Raudenbush, S. W. (1987). Application of hierarchical linear models to assessing change. *Psychological Bulletin, 101*, 147–158.

Bryk, A. S., & Raudenbush, S. W. (1988). On heterogeneity of variance in experimental studies: A challenge to conventional interpretations. *Psychological Bulletin, 104*, 396–404.

Bryk, A. S., & Raudenbush, S. W. (1992). *Hierarchical linear models: Applications and data analysis methods*. Newbury Park, CA: Sage.

Bullock, H. E., Harlow, L. L., & Mulaik, S. A. (1994). Causation issues in structural equation modeling research. *Structural Equation Modeling, 1*, 253–267.

Bunge, M. (1959). *Causality*. Cambridge, MA: Harvard University Press.

Bunge, M. (1979). *Causality and modern science*, 3rd edn. New York: Dover.

Burstein, L., Linn, R. L., & Capell, F. J. (1978). Analyzing multilevel data in the presence of heterogeneous within-class regressions. *Journal of Educational Statistics, 3*, 347–383.

Busing, F. M. T. A., Meijer, E., & Van der Leeden, R. (1994). MLA. *Software for multilevel analysis of data with two levels. User's guide for version 1.0b*. Tech. Rep. PRM 94-01, Leiden University, Department of Psychometrics and Research Methodology, Leiden, the Netherlands.

Busing, F. M. T. A., Meijer, E., & Van der Leeden, R. (1995). The MLA program for two-level analysis with resampling options. In T. A. B. Snijders, B. Engel, J. C. Van Houwelingen, A. Keen, G. J. Stemerdink, & M. Verbeek (Eds.), *Toeval zit overal* [Randomness is everywhere], (pp. 37–57). Groningen, the Netherlands: iec ProGAMMA.

Busing, F. M. T. A., Meijer, E., & Van der Leeden, R. (1997). *Delete-m jackknife for unequal m*. Tech. Rep. PRM 97-02, Leiden University, Department of Psychometrics and Research Methodology, Leiden, The Netherlands.

Byrne, B. M. (1994). *Structural equation modeling with EQS and EQS/Windows*. Thousand Oaks, CA: Sage.

Campbell, D. T., & Stanley, J. C. (1966). *Experimental and quasi-experimental designs for research*. Chicago: Rand McNally.

Carroll, J. D. (1968). Generalization of canonical correlation analysis to three or more sets of variables. In *Proceedings of the 76th Annual Convention of the American Psychological Association*, Vol. 5, (pp. 227–228).

Cattell, R. B. (1946). *Description and measurement of personality*. New York: World Book Company.

Cattell, R. B. (1952). The three basic factor-analytic research designs - their interrelations and derivatives. *Psychological Bulletin, 49*, 499–520.

Cattell, R. B. (1966). The data box: Its ordering of total resources in terms of relational systems. In R. B. Cattell (Ed.), *Handbook of multivariate experimental psychology*, (pp. 67–128). Chicago: Rand McNally.

Cattell, R. B. (1988). The data box: Its ordering of total resources in terms of possible relational systems. In J. R. Nesselroade, & R. B. Cattell (Eds.), *Handbook of multivariate experimental psychology*, 2nd edn, (pp. 69–130). New York, London: Plenum.

Caussinus, H. (1965). Contribution à l'analyse statistique des tableaux de corrélation. *Annales de la Faculté des Sciences de l'Université de Toulouse, 29*, 77–182.

Chatfield, C. (1989). *The analysis of time series: An introduction*. London: Chapman & Hall.

Cheung, K. C., Keeves, J. P., & Sellin, N. (1990). The analysis of multilevel data in educational research: Studies of problems and their solutions. *International Journal of Educational Research, 14*, 215–319.

Cliff, N. (1983). Some cautions concerning the application of causal modeling methods. *Multivariate Behavioral Research, 18*, 115–126.

Clogg, C. C. (Ed.) (1990). *Sociological methodology*. Washington, DC: American Sociological Association.

Clogg, C. C. (1995). Latent class models. In G. Arminger, C. C. Clogg, & M. E. Sobel (Eds.), *Handbook of statistical modeling in the social sciences*, (pp. 311–359). New York: Plenum.

Cohen, P., Cohen, J., Teresi, J., Marchi, M., & Velez, N. C. (1990). Problems in the measurement of latent variables in structural equations causal models. *Applied Psychological Measurement, 14*, 183–196.

Collins, L. M., Fidler, P. L., & Wugalter, S. E. (1996). Some practical issues related to estimation of latent class and latent transition parameters. In A. Von Eye, & C. C. Clogg (Eds.), *Analysis of categorical variables in developmental research*, (pp. 133–146). Thousand Oaks, CA: Sage.

Collins, L. M., Fidler, P. L., Wugalter, S. E., & Long, J. L. (1993). Goodness-of-fit testing for latent class models. *Multivariate Behavioral Research, 28*, 375–389.

Collins, L. M., & Horn, J. L. (Eds.) (1991). *Best methods for the analysis of change*. Washington, DC: American Psychological Association.

Collins, L. M., & Wugalter, S. E. (1992). Latent class models for stage-sequential dynamic latent variables. *Multivariate Behavioral Research, 27*, 131–157.

Converse, P. E. (1964). The nature of believe systems in mass publics. In D. E. Apter (Ed.), *Ideology and discontent*, (pp. 168–189). New York: Free Press.

Converse, P. E. (1970). Attitudes and non-attitudes: continuation of a dialogue. In E. R. Tufte (Ed.), *The quantitative analysis of social problems*. Reading, MA: Addison-Wesley.

Cook, N. R., & Ware, J. H. (1983). Design and analysis methods for longitudinal research. *Annual Review of Public Health, 4*, 1–23.

Cook, T. D., & Campbell, D. T. (1979). *Quasi–experimentation: Design and analysis issues for field settings*. Boston, MA: Houghton Mifflin.

Cook, T. D., Campbell, D. T., & Peracchio, L. (1990). Quasi experimentation. In *Handbook of industrial and organizational psychology*, 2nd edn, (pp. 491–576). Palo Alto, CA: Consulting Psychologists Press.

Cook, T. D., & Shadish, W. R. (1994). Social experiments: some developments over the past 15 years. *Annual Review of Psychology, 45*, 545–580.

Cronbach, L. J., & Furby, L. (1970). How we should measure 'change'– or should we? *Psychological Bulletin, 74*, 68–80, See also Errata, ibid, 74, 218.

Cronbach, L. J., Gleser, G. C., Nanda, H., & Rajaratnam, N. (1972). *The dependability of behavioral measurements*. New York: Wiley.

Crowder, M. J., & Hand, D. J. (1990). *Analysis of repeated measures*. London: Chapman & Hall.

Dale, A., & Davies, R. B. (Eds.) (1994). *Analysing social and political change: A casebook of methods*. London: Sage.

Dayton, C. M., & Macready, G. B. (1988a). Concomitant-variable latent class models. *Journal of the American Statistical Association, 83*, 173–178.

Dayton, C. M., & Macready, G. B. (1988b). A latent class covariate model with applications to criterion referenced testing. In R. Langeheine, & J. Rost (Eds.), *Latent trait and latent class models*, (pp. 129–143). New York: Plenum.

De Gruijter, D. N. M., & Van der Kamp, L. J. T. (1984). *Statistical models in psychological and educational testing*. Lisse, the Netherlands: Swets & Zeitlinger.

De Leeuw, J. (1983). The Gifi system of nonlinear multivariate analysis. In E. Diday (Ed.), *Data analysis and informatics IV*, (pp. 415–424). Amsterdam: North-Holland.

De Leeuw, J. (1989). Multivariate analysis with linearization of the regressions. *Psychometrika, 53*, 437–454.

De Leeuw, J., Bijleveld, C. C. J. H., Van Montfort, K., & Bijleveld, F. D. (1997). Latent variables, state spaces and mixing. *Kwantitatieve Methoden, 55*, 95–111.

De Leeuw, J., & Kreft, I. G. G. (1986). Random coefficient models for multilevel analysis. *Journal of Educational Statistics, 11*, 57–85.

De Lury, D. B. (1950). *Values and integrals of the orthogonal polynomials up to n = 50*. Toronto: University of Toronto Press.

Dembo, A., & Zeitouni, O. (1986). Parameter estimation of partially observed continuous time stochastic processes via the EM algorithm. *Stochastic Processes and their Applications, 23*, 91–113.

Dempster, A. P., Laird, N. M., & Rubin, D. B. (1977). Maximum likelihood from incomplete data via the EM algorithm. *Journal of the Royal Statistical Society, Series B, 38*, 1–38.

Dempster, A. P., Rubin, D. B., & Tsutakawa, R. D. (1981). Estimation in covariance components models. *Journal of the American Statistical Association, 76*, 341–353.

Dixon, W. J. (1988). *BMDP Statistical software manual, Vol. 2*. Berkely, CA: University of California Press.

Draper, N. R., & Smith, H. (1981). *Applied regression analysis*. New York: Wiley.

Duncan, O. D. (1966). Path analysis: Sociological examples. *American Journal of Sociology, 72*, 1–16.

Dunn, G., Everitt, B. S., & Pickles, A. (1993). *Modelling covariances and latent variables using EQS*. London: Chapman & Hall.

Du Toit, S. H. C. (1979). The analysis of growth curves. Unpublished doctoral thesis. Department of statistics, University of South Africa, Pretoria.

Edwards, A. E. (1985). *Multiple regression and the analysis of variance and covariance*. New York: Freeman.

Efron, B., & Tibshirani, R. J. (1993). *An introduction to the bootstrap*. New York: Chapman & Hall.

Embretson, S. E. (1991). A multidimensional latent trait model for measuring learning and change. *Psychometrika, 56*, 495–515.

Everitt, B. S. (1992). *The analysis of contingency tables*, 2nd edn. London: Chapman & Hall.

Fahrmeir, L. (1992). Posterior mode estimation by extended Kalman filtering for multivariate dynamic generalized linear models. *Journal of the American Statistical Association, 87*, 501–509.

Fahrmeir, L., & Tutz, G. (1996). *Multivariate statistical modelling based on generalized linear models*. New York: Springer-Verlag.

Farrington, D. P., Gallagher, B., Morley, L., Stledger, R. J., & West, D. J. (1990). Minimizing attrition in longitudinal research: Methods of tracing and securing co-operation in a 24–year follow–up study. In D. Magnusson, & L. R. Bergman (Eds.), *Data quality in longitudinal research*, (pp. 122–147). Cambridge: Cambridge University Press.

Fergusson, D. M., & Horwood, L. J. (1988). Structural equation modelling of measurement processes in longitudinal data. In M. Rutter (Ed.), *Studies of psychosocial risks: the power of longitudinal data*, (pp. 325–353). Cambridge: Cambridge University Press.

Fienberg, S. E. (1980). *The analysis of cross-classified categorical data*. Cambridge, MA: MIT Press.

Finkel, S. E. (1995). *Causal analysis with panel data*. Thousand Oaks, CA: Sage.

Firebaugh, G. (1997). *Analyzing repeated surveys*. Thousand Oaks, CA: Sage.

Fischer, G. H. (1976). Some probabilistic models for measuring change. In D. N. M. De Gruijter, & L. J. T. Van der Kamp (Eds.), *Advances in psychological and educational measurement*, (pp. 98–100). London: Wiley.

Fischer, G. H. (1977). Linear logistic test models: Theory and applications. In H. Spada, & W. F. Kempf (Eds.), *Structural models of thinking and learning*, (pp. 203–225). Bern: Hans Huber.

Fitzmaurice, G., Laird, N. M., & Rotnitsky, A. G. (1993). Regression models for discrete longitudinal responses. *Statistical Science*, *8*, 284–309.

Formann, A. K. (1992). Linear logistic latent class analysis for polytomous data. *Journal of the American Statistical Association*, *87*, 476–486.

Formann, A. K. (1994). Measuring change using latent class analysis. In A. Von Eye, & C. C. Clogg (Eds.), *Latent variables analysis: Applications for developmental research*, (pp. 294–312). Thousand Oaks, CA: Sage.

Freedman, D. A. (1987). As others see us: A case study in path analysis. *Journal of Educational Statistics*, *12*, 101–128.

Freedman, D. A. (1991). Statistical models and shoe leather (with discussion). *Sociological Methodology*, *21*, 291–358.

Games, P. A. (1990). Alternative analyses of repeated-measure designs by ANOVA and MANOVA. In A. Von Eye (Ed.), *Statistical methods in longitudinal research*, (pp. 81–121). Boston, MA: Academic Press.

Gifi, A. (1990). *Nonlinear multivariate analysis*. Chichester: Wiley.

Gilula, A., & Haberman, S. J. (1994). Conditional log-linear models for analyzing panel data. *Journal of the American Statistical Association*, *89*, 645–656.

Goldberger, A. S. (1971). Econometrics and psychometrics: a survey of communalities. *Psychometrika*, *36*, 83–107.

Goldberger, A. S., & Duncan, O. D. (1975). *Structural equation models in the social sciences*. New York: Seminar Press.

Goldstein, H. (1986a). Efficient statistical modelling of longitudinal data. *Annals of Human Biology*, *13*, 129–141.

Goldstein, H. (1986b). Multilevel mixed linear model analysis using iterative generalized least squares. *Biometrika*, *73*, 43–56.

Goldstein, H. (1989). Restricted (unbiased) iterative generalized least squares estimation. *Biometrika*, *76*, 622–623.

Goldstein, H. (1995). *Multilevel statistical models*, 2nd edn. London: Edward Arnold.

Goldstein, H., Healy, M. J. R., & Rasbash, J. (1994). Multilevel time series models with applications to repeated measures data. *Statistics in Medicine*, *13*, 1643–1655.

Goodman, L. A. (1968). The analysis of cross-classified data: Independence, quasi-independence, and interaction in contingency tables with or without missing cells. *Journal of the American Statistical Association*, *63*, 1019–1131.

Goodman, L. A. (1972). A general model for the analysis of surveys. *American Journal of Sociology*, *77*, 1035–1086.

Goodman, L. A. (1973). Causal analysis of panel studies and other kinds of surveys. *American Journal of Sociology*, *78*, 1135–1191.

Goodman, L. A. (1978). *Analysing qualitative/categorical variables: Loglinear models and latent structure analysis*. Cambridge: Abt.

Gottman, J. M. (Ed.) (1995). *The analysis of change*. Mahwah, NJ: Lawrence Erlbaum.

Greenacre, M. (1984). *Theory and applications of correspondence analysis*. New York: Academic Press.

Greenacre, M. (1993). *Correspondence analysis in practice*. London: Academic Press.

Greenhouse, S. W., & Geisser, S. (1959). On methods in the analysis of profile data. *Psychometrika, 25*, 213–323.

Guldenmund, F. W. (1991). *Single and two step approaches to modeling individual psychological growth*. Unpublished MA thesis, Leiden University: Department of Psychometrics and Research Methodology, Leiden, the Netherlands.

Guttman, L. (1941). The quantification of a class of attributes: A theory and method of scale construction. In P. e. Horst (Ed.), *The prediction of personal adjustment*, (pp. 319–348). New York: Social Science Research Council.

Haberman, S. J. (1978). *Analysis of qualitative data, Vol 1: Introduction topics*. New York: Academic Press.

Haberman, S. J. (1979). *Analysis of qualitative data, Vol 2: New Developments*. New York: Academic Press.

Hagenaars, J. A. (1990). *Categorical longitudinal data, log-linear panel, trend, and cohort analysis*. London: Sage.

Hagenaars, J. A. (1993). *Loglinear models with latent variables*. No. 07-094 in Sage University Paper series on quantitative applications in the social sciences, Newbury Park, CA: Sage.

Hagenaars, J. A. (1994). Latent variables in log-linear models of repeated observations. In A. Von Eye, & C. C. Clogg (Eds.), *Latent variables analysis: Applications for developmental research*, (pp. 329–352). Thousand Oaks, CA: Sage.

Hagenaars, J. A., & Luijkx, R. (1990). *LCAG*. Working Paper Series 17, Tilburg University, Department of Sociology, Tilburg, the Netherlands.

Hand, D. J., & Crowder, M. J. (1996). *Practical longitudinal data analysis*. London: Chapman & Hall.

Hand, D. J., & Taylor, C. C. (1987). *Multivariate analysis of variance and repeated measures*. London: Chapman & Hall.

Hannan, E. J., & Deistler, M. (1988). *The statistical theory of linear systems*. New York: Wiley.

Harvey, A. C., & Fernandes, C. (1989). Time series models for count or qualitative observations (with discussion). *Journal of Business and Economics Statistics, 7*, 407–422.

Harville, D. A. (1977). Maximum likelihood approaches to variance component estimation and to related problems. *Journal of the American Statistical Association, 72*, 320–340.

Hayduk, L. A. (1987). *Structural equation modeling with LISREL*. Baltimore and London: The Johns Hopkins University Press.

Hays, W. L. (1988). *Statistics*, 4th edn. New York: Holt, Rinehart, Winston.

Hedeker, D., & Gibbons, R. D. (1994). A random effects ordinal regression model for multilevel analysis. *Biometrics, 50*, 933–944.

Heinen, A. (1993). *Discrete latent variables models*. Tilburg, the Netherlands: Tilburg University Press.

Henning, H. J., & Rudinger, G. (1985). Analysis of qualitative data in developmental psychology. In J. R. Nesselroade, & A. Von Eye (Eds.), *Individual development and social change*, (pp. 295–341). Orlando, FL: Academic Press.

Hershberger, S. L. (1994). The specification of equivalent models before the collection of the data. In A. Von Eye, & C. C. Clogg (Eds.), *Latent variables analysis: Applications for developmental research*, (pp. 68–105). Thousand Oaks, CA: Sage.

Hershberger, S. L., Molenaar, P. C. M., & Corneal, S. E. (1996). A hierarchy of univariate and multivariate structural times series models. In G. A. Marcoulides, & R. E. Schumacker (Eds.), *Advanced structural equation modeling: Issues and techniques*, (pp. 159–194). Mahwah, NJ: Lawrence Erlbaum.

Hills, M. (1974). *Statistics for comparative studies*. New York: Wiley.

Ho, B. L., & Kalman, R. E. (1966). Effective construction of linear state-variable models from input/output functions. *Regelungstechnik*, *12*, 545–548.

Holland, P. W. (1988). Causal inference, path analysis and recursive structural equation models (with discussion). In C. C. Clogg (Ed.), *Sociological methodology*, (pp. 449–493). Oxford: American Sociological Association.

Hotelling, H. (1936). Relations between two sets of variates. *Biometrika*, *28*, 321–327.

Hox, J. J. (1994). *Applied multilevel analysis*. Amsterdam: TT-Publikaties.

Hox, J. J., Kreft, I. G. G., & Hermkens, P. L. J. (1990). Factorial surveys; multilevel by design. *Kwantitatieve Methoden*, *33*, 67–88.

Huck, S. W., & McLean, R. A. (1975). Using a repeated measures ANOVA to analyze the data from a pretest-posttest design: A potentially confusing task. *Psychological Bulletin*, *82*, 511–518.

Huyhn, H., & Feldt, L. S. (1976). Estimation of the box correction for degrees of freedom from sample data in the randomized block and split-plot designs. *Journal of Educational Statistics*, *1*, 69–82.

Hyman, H. H. (1955). *Survey design and analysis*. New York: Free Press.

Jansen, R. A. R. G., & Oud, J. H. L. (1995). Longitudinal LISREL model estimation from incomplete panel data using the EM algorithm and the Kalman smoother. *Statistica Neerlandica*, *49*, 362–377.

Janson, C. G. (1990). Retrospective data, undesirable behavior, and the longitudinal perspective. In D. Magnusson, & L. R. Bergman (Eds.), *Data quality in longitudinal research*, (pp. 100–121). Cambridge: Cambridge University Press.

Jennrich, R., & Schluchter, M. D. (1986). Unbalanced repeated measures models with structured covariance matrices. *Biometrics*, *42*, 805–820.

Jöreskog, K. G., & Goldberger, A. S. (1975). Estimation of a model with multiple indicators and multiple causes of a single latent variable. *Journal of the American Statistical Association*, *70*, 631–639.

Jöreskog, K. G., Gruvaeus, G. T., & Van Thillo, M. (1970). *ACOVS– A general computer program for analysis of covariance structures*. Research Bulletin 70-15, Educational Testing Service, Princeton, NJ.

Jöreskog, K. G., & Sörbom, D. (1993). *LISREL 8 user's reference guide*. Chicago: Scientific Software International.

Jöreskog, K. G., & Wold, H. (Eds.) (1982). *Systems under indirect observation, Part 1*. Amsterdam: North-Holland.

Judd, C. M., & Kenny, D. A. (1981). *Estimating the effects of social interventions*. Cambridge: Cambridge University Press.

Judd, C. M., McClelland, G. W., & Cutharie, S. E. (1995). Data analysis: Continuing issues in the everyday analysis of psychological data. *Annual Review of Psychology*, *46*, 433–465.

Kalbfleisch, J. D., & Prentice, R. L. (1980). *The statistical analysis of failure time data*. New York: Wiley.

Kalman, R. E. (1960). A new approach to linear filtering and prediction problems. *ASME transactions, Series D, Journal of Basic Engineering*, *82*, 35–45.

Keeves, J. P. (Ed.) (1997). *Educational research, methodology, and measurement: An international handbook*. Oxford: Pergamon Press.

Kendall, M. G., & Stuart, A. (1979). *The advanced theory of statistics: Inference and relationship*, 4th edn., Vol. 2. London: Griffin.

Kenny, D. A. (1979). *Correlation and causality*. New York: Wiley.

Keppel, G. (1982). *Design and analysis: A researcher's handbook*, 2nd edn. Englewood Cliffs, NJ: Prentice-Hall.

Kesselman, H. J., & Kesselman, J. C. (1993). Analysis of repeated measurements. In L. K. Edwards (Ed.), *Applied analysis of variance in behavioral science*, (pp. 105–146). New York: Dekker.

Kesselman, H. J., Kesselman, J. C., & Lix, L. M. (1995). The analysis of repeated measurements: Univariate tests, multivariate tests, or both? *British Journal of Mathematical and Statistical Psychology*, *48*, 319–338.

Kessler, R. C., & Greenberg, D. F. (1981). *Linear panel analysis: Models of quantitative change*. New York: Academic Press.

Kettenring, J. R. (1971). Canonical analysis of several sets of variables. *Biometrika*, *56*, 433–451.

Kirk, R. E. (1968). *Experimental design: Procedures for the behavioral sciences*, 1st edn. Monterey, CA: Brooks/Cole.

Kirk, R. E. (1981). *Experimental design: Procedures for the behavioral sciences*, 2nd edn. Monterey, CA: Brooks/Cole.

Kirk, R. E. (1982). *Experimental design: Procedures for the behavioral sciences*, 2nd edn. Monterey, CA: Brooks/Cole.

Kirk, R. E. (1995). *Experimental design: Procedures for the behavioral sciences*, 2nd edn. Monterey, CA: Brooks/Cole.

Kish, L. (1987). *Statistical design for research*. New York: Wiley.

Knapp, T. R. (1977). The unit of analysis problem in applications of simple correlational research. *Journal of Educational Statistics*, *2*, 171–186.

Kowalski, C. J., & Guire, K. E. (1974). Longitudinal data analysis. *Growth*, *38*, 131–169.

Kreft, I. G. G., & De Leeuw, J. (1991). Model based ranking of schools. *International Journal of Education*, *15*, 45–59.

Kreft, I. G. G., & De Leeuw, J. (1998). *Introduction to multilevel modelling*. London: Sage.

Kreft, I. G. G., De Leeuw, J., & Van der Leeden, R. (1994). A review of five multilevel analysis programs: BMDP-5V, GENMOD, HLM, ML3, VARCL. *The American Statistician, 48*, 324–335.

Kromrey, J. D., & Hines, C. V. (1994). Nonrandomly missing data in multiple regression: An empirical comparison of common missing-data treatments. *Educational and Psychological Measurement, 54*, 573–593.

Kuhfeld, W. F., & Young, F. W. (1988). New developments in psychometric and market research procedures. In S. U. G. 1988 (Ed.), *SUGI Proceedings*, Vol. 13, (pp. 1077–1081), SAS Institute, Cary, NC: SAS Institute.

Laird, N. M., & Ware, J. H. (1982). Random effects models for longitudinal data. *Biometrics, 38*, 963–974.

Langeheine, R. (1988). Manifest and latent Markov chain models for categorical panel data. *Journal of Educational Statistics, 13*, 299–312.

Langeheine, R. (1994). Latent variables Markov models. In A. Von Eye, & C. C. Clogg (Eds.), *Latent variables analysis: Applications for developmental research*, (pp. 373–395). Thousand Oaks, CA: Sage.

Langeheine, R., Pannekoek, J., & Van de Pol, F. (1996). Bootstrapping goodness-of-fit measures in categorical data analysis. *Sociological Methods & Research, 24*, 492–516.

Langeheine, R., & Van de Pol, F. (1990). A unifying framework for Markov modeling in discrete space and discrete time. *Sociological Methods & Research, 18*, 416–441.

Lazarsfeld, P. F. (1955). Interpretations of statistical relations as a research operation. In P. F. Lazarsfeld, & M. Rosenberg (Eds.), *The language of social research*, (pp. 115–125). New York: Free Press.

Liang, K. Y., Zeger, S. L., & Qaqish, B. (1992). Multivariate regression analyses for categorical data. *Journal of the Royal Statistical Society, Series B, 54*, 3–40.

Lindley, D. V., & Smith, A. F. M. (1972). Bayes estimates for the linear model. *Journal of the Royal Statistical Society, Series B, 34*, 1–41.

Little, R. J. A., & Rubin, D. B. (1987). *Statistical analysis with missing data*. New York: Wiley.

Little, R. J. A., & Rubin, D. B. (1989). The analysis of social science data with missing values. *Sociological Methods & Research, 18*, 292–326.

Little, R. J. A., & Schenker, N. (1995). Missing data. In G. Arminger, C. C. Clogg, & M. E. Sobel (Eds.), *Handbook of statistical modeling in the social sciences*, (pp. 39–75). New York: Plenum.

Loevinger, J. (1965). Person and population as psychometric concepts. *Psychological Review, 72*, 143–155.

Longford, N. T. (1987a). A fast scoring algorithm for maximum likelihood estimation in unbalanced mixed models with nested random effects. *Biometrika, 74*, 817–827.

Longford, N. T. (1987b). *VARCL: Software for variance component analysis of data with hierarchically nested random effects (maximum likelihood)*. Princeton, NJ: Educational Testing Service.

Longford, N. T. (1993). *Random coefficient models*. Oxford: Clarendon Press.

Longford, N. T. (1995). Random coefficient models. In G. Arminger, C. C. Clogg, & M. E. Sobel (Eds.), *Handbook of statistical modeling in the social sciences*, (pp. 519–577). New York: Plenum.

Longford, N. T., & Muthén, B. O. (1991). Factor analysis for clustered observations. Paper presented at the 7th European Meeting of the Psychometric Society in Trier, 1991.

Lord, F. M., & Novick, M. R. (1968). *Statistical theories of mental test scores*. Reading, MA: Addison-Wesley.

MacCallum, R. C., & Ashby, F. G. (1986). Relationship between linear systems theory and covariance structure modeling. *Journal of Mathematical Psychology, 30*, 1–27.

MacCallum, R. C., Wegener, D. T., Uchino, B. N., & Fabrigar, L. R. (1993). The problem of equivalent models in applications of covariance structure analysis. *Psychological Bulletin, 14*, 185–199.

Mackie, J. L. (1974). *The cement of the universe*. Oxford: Oxford University Press.

Magnusson, D., & Bergman, L. R. (Eds.) (1990). *Data quality in longitudinal research*. Cambridge: Cambridge University Press.

Magnusson, D., Bergman, L. R., Rudinger, G., & Törestad, B. (Eds.) (1991). *Problems and methods in longitudinal research: Stability and change*. Cambridge: Cambridge University Press.

Marcoulides, G. A., & Schumacker, R. E. (Eds.) (1996). *Advanced structural equation modeling: Issues and techniques*. Mahwah, NJ: Lawrence Erlbaum.

Marsh, H. W., Balla, J. R., & Hau, K. T. (1996). An evaluation of incremental fit indices: a clarification of mathematical and empirical properties. In G. A. Marcoulides, & R. E. Schumacker (Eds.), *Advanced structural equation modeling: Issues and techniques*, (pp. 315–353). Mahwah, NJ: Lawrence Erlbaum.

Maruyama, G. M. (1998). *Basics of structural equation modeling*. Thousand Oaks, CA: Sage.

Mason, W. M., Anderson, A. F., & Hayat, N. (1988). *Manual for GENMOD*. Ann Arbor, MI: University of Michigan, Population Studies Center.

Mason, W. M., & Fienberg, S. E. (Eds.) (1985). *Cohort analysis in social research*, Vol. 2. New York: Springer-Verlag.

Mason, W. M., Wong, G. Y., & Entwisle, B. (1984). Contextual analysis through the multilevel linear model. *Sociological Methodology*, (pp. 72–103).

Mauchly, J. W. (1940). Significance tests for sphericity of a normal n-variate distribution. *Annals of Mathematical Statistics, 11*, 204–209.

Maxwell, S. E., & Delaney, H. D. (1990). *Designing experiments and analyzing data: A model comparison perspective*. Belmont, CA: Wadsworth.

McArdle, J. J. (1986). Latent growth within behavior genetic models. *Behavior Genetics, 16*, 163–200.

McArdle, J. J. (1988). Dynamic but structural equation modeling of repeated measures data. In J. R. Nesselroade, & R. B. Cattell (Eds.), *Handbook of multivariate experimental psychology*, 2nd edn, (pp. 561–614). New York, London: Plenum.

McArdle, J. J., & Epstein, D. (1987). Latent growth curves within developmental structural equation models. *Child Development, 58*, 110–133.

McArdle, J. J., & Hamagami, F. (1996). Multilevel models from a multiple group structural equation perspective. In G. A. Marcoulides, & R. E. Schumacker (Eds.), *Advanced structural equation modeling: Issues and techniques*, (pp. 89–124). Mahwah, NJ: Lawrence Erlbaum.

McDonald, R. P., & Goldstein, H. (1989). Balanced versus unbalanced designs for linear structural relations in 2-level data. *British Journal of Mathematical and Statistical Psychology, 42*, 215–232.

Menard, S. (1991). *Longitudinal research*. Newbury Park, CA: Sage.

Meredith, W., & Tisak, J. (1990). Latent curve analysis. *Psychometrika, 55*, 107–122.

Messick, S. (1989). Validity. In R. L. Linn (Ed.), *Educational measurement*, 3rd edn, (pp. 13–103). New York: American Council on Education, Macmillan.

Michailides, G. (1996). *Multilevel homogeneity analysis*. Ph.D. thesis, University of California at Los Angeles, Los Angeles.

Mislevy, R. J., & Bock, R. D. (1989). A hierarchical item-response model for educational testing. In R. D. Bock (Ed.), *Multilevel analysis of educational data*, (pp. 57–74). San Diego, CA: Academic Press.

Molenaar, P. C. M. (1985). A dynamic factor model for the analysis of multivariate time series. *Psychometrika, 50*, 181–202.

Molenaar, P. C. M., De Gooijer, J. G., & Schmitz, B. (1992). Dynamic factor analysis of nonstationary multivariate time series. *Psychometrika, 57*, 333–349.

Mooijaart, A., & Van der Heijden, P. G. M. (1992). The EM algorithm for latent class analysis with equality constraints. *Psychometrika, 57*, 261–269.

Mooijaart, A., & Van Montfort, K. (1997). State space models for categorical variables. *Kwantitatieve Methoden, 55*, 73–94.

Moos, R. H. (1968). The development of a menstrual distress questionnaire. *Psychosomatic Medicine, 30*, 853–867.

Morgan, T. M., Aneshensel, C. S., & Clark, V. A. (1983). Parameter estimation for mover-stayer models: analyzing depression over time. *Sociological Methods & Research, 11*, 345–366.

Morrison, D. F. (1990). *Multivariate statistical methods*, 3rd edn. New York: McGraw-Hill.

Murphy, M. (1990). Minimizing attrition in longitudinal studies: Means or end? In D. Magnusson, & L. R. Bergman (Eds.), *Data quality in longitudinal research*, (pp. 148–156). Cambridge: Cambridge University Press.

Muthén, B. O. (1987). *LISCOMP: Analysis of linear structural equations with a comprehensive measurement model*. Mooresville, IN: Scientific Software, Inc.

Muthén, B. O. (1989). Latent variable modeling in heterogeneous populations. *Psychometrika, 54*, 557–585.

Muthén, B. O. (1997). Latent variable modeling of longitudinal and multilevel data. In A. E. Raftery (Ed.), *Sociological methodology 1997*, (pp. 453–480). Washington, DC: American Sociological Association.

Muthén, B. O., Kaplan, D., & Hollis, M. (1987). On structural equation modeling with data that are not missing completely at random. *Psychometrika*, *52*, 431–462.

Muthén, B. O., & Satorra, A. (1989). Multilevel aspects of varying parameters in structural models. In R. D. Bock (Ed.), *Multilevel analysis of educational data*, (pp. 87–99). San Diego, CA: Academic Press.

Neale, M. C. (1994). *Mx: Statistical modeling*, 2nd edn. Richmond, VA: Department Psychology, Medical College Virginia.

Nesselroade, J. R. (1988). Sampling and generalizability: Adult development and aging research issues examined within the general methodological framework of selection. In K. W. Schaie, R. T. Campbell, W. Meredith, & S. C. Rawlings (Eds.), *Methodological issues in aging research*, (pp. 13–42). New York: Springer-Verlag.

Nesselroade, J. R. (1991). Interindividual differences in intraindividual change. In L. M. Collins, & J. L. Horn (Eds.), *Best methods for the analysis of change*, (pp. 92–105). Washington, DC: American Psychological Association.

Nesselroade, J. R., & Baltes, P. B. (Eds.) (1979). *Longitudinal research in the study of behavior and development*. New York: Academic Press.

Nesselroade, J. R., & Cattell, R. B. (Eds.) (1988). *Handbook of multivariate experimental psychology*, 2nd edn. New York, London: Plenum.

Nesselroade, J. R., & Featherman, D. L. (1991). Intraindividual variability in older adults' depression scores: some implications for developmental theory and longitudinal research. In D. Magnusson, L. R. Bergman, G. Rudinger, & B. Törestad (Eds.), *Problems and methods in longitudinal research: Stability and change*, (pp. 47–66). Cambridge: Cambridge University Press.

Nesselroade, J. R., & Ford, D. H. (1985). P-technique comes of age. *Research on Aging*, *7*, 46–80.

Nesselroade, J. R., & Ford, D. H. (1987). Methodological considerations in modeling living systems. In M. E. Ford, & D. H. Ford (Eds.), *Humans as self–constructing living systems: Putting the framework to work*, (pp. 47–79). Hillsdale, NJ: Lawrence Erlbaum.

Nesselroade, J. R., & Jones, C. J. (1991). Multi-modal selection effects in the study of adult development: A perspective on multivariate, replicated, single–subject, repeated measures designs. *Experimental Aging Research*, *17*, 21–27.

Nesselroade, J. R., & Labouvie, E. W. (1985). Experimental design in research on aging. In J. E. Birren, & K. W. Schaie (Eds.), *Handbook of the psychology of aging*, 2nd edn, (pp. 35–60). New York: Van Nostrand Reinhold.

Nesselroade, J. R., & Von Eye, A. (Eds.) (1985). *Individual development and social change*. Orlando, FL: Academic Press.

Nishisato, S. (1980). *Analysis of categorical data: Dual scaling and its applications*. Toronto: University of Toronto Press.

Nishisato, S. (1994). *Elements of dual scaling: An introduction to practical data analysis*. Hillsdale, NJ: Lawrence Erlbaum.

O'Brien, R. G., & Kaiser, M. K. (1985). MANOVA method for analyzing repeated measures designs: An extensive primer. *Psychological Bulletin*, *97*, 316–333.

Olmstead, R. E. (1996). *Diurnal associations of smoking and nicotine with mood.* Tech. Rep. UMI Number 9704609, UMI, Ann Arbor, MI.

Ord, K., Fernandes, C., & Harvey, A. C. (1993). Time series models for multivariate series of count data. In T. S. Rao (Ed.), *Developments in time series analysis. In honour of Maurice B. Priestly*, (pp. 295–309). London: Chapman & Hall.

Oud, J. H. L., & Jansen, R. A. R. G. (1996). Nonstationary longitudinal model estimation from incomplete data using EM and the Kalman smoother. In U. Engel, & J. Reinecke (Eds.), *Analysis of change: Advanced techniques in panel analysis*, (pp. 135–159). Berlin: Walter de Gruyter.

Oud, J. H. L., Van den Bercken, J. H., & Essers, R. J. (1990). Longitudinal factor score estimation using the Kalman filter. *Applied Psychological Measurement, 14*, 395–418.

Ouweneel, A., & Bijleveld, C. C. J. H. (1989). The economic cycle in Bourbon central Mexico: A critique of the 'recaudación del diezmo líquido en pesos'. *Hispanic American Historical Review, 69*, 479–530.

Pedhazur, E. J., & Pedhazur Schmelkin, L. (1991). *Measurement, design, and analysis: An integrated approach.* Hillsdale, NJ: Lawrence Erlbaum.

Perenboom, R. J. M., & Zaal, K. (1991). *Het Zorghuis dr. W. Drees: een nieuwe woon/zorgvoorziening voor ouderen [The Care Home dr. W. Drees: a new living/care facility for the elderly].* Tech. rep., NIPG-TNO, P.O. Box 2215, 2301 CE Leiden, the Netherlands.

Petersen, T. (1995). Analysis of event histories. In G. Arminger, C. C. Clogg, & M. E. Sobel (Eds.), *Handbook of statistical modeling in the social sciences*, (pp. 453–517). New York: Plenum.

Plewis, I. (1985). *Analysing change. Measurement and explanation using longitudinal data.* Chichester: Wiley.

Potthoff, R. F., & Roy, S. N. (1964). A generalized multivariate analysis of variance model useful especially for growth curve problems. *Biometrika, 51*, 313–326.

Poulsen, C. S. (1982). *Latent structure analysis with choice modeling applications.* Ph.D. thesis, Wharton School, University of Pennsylvania.

Prosser, R., Rasbash, J., & Goldstein, H. (1991). *ML3. Software for three-level analysis. User's guide for V. 2.* London: Institute of Education, University of London.

Rao, C. R. (1965). The theory of least squares when the parameters are stochastic and its application to the analysis of growth curves. *Biometrika, 52*, 447–458.

Rasbash, J., Yang, M., Woodhouse, G., & Goldstein, H. (1995). *MLn: Command reference guide.* London: Institute of Education, University of London.

Raudenbush, S. W. (1988). Educational applications of hierarchical linear models: A review. *Journal of Educational Statistics, 13*, 85–1160.

Raudenbush, S. W. (1989). The analysis of longitudinal, multilevel data. *International Journal of Educational Research, 13*, 721–740.

Rindskopf, D. (1984a). Structural equation models: Empirical identification, Heywood cases, and related problems. *Sociological Methods & Research, 13*, 109–119.

Rindskopf, D. (1984b). Using phantom and imaginary variables to parametric constraints in linear structural models. *Psychometrika, 49*, 37–47.

Rogosa, D. R. (1979). Causal models in longitudinal research: Rationale, formulation and interpretation. In J. R. Nesselroade, & P. B. Baltes (Eds.), *Longitudinal research in the study of behavior and development*, (pp. 261–302). New York: Academic Press.

Rogosa, D. R. (1995). Myths and methods: 'myths about longitudinal research' plus supplemental questions. In J. M. Gottman (Ed.), *The analysis of change*, (pp. 3–66). Mahwah, NJ: Lawrence Erlbaum.

Rogosa, D. R., Brandt, D., & Zimowski, M. (1982). A growth curve approach to the measurement of change. *Psychological Bulletin, 92*, 726–748.

Rogosa, D. R., & Willett, J. B. (1985). Understanding correlates of change by modeling individual differences in growth. *Psychometrika, 50*, 203–228.

Rossi, P. H., Wright, J. D., & Anderson, A. B. (Eds.) (1983). *Handbook of survey research*. New York: Academic Press.

Rouanet, H., & Lépine, D. (1970). Comparison between treatments in a repeated-measurement design: ANOVA and multivariate methods. *British Journal of Mathematical and Statistical Psychology, 23*, 147–163.

Rovine, M. J. (1994). Latent variable models and missing data analysis. In A. Von Eye, & C. C. Clogg (Eds.), *Latent variables analysis: Applications for developmental research*, (pp. 181–215). Thousand Oaks, CA: Sage.

Rovine, M. J., & Delaney, M. (1990). Missing data estimation in developmental research. In A. Von Eye (Ed.), *Statistical methods in longitudinal research*. Boston, MA: Academic Press.

Rovine, M. J., & Von Eye, A. (1991). *Applied computational statistics in longitudinal research*. Boston, MA: Academic Press.

Rudinger, G. (1979). Erfassung von Entwicklungsverlaufen im Lebenslauf. In H. Rauh (Ed.), *Jahrbuch für Entwicklungspsychologie*. Stuttgart: Klett-Cotta.

Rudinger, G., & Wood, P. K. (1990). N's, times, and number of variables in longitudinal research. In D. Magnusson, & L. R. Bergman (Eds.), *Data quality in longitudinal research*, (pp. 157–180). Cambridge: Cambridge University Press.

Rutter, M., & Pickles, A. (1990). Improving the quality of psychiatric data: Classification, cause, and course. In D. Magnusson, & L. R. Bergman (Eds.), *Data quality in longitudinal research*, (pp. 32–57). Cambridge: Cambridge University Press.

Saris, W. E., & Stronkhorst, L. H. (1984). *Causal modeling in nonexperimental research*. Amsterdam: Sociometric Research Foundation.

SAS Institute (1992). *SAS/STAT software: Changes and enhancements release 6.0.7*. SAS Technical Report P-229, SAS Institute, Cary, NC.

Satorra, A., & Saris, W. E. (1985). Power of the likelihood ratio test. *Psychometrika, 50*, 83–90.

Schaie, K. W., Campbell, R. T., Meredith, W., & Rawlings, S. C. (Eds.) (1988). *Methodological issues in aging research*. New York: Springer-Verlag.

Schaie, K. W., & Hertzog, C. (1982). Longitudinal methods. In B. B. Wolman (Ed.), *Handbook of developmental psychology*, (pp. 91–115). Englewood Cliffs, NJ: Prentice-Hall.

Schaie, K. W., & Hertzog, C. (1985). Measurement in the psychology of adulthood and aging. In J. E. Birren, & K. W. Schaie (Eds.), *Handbook of the psychology of aging*, 2nd edn, (pp. 61–92). New York: Van Nostrand Reinhold.

Scheffé, H. A. (1959). *The analysis of variance*. New York: Wiley.

Schluchter, M. D. (1988). *BMDP5V–unbalanced repeated measures models with structured covariance matrices*. Tech. Rep. 86, BMDP Statistical Software, Los Angeles.

Schmidt, P., & Wytte, A. D. (1988). *Predicting recidivism using survival models*. Berlin: Springer-Verlag.

Schoon, I. (1992). *Creative achievement in architecture: A psychological study*. Ph.D. thesis. Leiden, the Netherlands: DSWO Press.

Searle, S. R., Casella, G., & McCulloch, C. E. (1992). *Variance components*. New York: Wiley.

Seltzer, M. (1990). *The use of data augmentation in fitting hierarchical models to educational data*. Ph.D. thesis, University of Chicago, Chicago, Unpublished dissertation.

Shao, J., & Tu, D. (1995). *The jackknife and bootstrap*. New York: Springer-Verlag.

Shavelson, R. J., Webb, N. M., & Rowley, G. L. (1989). Generalizability theory. *American Psychologist, 44*, 922–932.

Simon, H. A. (1954). Spurious correlation: a causal interpretation. *Journal of the American Statistical Association, 49*, 467–479.

Singer, H. (1993). Continuous-time dynamical systems with sampled data, errors of measurement and unobserved components. *Journal of Time Series Analysis, 14*, 527–545.

Singer, J. D., & Willett, J. B. (1991). Modeling the days of our lives: Using survival analysis when designing and analyzing studies of duration and the timing of events. *Psychological Bulletin, 110*, 268–290.

Singh, A. C., & Roberts, G. R. (1990). State space generalized linear modeling with a quasi-Kalman filter. *ASA Proceedings of the Section of Social Statistics*, (pp. 165–169).

Singh, A. C., & Roberts, G. R. (1992). State space modelling of cross-classified time series of counts. *International Statistical Review, 60*, 321–335.

Skinner, C. J., Holt, D., & Smith, T. M. (Eds.) (1989). *Analysis of complex surveys*. New York: Wiley.

Sloane, D., & Morgan, S. P. (1996). An introduction to categorical data analysis. *Annual Review of Sociology, 22*, 351–375.

Sobel, M. E. (1994). Causal inference in latent variable models. In A. Von Eye, & C. C. Clogg (Eds.), *Latent variables analysis: Applications for developmental research*, (pp. 3–35). Thousand Oaks, CA: Sage.

Sobel, M. E. (1995). The analysis of contingency tables. In G. Arminger, C. C. Clogg, & M. E. Sobel (Eds.), *Handbook of statistical modeling in the social sciences*, (pp. 251–310). New York: Plenum.

Sörbom, D. (1982). Structural equation models with structural means. In K. G. Jöreskog, & H. Wold (Eds.), *Systems under indirect observation, Part 1*, (pp. 183–195). Amsterdam: North-Holland.

Spiel, C. (1994). Latent trait models for measuring change. In A. Von Eye, & C. C. Clogg (Eds.), *Latent variables analysis: Applications for developmental research*, (pp. 274–293). Thousand Oaks, CA: Sage.

SPSS (1990). *SPSS Categories, user's manual*. Chicago: SPSS Inc.

Stevens, J. P. (1990). *Intermediary statistics*. Hillsdale, NJ: Lawrence Erlbaum.

Stevens, J. P. (1992). *Applied multivariate statistics for the social sciences*, 2nd edn. Hillsdale, NJ: Lawrence Erlbaum.

Stevens, J. P. (1996). *Applied multivariate statistics for the social sciences*, 3rd edn. Mahwah, NJ: Lawrence Erlbaum.

Stoolmiller, M., & Bank, L. (1995). Autoregressive effects in structural equation models: We see some problems. In J. M. Gottman (Ed.), *The analysis of change*, (pp. 261–278). Mahwah, NJ: Lawrence Erlbaum.

Strenio, J. F. (1981). *Empirical Bayes estimation for a hierarchical linear model*. Ph.D. thesis, Harvard University.

Strenio, J. F., Weisberg, H. I., & Bryk, A. S. (1983). Empirical Bayes estimation of individual growth curve parameters and their relationship to covariates. *Biometrics*, *39*, 71–86.

Svalastoga, K. (1959). *Prestige, class, and mobility*. London: Heinemann.

Tabachnik, B. G., & Fidell, L. S. (1989). *Using multivariate statistics*, 2nd edn. New York: Harper and Row.

Tate, R. L., & Wongbundit, Y. (1983). Random versus non-random coefficient models for multilevel analysis. *Journal of Educational Statistics*, *8*, 103–120.

Tatsuoka, M. M. (1988). *Multivariate analysis: Techniques for educational and psychological research*. New York: Macmillan.

Tenenhaus, M., & Young, F. W. (1985). An analysis and synthesis of multiple correspondence analysis, optimal scaling, homogeneity analysis, and other methods for quantifying categorical multivariate data. *Psychometrika*, *50*, 91–119.

Tibben, A., Timman, R., Bannink, E. C., & Duivenvoorde, H. J. (1997). Three-year follow-up after presymptomatic testing for Huntingtons's disease in tested individuals and partners. *Health Psychology*, *16*, 20–35.

Timm, N. H. (1975). *Multivariate analysis with applications in education and psychology*. Monterey, CA: Brooks/Cole, Formerly publised by Wadsworth, Belmont: CA.

Timman, R., & Bijleveld, C. C. J. H. (1996). *Nonlinear longitudinal discriminant analysis of the psychological aftermath of presymptomatic DNA testing for Huntington disease*. Tech. Rep. PRM-96-02, Leiden University: Department of Psychometrics, Leiden, the Netherlands.

Traub, R. E. (1994). *Reliability for the social sciences*. Newbury Park, CA: Sage.

Tukey, J. W. (1954). Causation, regression and path analysis. In O. Kempthorne (Ed.), *Statistics and mathematics in biology*, (pp. 35–66). Ames, IA: Iowa State University Press.

Van Buuren, S. (1990). *Optimal scaling of time series*. Ph.D. thesis. Leiden, the Netherlands: DSWO Press.

Van Buuren, S. (1997a). Fitting ARMA time series by structural equation models. *Psychometrika*, *62*, 215–236.

Van Buuren, S. (1997b). Optimal transformations for categorical autoregressive time series. *Statistica Neerlandica*, *51*, 90–106.

Van de Geer, J. P. (1984). Linear relations between k sets of variables. *Psychometrika*, *49*, 79–94.

Van de Geer, J. P. (1985). *HOMALS user's guide*. Tech. Rep. UG-85-02, Leiden University: Department of Data Theory.

Van de Geer, J. P. (1993). *Multivariate analysis of categorical data: Theory and applications*. London: Sage.

Van de Pol, F., & De Leeuw, J. (1986). A latent Markov model to correct for measurement error. *Sociological Methods & Research*, *15*, 118–141.

Van de Pol, F., & Langeheine, R. (1989). Mixed Markov models, mover-stayer models, and the EM algorithm, with an application to labour market data from the Netherlands socioeconomic panel. In R. Coppi, & S. Bolasco (Eds.), *Multiway data analysis*, (pp. 485–495). Amsterdam: North-Holland.

Van de Pol, F., & Langeheine, R. (1990). Mixed Markov latent class models. In C. C. Clogg (Ed.), *Sociological methodology*, (pp. 213–247). Washington, DC: American Sociological Association.

Van de Pol, F., Langeheine, R., & De Jong, W. (1989). *PANMARK user manual: PANel analysis using MARKov chains*. Voorburg, the Netherlands: Netherlands Central Bureau of Statistics.

Van den Boogaard, T. G. H. M., & Bijleveld, C. C. J. H. (1988). Daily menstrual symptoms measures in women and men using an extended version of Moos's instrument. *Journal of Psychosomatic Obstetrics and Gynaecology*, *9*, 103–110.

Van den Boom, D. (1988). *Neonatal irritability and the development of attachment: Observation and intervention*. Ph.D. thesis, Leiden University, Leiden, the Netherlands, Unpublished PhD thesis.

Van der Burg, E., & De Leeuw, J. (1983). Non-linear canonical correlation. *British Journal of Mathematical and Statistical Psychology*, *36*, 54–80.

Van der Burg, E., De Leeuw, J., & Dijksterhuis, G. M. (1994). OVERALS, nonlinear canonical correlation with K sets of variables. *Computational Statistics & Data Analysis*, *18*, 141–163.

Van der Burg, E., De Leeuw, J., & Verdegaal, R. (1988). Homogeneity analysis with k sets of variables: An alternating least squares method with optimal scaling features. *Psychometrika*, *53*, 177–197.

Van der Heijden, P. G. M. (1987). *Correspondence analysis of longitudinal categorical data*. Ph.D. thesis. Leiden, the Netherlands: DSWO Press.

Van der Heijden, P. G. M., & De Leeuw, J. (1985). Correspondence analysis: a complement to log-linear analysis. *Psychometrika*, *50*, 429–447.

Van der Kloot, W. A. (1981). Multidimensional scaling of repertory grid responses: two applications of homals. In H. Bonatius, R. Holland, & S. Rosenberg (Eds.), *Personal construct psychology*, (pp. 177–186). London: Macmillan.

Van der Leeden, R. (1990). *Reduced rank regression with structured residuals*. Ph.D. thesis. Leiden, the Netherlands: DSWO Press.

Van der Leeden, R., Busing, F. M. T. A., & Meijer, E. (1995). *Bootstrap methods for two-level models*. Tech. Rep. PRM 95-04, Leiden University, Department of Psychometrics and Research Methodology, Leiden, The Netherlands.

Van der Leeden, R., Vrijburg, K. E., & De Leeuw, J. (1996). A review of two different approaches for the analysis of growth data using longitudinal mixed linear models: comparing hierarchical linear regression (ML3, HLM) and repeated measures designs with structured covariance matrices (BMDP5V). *Computational Statistics & Data Analysis, 21*, 583–605.

Vermunt, J. K. (1993). *LEM: Log-linear and event history analysis with missing data using EM algorithm*. WORC PAPER 93. 909. 015/7, Tilburg University, Tilburg, the Netherlands.

Vermunt, J. K. (1996). *Log-linear event history analysis: A general approach with missing data, latent variables, and unobserved heterogeneity*. Tilburg, the Netherlands: Tilburg University Press.

Vermunt, J. K. (1997). *Log-linear models for event histories*. London: Sage.

Visser, R. A. (1982). *On quantitative longitudinal data in psychological research*. Ph.D. thesis, Leiden University, Unpublished PhD thesis.

Visser, R. A. (1985). *Analysis of longitudinal data in behavioural and social research*. Leiden, the Netherlands: DSWO Press.

Voeten, M. J. M. (1991). Beschrijving van de individuele ontwikkeling van leervorderingen [description of the individual development of learning progress]. In J. Hoogstraten, & W. J. Van der Linden (Eds.), *Bundel onderwijsresearchdagen '91 [Reader educational research days 1991]*, (pp. 79–88). Amsterdam: Stichting Centrum voor Onderwijsonderzoek.

Von Eye, A. (1985). Longitudinal research methods. In T. Husén, & T. N. Postlethwaite (Eds.), *The international encyclopedia of education*, (pp. 3140–3152). Oxford: Pergamon.

Von Eye, A. (Ed.) (1990). *Statistical methods in longitudinal research*, Vol. 1. Boston, MA: Academic Press.

Von Eye, A., & Clogg, C. C. (Eds.) (1994). *Latent variables analysis: Applications for developmental research*. Thousand Oaks, CA: Sage.

Ware, J. H. (1985). Linear models for the analysis of longitudinal studies. *Journal of the American Statistical Association, 80*, 95–101.

Werts, C. E., & Linn, R. L. (1970). Path analysis: Psychological examples. *Psychological Bulletin, 74*, 193–212.

White, P. (1990). Ideas about causation in philosophy and psychology. *Psychological Bulletin, 108*, 3–18.

Wiggins, L. M. (1973). *Panel analysis, latent probability models for attitude and behavior processes*. Amsterdam: Elsevier.

Willett, J. B. (1988). Questions and answers in the measurement of change. In E. Z. Rothkopf (Ed.), *Review of research in education*, (pp. 345–422). Washington, DC: American Educational Research Association.

Willett, J. B., & Sayer, A. G. (1996). Cross-domain analysis of change over time: Combining growth modeling and covariance structure analysis. In G. A. Marcoulides, & R. E. Schumacker (Eds.), *Advanced structural equation modeling: Issues and techniques*, (pp. 125–158). Mahwah, NJ: Lawrence Erlbaum.

Willett, J. B., & Singer, J. D. (1991). How long did it take? Using survival analysis in educational and psychological research. In L. M. Collins, & J. L. Horn (Eds.), *Best methods for the analysis of change*, (pp. 310–328). Washington, DC: American Psychological Association.

Willms, J. D. (1986). Social class segregation and its relationship to pupils' examination results in Scotland. *American Sociological Review*, *55*, 224–241.

Winer, B. J. (1962). *Statistical principles in experimental design*. New York: McGraw-Hill.

Winer, B. J. (1971). *Statistical principles in experimental design*, 2nd edn. New York: McGraw-Hill.

Winer, B. J., Brown, D. R., & Michels, K. M. (1991). *Statistical principles in experimental design*, 3rd edn. New York: McGraw-Hill.

Wood, P. K., & Brown, D. (1994). The study of intraindividual differences by means of dynamic factor models: Rationale, implementation and interpretation. *Psychological Bulletin*, *116*, 166–186.

Wright, S. (1918). On the nature of size factors. *Genetics*, *3*, 367–374.

Wright, S. (1934). The method of path coefficients. *Annals of Mathematical Statistics*, *5*, 161–215.

Wright, S. (1960). Path coefficients and regressions: alternative or complementary concepts? *Biometrics*, *16*, 189–202.

Yamaguchi, K. (1996). Some log-linear fixed-effect latent trait Markov-chain models: A dynamic analysis of personal efficacy under the influence of divorce/widowhood. In A. E. Raftery (Ed.), *Sociological Methodology 1996*, (pp. 39–78). Oxford: American Sociological Association.

Young, F. W. (1981). Quantitative analysis of qualitative data. *Psychometrika*, *46*, 347–388.

Young, F. W., De Leeuw, J., & Takane, Y. (1976). Regression with qualitative and quantitative variables: An alternating least squares method with optimal scaling features. *Psychometrika*, *41*, 505–529.

Young, F. W., Takane, Y., & De Leeuw, J. (1978). The principal components of mixed measurement multivariate data: An alternating least squares method with optimal scaling features. *Psychometrika*, *43*, 279–281.

Notes on contributors

Catrien Bijleveld is now Programme Coordinator at the Department of Research, Research and Documentation Centre, Ministry of Justice. She studied psychometrics at Leiden University and obtained her doctoral degree with her thesis 'Exploratory Linear Dynamic Systems Analysis'. Her research interests are longitudinal data analysis, research methods in criminology, as well as applied research in various areas. She has taught many courses, introductory as well as advanced, on research methodology and longitudinal data analysis. Some publications are:

Bijleveld, C. C. J. H. & De Leeuw, J. (1991). Fitting longitudinal reduced rank regression models by alternating least squares. *Psychometrika, 56*, 433–447.

Van de Water, H. P. A., Bijleveld, C. C. J. H., Wiggers, C. C. M. C. & Berkane, M. (1992). Is the worst of the epidemic over? Back calculation of HIV seroprevalence in the Netherlands. *Health Policy and Planning, 21*, 211–221.

Bijleveld, C. C. J. H. (1993). The evaluation of the impact of adult education on abolishing female circumcision in the northern Sudan. *Arab Medical Bulletin, 12*, 22–36.

Hentschel, U. & Bijleveld, C. C. J. H. (1995). It takes two to do therapy: differential aspects in the formation of therapeutic alliance. *Psychotherapy Research, 5*, 22–32.

Leo van der Kamp is Professor of Psychology at Leiden University. His research interests include research methodology for psychology and education, psychological test theory and multivariate analysis. His publications are in the area of generalizability theory, item response theory, and the application of multilevel modelling and structural equation modelling in health psychology and education. He has taught many undergraduate, graduate and postgraduate courses on these topics. Relevant publications are:

De Gruijter, D. N. M. & Van der Kamp, L. J. Th. (1991). Generalizability theory. In R. K. Hambleton & J. N. Zaal (Eds.) *Advances in educational and psychological testing*, (pp. 45–68). Boston: Kluwer.

Vooijs, M. W. & Van der Kamp, L. J. Th. (1991). Linear versus nonlinear effects in the measurement of effects in a quasi-experimental design. *Evaluation Review, 15*, 625–638.

Van der Kamp, L. J. Th. (1992). Some issues and problems in measuring the quality of education. In P. Vedder (Ed.) *Measuring the quality of education*, (pp. 149–166). Amsterdam/Lisse: Swets & Zeitlinger.

Ab Mooijaart has a Master's degree in psychology. His PhD thesis was titled 'Latent Structure Analysis'. He is Associate Professor at the Unit of Psychometrics and Research Methodology of the Department of Psychology, Leiden University. His research interests are structural equation models, numerical algorithms and categorical data analysis. He has taught many courses on multivariate analysis, categorical data analysis and mathematical statistics. Recent publications include:

Mooijaart, A., & Van der Heijden, P. G. M. (1992). The EM-algorithm for latent class analysis with equality constraints. *Psychometrika, 57,* 261–269.

Van der Heijden, P. G. M., & Mooijaart, A. (1995). Some new log-bilinear models for the analysis of asymmetric in a square contingency table. *Sociological Methods and Research, 24,* 7–29.

Meijer, E. & Mooijaart, A. (1996). Factor analysis with heteroskedastic errors. *British Journal of Mathematical and Statistical Psychology, 49,* 189–202.

Siciliano, R. & Mooijaart, A. (1997). Three-factor association models for three-way contingency tables. *Computational Statistics and Data Analysis, 24,* 337–356.

Willem van der Kloot studied psychometrics and social psychology at Leiden University and obtained his doctoral degree with his thesis 'A Cognitive Structure Approach to Person Perception'. He is Associate Professor in the Unit of Psychometrics and Research Methodology of the Department of Psychology, Leiden University. He teaches regression analysis, analysis of variance, multivariate analysis and multidimensional scaling. He conducts research on fundamental issues and applications of multidimensional scaling, and on the measurement of pain. Relevant publications are:

Verkes, R. J. , Van der Kloot, W. A., & Van der Meij, J. (1989). The perceived structure of 176 pain descriptive words. *Pain, 38,* 219–229.

Van der Kloot, W. A., & Van Herk, H. (1991). Multidimensional scaling of sorting data: A comparison of three procedures. *Multivariate Behavioral Research, 26,* 563–581.

Van der Kloot, W. A., & Willemsen, T. M. (1991). The measurement, representation and predictive use of implicit personality theories. *Cahiers de Psychologie Cognitive/ European Bulletin of Cognitive Psychology, 11,* 137–153.

Van der Kloot, W. A. (1997). *Multidimensionale schaaltechnieken voor gelijkenis- en keuzedata* [Multidimensional scaling of similarity and choice data]. Utrecht: Lemma.

Rien van der Leeden is Assistant Professor at the Unit of Psychometrics and Research Methodology of the Department of Psychology, Leiden University. He obtained his doctoral degree with the thesis 'Reduced Rank Regression with Structured Residuals'. His research interests are mainly in multilevel analysis and structural relations modeling, with recent work focussing on bootstrap estimation methods for two-level models. Other research interests include social psychology and criminology. Since 1986 he has taught many undergraduate, graduate and postgraduate courses on research methodology and psychometrics, mostly on the theory and application of nonlinear multivariate analysis and multilevel modeling. Recent publications include:

Kreft, I. G. G., De Leeuw, J., & Van der Leeden, R. (1994). Review of five multilevel analysis programs: BMDP5V, GENMOD, HLM, ML3 and VARCL. *American Statistician, 48*, 324–335.

De Heus, P., Van der Leeden, R., & Gazendam, B. (1995). *Toegepaste data-analyse* [Applied data analysis]. Utrecht: Lemma.

Wemmers, J. -A., Van der Leeden, R., & Steensma, H. (1995). What is procedural justice: criteria used by Dutch victims to assess the fairness of criminal justice procedures. *Social Justice Research, 8*, 329–350.

Van der Leeden, R., Vrijburg, K., & De Leeuw, J. (1996). A review of two different approaches for the analysis of growth data using longitudinal mixed linear models. *Computational Statistics and Data Analysis, 21*, 583–605.

Eeke van der Burg is Assistant Professor at the Unit of Psychometrics and Research Methodology of the Department of Psychology, Leiden University. Before that she worked at different methodology departments of several universities, all concerning social or behavioural sciences. She studied mathematics at Leiden University. Her PhD thesis was titled 'Nonlinear Canonical Correlation Analysis and Some Related Techniques'. Her research concerns multivariate analysis models for data that consist of two or more sets of variables. She has taught graduate courses on advanced statistics and multivariate analysis methods, and shared in teaching several postgraduate courses. Publications since 1993 include:

Van der Burg, E. & Bijleveld C. C. J. H. (1993). Longitudinal k-sets analysis using a dummy time variable. *Qüestiio, 17*, 333–345.

Van der Burg, E. & Dijksterhuis, G. B. (1993). An application of nonlinear redundancy analysis and canonical correlation analysis. In R. Steyer, K. F. Wender and K. F. Widaman (Eds.), *Psychometric Methodology, Proceedings of the 7th European Meeting of the Psychometric Society in Trier*, (pp. 74–79). Stuttgart: Gustav Fischer Verlag.

Van der Burg, E., De Leeuw, J., & Dijksterhuis, G. B. (1994). OVERALS: nonlinear canonical correlation analysis with k sets of variables. *Computational Statistics and Data Analysis, 18*, 141–163.

Van der Burg, E. & Dijksterhuis, G. B. (1996). Generalised canonical analysis of individual sensory profiles and instrumental data. In T. Naes & E. Risvik (Eds.), *Multivariate analysis of data in sensory research*, (pp. 221–258). Amsterdam: Elsevier Science Publishers.

Author index

Subject index